PETER MAHON

Imagining Joyce and Derrida

Between *Finnegans Wake* and *Glas*

UNIVERSITY OF TORONTO PRESS
Toronto Buffalo London

© University of Toronto Press Incorporated 2007
Toronto Buffalo London
Printed in Canada

ISBN 978-0-8020-9249-6

Printed on acid-free paper

Library and Archives Canada Cataloguing in Publication

Mahon, Peter, 1971–
    Imagining Joyce and Derrida : between Finnegans wake and
Glas / Peter Mahon.

    Includes bibliographical references and index.
    ISBN 978-0-8020-9249-6

    1. Joyce, James, 1882–1941. Finnegans wake.   2. Derrida, Jacques. Glas.
3. Joyce, James, 1882–1941 – Criticism and interpretation.   4. Derrida,
Jacques – Criticism and interpretation.   I. Title.

PR6019.O9Z7254 2007   823'.912   C2006-906663-9

University of Toronto Press acknowledges the financial assistance to
its publishing program of the Canada Council for the Arts and the
Ontario Arts Council.

This book has been published with the help of a grant from the
Canadian Federation for the Humanities and Social Sciences, through the
Aid to Scholarly Publications Programme, using funds provided by
the Social Sciences and Humanities Research Council of Canada.

University of Toronto Press acknowledges the financial support for
its publishing activities of the Government of Canada through the
Book Publishing Industry Development Program (BPIDP).

Pour Darcy, pour tout.
... tiger, my eagle eye.

Contents

Acknowledgments

I would like to thank Lorraine Weir of the department of English at the University of British Columbia for all her help, insight, advice, and support during the formative stages of this project. I would also like to thank Ralph Sarkonak of the French, Hispanic, and Italian Studies department at UBC for his careful reading of the text and his support at a time when it was needed.

Special thanks are due to Jill McConkey at University of Toronto Press for her hard work on behalf of this book. I would also like to thank the other staff at UTP involved in seeing the manuscript into print. Thanks also to the anonymous readers of the manuscript for their insightful comments and the Board of Trinity College, Dublin, for giving me permission to reproduce folio 124r of the Book of Kells.

Last, but certainly not least, I would like to thank my family in Ireland, especially Karen, Colm, Gran, and Brian. A very special thanks must go to my mother, Joan Mahon, for all her sacrifices over the years. Thanks, Mam.

The *'Tunc'* page (124r) of the Book of Kells (Trinity College, Dublin)

IMAGINING JOYCE AND DERRIDA:
BETWEEN *FINNEGANS WAKE* AND *GLAS*

Introduction: A Brief Sketch of Joyce-Derrida Intertextuality

Yes, everything has already happened to us with *Ulysses* and has been signed in advance by Joyce.

Jacques Derrida, 'Ulysses Gramophone'

The all-riddle of it? That that is allruddy with us, ahead of schedule, which already is plan accomplished from and syne.

Finnegans Wake 274.2–5

This study argues that James Joyce's *Finnegans Wake*[1] can be read as a text that disrupts and reinscribes the philosophical understanding of the process of *mimēsis*, a process of imitating (expressing, describing, representing, illustrating) a pre-existent 'reality,' whether that reality is understood as the thing itself or an *eidos* or *idea*.[2] In place of this process of *mimēsis*, *Finnegans Wake* proposes the problematic of the 'immargination' (4.19) – a sort of unlimited imagination – which tries to picture the ever-receding figure of Finnegan, who is lost in a past that has never been present or a future that never arrives.[3] Thus, this study will argue that, to the extent that Finnegan never presents himself, the imagination in *Finnegans Wake* imitates 'nothing.' In order to give the *Wake*an imagination conceptual rigour, I will reconsider some of Derrida's earlier, so-called more philosophical texts – *Dissemination*, *The Margins of Philosophy*, *Speech and Phenomena*, and *Writing and Difference*[4] – in conjunction with the textual practice of *Finnegans Wake*. This entails mobilizing some of the key textual strategies employed in those texts – *différance*, catachresis, repetition, and so on – and mapping them onto the *Wake*an 'immargination' in order to develop a theoretical framework that will enable readers of Joyce and/or Derrida to theorize and negotiate a broadened conception of Joyce-Derrida intertextuality. This theoretical framework also has the effect of broadening the hitherto received Joyce-Derrida intertext by building upon and generalizing Derrida's contribution to Joyce studies by considering those texts where Derrida does not explicitly address Joyce. This approach, when coupled with Derrida's designation of Hegel as the privileged heading under which 'the very project of philosophy' is 'displaced and reinscribed' (M 19), paves the way for a sustained comparison of *Finnegans Wake* to Derrida's fullest meditation on Hegel, *Glas*.

In arguing that *Finnegans Wake* may be understood as a sort of 'proto-deconstruction' that shares much with Derrida's careful tracing of the disruption of presence and philosophical mimesis, I am endebted to Derrida's direct engagements with Joyce's work,[5] 'Two Words for Joyce'[6] and his 1984 address to the James Joyce Symposium, 'Ulysses Gramophone: Hear say yes in Joyce.'[7] It also owes much to the work carried out over the last two decades or so by Joyceans who have produced generous readings of Joyce and Derrida. For example, Joyceans such as Sam Slote, Claudette Sartiliot, and Susan Shaw Sailer have explored Derrida's texts on Joyce and have taken seriously some of their implications for the field of Joycean studies.[8] These explorations are invaluable for Joyce studies in that they illustrate the possibility of reading Derrida and Joyce in theoretically fruitful and sophisticated ways. In the same spirit, still other Joyceans have offered surveys of Joycean-Derridean intertextuality based on Derrida's other, less systematic references to Joyce and his texts.[9] In addition to the work of Joyceans, this study owes a debt to the work of several authors active in the field of Derridean scholarship who have recognized Derrida's indebtedness to Joyce's texts. For example, Reed-Way Dasenbrock, Herman Rapaport, Christopher Norris, and Geoffrey Bennington all note the importance of Joyce in their considerations of different facets of Derrida's thought.[10]

Even though it situates itself in the wake of Derrida's analysis of both *Finnegans Wake* and *Ulysses*, the present study differs from all these efforts primarily in terms of focus and scope if not in spirit. It does not content itself with explicating Derrida's readings of either *Ulysses* or *Finnegans Wake*, a practice that is at least partly responsible for constraining much of what has been written on Joyce and Derrida. Rather, in setting itself the task of creating a theoretical framework that will enable readers of Joyce and/or Derrida to theorize and negotiate a broadened conception of Joyce-Derrida intertextuality and to unlock the rigorously deconstructive potential of the *Wake*'s textual practice, this study can usefully be seen as an attempt to address the situation that Laurent Milesi has also recently noticed in his collection *James Joyce and the Difference of Language*: 'the strategic pervasiveness of the Joycean approach to language in Derrida's style has received numerous treatments, among which see especially Alan Roughley, *Reading Derrida Reading Joyce*, and, to a minor extent, Sailer, *On the Void of To Be* ... Although these are more commendable than Lernout's unsympathetic, nit-picking summaries in *The French Joyce*,[11] I feel that a greater degree of analytic sophistication is still required to approach the vast topic of Joyce's "influence" on Derrida' (23). It is precisely the 'gap' that Milesi alludes to here that this study seeks to supplement.

According to Derrida, *mimēsis* has traditionally been interpreted by Western philosophy – from Plato to Hegel – as the imitation of an *eidos* or idea:[12]

> But what is the idea? What is the ideality of the idea? When it is no longer the *ontōs on* in the form of the thing itself, it is, to speak in a post-Cartesian manner, the copy inside me, the representation of the thing through thought, the ideality – *for* a subject – of what is. In this sense, whether one conceives it in its 'Cartesian' or in its 'Hegelian' modification, the idea is the presence of what is, and we aren't yet out of Platonism. It is still a matter of imitating (expressing, describing, representing, illustrating an *eidos* or *idea*, whether it is a figure of the thing itself, as in Plato, a subjective representation, as in Descartes, or both, as in Hegel. (D 194)

Here, Derrida's genealogy lays bare the 'eidetic schema' that structures and controls the thinking of the major names of Western philosophy. These thinkers share a thought that is controlled by the presence of the *eidos* insofar as it is still subject to the radical opposition between a fully present 'reality' and its pale representation or copy. Derrida accords 'Platonism' a certain privilege precisely because it can stand 'more or less immediately for the whole history of Western philosophy, including the anti-Platonisms that regularly feed it.' What binds all these Platonisms and anti-Platonisms together *as* Platonism is their shared desire to maintain the priority of 'what is, "reality," the thing itself' over the 'painting, the portrait, ... the inscription or transcription of the thing itself' (D 191). In other words, the Platonic *eidos* structures

any conception of 'reality' as that which is prior to inscription or reproduction is interpreted by Western thought in terms of a temporal
presentness/presence – a 'now.'[13] To the extent that Western philosophy maintains the prior presence of 'what is' over its 'inscription' it
remains within Platonism and its powerful conception of the process
of *mimēsis*: the imitation (expression, description, representation, illustration, etc.) of a 'reality' – be it the *eidos* or *idea* (D 194) or the thing
itself (D 191). It is this conception of presence that *Finnegans Wake* displaces and disrupts. In doing so, the *Wake* also displaces other key concepts associated with the concept of presence.

Putting the privilege of presence/reality into question has a profound bearing on what is called 'literature,' since it has traditionally
been understood to 'copy' pre-existent 'reality.' In this form of questioning, reality, as 'that which is, the being-present (the matrix-form
of substance, of reality, of the opposition between matter and form,
essence and existence, objectivity and subjectivity, etc.)' can no longer
be rigorously 'distinguished from the appearance, the image, the phenomenon, etc., that is, from anything that, presenting it *as* being
present, doubles it, re-presents it, and can therefore replace and de-
present it' (D 191). It not only puts into question the distinction
between the realm of that which is and that which is imitated, but also
what constitutes the 'order of appearance': 'the very process of appearing in general' where 'the precedence [*pré-séance*][14] of the imitated ...
governs the philosophical or critical interpretation of literature' (D
192). This study will argue that it is precisely the 'order of appearance'
that *Finnegans Wake* both displaces and reinscribes and it is this displacement that prevents one from considering the *Wake* as literature in
any simple sense.

However, arguing that the *Wake* shares similarities with Derrida's
disruption of presence and the philosophical mechanism of *mimēsis*
poses a theoretical problem for a reader of Joyce and Derrida. This theoretical problem can be clarified by considering both Plato's and
Hegel's eidetic philosophies and their relations to what is at stake in
this study's engagement with *Finnegans Wake*. The role Hegel's philosophy plays in Derrida's writing is particularly useful for grasping the
problem I am alluding to because it 'both include[s] within itself and
anticipate[s] all the figures of its beyond, all the forms and resources of
its exterior' (WD 252). Hegel's philosophy, insofar as it anticipates its
exterior, or beyond, is remarkably similar to Derrida's formulation of
what he calls 'yes-laughter' and the 'Ulyssean circle of *self-sending*': 'I

will say in conclusion that the Ulyssean circle of *self-sending* commands a reactive yes-laughter, the manipulatory operation of hypermnesic reappropriation' (AL 304). What Derrida is making legible here, I want to suggest, is the 'Hegelianism' of Joyce's *Ulysses* under the heading of 'hypermnesia,' which may be understood as a particularly powerful form of memory that is 'capable of storing in an immense epic work Western memory and virtually all the languages in the world *including traces of the future*' (281, Derrida's emphasis). This hypermnesic laughter is no mere 'remembering,' and it cannot be confined to *Ulysses* because it finds an even more powerful expression in the *Wake*, where the reader of Joyce is forced 'to be in his memory, to inhabit his memory, which is henceforth greater than all your finite memory can, in a single instant or a single vocable, gather up of cultures, mythologies, religions, philosophies, sciences, history of mind and of literatures' (PSJ 147). Both the anticipation of the Ulyssean circle and the 'yes-laughter' of hypermnesic appropriation wherein 'all the histories, stories, discourses, knowledges' would be prescribed in advance (292) are variations of the Hegelian *eidos*, which is 'oriented from the unknown to the known or knowable, to the always already known or to anticipated knowledge' (WD 271).[15] In other words, the question of hypermnesia as it surfaces in Derrida's analyses of Joyce's text finds it roots in Derrida's consideration of the circuit of reappropriative return to the *eidos* as it is found in Hegelian philosophy (WD 251–77) and, given Hegel's closeness to Plato, the role the *eidos* plays in Platonic 'anamnesis' (AL 276, 281).[16]

It is with respect to this Joycean, or, to be more accurate, the Joycean variant of the Hegelian appropriation, then, that the relation between Joyce and Derrida is at its most complex, and such complexity demands a reconception of the textual relations of reading Joyce and Derrida together. If the reader of Joyce and Derrida is to avoid simply making Derrida's texts into mere 'moments' that are anticipated and appropriated in advance by either *Ulysses* or *Finnegans Wake*, account must be taken of the manner in which the Derridean texts negotiate this Hegelian circle. It would not be sufficient to invoke the *Wake*'s multiple languages as a way of 'stepping outside' that circle. This is because, as Derrida points out in 'Two Words for Joyce,' the Babelian motif of multiple languages is already a part of the Joycean hypermnesic circle. This is perfectly illustrated by the *Wake*'s description of the hen's letter, her famous 'polyhedron of scripture' (107.8), written to try and clear her husband's name of wrongdoing, as an artefact that is composed in many different languages (117.12–16). The *Wake* goes on to designate the letter's writing – and by extension its own 'lingo' – as a writing that is incommensurable with the 'practice' of 'metaphysicians':

> For if the lingo gasped between kicksheets, however basically English, were to be preached from the mouths of wickerchurchwardens and metaphysicians in the row and advokaatoes, allvoyous, demivoyelles, languoaths, lesbiels, dentelles, gutterhowls and furtz, where would their practice be or where the human race itself were the Pythagorean sesquipedalia of the panepistemion, however apically Volapucky, grunted and gromwelled, ichabod, habakuk, opanoff, uggamyg, hapaxle, gomenon, ppppfff, over country stiles, behind slated dwellinghouses, down blind lanes, or, when all fruit fails, under some sacking left on a coarse cart? (116.25–35)

That is to say, the *Wake*'s idiomatic lingo – its 'hapaxle, gomenon' (or *hapax legomenon*, or 'once said') – 'however basically English,' is a multiplicity of 'languoaths' that disrupts the practice of metaphysicians. If the reader of Joyce cannot disrupt the underlying Hegelianism of the Joycean circle by citing the *Wake*'s multiplicity of languages, and if it appears that the text takes the disruption of metaphysics into account, then it would appear that the *Wake* has somehow already anticipated the Derridean 'project' of the deconstruction of metaphysics.[17] This also implies that when the reader of the *Wake* tries to find how 'deconstructive' Joyce's text is, s/he can only ever risk making Derrida's texts into a moment of the Hegelian-Joycean circle.

In order to minimize this risk, this study adopts a two-fold approach to the problem of not making Derrida's work into a mere exterior or beyond to be appropriated by the Joycean text. The first aspect of this approach I will treat as axiomatic throughout this study. It involves employing the motifs of *différantial* spacing, doubling, and catachresis utilized by Derrida to disrupt other 'hypermnesias' – the Platonic,[18] and particularly the Hegelian philosophies of eidetic mimesis – that underlie and structure Joycean appropriation, and treating them as a guide for disrupting the structure of hypermnesia *itself*. Insofar as these motifs disrupt more than one circle of hypermnesia, they offer the possibility of disrupting Joycean appropriation. The second aspect of this study's approach derives from the first in that it pays careful attention to the motifs just mentioned that constitute the theoretical matrix of the spacing inherent in the laughter of the *yes, yes* that Derrida elaborates in both 'Ulysses Gramophone: Hearsay Yes in Joyce' and 'Two Words for Joyce.' In addition to the *yes*-laughter of mastery, Derrida locates a non-appropriative *yes*, another laughter which is always multiple, dialogical, and directed to another: 'But when, and it is only a question of rhythm, the circle opens, reappropriation is renounced, the specular gathering together of the sending lets itself be joyfully dispersed in a multiplicity of unique yet numberless sendings, then the other *yes* laughs, the other, yes, laughs' (AL 304). The (other) *yes*-laughter affirms 'the Other' and opens and disrupts (however momentarily) the circle of appropriative memory, which would attempt to appropriate all others to itself (ibid). In other words, the *yes* of hypermnesic mastery is always doubled – spaced out – by its non-appropriative other in a '*yes, yes*' (AL 296) that cannot be reduced to a singular *yes* since both 'call for and imply each other irresistibly,' contaminating each other from the very start (307). The laughter of the '*yes, yes*' is therefore the caught up in writing, the irreducible 'ambiguity of written and oral marks' (AL 282) that constitutes the 'spacing' of the written archive (PSJ 156).[19] It is this spacing therefore that breaches the circle of appropriation. However, this approach remains risky insofar as the joyful *yes*-laughter that disrupts Joycean appropriation is, as Derrida makes clear throughout 'Ulysses Gramophone,' always 'gramophoned' by its double – 'an internal telephone which parasites it like its mimetic, mechanical double, like its incessant parody' (276). Using this approach, this analysis will try to avoid seeing Derrida's work – despite the remarkable similarities they appear to share – as a mere moment of the Joycean text. It seeks to view the Joycean and Derridean texts in a double relationship, where their writing is open-endedly 'selfpenned to one's other, ... neverperfect everplanned' (489.33–4).

Even though careful consideration of the disruptions of both Platonic anamnesis and the Hegelian dialectic are critically important for this study, the Hegelian dialectic will be given a certain priority later on since it is, as was mentioned above, the privileged heading under which the project of philosophy is displaced and reinscribed (M 19). For Derrida, this priority has to do with the manner in which Hegelian philosophy 'include[s] within itself and anticipate[s] all the figures of its beyond, all the forms and resources of its exterior' (WD 252). This situation makes the recourse to Hegelianism indispensable not only for this analysis, but also for a reader of Joyce and Derrida. This is not just because Hegel provides a context for understanding the powerful sway that appropriative hypermnesia holds over Derrida's analysis of Joyce's texts and Derrida's textual strategies, but also because Hegel is the privileged site where the appropriative structure of the hypermnesic circle is put into question by Derrida.

Thus, it is in view of the privileged Hegelian site that chapter 1 sketches the theoretical groundwork for the entire study by examining in detail how certain deconstructive strategies employed by Derrida – *différance*, catachresis, doubling, for example – form the theoretical underpinnings of the *yes*-laughter that Derrida reads in Joyce, since they mark what cannot easily be anticipated by either Hegelian or Platonic philosophy. These strategies are then grafted onto what I will argue is the crucially important role the non-eidetic imagination plays for a reader of *Finnegans Wake*. In order to clarify how this 'immargination' works, and in order to theorize what role the reader plays in the operation of this imaginative framework, chapter 1 examines one of Joyce's most celebrated sources for *Finnegans Wake*: Giambattista Vico's 1744 edition of *The New Science*. Vico's conception of the power of the imagination, the role the reader plays in writing the text of *The New Science*, and his exploration of the ancient religious art of augury are used to clarify the enabling and active role the reader plays in generating or writing the text of *Finnegans Wake*. In other words, Vico will make it possible to begin the task of theorizing both the theoretical framework of the non-present imagination and the reader's role in it as a site of what will be termed 'deconstructive performance.' Since the operation of the imagination shares a structural affinity with certain key textual strategies found in Derrida's writing, which are, to a certain degree, 'outside' what is taken to be the 'usual' terrain of Joyce-Derrida intertextuality – that is to say, 'outside' of the texts where Derrida either explicitly writes on Joyce or mentions him by name – the chapter concludes by suggesting that there is an expanded zone of Joycean-Derridean intertextuality that stands in need of exploration by those with an interest in the work of both these authors. Further, since Derrida's examination of *différance* accords a privileged position to both Hegel's philosophy and the role laughter plays in disrupting it, chapter 1 concludes by arguing that Hegel and laughter are indispensable for understanding the role that Derrida assigns the laughter of the '*yes, yes*' in his analysis of Joyce, as well as to the expanded zone of intertextuality outlined in this study.

Chapters 2 to 6 essentially test the general applicability and flexibility of the imaginative framework arrived at in chapter 1. The expanded understanding of Joyce-Derrida intertext is used to shape and guide a sustained comparative analysis of *Finnegans Wake* and Derrida's most overlooked text, *Glas*, which Derrida has said 'is also a sort of a wake' (PSJ 150).[20] Typographically speaking, *Glas* is an unusual text: each page is square, and consists of two columns, each using a different-sized font: the left-hand column (a) examines Hegel, and the right-hand column (b) examines Jean Genet.[21] Each column has additional insertions (i) that can either cut into a column or interrupt it completely; they deal with a broad range of other authors such as Freud, Feuerbach, and Kierkegaard. *Glas* is chosen here to test chapter 1's imaginative framework not simply because of its unusual textual layout, although this will be important later; *Glas* is chosen primarily because it is Derrida's most sustained analysis of the Hegelian philosophical system and because, as is argued throughout this study, it can be read as Derrida's most sustained meditation on the imagination, time, and the body.

Chapters 2 to 6 explore how the imaginative framework may be used to identify, isolate, and theorize the remarkable similarity of key traits and textual strategies employed in both *Finnegans Wake* and *Glas*. Chapter 2 centres on the relations between the imagination and the hen's celebrated letter of book I, section 5 of *Finnegans Wake*. This chapter argues that the hen's writing of the letter should be given paradigmatic status in the study of *Finnegans Wake* due to its close relation to one of Joyce's most important intertexts, Giambattista Vico's *The New Science*. By directing the reader's attention to the actions of the hen on the mound, the *Wake* parodies the central status that Vico accords to the practice of *auspicium*, or augury, in the emergence of what he calls the human institutions. This chapter then utilizes Derrida's consideration of what Heidegger in *Kant and the Problem of Metaphysics* calls 'autoaffection' – an imaginative mode of time derived from a reading of Kant's *Critique of Pure Reason* – in order to analyse and give theoretical rigour to the structure of this Vichian imaginative framework.[22] The second part of this chapter entails the the study's first detailed comparison of some of the key writing techniques employed by the hen in her letter with the written techniques of Derrida's *Glas*.

Chapter 3 considers how the framework of the imagination examined in chapter 2 may be understood to operate in the *Wake*. It compares the hen's 'writing-gathering,' as she hops about on the primal rubbish heap, to what Heidegger calls the imagination – the 'synthesizing power' that precedes knowledge. It considers how the *Wake* offers the reader a parodic double of philosophical *logos* – speech, reason, account, discourse, and so on – which is derived from the Greek word *legein*, to gather, collect. Read in this way, the hen's 'gathering' may be seen as a non-philosophical simulacrum of the gathering *logos* of philosophy. As such, she corresponds to the process of 'agglutination' that characterizes the textual procedure of *Glas* (139–40b). The chapter then goes on to explore how the texts of both *Finnegans Wake* and *Glas* joyfully fuse both writing and reading with the obscene processes and rhythms of bodily discharge.

Chapter 4 continues the analysis of the textual rhythms examined in chapter 3 by examining the relations that these textual rhythms have with the 'imaginative' and 'inventive' aspects of what Vico calls 'the topics.' Topics are, for Vico, that imaginative base that conceptual thought must constantly presuppose. Both the topics and the 'imagination' have their 'roots in the body' (NS 819). This chapter then considers what these aspects of Vichian *memoria* share with what Derrida in his essay 'The White Mythology' calls 'catachresis,' the 'abusive inscription of a sign' (M 255). The analysis goes on to explore how the body may be said to act as the site of imaginative catachresis in order to account for *Finnegans Wake*'s frequent association of its writing processes with the rhythms of bodily discharge. It finishes by suggesting that this bodily writing is indispensable for coming to terms with the textual process of Derrida's *Glas* due to its incommensurability with philosophical dialectics.

Chapter 5 returns to the process of bodily writing explored in chapter 4 in order to compare it to what *Glas* calls 'repression.' 'Repression' is not simply understood in the psychoanalytical sense of the word. In *Glas*, repression 'remains a confused imagination' that is 'not-yet,' or prior to, speculative dialectics (191a). This 'confused imagination' both mimics and disrupts the roles that marriage, the family, and religion play in Hegelian speculative dialectics. This chapter then considers how the institutions of family, marriage, and religion in *Glas* may be mapped onto the roles they play in *Finnegans Wake*. It explores in detail how the play of these institutions in each text displaces the processes of dialectical thinking by drawing attention to a certain nonpresence that takes the form of a 'not-yet' that is never present in the text.

Finally, chapter 6 compares the elaboration of time in both *Finnegans Wake* and *Glas* in order to consider how time may be thought about in conjunction with the rhythm discussed in the previous chapters. It does so by examining the peculiar temporality of the 'not yet' that never arrives as it functions in both *Finnegans Wake* and *Glas*. This mode of time, I will argue, is only graspable as a sort of 'empty time' that cannot be reduced to presence. As a temporal non-present, it remains steadfastly incommensurable with the philosophical understanding of sense and meaning as presence. By considering both *Finnegans Wake* and *Glas* together on the basis of temporality, or, better, temporalization, I hope to show how in this chapter how time provides an important context for the imaginative framework that underlies this study's broadened understanding of the shared intertextual 'laughter' of both *Glas* and *Finnegans Wake* that resists being appropriated by philosophical meaning. It is to be hoped that this broadened conception of Joyce-Derrida intertextuality will enable the reader to appreciate *Finnegans Wake* as a text that not only deserves to be read alongside the texts of Heidegger, Nietzsche, and Bataille, but also deserves to be considered as a major text in the genealogy of Derridean deconstructive strategy.

1 'Immargination': The Site of the Imagination

'Presence'/'Absence'

Finnegans Wake can be read as a text that puts the 'Platonist' order of appearance into question by displacing the value of presence on which it relies. In order to get a sense of what is at stake in the *Wake*'s radical displacement and reinscription of both the 'Platonist' order of appearance and the privileged role it plays in the literary-philosophical understanding of *mimēsis*, it is necessary to understand something of the various components that constitute it. According to Derrida in 'The Double Session,' Platonism acts as something of a privileged heading that can stand 'more or less immediately for the whole history of Western philosophy, including the anti-Platonisms that regularly feed it' (D 191).[1] Platonism can stand in for all of Western philosophy precisely to the extent that it wishes to maintain the priority of 'what is, "reality," the thing itself' over the 'painting, the portrait, ... the inscription or transcription of the thing itself' (ibid). In maintaining the priority of 'what is' over its 'inscription,' Platonism has bequeathed to Western philosophy its powerful conception of the process of *mimēsis*: the imitation (expression, description, representation, illustration, etc.) of 'an *eidos* or *idea*' (D 194). The *eidos* or idea, since it is understood to be 'already in the mind like a grid without a word' (M 257),[2] is the paradigm for any 'reality' that is imitated. Platonic 'reality' – the *eidos* – therefore informs and structures Western philosophy's conception of any 'reality' as that which is understood to exist prior to being copied. If reality is 'eidetic' – that is, exists prior to imitation – then that reality must also be understood on the basis of its coordination with 'the historical determination of the meaning of being in general as *presence* (presence of the thing to the sight as *eidos*, presence as substance/essence/existence [*ousia*], temporal presence as point [*stigmē*] of the now or the moment [*nun*], the self-presence of the *cogito*, consciousness, subjectivity, the co-presence of the other and of the self, intersubjectivity as the intentional phenomenon of the ego, and so forth)' (OG 12). In other words, 'reality' is always interpreted in terms of 'the *on* (being-present),' the undisturbed presence that precedes (its) imitation, and this is what permits the *eidos* to stand in for all the historical forms of that which is (present) insofar as they are 'distinguished from the appearance, the image, the phenomenon, etc., that is, from anything that, presenting it *as* being present, doubles it, re-presents it' (D 191). It is through the *eidos* that Platonism (and thus Western philosophy) defines the realm of that which is – 'reality' – as that presence which precedes imitation.

The *eidos* therefore plays a central role in constituting what Derrida refers to as the 'order of appearance,' which organizes the literary-philosophical interpretation of *mimēsis*. The 'order of appearance' is 'the very process of appearing in general' where 'the precedence [*préséance*] of the imitated ... governs the philosophical or critical interpretation of literature' (D 192). Despite the proliferation of anti-Platonisms that appear to contest or invert the order of appearance founded on the present (meaning), the 'absolute distinguishability between imitated and imitator, and the anteriority of the first over the second,' has not 'been displaced by any metaphysical system' (D 192).[3] It is precisely this space of displacement, I will argue, that the text of *Finnegans Wake* insistently sketches for its reader.

The central role the *eidos* plays in the Platonist order of appearance can be further clarified by considering the relation it bears with what Derrida calls the *logos*. Derrida posits a continuum between Aristotle's conception of *logos* as thought – that is, the 'universal language' of the mental experiences shared by all men[4] – and the 'absolute *logos*' of the 'infinite creative subjectivity in medieval theology' (OG 13) – God – who creates the *res* (or actual 'thing') from 'its *eidos*, from its *sense* thought in the logos or in [his] infinite understanding' (OG 11, my emphasis). In both God's and man's cases, the *logos* is the realm of transparent sense or universal meaning and its proper object is the *eidos* whose present meaning is beyond the spoken and written differences between languages (ibid.). Derrida implies that God and man share a space of creative subjectivity that is shaped and guided by the *eidos*, which is itself primarily conceived in terms of intended meaning or sense. In other words, that which is made has an intended meaning (the *eidos*), and is therefore structured like a sign. The *eidos* is therefore the meaningful intention that binds not only God and man but also the relations between the *res* and *logos* in the act or process of making/ production to the problematic of meaning.[5]

Eidetic meaning (or sense) also has an 'original and essential link [of *logos*] to the *phonē* [Greek, "speech"]' that, says Derrida, 'has never been broken' in Western thought (ibid.).[6] The relation between meaning and speech both in and as the *logos* organizes a hierarchy that structures Saussure's conception of the sign in terms of signifier/signified along the same lines as Platonist *mimēsis*. Like the voice or speech, the signified has 'an immediate relation with the *logos* in general (finite or infinite), and a mediated one with the signifier, that is to say with the exteriority of writing' (OG 15). This hierarchical organization holds even if 'the thing, the "referent," is not immediately related to the *logos* of a creator God where it began by being the spoken/thought sense' (OG 14–15). In other words, this confirms what was said above: what is understood by the thing, the referent, reality, etc., has already been pre-determined and pre-interpreted as present meaning or 'sense' by the *eidos* produced in the *logos*. Not only is the entire province of present meaning produced in the *logos* according to the structure of the Platonist *eidos*, the power of the *eidos* is such that it also provides the model for, and thus guides the interpretation of, the 'thing' or 'referent': 'reality' itself. The *eidos* is therefore the 'model' for both meaning *and* 'reality.' Further, as this brief consideration of the signifier and signified should serve to confirm, the order of appearance is not simply confined to the 'imitative' arts: it extends to incorporate into its realm the so-called arbitrary relation between the signifier and the signified. To the extent that both the signifier and writing are expelled outside the realm of thoughtful speech, relegated to secondarity or exteriority in that they merely 'represent' the meaning of the spoken signified, the relation of the signified to the signifier remains governed by the Platonist order of appearance. Derrida gives the name 'logocentrism' to all the forms of present meaning that bear this privileged relation to thought understood as speech.

What should be becoming clear is that what is understood to be 'reality' modelled upon the *eidos* is not simply something immediate and intuitive. There are at least three reasons for saying this. First, 'reality,' since it is taken to be present already partakes in the 'formal essence' of the 'signified (sense or thing, noeme or reality),' 'is *presence*' (OG 18). In other words, the order of appearance already entails an understanding of 'reality' that is itself already predetermined by a concept of presence derived from the *eidos* understood as meaning or sense. Second, the interpretation of reality in the order of appearance is further dependent upon an interpretation of the *eidos* derived from the role that meaning and speech play in the philosophical understanding of the *logos*. Third, through a consideration of the *eidos*, the order of appearance is further revealed to be dependent upon a covert interpretation of the process of creation or production as a guiding metaphor for interpreting and ordering the relations that obtain between the *eidos*, the *logos*, and the *res*. Thus, what is understood by 'reality' is already predetermined by a series of complex metaphors and/or philosophical concepts that can be traced back to the *eidos* and its relation to presence, meaning, and production. It is this 'reality' as it is thus determined and held in place that is necessary to the constitution of the Platonist 'order of appearance' that designates 'reality' as a meaningful presence that is prior to and independent of any imitative/representative act.

In what follows, I want to consider how *Finnegans Wake* displaces the Platonist order of appearance by focusing on its treatment of the value of presence and the *eidos* that constitutes 'reality.' By displacing the meaning and reality that hinge on the *eidos* and presence, the *Wake* also marks the limits of the ability of the Platonist order of appearance to account for its textual practice. This is not to suggest, however, that *Finnegans Wake* simply rejects the Platonist *eidos* for another 'more truthful' or 'accurate' model of 'reality': this is impossible precisely because 'reality' is always already inextricably bound up with the concepts and metaphors just outlined. On the contrary, this analysis will pay close attention to how this displacement of presence permits the *Wake* to *avoid* simply rejecting Platonism by considering how it offers its reader a non-Platonist 'double' for the *eidos*, which gives rise to alternative modes of textual practice. This 'double,' which 'doubles' and 'doubles *for*' the *eidos* is absolutely necessary for coming to grips with the operation of the 'immargination' in *Finnegans Wake*. A comparative reading of both the 'immargination' and the 'double' will suggest that the textual practice of *Finnegans Wake* shares a great deal with the strategies and resources of the Derridean project of deconstruction. As a result, the 'immargination' suggests itself as a site for theorizing, and therefore guiding, a more detailed comparative exploration of *Wake*an textual practice and the radical Derridean textuality that interminably deconstructs the philosophy of presence. This also means that what follows here is not, in any simple sense, a 'philosophical,' 'conscious,' or even 'truthful' comparative reading of *Finnegans Wake* and the texts of Jacques Derrida precisely because, as Derrida himself notes in his discussion of Husserl and temporality, 'within philosophy there is no possible objection concerning this privilege of the present-now; it defines the very element of philosophical thought, it is *evidence* itself, conscious thought itself, it governs every possible concept of truth and sense' (SP 62, Derrida's italics).

The (dis)Order of Appearance: Finnegan ... Différance

To the extent that *Finnegans Wake* can be read as a text that defers and displaces presence on its very 'first' page with the 'loss' of Finnegan, it marks itself as a text that is no longer adequately understandable in terms of the order of appearance that constitutes the literary-philosophical conceptions of *mimēsis*, evidence, consciousness, truth, and sense. The displacement of presence first becomes legible to the reader of the *Wake* through the text's treatment and conception of the figure of Finnegan, the eponymous hero of the text, who, after a 'great fall of the offwall' he has been building in the Phoenix Park, is effectively lost as substantial presence. In fact, the only trace of Finnegan's 'presence' in the text is marked by a stuttering roll of thunder within which is discernible the sound of his screams as he falls:

> The fall (bababadalgharaghtakamminarronnkonnbronntonner-
> ronntuonnthunntrovarrhounawnskawntoohoohoordenenthur-
> nuk!) of a once wallstrait oldparr is retaled early in bed and later
> on life down through all christian minstrelsy. The great fall of the
> offwall entailed at such short notice the pftjschute of Finnegan,
> erse solid man, that the humptyhillhead of humself prumptly sends
> an unquiring one well to the west in quest of his tumptytumtoes:
> and their upturnpikepointandplace is at the knock out in the park
> where oranges have been laid to rust upon the green since dev-
> linsfirst loved livvy. (3.15–24)

It is not the case that Finnegan appears in the text only to disappear again: Finnegan never actually presents himself in *propria persona* in the text: even when he is spoken to, it is only through proxies. He forever remains a trace, only legible in his wake. His 'fall,' therefore, marks therefore not so much the 'loss' of a pristine presence, but rather the manner in which the lack of presence constitutes the 'figure' (a term that is now rendered problematic for obvious reasons) of Finnegan in the text of the *Wake*.

The power of Finnegan's wake to actually generate text is underlined in the text: it is his 'fall' that drives the narrative level of the text, which, at the end of book I, section 1, takes on the character of a sort of 'investigation' into his 'disappearance.' This investigation, conducted by the 'Mamalujo' (the four old men of the Gospel, Matthew, Mark, Luke, and John), seeks Finnegan in order to restore him to presence. The futility of their attempt starts to become obvious as I.2 tries to trace the (true) circumstances of Finnegan's fall through the popular oral history of 'The Ballad of Persse O'Reilly' written by Hosty (44.24–47.29). However, the ballad not only changes Finnegan's name to Persse O'Reilly, and associates him with Humpty's fall from the wall, but also accuses him of both rape and the solicitation of homosexual favours in the Phoenix Park. Through the ballad, the fall becomes a crime that only adds to the confusion surrounding Finnegan/Persse O'Reilly's 'fall.' The situation goes from bad to worse when I.2 finally gives way to I.3's free-for-all rumour mongering and presents three very different reconstructions of the crime, and the Phoenix Park becomes the setting for a fight on a plain in Ireland. Things are further clouded when a *vox pop* is taken, and all and sundry offer their interpretations and opinions as to the circumstances surrounding the fall/crime. Section I.4 then tries to arrive at the 'true truth' (96.27) of the situation by setting up the juridical structure of a trial. The fact that what started out as an investigation into Finnegan's disappearance has now taken the form of a trial presided over by the Mamalujo indicates how powerful the rumours and speculation of I.2 and I.3 have been. The trial, in its attempt to arrive at the 'true truth' of Finnegan's situation, also constitutes Finnegan as the ever-receding paradigm for truth and meaning in the book. Despite its best efforts and its power to call forward what can only be described as unreliable 'witnesses' who 'saw' the fall/crime, the trial becomes bogged down in conflicting testimony from its witnesses and a host of other 'unfacts' (57.16). During the trial and investigation the text also explicitly equates truth with the unveiling of presence when it explicitly characterizes the 'true truth' as that which would 'unhume the great shipping mogul and underlinen overlord' (97.24). Despite these claims, the judges are forced to admit their inability to arrive at the truth about Finnegan and decide that the best bet is to wait for his wife the hen to write a letter that will tell the 'cock's trootabout him' (113.12).[7] It should be clear from this brief outline of the first half of book I that the desire to restore Finnegan's presence constitutes a major structural element of *Finnegans Wake*.

But the *Wake*, even as it treats Finnegan's withdrawal from the text as a major structural and generative principle in the text, also uses that withdrawal as a sort of 'lure' for the reader. This lure can be understood to play a double and contradictory function. On the one hand, it would appear to permit the text to hold out the possibility of a more originary conception of Finnegan's presence by diffusing it throughout his many names, avatars, initials, and attributes.[8] This would appear to equate Finnegan with the sort of meaningful presence Derrida calls 'the "primum signatum"': the "transcendental" signified': 'implied by all lexicons and all syntax, and therefore by all linguistic signifiers, though not to be identified simply with any one of those signifiers, allowing itself to be precomprehended through each of them' (OG 20). Such a transcendental signified would also guarantee the binary opposition that structures the sign as 'the difference between signifier and signified,' a difference that is both 'absolute and irrefutable' (OG 20). In other words, Finnegan could be seen to function as that which guarantees the concept of sign: since he is not reducible to any one signifier in the text, he must act as a sort of transcendental signified that offers the possibility of an eternally present meaning/truth that would remain outside of the plays of the signifier, thereby regulating and maintaining the structure of the sign (signifier/signified), and guaranteeing that the 'signified' (eidetic meaning) is never to be reduced to a mere 'signifier' (OG 20).

The *Wake* also inscribes its reader in the text as one who is caught in this 'closure' to the extent that the text places upon him/her part of the burden of the responsibility for 'framing up the figments' of Finnegan's situation 'in the evidential order' and 'bring[ing] the true truth to light' (96.26–7). This responsibility is made explicit in I.5, where the reader is offered all sorts of advice and encouragement in his/her textual pursuit of the truth.[9] Even though the text performs and encourages the reader to pursue the inquiry into Finnegan's whereabouts after his withdrawal from the text, it also frames that inquiry as an '*un*quiry' (3.22).[10] This 'un' creates doubt that there will ever be a successful arrival at his presence despite the textually sanctioned search for Finnegan. Finnegan's withdrawal from presence makes possible the search for the 'facts' (31.33) or the 'true truth' (96.27) regarding his disappearance. At the same time, however, his withdrawal pulls him towards absence, and as it does so, it thwarts the search for those 'facts' by multiplying all the distracting 'unfacts' (57.16) that overcome the search for him. This suggests that the search for the 'true truth' is not simply plagued by 'unfacts' that would happen to the truth accidentally, but rather that everywhere in the text where there is an attempt to arrive at the truth in the form of proximal presence, there is also a pull towards absence. However, these tensions cannot be simply understood as being localized. They adhere to the structural principle of ever-receding withdrawal and pursuit that shapes not only book I but also the paradigm for the pursuit of truth as presence across the entire text of the *Wake*. Finnegan's 'wake' simultaneously makes both possible and impossible the search for truth understood as proximal presence in the text. It also makes legible the structural tensions between presence and absence. For this reason, Finnegan's wake cannot be reduced to either presence or absence, and it is the condition of being 'between' presence and absence that will align Finnegan, as I will be arguing shortly, with what Derrida calls '*différance.*'

If one reads the 'fall' at the beginning of *Finnegans Wake* as a scene that 'begins' by displacing presence by reinscribing it in a scene of loss and non-presence, then the presence that would guarantee the transcendental signified must also be disrupted. This effectively removes the guarantee that would make a signified essentially different from a signifier; their distinction becomes problematic. Once the presence of the transcendental signified is displaced, 'one recognizes that every signified is also in the position of a signifier.'[11] Problematizing the binary opposition of signifier/signified is not a simple 'confusion' of both terms: the fact that 'this opposition or difference cannot be radical or absolute does not stop it from functioning' (P 20). In other words, there is still a 'difference' that remains between the signifier/signified that owes something to the concept of the sign. This is why it can never be a case of simply 'rejecting' (OG 13) or 'junking' these concepts (P 24), since they 'are indispensable for unsettling the heritage to which they belong' (OG 14). It is here that the problematic of what Derrida calls the 'closure of metaphysics' asserts itself. The closure of metaphysics is not 'a circle surrounding a homogeneous field, a field homogeneous with itself on its inside, whose outside would be homogeneous also. The limit has the form of always different faults, of fissures whose mark or scar is borne by all the texts of philosophy' (P 56; see also OG 14 and D

193). In other words, 'closure' is marked by certain key concepts – such as the concept of the sign – that can 'simultaneously confirm and shake' logocentrism (P 24). That is why using these double concepts constantly runs the risk of 'falling back within what is being deconstructed' (OG 14). This can be illustrated as follows: the 'reduction of writing – as the reduction of the exteriority of the signifier – was part and parcel of phonologism and logocentrism' (P 24) in which the 'voice is *heard* (understood) ... closest to the self as the absolute effacement of the signifier' (OG 20). The signifier vanishes in the signified in logocentrism. The deconstruction of logocentrism takes us to the very 'edge' of the erasure of the signifier; however, it does not erase the signifier because to do so would be to simply return to a uncritical logocentrism. Deconstruction, therefore, respects and retains the trace of difference inherent in the concept of sign, and logocentrism and its deconstruction are separated by the smallest of differences. In the context of *Finnegans Wake*, this doubleness plays itself out in the 'figure' of 'Finnegan's wake,' which can be read simultaneously as the displacement of presence and the transcendental signified: 'Finnegan's wake' marks, like the concept of the sign, the 'break' with metaphysics as well as the risk of falling back into it.

Recognizing that every signified is also in the place of the signifier has other consequences. The 'epoch of the logos' 'debases' writing and the signifier – 'text in general' – as 'secondarity' or 'exteriority.' Text is always 'second' or 'exterior' because it is 'preceded by a truth, or a meaning already constituted by and within the element of the logos' (OG 14). Text is both outside and comes after the *eidos*. As such, its writing becomes articulated with the spacing of *différance*:

> The gram as *différance*, then, is a structure and a movement no longer conceivable on the basis of the opposition of presence/absence. *Différance* is the systematic play of differences, of the *spacing* by means of which elements are related to each other. This spacing is the simultaneously active and passive ... production of the intervals without which the 'full' terms could not signify, would not function. It is also the becoming-space of the spoken chain – which has been called temporal or linear; a becoming space which makes possible both writing and every correspondence between speech and writing, every passage from the one to the other. (P 27)

Neither present nor absent, *différantial* spacing is found in both speech and writing. Spacing – the exteriority of writing and the signifier –

puts speech in the place of a more general writing, a general spacing. This displacement was already glimpsed when the displacement of the transcendental signified had the effect of putting the signified in the place of the signifier; what spacing does is permit a general displacement of (the) presence (of the signified) and its reinscription within (the) writing (of signifiers): 'what I call *text* is also that which "practically" inscribes and overflows the limits' of a discourse that is governed by 'essence, sense, truth, meaning, consciousness, ideality, etc.,' each of which is 'put back into the position of a *mark* in a chain that this authority intrinsically and illusorily believes it wishes to, and does in fact, govern' (P 59–60; see also D 193). 'Presence' in all its forms is displaced and reinscribed as an effect of textual *différance* or writing (M 16–17). It is not surprising that textuality in the form of the hen's letter presents itself at the point where the attempt to reconstruct the past unravels in book I.

Finnegan's liminal position between presence/absence is further underlined in book I, where he is served up as a fish for ritualistic consumption, only to disappear again:

> But,
> lo, as you would quaffoff his fraudstuff and sink teeth through
> that pyth of a flowerwhite bodey behold of him as behemoth for
> he is noewhemoe. Finiche! Only a fadograph of a yestern scene.
> Almost rubicund Salmosalar, ancient fromout the ages of the Ag-
> apemonides, he is smolten in our mist, woebecanned and packt
> away. So that meal's dead off for summan, schlook, schlice and
> goodridhirring. (7.12–18)

Instead of appearing in the feast of the text according to the structure of the doctrinal belief in the 'Real Presence' of God during the Eucharist, Finnegan is the 'goodridhirring' who does not 'appear' as present at all. Finnegan does not hold out any substantial 'Real Presence,' because he is 'noewhemoe.' The foodstuff he provides for consumption is precisely not flesh; it is only a 'fraudstuff.' This implies that 'Real Presence' in the text is fraudulent, a 'good red herring,'[12] a false lead, and underscores Finnegan's peculiar form of 'presence' as something that never amounts to much more than a 'fadograph.' But Finnegan is not simply absent either; his remains take the form of a faded photograph, and are elsewhere allied with the faded presence of a 'ghost' (24.27). Finnegan, as neither present nor absent, is only ever registered in the text in the mode of a withdrawal that creates a 'wake,' and it is this wake that gives rise to both 'truth' and 'untruth' and exposes their relation to the value of proximal presence. The text therefore plays in a realm of 'non-presence,' which is not-simply-absent, dangling and withdrawing Finnegan as the paradigm for truth and meaning.[13]

Immargination

By withdrawing from the text, Finnegan erases himself as (present) paradigm or model: the 'fall' marks Finnegan with a 'pastness' that is not a modification of a 'present,' and this goes a long way towards accounting for the immense difficulties that surround the book's (vain) attempts at restoring or recovering any certitude regarding him. But the mode of non-presence at the beginning of the *Wake* does not attach itself only to Finnegan's withdrawal from proximal presence into a past that cannot be determined. Non-presence, or non-presentness, in the sense of nearness or proximity, is brought into contact with its other sense: temporal presentness or presence. In the *Wake* this disruption of temporal presentness stretches into a future that is marked repeatedly in the opening pages of the book. This form of temporality is subjected to a further twist in the text in that it is a time that has itself not arrived into proximal presence. It is the non-present time of the 'not yet':

> not yet, though venissoon after, had a
> kidscad buttended a bland old isaac: not yet, though all's fair in
> vanessy, were sosie sesthers wroth with twone nathandjoe. Rot a
> peck of pa's malt had Jhem or Shen brewed by arclight and rory
> end to the regginbrow was to be seen ringsome on the aquaface.
> (3.10–14)

This 'not yet' defers (incessantly) the 'events' of *Finnegans Wake* by putting the designating of such events as what comes *after* writing:

> Then, pious Eneas, conformant to the fulminant firman which
> enjoins on the tremylose terrian that, when the call comes, he
> shall produce nichthemerically from his unheavenly body a no
> uncertain quantity of obscene matter not protected by copriright
> in the United Stars of Ourania or bedeed and bedood and bedang
> and bedung to him, with this double dye, brought to blood heat,

gallic acid on iron ore, through the bowels of his misery, flashly,
faithly, nastily, appropriately, this Esuan Menschavik and the first
till last alshemist wrote over every square inch of the only fools- ˙
cap available, his own body, till by its corrosive sublimation one
continuous present tense integument slowly unfolded all marryvoising moodmoulded cyclewheeling history (thereby, he said,
reflecting from his own individual person-life unlivable, trans-
accidented through the slow fires of consciousness into a dividual chaos, perilous, potent, common to allflesh, human, only,
mortal) but with each word that would not pass away the squid-
self which he had squirtscreened from the crystalline world
waned chagreenold and doriangrayer in its dudhud. This exists
that isits after having been said we know. (185.27–86.9)

Like the 'events' of the narrative, the shell of 'continuous present
tense' does not come 'first': it is always *after* Shem's act of writing. In
other words, the present (and, by extension, consciousness and the self)
occurs after the body, its effluvia, (re)writing, alchemy, and so on. Thus,
what I am calling the 'not yet' is inextricable from Shem's act of bodily
writing, which is not governed by a preceding present. However, what
is called the future is also already past. This strange temporality affects
the major events the *Wake* goes on to consider – the 'arrival' of a
stranger, the emergence of the very strange 'sosie sisters,' the rivalry of
the male twins 'Jhem or Shen,' the guilty fall of the builder Finnegan,
and so forth. These events have not happened yet, even though they are
said to have *already* happened. The deferred temporality of the 'not yet'
is therefore allied to what Derrida calls the trace – 'a past that has never
been present' (M 21)[14] – which is to say, a textual 'past' since the present
only comes after the written text, which nevertheless lies somewhere in
the future since these traces 'always remain, as it were, to come – come
from the future, from the *to come*' (Mem 58). The traces or remains of
'time' (the quotes here serve to indicate that the 'time' referred to is not
time as it is perhaps normally understood) in the *Wake* is simultaneously 'past' and 'to come.' Neither the 'past' nor the 'to come' can be
understood to modify a present, since the 'not-yet' is held in the future
and in the past that never comes to (be) present. The not-yet is both the
non-present origin and the exhaustion of the present; as such it functions as an empty form of time that seems to mark nothing. This temporality affects the entire structure of the *Wake*an textual 'unquiry' into
Finnegan's withdrawal: it not only erases Finnegan as it erases itself but
also constitutes the 'medium' of any possible *Wake*an events, opening

the space of their possibility. *Wake*an non-presence is therefore con-structed as two different 'times' – the 'past' and the 'future,' neither of which are modifications of either a temporal or proximal 'present.' In this temporal void, a 'signified' comes to presence, and this is why any attempt to gather evidence regarding Finnegan and his alleged miscon-duct fails.[15] When taken in conjunction with Derrida's above observa-tion that 'within philosophy there is no possible objection concerning this privilege to the present-now,' it starts to become clear how the *Wake* sets itself the task of exploring a non-literary-philosophical textuality without presence.

However, it should not be thought that *Finnegans Wake* disables its reader by withdrawing the temporal and spatial modes of presence from the text in its opening pages. Despite these withdrawals, the text outlines a mode for proceeding within the empty time and space of its non-present 'unquiry' into the withdrawal of presence into non-presence: the 'immargination':

> Bygmester Finnegan, of the Stuttering Hand, freemen's mau-rer, lived in the broadest way immarginable in his rushlit toofar-back for messuages before joshuan judges had given us numbers or Helviticus committed deuteronomy (one yeastyday he sternely struxk his tete in a tub for to watsch the future of his fates but ere he swiftly stook it out again, by the might of moses, the very wat-er was eviparated and all the guennesses had met their exodus so that ought to show you what a pentschanjeuchy chap he was!) and during mighty odd years this man of hod, cement and edi-fices in Toper's Thorp piled buildung supra buildung pon the banks for the livers by the Soangso. (4.18–27)

This passage offers what it calls the 'immargination' as that power through which the text 'pictures' how 'Bygmester' – 'master builder' – Finnegan, a man of 'hod, cement and edifices,' lived as a builder. The 'immargination' does this despite the fact that the *différantial* Finnegan is ungraspable in terms of presence. In other words, the 'immargin-ation' pictures Finnegan according to an operation that is no longer graspable in terms of the imitation of a 'presence': the 'immargination' pictures a 'past' that was never 'present,' and is in no way a modifica-tion of any present/presence, since Finnegan is *différantial* and so too is the activity he is engaged in. Nor is the operation of the immargination graspable in terms of the mechanism of the 'message' – a chain of signifiers whose meaning is guided by the presence of an animating intention, even if that animating presence is the paradigmatic one of the author-God of the Pentateuch: the operation of the immargination precedes the intention of an animating presence, since it reaches into a past 'toofarback for messuages' (4.19–21).[16]

The scene of immarginative 'buildung' also invites further considerations, all of which point to the text's concern with the dislocation and reinscription of the Platonist order of appearance discussed above. Finnegan builds by piling 'buildung supra buildung' in a scene where 'buildung' can designate both Finnegan's activity and his 'product' – a concept that is, for reasons that will soon become clear, problematic. 'Buildung' is of course a complex portmanteau word that, in combining the English word 'building' with the German word *Bildung* (education, culture, creation, formation), draws attention to the lexical richness of its components. 'Buildung' not only underscores the 'immarginative' nature of Finnegan's creation/formation by recalling a German word for the imagination – *die Einbildung* – it also draws attention to the traces of other German words that have to do with forming and picturing: *Bild* – picture, image, photo, frame, drawing, painting, appearance, metaphor – and *Bilden*, form. In so doing, the text brings Finnegan's activity into contact with the complicated network of meanings that encompass the technology of reproduction and representation in order to make his 'b(u)ildungs' legible as 'immarginative' 'products,' if one can even call that which never amounts to an object a 'product.' The series of German words *Bild, Bilden, Bildung,* and *die Einbildung* is of particular use here in teasing out what is at stake in what Finnegan does, since it also reassembles the network of meanings and associations that constitute the *eidos* (Greek: look, semblance, form, kind, nature, ideal form, model). Once attention is paid to the lexical resources of both the *-bild-* and the *eidos*, it becomes clear that they are at once capable of evoking *both* the imitated ('form') *and* the imitation ('copy,' 'look,' 'picture'); as such, these words already mark the dislocation of the Platonist order of appearance maintains the priority of 'what is, "reality," the thing itself' over the 'painting, the portrait, ... the inscription or transcription of the thing itself' (D 191). Since 'buildung' names both the 'product' and the activity of the text's eponymous hero, the network of associations that constitutes both the *-bild-* and the *eidos* are accorded a role of some importance for reading the *Wake*. On this reading, what *Finnegans Wake* makes legible through its 'immarginative' employment of the resources of *-bild-* and *eidos*, therefore, is its concern with the displacement of both the order of appearance and the presence of the present, which have traditionally controlled the literary-philosophical conception of *mimēsis*.

An even closer consideration of the scene of immarginative build-ung, however, seems to confront the reader with a sort of legible era-sure: the displacement of the order of appearance does not entail the *simple* loss or rejection of the entire network of meanings associated with *mimēsis*. What the scene of immarginative buildung makes legible is actually the 'remains' of *mimēsis* without presence, the *eidos* or the order of appearance. In the order of appearance, 'the anteriority of the first over the second' is maintained, and that which represents or imi-tates comes second: 'The double comes after the *simple*; it multiplies it as a *follow up*' (D 191). Once this is recognized, it then becomes possible to see that the text of the *Wake* actively maintains itself in the place of the imitation, the double. From its very first page, *Finnegans Wake* announces itself as a text that is obsessed with the motif of 'doubling': it is a text in which things go 'doublin their mumper all the time' (3.8–9). To the extent that the *Wake*'s text make legible both displacing the order of appearance and maintaining the mark of exteriority, secondar-ity, and doubleness, any site that manages to yoke these forces together must be a site of tremendous importance for reading *Finnegans Wake*. Once again, the scene of immarginative buildung offers itself to the reader as such a site.

What is at stake in the operation of the immargination can be clari-fied by marking out how its displacement of the metaphysical order of appearance is bound up with its dislocation of the priority of presence and its power to double. First, since Finnegan never presents himself in the text, the operation of the immargination contests the order of appearance by picturing without a present model: in it there is no present (to be) 'imitated.' There is no 'simple.' Second, since the value of presence has already been displaced in the immarginative opera-tion, what happens to the order of appearance is the same as was seen to occur with the distinction between signifier/signifier once the tran-scendental signified was put in the place of the signifier. The imitator – the double – is 'delayed' and in the same position of 'secondarity' or 'exteriority' as writing and the signifier discussed above. This is why, even though the scene of the immarginative buildung quickly sketches the subversion of the metaphysical order of appearance, it nevertheless holds or maintains itself in the space of the double, the imitator. The centrality of doubling to the scene of immarginative buildung is also marked from its 'first' appearance in the text as a scene of doubling/ repetition: Finnegan piles 'buildung supra buildung.' In the immargination, the simple is displaced and reinscribed in the position of the double.

Still other doubling effects that are indissociable from the operation of the immargination and that further serve to make legible the peculiarity of immarginative b(u)ildung can be read in the abyssal nature of this scene. The scene of 'buildung' is abyssal insofar as it immargines a scene of immargination: in 'immargining' a *différantial* Finnegan – that is, a Finnegan beyond the opposition of presence/absence – the scene also immargines the activity of 'immargination.' Finnegan 'builds' 'from next to nothing,' and he does so without a present model. However, Finnegan's activity is not simply creation from nothing. It is creation from *next* to nothing: the absence of nothing is marked with the trace of presence and cannot be reduced to the simple opposition of presence/absence, since they are articulated by the next to nothingness of *différance*. The other abyssal aspect of this scene of immarginative doubling has already been mentioned in passing above: the scene blurs the 'operation' of the immargination with its 'object' – the ever-receding Finnegan b(u)ildung – and points to the immargination as the site of originary contamination, where the margin between the 'imagined' (Finnegan 'b(u)ildung' without model) and the 'immargination' (the buildung of images without a present model) is erased, making it possible for each to double for the other. And since Finnegan is also the paradigmatic receding object in the text, his contaminative association with the immargination makes it possible to generalize the immarginative process in the text. Yet, it also makes it impossible to consider the immarginary process (itself), as it is given in the *Wake*, as a present 'model' to be imitated, since it withdraws itself into *différance*: not only can the imagined object substitute itself for the imagination that is supposed to be imagining it, there is no longer a present object that can be clearly imagined.

The immarginative scene of Finnegan's 'buildung' can now be read in terms of the displacement of the order of appearance. Once the order of appearance is displaced, doubling emerges as a structuring force in the text. Finnegan the master builder piles 'buildung' – simultaneously the final form ('buildung') and the material ('buildungs' used as 'blocks') – 'supra buildung.' The order of appearance is irretrievably displaced by the double: that which is to be made – the buildung – is *already* made insofar as it is used as part of the buildung (materials) – 'buildung supra buildung.' At the same time, however, what is made is also *un*made: the 'final product' is always only a 'part' of itself as 'final product.' Buildung is therefore indissociable from the double to the extent that it proceeds by using what it has made as its material to make what it has already made, with the result that it is impossible to discern here the order of appearance: where is the 'buildung' to be imitated if it is already part of the 'imitation'? In fact, this 'buildung' 'produces' precisely nothing: the 'finished product' subtracts or withdraws itself as 'finished product' by being included in the 'process.' However, just because 'nothing' is 'produced' in this scene does the text thereby paralyse its reader. On the contrary, despite both the displacement of the order of appearance, caught between the imitated and imitation, and the lack of any clearly discernible final finished 'product' or 'materials,' Finnegan's praxis is anything but paralysed or inactive. Finnegan still 'builds.' And he does so without presence: for in buildung as doubling, Finnegan remains *within* the secondarity or exteriority of the double (and hence the signifier and writing). What he builds does not imitate any prior presence (*eidos*), even as it bears the traces of the double. Thus, it has much in common with the praxis sketched by Derrida in the essay 'Dissemination':

> What is to be said about this praxis? If to produce is to draw out of darkness, to bring to light, to unveil or to manifest, then this 'practice' does not content itself with the act of making or producing. It cannot be governed by the motif of truth whose very horizon it *frames*, for it is just as rigorously accountable for *non*production, for operations of nullification and deduction, and the working of a certain textual zero. (D 296; Derrida's italics)

This praxis is a 'making' that is no longer simply a 'making,' a praxis that is no longer simple 'production.' Rather, it is a dynamic *praxis* that is intimately bound up with secondarity and doubling, which are no longer bound by the literary-philosophical Platonist order of appearance. That is to say: the *différantial* immargination is a dynamic praxis that 'produces' nothing (present) and thereby retains the traces of the double without presence.

What the *différantial* immargination marks in the *Wake*, then, is not just the displacement and reinscription of eidetic presence and meaning, but also the literary-philosophical order of appearance that depends upon it. By putting presence – the formal essence of the signified – into question and thereby putting the precedence of the imitated into question, the operation of the immargination in the text of *Finnegans Wake* both displaces and exceeds the Platonist order of appearance. And once the value of presence is put into question, the entire schema of 'reality' – which, as I have been arguing, is modelled upon the *eidos* and held in place by a series of complex metaphors and concepts constituting the order of appearance – is dislocated, not rejected. In other words, it now becomes possible to read the *Wake*'s radical textual practice as the problematical space where it is no longer possible to maintain the priority of 'what is, "reality," the thing itself' over the 'painting, the portrait, ... the inscription or transcription of the thing itself' (D 191). In reinscribing this order through the disorienting effects of the 'immargination,' *Finnegans Wake* displaces the Platonist *mimēsis* which that order takes for granted. Further, the displacement of the order of appearance also recasts the guiding metaphor of the act of creation or production that predetermines the relations that obtain between the *eidos*, the *logos*, and the *res* as non-production. Insofar as it utilizes these strategies, the radical textuality of *Finnegans Wake* can no longer be called 'literature,' inasmuch as that concept still denotes a body of text that is a 'copy' of a pre-existent 'reality' that is present somewhere else. The *Wake*'s radical textual practice calls for a response that is no longer simply literary-philosophical criticism: it calls for a *différantial* and 'immarginative' approach. The *différantial* immargination opens an affirmative pathway that permits the reader to read Joyce writing Derrida: *différance*, the systematic play of differences or 'spacing' by means of which elements are related to each other' (P 27), facilitates both texts in their opening up to each other only by passing through the *yes, yes* that affirms 'the Other,' in a spacing that '*at the same time* institutes, forbids *and* interferes with the so-called monologue' (AL 271–2).

'a waalworth of skyerscape': The Metaphors of Metaphor

If, as I have been arguing, the text of the *Wake* can be said to displace the privilege accorded to the various forms of presence in Western philosophy – what I have referred to variously as 'reality,' 'referent,' *eidos*, signified, and so on – might the various mentions of the body in the text of the *Wake* be taken as an attempt to resurrect the inherent metaphoricity of philosophical language? On the contrary, it would appear that *Finnegans Wake* can be read as a text that displaces and reinscribes 'metaphor.'

This situation can be clarified by a closer consideration of the buildung that Finnegan builds in the non-present space-time of the imagination – a burning skyscraper, which is also a sort of 'beacon' or 'lighthouse' (4.36–5.4) – alongside Derrida's analysis of metaphor in 'White Mythology' (M 207–71). Finnegan's immarginary uninhabitable lighthouse neatly combines in one figure what Derrida analyses as the 'the metaphors of metaphor': 'the (artificial) light and (displaced) habitat' (253).

What Derrida calls here the 'metaphors of metaphor' marks the difference between Derrida's approach to the question of metaphor in philosophy and the tradition of texts that would seek to criticize philosophy as a fund of 'worn-out' metaphors.[17] On the contrary, Derrida is interested in the tropes that cannot be understood from the point of view of the concept of metaphor. The concept of metaphor is itself nothing other than 'a classical philosopheme' (219, 228). What Derrida is interested in are those tropes that 'produce philosophemes' – philosophical concepts – *themselves*. Those tropes that are responsible for giving more powerful philosophical concepts than metaphor – for example, the concepts of concept, the fundamental, *theoria, eidos, logos, arkhe,* and so on (M 224) – are therefore 'prior to all philosophical rhetoric' that would be 'derivative' with respect to these philosophemes (255): 'Metaphor has been issued from a network of philosophemes which themeselves correspond to tropes or to figures, and these philosophemes are contemporaneous to or in systematic solidarity with these tropes or figures' (219). In other words, to the extent that they produce philosophical concepts, the 'metaphors of metaphor' define the entire conceptual field of philosophy itself that generates the concept of metaphor (ibid.; cf. 228). The concept of metaphor is therefore derivative with respect to 'the layer of primary philosophemes' and the tropes that generate that layer. Further, this 'stratum of "tutelary" tropes' (219) can no longer be understood to be made up of 'metaphors,' if metaphor is understood in terms of the concept of metaphor, because they give rise to *every concept* in the field of philosophy.

This results in a complex situation. The attempt to take philosophy back to its 'metaphorical roots' reaches a point where it discovers its limitations with respect to the field of philosophy. Nevertheless, the attempt to return to the metaphorical roots of philosophy opens a space of figures that are not simply graspable as metaphors:

If one wished to conceive and to class all the metaphorical possibilities of philosophy, one metaphor, at least, always would remain excluded, out-

side the system: the metaphor, at the very least, without which the concept of metaphor could not be constructed, or, to syncopate an entire
chain of reasoning, the metaphor of metaphor. This extra metaphor,
remaining outside the field that it allows to be circumscribed, extracts or
abstracts itself from this field, thus subtracting itself as a metaphor less.
By virtue of what we might entitle, for economic reasons, tropic supplementarity, since the extra turn of speech becomes the missing turn of
speech, the taxonomy or history of philosophical metaphors will never
trun a profit ... The field is never saturated. (220)

Here, in the play of the 'more' and the 'less,' the 'metaphor of metaphor' no longer designates 'metaphor.' It rather designates the displacement and reinscription of metaphor that exposes the limits of
metaphor as a derivative philosophical concept. The concept of metaphor 'which remains a philosophical product' cannot 'dominate philosophical metaphorics as such.' At the same time, 'philosophy is
deprived of what it provides itself': because its 'instruments belong to
its field, philosophy is incapable of dominating its general tropology
and metaphorics. It could percieve its metaphorics only around a
blindspot or central deafness,' a contour described by 'the concept of
metaphor' (M 228).[18] The condensation of the 'metaphor of metaphor'
thus neatly combines what was referred to above as the 'general economy' – the 'expenditure without reserve' that involves an irreducible
loss of (present) meaning, and does not turn a profit – with what Derrida nicknames 'the supplement.' The supplement, like the general
economy, never generates a profit because it is both that which adds a
surplus and that which marks a loss insofar as it takes the place of
something: in the supplement, the 'play of substitution fills and marks
a determined lack' (OG 157; cf. 144–5).

   The two 'metaphors of metaphor' – 'the light and the house' – mentioned above play privileged roles in defining metaphor 'itself,' even
though they do not, says Derrida, 'have the same function' (253). The
first – the light – is caught up in the '"idealizing" metaphor which is
constitutive of the philosopheme in general' (254); it is 'indispensable
to the general system in which the concept of metaphor is inscribed'
(253):

Thought is composed of ideas, and the expression of thought by speech is
composed of words. First then, let us see what ideas are in themselves:
following this we will see what words are relative to ideas, or, if you will,

what ideas are as represented by words. A. – IDEAS. The word *Idea* (from the Greek *eidō*, to see) signifies relative to the object seen by the spirit the same thing as image; and relative to the spirit which sees the same things as *seen* or *perception*. But the objects seen by our spirit are either physical and material objects that affect our senses, or metaphysical and purely intellectual objects completely above our senses. (M 254, citing Fontanier, *Figures of Discourse*, 41; emphasis in original)

The 'metaphor' of idealizing is therefore also a metaphor derived from the play of sunlight and sight: the 'first light we have known is doubtless the light of day,' and such light allows me to see (*eidō*), and that which the light of the intelligence or enlightenment allows to be 'seen' is the *eidos* or idea (M 257). And since all philosophical ideas – including the philosophical 'idea' of metaphor itself – are derived from this 'tutelary trope' (219) of light and sight, the space of the *eidō* – idealization – is a metaphor of metaphor.

But things are more complicated still. Fontanier can only point to that which is supposed to be prior to language – that is, the supposedly wordless 'ideas' that compose thought – by 'recalling the history of the signifier "idea"' (254). That is, the tutelary trope is indissociable from a consideration of language. It is the signifier/*word* 'idea' that is etymologically derived from another (Greek) *word* – *eidō* – that makes clear the 'vehicle' of the 'metaphorical' 'idea.' This derivation has the effect of displacing and reinscribing the presence of the 'idea'/'signified' by putting it in the place of the 'signifier.' Thus, the philosophical divisions of the '*idea* and the *word*,' 'thought and language,' 'sense and the sensory' (254) are undone because '*eidos*' is already an uneasy mixture of both 'language' and 'thought,' 'signifier' and 'signified.' It is no longer simply 'present' outside the workings of the signifier; it is rather inscribed in them, and the philosophical project that would attempt to secure the conceptual division word and *eidos* is undermined from the very beginning. If Fontanier can pass over the entanglement of the *eidō*/*eidos* – 'as if this was nothing at all' – it is precisely because his analysis is governed by the same philosophical system that seeks to maintain an absolute distinction between 'the signified and the signifier, sense and the sensory, thought and language, and primarily the division between the *idea* and the *word*' (ibid.). What he does not appear to 'see' is that 'an entire stratification of metaphors and of philosophical interpretations ... supports the concept of that which is called upon to precede language or words, that which is called upon to be previous, exterior, and superior to language and words, as meaning is to expressing, the represented to representation' (ibid.). To the extent that Fontanier does not 'see' this 'metaphor of metaphor' he is somewhat emblematic both of philosophy's inability to dominate 'its general tropology and metaphorics' with the concept of metaphor, and of what was just referred to as its ability to perceive its metaphorics around a blind spot or central deafness.

If it is recalled here that Finnegan's tower is built in the *Wakean* 'immargination' without presence, it can already be supposed that it no longer functions in terms of the philosophical division of 'signifier and signified' that tries to point to a purely eidetic realm outside language. This situation is underlined to the extent that the scene of the tower's construction cannot be understood to distinguish clearly between words, seeing and ideas:

> a waalworth
> of a skyerscape of most eyeful hoyth entowerly, erigenating from
> next to nothing and celescalating the himals and all, hierarchitec-
> titiptitoploftical, with a burning bush abob off its baubletop
> (4.35–5.2)

The tower's 'eyeful hoyth' that 'erigenates' 'from next to nothing' evokes the Tower of Babel by its 'baubletop.' Language is therefore always an issue in this erection. At the same time, languages are indissociable from thought in the form of 'calculation': Finnegan must also 'caligulate by multiplicables' (4.32–3). The small stones of calculus fuse with the fiery baubletop because the 'end product' is also the 'raw material' in this scene of 'buildung.' Finnegan's tower/lighthouse burns with a 'light' that is *already* a fiery Babelian conflagration of words/languages and thought/calculations, and the peculiar 'light' it sheds cannot become a pure light that would somehow exist 'outside' of language(s). To the extent that there is no light 'outside' of language in the scene of immarginative buildung, *Finnegans Wake* can be understood to sketch the problematic space of the *eidō/eidos* where language and thought are entangled.

But that is not all. Finnegan's tower may also be said to displace and reinscribe the other 'metaphor of metaphor' discussed by Derrida: the circular trajectory of 'reappropriation.' This time, however, Finnegan's tower explicitly distorts this second metaphor of metaphor by opening up within it an irretrievable loss of present meaning that makes clear the structure of general supplementarity inherent in the 'wake.' Reappropriation constitutes metaphor to the extent that metaphor 'has always been defined as the trope of resemblance; not simply as the resemblance between two signs one of which designates the other' (215). This can be made clearer by considering how the 'metaphor' of idealization goes hand in hand with that of reappropriation. Everything, says Derrida, 'in the discourse on metaphor' that 'passes through the sign *eidos*, with its entire system,' is 'articulated with the analogy between the vision of the *nous* and sensory vision, between the intelligible sun and the visible sun' (M 253–4). Philosophical discourse 'describes a metaphor which is displaced and reabsorbed between two suns' (269).

This similarity gives rise to the second example of 'metaphor of metaphor' discussed by Derrida: 'the metaphor of the borrowed dwelling' (M 253). This housing metaphor is not 'one figure among others':

> it is there in order to signify metaphor *itself*; it is a metaphor of metaphor; an expropriation, a being-outside-one's-own-residence, but still in a dwelling, outside its own residence but still in a residence in which one comes back to oneself, recognizes oneself, reassembles oneself or resembles oneself, outside oneself in oneself. This is the philosophical metaphor as a detour within (or in sight of) reappropriation, *parousia*, the self-presence of the idea in its own light. The metaphorical trajectory from the Platonic *eidos* to the Hegelian Idea. (Ibid.)

It is the 'recourse to a metaphor in order to give the "idea" of metaphor [that] prohibits a definition, but nevertheless metaphorically assigns a checkpoint, a limit, a fixed place: the metaphor/dwelling' (ibid.). The metaphor of the borrowed dwelling provides the place where meaning understood as presence – the 'signified' of the Platonic *eidos* or the Hegelian 'Idea' – can metaphorically reside. This 'return' to sense can be illustrated by taking up Derrida's consideration of Aristotelian metaphor. Only that which has meaning can be subject to metaphor. Meaning and reference are the possibility of signifying by means of a noun (236–7). A noun, says Aristotle, signifies the presence of 'an independent being identical to itself,' which articulates 'the theory of the name' with 'ontology' (237). Metaphor consists in giving 'the thing a name (*onomatos*) that belongs to something else (*allotriou*)' (231). Since to 'produce a good metaphor is to see a likeness' (*Poetics* 1459a7–8, cited at 237), metaphor cannot be seperated from the concept of *mimēsis*, which is 'never without the *theoretical* perception of resemblance,' *homoiōsis*, which is 'constitutive of the value of truth (*alētheia*)' (237), or the 'proper appearing of the propriety of what is' (244), *logos*, the meaning and truth in discourse that separates man from animal and *physis*, which 'is revealed in *mimēsis*' (237).

It can easily be seen that the 'return' of metaphor is held firmly in check by the entire philosophy of meaning that constructs it as the meaningful and appropriate (proper) resemblance of two terms. Meaning can reside in the borrowed dwelling because that dwelling is also 'proper':

> Metaphor, therefore, is determined by philosophy as a provisional loss of meaning, an economy of the proper without irreparable damage, a certainly ineveitable detour, but also a history with its sights set on, and within the horizon of, the circular reappropriation of literal, proper meaning. This is why the philosophical evaluation of metaphor always has been ambiguous: metaphor is dangerous and foreign as concerns *intuition* (vision or contact), *concept* (the grasping or proper presence of the signified), and *consciousness* (proximity or self-presence); but it is in complicity with what it endangers, is necessary to it in the extent to which the de-tour is a re-turn [*re-tour*] guided by the function of resemblance (*mimēsis* or *homoiōsis*), under the law of the same. The opposition of intuition, the concept, and consciousness at this point no longer has any pertinence. The three values belong to the order and to the movement of meaning. (M 270)

Since the operation of metaphor is strictly controlled by philosophy, the 'loss' of meaning in it is only ever provisional, controlled. Every 'borrowed dwelling' is also a 'proper dwelling': Hegel in his discussion of metaphor in the *Aesthetics* traces this trajectory. For him, a metaphor occurs when a 'word which originally signifies something sensuous ... is carried over ... into the spiritual sphere.' The proper or 'literal meaning' – *eigentliche Bedeutung, sense propre* – 'is lost and exchanged for a spiritual meaning.' But gradually the 'metaphorical element' in the use of such a word vanishes and the 'word changes from a metaphorical (*uneigentliche, non propre*) to a literal expression (*eigentlichen Ausdruck, expression propre*), because owing to readiness to grasp in the image only the meaning, image and meaning are no longer distinguished, and the image directly affords only the abstract meaning itself instead of a concrete picture.' The example Hegel uses to illustrate this is the German word *begreifen* – to grasp. When this word is used, it is usually taken in its 'spiritual sense' – the sense of grasping or apprehending an idea – and 'it does not occur to us at all to think of a perceptible grasping of the hand' (M 225 citing Hegel, *Aesthetics* 404–5). Here, Derrida's description of the process of metaphorization as *'usure'* is instructive.[19] *Usure* is both profit and loss insofar as it suggests simultaneously both the 'use' that erases by rubbing away, and the 'usury' that turns a profit (M 210). In the philosophical/dialectical interpretation of metaphor, the proper sensual meaning – grasping with the hand – is 'worn away' to reveal the proper spiritual meaning – grasping with the mind. This gradual 'wearing away' of the sensual meaning in the revelation of the spiritual meaning is what guides the Hegelian dialectic of metaphor. But, since the movement of metaphorization can be understood as the movement of dialectics itself, metaphor is once again made derivative: the 'origin and erasure of the metaphor, transition from the proper sensory meaning to the proper spiritual meaning by means of the detour of figures' is 'nothing other than a movement of idealization' (M 226). This is why metaphor originates and ends in philosophy: the operation of metaphor is *already* engulfed by the master category of the Hegelian *relève/Aufhebung*, the 'memory (*Erinnerung*) that produces signs, interiorizes them in elevating, suppressing, and conserving the sensory exterior,' using the oppositions of nature/spirit and sensory/sense (*sinnlich/Sinn*) to do so (ibid.). Further, metaphor is already caught in the problematic space of meaning in general discussed above: the opposition of signifier/signified here recast as the opposition of 'the atemporal and nonspatial signified as meaning, content' to the 'metaphorical signifier' (M 228). For reasons already discussed, metaphor is derivative with respect to both the operation of idealization and these master oppositions. Idealization is not confined to Hegel, however, since idealization sketches the 'metaphorical trajectory from the Platonic *eidos* to the Hegelian Idea' (253). The wearing away of the sensual reveals the spiritual, which philosophy then interprets as 'the twisting return toward the already-there of a meaning, *production* ... but as *revelation*, unveiling, bringing to light, truth' (257). Metaphor, as the movement from sensual meaning to spiritual meaning, is dominated by this process of wearing away and revelation of the already-there of meaning; it cannot therefore disrupt the circuit of (philosophical) sense's return to itself.

If the philosophical operation of metaphor always provides a dwelling that is (re)appropriated by the signified, philosophical sense, then it may be said that an uninhabitable place cannot enter into this signif-

icant play of dwellings. Such a (non)dwelling would displace the relations between signifier and signified. Without a home, the signified is
condemned to wander in the desert without any possibility of returning to its proper dwelling. The loss of the dwelling is also legible in the
tower that Finnegan b(u)ilds in the space before presence. Finnegan's
tower is not a dwelling precisely because it is more 'ancient' than the
very property of 'messuages' (4.20) – dwelling houses and their adjacent land and buildings. This is why the 'skyerscape of most eyeful
hoyth entowerly,' a cross between a wall and a burning tower that is
built in the imagination before dwellings and property, remains uninhabitable. And since it is in no sense a 'dwelling,' it cannot even be
modified into a 'borrowed' one. As a structure, this tower cannot be
considered a home. The beacon/lighthouse loses the property of being
a home on the one hand because it is literally uninhabitable, and on the
other because it is given prior to the dwelling understood as property.

It is this uninhabitable tower that both sets Finnegan on his way in
non-presence and keeps him there. Finnegan falls from the tower in the
first instance because it is uninhabitable (by him): the tower was never,
is not, and will never be a home. This suggests that he is lost as presence precisely to the extent that he could not live in the tower and cannot return home to it as a (proper) dwelling. Without such a home,
'Finnegan' must also do without a proper name. Without a proper
name, he falls from the world of propriety and property, and succumbs
to the exhaustive series of names in both I.3 and I.6 that reach after him
without ever reaching him. These names, as I mentioned above, multi-
ply in the wake of a figure who never presents himself. This multipli-
cation conforms to what Derrida says about the absence of the proper
name in Aristotle's discussion of metaphor. Aristotle moves from a
consideration of 'the cup of Ares' as a metaphor of a shield to 'a cup
that holds no wine.' In this doubling of metaphor ('the metaphorization of metaphor'), Aristotle enacts the loss of the proper name –
'Ares,' the Greek god of war – in a field of generalized metaphoricity:

> But this procedure can be pursued and complicated infinitely, although
> Aristotle does not say so. No reference properly being named in such a
> metaphor, the figure is carried off into the adventure of a long, implicit
> sentence, a secret narrative which nothing assures us will lead us back to
> the proper name. The metaphorization of metaphor, its bottomless over-
> determinability, seems to be inscribed in the structure of metaphor, but as
> its negativity. (M 243)

Here, the 'proper' is reinscribed in the 'figurative,' and according to a process that should be familiar by now, the 'secondarity' of the 'figurative' remains. Section I.6 of the *Wake* can be understood to enact this doubling of metaphor insofar as it multiplies the 'proper' name of each figure in the text to the point where there is no longer any 'proper' name: this is how 'Finnegan' can become, for example, the 'secondtonone mytherector and maximost bridgemaker' who 'was the first to rise taller through his beanstale than the bluegum buaboababbum or the giganteous Wellingtonia Sequoia' (126.10–12), and, at the same time, a village in County Clare and piece of clothing – 'Finvara for my shawlders' (621.11–12). This loss of 'Finnegan's' 'proper' 'name' is further complicated by the fact that, as Glasheen notes, 'Finnuala' as a 'name' is usually merely 'indicated' by certain of her attributes rather than properly 'named.'[20] Here 'Finnegan' becomes a variation on the (hidden) feminine 'Finnuala' (Irish, 'white- or fairshouldered'). This variation robs him of masculinity through a fragmentry echo of 'his' 'name' – 'Finn-.' Section I.6 then generalizes the loss of the proper name to each of the figures in the book and subjects each of them to an exhaustive series of names that can only mark their lack of a 'proper' one, a situation marked by the commonplace observation that every named figure at the *Wake* quickly becomes someone else. What the *Wake* stages, therefore, is not simply the trajectory of philosophical metaphor – the de-tour is a re-turn [*re-tour*] – but that trajectory as it is affected by yet another 'turn' – the *tour* that Finnegan builds – that displaces (the) *proper* (name(s)). Here, the value of propriety is displaced in a manner analogous to the reinscription of the *eidō/eidos* in language. The *tour*, like the *eidō* discussed above, since it describes the trajectory/movement of meaning in general, cannot be contained with metaphor: it is a metaphor of metaphor.

What is called the 'proper' – in dialectical meaning – loses itself as proper sensual meaning, only to refind itself as proper spiritual meaning. As such, proper meaning overlooks the 'double turn' that opens 'metaphor and dialectics' (228). Proper meaning guides and interprets 'the separation between sense (the signified) and the senses (sensory signifier) [that] is enunciated by the same root (*sensus/Sinn*)' as being due to the 'generous stock' of semantic richness contained in that root. The semantic richness of the root is thus read speculatively, dialectically (M 228): the movement from proper sensual meaning is also a process of 'wearing away' that 'reveals' the proper spiritual meaning. The dialectic is stretched between two proper meanings: one sensual, the other spiritual. This is how it is possible for Hegel to identify the 'generous stock' at work not only in words like *sinnlich/Sinn* (sensory/ Sense) (M 226), but also in certain German words that name the key concepts of speculative philosophy: '*Aufhebung, Urteil, Meinen, Beispel,* etc.' This is the 'lucky accident that installs a natural language in speculative dialectics' (D 220).

At the same time, however, this situation can be interpreted as the inscription of dialectics in the play of language.[21] If one is not to interpret 'speculatively, dialectically' – that is, if one is not to read metaphor purely philosophically by focusing on the gradual wearing away (*usure*) of proper sensual sense in order to uncover the proper spiritual sense of a word – then one must read that which the proper and the dialectic cover up in the 'double turn.' Instead of wearing the sensual away to discover a spiritual that was somehow always already there, the 'double turn' must be understood in terms of what Derrida calls 'syntax' in 'The Double Session,' where the point is not to share Hegel's 'fascination' with 'the lexical richness, the semantic infiniteness of a word or concept, its depth or breadth, the sedimentation that produced inside it two contradictory layers of signification.' Rather, what 'counts here is the formal or syntactic *praxis* that composes or decomposes' those contradictory layers. This syntax is 'the "between" whether it names fusion or separation,' and it 'carries all the force of this operation.' It has no full meaning of its own because it 'forms a syntactical plug' (D 221). It is 'not a categorem, but a syncategorem: what philosophers from the Middle Ages to Husserl's *Logical Investigations* have called an incomplete signification.' This 'betweenness' is syntactic and it affects

> all other signs which, like *pharmakon, supplément, différance,* and others, have a double, contradictory, undecidable value that always derives from their syntax, whether the latter is in a sense 'internal,' articulating and combining under the same yoke, *huph' hen,* two incompatible meanings or 'external,' dependent on the code in which the word is made to function. But the syntactical composition and decomposition of a sign renders this alternative between internal and external inoperative. One is simply dealing with greater or lesser syntactical units at work, and with economic differences in condensation. Without reducing all these to the same, quite the contrary, it is possible to recognize a certain serial law in these points of indefinite pivoting: they mark the spot which can never be mediated, mastered, sublated, or dialecticized through any *Erinnerung* or *Aufhebung.* (D 221)

But 'betweenness' is not simply 'without meaning': it contains as its 'meaning' a 'semantic quasi-emptiness; it signifies the spacing relation, the articulation, the interval.'[22] As such, the 'between' is no longer 'a purely syntactic function': its 'semantic void' begins to signify 'spacing and articulation; it has as its meaning the possibility of syntax' (D 222). It is neither purely syntactic nor purely semantic.

It is this 'syntax' that breaks the 'continuist supposition' that governs the loss of meaning in the philosophical concept of metaphor that destroys itself in becoming 'proper' once more. Metaphor is always organized within the syntactics of a doubled 'loss of meaning' that destroys metaphor. The destruction of metaphor, says Derrida, 'will always have been able to take two courses which are almost tangent, and yet different, repeating, miming, and separating from each other according to certain laws.' This path is the also the circle of *anamnesis* or *Erinnerung* from Plato to Hegel, which takes the form of a 'specular circle, a return to itself without loss of meaning, without irreversible expenditure': it finishes by discovering the origin of its truth (M 268). The other destruction of metaphor makes legible the limits of metaphor and philosophy's 'general tropology.' In 'traversing and doubling the first self-destruction, it passes through the supplement of syntactic resistance through everything (for example in modern linguistics) that disrupts the opposition of the semantic and the syntactic, and especially the philosophical hierarchy that submits the latter to the former.' It is no longer a question of 'extending and confirming a philosopheme, but rather, of unfolding it without limit, and wresting the borders of propriety from it. And consequently to explode the reassuring opposition of the metaphoric and the proper, the opposition in which the one and the other have never done anything but reflect and refer to each other in their radiance' (M 270–1). It is this other destruction without propriety that Derrida names 'catachresis.'

Catachrestic Writing

The *Wake*an beacon/lighthouse displaces and reinscribes the concept of metaphor as it describes the 'metaphors of metaphor': the space of the *eidō* and that of the *'tour'* – turn and tower. Its disruptive double nature as lighthouse necessitates a peculiar language-light that displaces the value of a dwelling (be it 'proper' or 'borrowed'). It also affects 'Finnegan' with the lack of a proper name by displacing and reinscribing his 'presence.' And yet, even though the space of the *eidō* and the *tour* is not 'metaphoric,' it corresponds to the space of '"tropic" movements which, no longer capable of being called by a philosophical name – i.e. metaphors – nevertheless, and for the same reason, do not make up a "proper" [*propre* – "literal"] language' (229). It is this problematic space that the light from 'Finnegan's' lighthouse 'illuminates.' Since the 'materials' 'Finnegan' 'builds' with are 'already' the 'final product,' and the 'tower' he 'builds' 'erigenates' 'from next to nothing' (4.36–5.1) 'in' a 'scene' of 'buildung' 'without' 'presence,' it becomes clear that the only way of 'describing' this very peculiar scene at the start of *Finnegans Wake* is through an abuse of 'proper' terms that I have tried to mark here with quotation marks. Catachresis is the only possible way of sketching this scene.

Catachresis also intervenes in Derrida's analysis in response to his question on the metaphors of metaphor: '[C]an these defining tropes that are prior to all philosophical rhetoric and that produce philosophemes still be called metaphors?' Catachresis 'concerns first the violent and, forced, abusive inscription of a sign, the imposition of a sign upon a meaning which did not yet have its own proper sign in language. So much so that there is no substitution here, no transport of proper signs, but rather the irruptive extension of a sign proper to an idea, a meaning, deprived of their signifier. A "secondary origin"' (M 255).[23] This 'secondary origin' produces 'a new kind of proper sense, by means of a catachresis whose intermediary status tends to escape the opposition of the primitive [sense] and the figurative [sense], standing between them as a "middle"' (M 256). Catachresis, as the 'middle,' is here also a 'between,' a syncategorem: an interval that is neither purely semantic nor purely syntactic; a spacing.

Catachresis comes to bear where there is no longer a proper name for an idea, but this is not to say that such an idea already exists 'in the mind like a grid without a word.' On the contrary, the point here is precisely *not* 'to interpret the situation in philosophical terms' (M 257).[24] It must be borne in mind that these ideas 'could not have been retraced, tracked down, brought to daylight without the twisting which goes *against usage*, without the infraction of a catachresis' (ibid., Derrida's italics). Language and words are called upon to name the *eidos*/idea that is believed to precede their operation. The irony of course is that the *eidos*/idea could never have been found without the catachrestic use of language. For this reason, catachresis cannot be read in philosophical terms as the twisting return towards the already-there of a meaning. Rather, this 'irruptive extension' is called for by the *lack* of a prior/proper meaning or *eidos* that Western philosophy requires; whence the ambiguity that Derrida locates in discussions of catchresis that are governed by the philosophical distinction between signifier and signified, thought and language, and so forth (M 254). This ambiguity interprets the operation of catachresis as that which, on the one hand, 'does not emerge from language, does not create new signs, does not enrich the code' and yet, on the other, 'transforms its [language's] functioning, producing, with the same material, new rules of exchange, new values' (257). Understood in this way, it becomes clear that catachresis, like the 'immargination' discussed above, also 'produces' without (the) presence (of the signified).

Finnegans Wake explicitly pushes the operation of catachresis in the direction of language and a scene of writing during a scene of infantile composition in book II.2, which also reinscribes the interplay of the Same and Other in the scene of 'demiurgic' creation from Plato's *Timaeus* (36b–d).[25] As it does so, the text of the *Wake* also extends the effects of catachresis to words that pass from one person to another:[26]

> chanching letters for them vice o'verse
> to bronze mottes and blending tschemes for em in tropadores and
> doublecressing twofold thruths and devising tingling tailwords
> too whilest, cunctant that another would finish his sentence for
> him, he druider would smilabit eggways ned, he, to don't say
> nothing, would, so prim, and pick upon his ten ordinailed ungles,
> trying to undo with his teeth the knots made by his tongue,
> retelling humself by the math hour, long as he's brood reel of
> funnish ficts apout the shee, how faust of all and on segund
> thoughts and the thirds the charmhim girlalove and further-
> more and filthily with bag from Oxatown and baroccidents and
> proper accidence and hoptohill and hexenshoes, in fine the whole
> damning letter; and, in point of feet, when he landed in ourland's
> leinster of saved and solomnones for the twicedhecame time ...
> (288.1–14)

Here, in the *Wake*an recasting of the scene of demiurgic creation, the childish creator – 'Dolph, dean of idlers' (287.18) – performs a scene of composition as he lies in his cot that also doubles for the composition of the text of *Finnegans Wake* 'itself.' In this abyssal scene of composition, the infant Dolph uses his fingers to joyously and dextrously recount the stories he has heard from others. Unable to reproduce them orally, Dolph gleefully (re)composes the words of others by means of the figure of catachresis: the words he hears from others are twisted from their initially intended signified meaning. Dolph 'extends' the proper meaning of those stories, not in order to produce a truthful narrative, but rather to give a 'stolentelling' (424.35) that is no longer concerned with simply presenting truth. In Dolph's hands, the stories become an elaborate dance of 'funnish ficts' and 'doublecressing twofold truths' that are no longer concerned with establishing the prior 'true' meaning of the words of others before they are catachrestically 'changed' through their 'chance' (288.1) similarity to yet more (other) words.[27] Here, then is an infant who finger-writes against present truth by 'tscheme[-ing]' catachrestically, irruptively extending the signs and words of others, 'chanching' them into other words that they resemble by 'chance.' This scene is also, as I have mentioned, the scene that composes the *Wake*.

The reader is invited to hear in the chance resemblance of words a writing that is motivated by a 'tingle' in its 'tailwords,' the chime of 'bronze mottes' in complex and seductive tropes ('tropadores'). The reader is invited to hear in the irruptive extension that gives the 'tingling tailwords' a writing that is no longer governed by the (intended) signified (meaning).[28] Paradoxically, hearing these tingling tailwords also allows the reader to hear that Dolph's writing says 'nothing' (288.6). In other words, the 'nothing' that Dolph composes and that has little to do with a fully present intended meaning or idea that could be understood to pre-exist those words – including his own, since he is always 'cunctant' to let another 'finish his sentence for him' (288.4) – is itself a catachresis that names a 'next to nothing.' What the reader 'hears,' like Dolph in his crib, is the remainder of the words of others – that is, what is left over after present animating intention or meaning has been displaced and reinscribed in (finger) writing – the play of the non-present, non-true residue of the words of others stripped of their pre-existent eidetic meaning or intention that is heard as 'tingling' through their chance similarities. Dolph's 'nothing' is not simply silence; it is akin to what Derrida in his reading of *Ulysses* calls the affirmative *yes, yes* which 'describes nothing, states nothing, even if it is a sort of performative implied in all statements' (AL 297). Listening to this absence of eidetic meaning, one hears the echo of the 'nothing' at the heart of the scene of Dolph's pleasurable composition that corresponds to the b(u)ildung of Finnegan's tower analysed above. In bringing the scene of Finnegan's b(u)ildung into contact with Dolph's scene of writing, the *Wake* invites the reader to hear the catachrestic use of the affirmative – the words of others – as the medium that is 'immarginatively' excessive with respect to the philosophy of presence.

What I am referring to here as 'tingling' draws together a number of motifs that will be important later in this analysis. The first of these is directly connected to what I have been referring to here as the notion of 'tingling' understood as a bodily sensation that is neither simply pleasurable nor simply unpleasurable. I will consider this bodily sensation in conjunction with what has already been said about the 'secondary origin' of catachresis in order to sketch what I will call a 'textual' body.[29] The second of these is of major importance here in that it can be used to draw an analogy between the operation of the entire textual surface of *Finnegans Wake* and Derrida's entire textual procedure after *Dissemination*. As such it is of particular importance in a study that has as its stated aim a reconsideration and expansion of what constitutes Joyce-Derrida intertextuality. It is announced by the notion of 'tingling' as a 'tinkling,'[30] the similar 'ring' of signifiers that Dolph explores:

> Rhyme – which is the general law of textual effects – is the folding-together of an identity and a difference. The raw material for this operation is no longer merely the sound of the end of a word: all 'substances' (phonic and graphic) and all 'forms' can be linked together at any distance and under any rule in order to produce new versions of 'that which in discourse does not speak.' For difference is the necessary interval, the suspense between two outcomes, the 'lapse of time' between two shots, two rolls, two chances. Without it being possible in advance to *decide* the limits of this sort of propagation, a different effect is produced each time, an effect that is each time new [*neuf*], a game [*jeu*] of chance forever new, a play of fire [*feu*] forever young [*jeune*] – fire and games being always, as Heraclitus and Nietzsche have said, a play of luck with necessity, of contingency with law. (D 277)

Rhyme inscribes spacing in both speech/writing: it therefore functions as what Derrida refers to as 'general writing.'[31] Dolph's 'tingling tail-words' are therefore analogous to the 'repercussions set off among signifiers' that Derrida finds at work in Mallarmé's texts, which are 'in no way dictated or decided in advance by any thematic intentionality' (ibid.).[32] Through the scene with Dolph in his cot, *Finnegans Wake* invites the reader to read its textual surface as a catachrestic generalized writing, a 'twofold' that 'tingles' and 'changes' with the 'chance' resemblances between the words of others that are no longer governed by present meaning in the form of an intended meaning.

Insofar as it is no longer governed by the value of present-meaning-as-intention, Dolph's writing slides towards a doubling 'unconsciousness' where its 'doublecressing twofold thruths' play upon the sort of 'double stage' Derrida explores in 'The Double Session.' This double stage also marks the limits of Hegelian meaning:[33]

> These 'words' [e.g., *pharmakon*, *supplément*, *différance*] admit into their games both contradiction and noncontradiction (and the contradiction and noncontradiction *between* contradiction and noncontradiction). Without any dialectical *Aufhebung*, without any time off, they belong in a sense both to consciousness and the unconscious, which Freud tells us can tolerate or remain insensitive to contradiction. Insofar as the text depends upon them, *bends* to them [*s'y plie*], it thus plays a double scene upon a double stage. It operates in two absolutely different places at once, even if these are only separated by a veil, which is both traversed and not traversed, *inter*sected [*entr'ouvert*]. (D 221)

Here, the action of the *Aufhebung* is halted in those words that are shot through with the syntax of writing, that irreducible spacing that prevents meaning from becoming fully conscious. Through these words, or rather, their 'betweenness' as neither purely semantic nor purely syntactic, the '*Aufhebung – la relève –* is constrained into writing itself otherwise. Or perhaps simply into writing itself. Or, better, into taking account of its consumption of writing' (M 19). It will be for the same reasons that the 'doublecressed twofold' that displaces and reinscribes 'intention' – yet another figure for the presence of signified meaning – will provide a general background within which the *Aufhebung* is displaced and reinscribed.[34] It is this double space that will also provide the stage on which Derrida's *Glas* may be considered in conjunction with *Finnegans Wake*. It is the motif of the 'double scene' and the 'double stage' that also displaces and reinscribes the *eidos*.

From Imitation to Mimicry: From eidos *to* 'eidos'

The type of composition carried out by Dolph or by 'Finnegan' recurs throughout Joyce's texts. One such example is found in the first chapter of *Ulysses*, where Stephen composes the scene of Clive Kempthorpe's 'debagging' after just having caught Buck Mulligan's passing reference to it in his attempt to reconcile with Stephen:

– And to think of your having to beg from these swine. I'm the only one that knows what you are. Why don't you trust me more? What have you up your nose against me? Is it Haines? If he makes any noise here I'll bring down Seymour and we'll give him a ragging worse than they gave Clive Kempthorpe.

Young shouts of moneyed voices in Clive Kempthorpe's rooms.

Palefaces: they hold their ribs with laughter, one clasping another. O, I shall expire! Break the news to her gently, Aubrey! I shall die! With slit ribbons of his shirt whipping the air he hops and hobbles round the table, with trousers down at heels, chased by Ades of Magdalen with the tailor's shears. A scared calf's face gilded with marmalade. I don't want to be debagged! Don't you play the giddy ox with me!

Shouts from the open window startling evening in the quadrangle. A deaf gardener, aproned, masked with Matthew Arnold's face, pushes his mower on the sombre lawn watching narrowly the dancing motes of grasshalms. (*Ulysses* 1.160–75)[35]

Stephen's process of composition breaks from Mulligan's intention to reconcile; is purely imaginative insofar as it cannot be said to arise out of any particular past-present or present experience he has had of Oxford; and has little to do with the real reason for his problems with Mulligan. As such, Stephen's play with 'funnish ficts' arises from the next to nothing of Buck's passing remark about Kempthorpe. From this meagre offering, from the words of another, from next to nothing, Stephen reproduces a hilarious reinscription of Oxford's quadrangle. Stephen's composition is therefore catachrestic in precisely the sense Derrida gives that word because it 'eriginates,' like the b(u)ildung of Finnegan's tower or Dolph's 'handwriting' 'from next to nothing.' Here, the next to nothing is only Buck's passing remark about Kempthorpe.

The words of another can also be understood as next to nothing if, like Dolph in his crib, one considers them as just language without the presence of intention, meaning, the *eidos*. In other words, language in the scene of catachresis can be understood as pure text. This can be made clearer by returning to Derrida's reading of Stéphane Mallarmé's 'Mimique,' a short work on mime in 'The Double Session' (D 173–286). As Derrida reads it, 'Mimique' sketches the non-philosophical 'other' of Platonic *mimēsis*. If the Platonic *eidos* is accorded a certain privilege in this analysis, it is because I take it as axiomatic that 'Platonism' can stand 'more or less immediately for the whole history of Western philosophy, including the anti-Platonisms that regularly feed it.'[36] Platonism can stand in for all of Western philosophy first and foremost because it wishes to maintain the priority of 'what is, "reality," the thing itself' over the 'painting, the portrait, ... the inscription or transcription of the thing itself' (D 191). In maintaining the priority of 'what is' over its 'inscription,' Platonism has bequeathed to Western philosophy its powerful conception of the process of *mimēsis*: the imitation (expression, description, representation, illustration, etc.) of 'an *eidos* or *idea*' (D 194). The *eidos* or idea, since it is 'already in the mind like a grid without a word,'[37] is the 'reality' that is then imitated. As such, the *eidos* can stand in for all forms of 'that which is, the being-present (the matrix-form of substance, of reality, of the opposition between matter and form, essence and existence, objectivity and subjectivity, etc.)' insofar as they are 'distinguished from the appearance, the image, the phenomenon, etc., that is, from anything that, presenting it *as* being present, doubles it, re-presents it, and can therefore replace and de-present it' (D 191). It is through the *eidos* that Platonism (and thus Western philosophy) defines the realm of that which is as that which is imitated, and constitutes what Derrida calls the 'order of appearance,' 'the very process of appearing in general' where 'the precedence [*pré-séance*] of the imitated ... governs the philosophical or critical interpretation of literature' (D 192).

In 'Mimique,' Mallarmé's mime – in the guise of a Pierrot – not only displaces the imitation of the *eidos*, but also inscribes what is mimed without (the) prior presence (of the *logos* – 'meaning, word, voice, discourse,' D 198):

There is no imitation. The Mime imitates nothing. And to begin with, he doesn't imitate. There is nothing prior to the writing of his gestures. Nothing is prescribed for him. No present has preceded or supervised the tracing of his writing. His movements form a figure that no speech anticipates or accompanies. They are not linked with *logos* in any order of consequence. '*Such is this PIERROT MURDERER OF HIS WIFE composed and set down by himself, a mute soliloquy ...* '[38]

'Composed and set down by himself ... ' Here we enter a textual labyrinth panelled with mirrors. The Mime *follows* no preestablished script, no program obtained elsewhere. Not that he improvises or lets himself go spontaneously: he simply does not obey any verbal order. His gestures, his gestural writing (and Mallarmé's insistence on describing the regulated gesture of dance or pantomime as a hieroglyphic inscription is legendary), are not dictated by any verbal discourse or imposed by any diction. The Mime inaugurates; he breaks into a white page: ' ... *a mute soliloquy that the phantom, white as a yet unwritten page, holds in both face and gesture at full length to his soul.*' (D 194–5)

Mime differs from imitation in that it, like the 'immargination' in the *Wake*, imitates 'nothing.' In imitating nothing, mime therefore differs from all sorts of Platonism, including all its Cartesian and Hegelian forms. But Mallarmé still calls this nothing, which 'is' not anything that can present itself (D 126), an 'Idea.' In other words, the Mime recounted in *Mimique* '*illustrates but the idea, not any actual action*' (194, Mallarmé's italics). Thus, Mallarmé's Mime's gestural writing mimes a simulacrum, a double of an idea or *eidos*, and such simulation robs the idea or *eidos* of its presence: the Mallarméan 'Idea' is now a simulated '*eidos*,' a nothing that nowhere presents itself. It is an *eidos* without *logos*, and the Mime 'is not subjected to the authority of any book' (195). Nevertheless, it was 'in a booklet, upon a page, that Mallarmé must have read the effacement of the booklet before the gestural initiative of the Mime'[39] (196). This effacement opens mime and gestural writing, and this effacement echoes that of the *Wake*'s opening page:

> What Mallarmé *read*, then, in this little book is a prescription that *effaces itself through its very existence*, the order given to the Mime to imitate nothing that in any way preexists his operation: neither an act ('*the scene illustrates but the idea, not any actual action*') nor a word ('*stilled ode ... mute soliloquy that the phantom, white as a yet unwritten page, holds in both face and gesture at full length to his soul*').
>
> In the beginning of this mime was neither the deed nor the word. It is prescribed (we will define this word in a moment) to the Mime that he not let anything be prescribed to him but his own writing, that he not reproduce by imitation any action (*pragma*: affair, thing, act) or any speech (*logos*: word, voice, discourse). The Mime ought only to write himself on the white page he is; he must *himself* inscribe *himself* through gestures and plays of facial expression. At once page and quill, Pierrot is both passive and active, matter and form, the author, the means, and the raw material of his mimodrama. The histrion produces himself here. (198)

The auto-effacement of the booklet also entails the loss of the present *logos*, the inward discourse of speech, or the 'hearing-oneself-speak,' that constitutes the very mode of phenomenological and philosophical self-present 'identity' (SP 70–87).[40] This is because the Mime's gestures no longer imitate the self-present *logos* that is 'shaped according to the model of the [Platonic] *eidos*' (D 188). In this simulated double space, therefore, both the *eidos* and the *logos* it shapes are displaced by a simulated double that imitates nothing. The Mime is both active and passive in the face of these prescriptions: he 'writes' ('is written') because he 'reads' (D 198) (and 'is read' by [D 224]) the text. In the realm of the non-Platonic *eidos*, reading is both the prescription to erase the *eidos* and the prescription to write or 'produce' oneself.[41]

Despite all this, it is still an 'Idea' that comes to substitute for the *eidos* (see also D 192–8). However, since 'no present' 'precede[s] or supervise[s] the tracing of [the Mime's] writing' (194), this 'Idea' cannot be understood to present itself at all. Because this reconfigured 'Idea' does not present itself, it gives itself as nothing to be read. This nothing, which is still legible, is constituted by *différance*. As nothing, it is not, and is nowhere subject to the realm of Being, the 'is':

> Perhaps we must attempt to think this unheard-of thought, this silent tracing: that the history of Being, whose thought engages the Greco-Western *logos* such as it is produced via the ontological difference, is but an epoch of the *diapherein*. Henceforth one could no longer even call this an 'epoch,' the concept of epochality belonging to what is within history as the history of Being. Since Being has never had a 'meaning,' has never been thought or said as such, except by dissimulating itself in beings, then *différance*, in a certain and very strange way, (is) 'older' than the ontological difference or than the truth of Being. When it has this age it can be called the play of the trace. The play of a trace which no longer belongs to the horizon of Being, but whose play transports and encloses the meaning of Being: the play of the trace, of the *différance*, which has no meaning and is not. Which does not belong. There is no maintaining, and no depth to, this bottomless chessboard on which Being is put into play. (M 22)[42]

That which comes about through the *différantial* play of traces is, for Derrida, the text of writing: '[It] is this constitution of the present, as an "originary" and irreducibly nonsimple (and therefore, *stricto sensu* nonoriginary) synthesis of marks, or traces (to reproduce analogically and provisionally a phenomenological and transcendental language that will soon reveal itself to be inadequate), that I propose to call archi-writing, archi-trace, or *différance*. Which (is) (simultaneously) spacing (and) temporization' (M 13). It is now easy to see that it is the written text, text composed of *différantial* traces, which is not. Thus if it is text that is imitated, then the one imitating it imitates nothing, and stays within the space of the non-Platonic *eidos*.

This goes to the heart of a difficulty of writing. Writing, according to *Dissemination*, 'refers only to itself,' but also refers 'each time to another text': 'It is necessary that while referring each time to another text, to another determinate system, each organism refer to *itself* as a determinate structure; a structure that is open and closed *at the same time*' (D 202). The written text is 'haunted by the ghost or grafted onto the arborescence of another text' (202). This odd situation is merely the extension of the principle of *différance* to include the situation of other written texts which also do not 'exist' in any present sense within a more generalized text. In other words, writing is itself – from top to bottom – *différantial*.

But this mirroring of writing and the written that imitates nothing is not to be taken for the unveiling of an ancient Greek or Heideggerian *aletheia*:

> One could indeed push Mallarmé back into the most 'originary' metaphysics of truth if all mimicry [*mimique*] had indeed disappeared, if it had effaced itself in the scriptural production of truth.
>
> But such is not the case. *There is* mimicry. Mallarmé sets great store by it, along with simulacrum ... We are faced then with mimicry imitating nothing; faced, so to speak, with a double that doubles no simple, a double that nothing anticipates, nothing at least that is not already double. There is no simple reference. It is in this that the mime's operation does allude, but alludes to nothing, alludes without breaking the mirror, without reaching beyond the looking-glass. *'That is how the Mime operates, whose act is confined to a perpetual allusion without breaking the ice or the mirror.'* This speculum reflects no reality; it produces mere 'reality-effects.' (D 206)

The mime that remains 'thus preserves the differential structure of mimicry or *mimesis*, but without its Platonic or metaphysical interpretation, which implies that somewhere the being of something that *is*, is being imitated' (206). Mime, mimicry, maintains 'the structure of the *phantasma* as it is defined by Plato: the simulacrum as the copy of the copy. With the exception that there is no longer any model, and hence no copy, and that this structure (which encompasses Plato's text, including his attempt to escape it) is no longer being referred back to any ontology or even to any dialectic' (D 206–7).

In other words, the phantasma, simulacrum, or eidolon is 'produced' in the imagination, which doubles (for) the Platonic *eidos*. The doubleness that simultaneously connects and separates the Platonic and non-Platonic *eidos* is maintained in the face of the dialectical suppression that would make it simply philosophical. Rather, the non-Platonic *eidos* 'is a simulacrum of Platonism or Hegelianism, which is separated from what it simulates only by a barely perceptible veil, about which one can just as well say that it already runs – unnoticed – between Platonism and itself, between Hegelianism and itself' (207): as such, the *eidos* begins to play in the space on the double stage of the unconscious as it was just discussed above. All of this forms an operation

> which no longer belongs to the systems of truth, does not manifest, produce, or unveil any presence; nor does it constitute any conformity, resemblance, or adequation between a presence and representation. And yet this operation is not a unified entity but the manifold play of a scene that, illustrating nothing – neither word nor deed – beyond itself, illustrates nothing. Nothing but the many-faceted multiplicity of a lustre which itself is nothing beyond its own fragmented light. Nothing but the idea which is nothing. The ideality of the idea is here for Mallarmé the still metaphysical name that is still necessary in order to mark non-being, the nonreal, the nonpresent. This mark points, alludes without breaking the glass, to the beyond of beingness, toward the *epekeina tes ousias*: a hymen (a closeness and a veil) between Plato's sun and Mallarmé's lustre this 'materialism of the idea' is nothing other than the staging, the theater, the visibility of nothing or of the self. It is a dramatization which *illustrates nothing*, which illustrates *the nothing*, lights up a space, re-marks a spacing as a nothing, a blank. (D 208)

It is this catachrestic reinscription of the *eidos* that I will follow throughout the remainder of this text.

However, this mode of non-eidetic reading, no matter how strange it might seem at first, is also a part of a long tradition of reading texts. That tradition is itself referred to by the *Wake* in relation to the scene of demiurgic creation discussed above:

> *antiquissimam flaminum amborium Jordani et Jambaptistae mentibus revolvamus sapientiam: totum tute fluvii modo mundo fluere, eadem quae exaggere fututa iterum inter alveum fore futura, quodlibet sese ipsum per aliudpiam agnoscere contrarium, omnem demun amnem ripis rivalibus amplecti.*

[translation: '... let us turn over in our minds that most ancient wisdom of Giordano and Giambattista: the fact that the whole of the river flows safely, with a clear stream, and that those thing which were to have been on the bank would later be in the bed; finally that everything recognizes itself through something opposite and that the stream is embraced by rival banks.' (*Annotations*)] (287.23–8)

In other words, Dolph's catachrestic 'stolentellings' in the crib can be understood to fit into the tradition of reading-writing exemplified by Giordano Bruno and Giambattista Vico. In the next section of this chapter, I will examine some of the ways in which both Derrida's writing and Joyce's writing relate to Vico's *The New Science*.

The (Quasi-) Vichian Reader-Writer

The loss of the *eidos* as a present model to be imitated in imaginary writing also means there can no longer be any imitation of that philosophical *eidos* (signified meaning, referent, thing-in-itself). In this way, a reader of a text that stages the scene of either immargination or writing also becomes a writer of that text to the extent that the text does not simply exist before the act of reading. Joyce's tower b(u)ildung and Derrida's discussions of both Mallarmé's text and catachresis share a great deal with Giambattista Vico's *The New Science*.[43] Vico's cyclical ideal eternal history of mankind is a powerful statement of the tradition of non-eidetic reading, which sees itself as a productive writing. In this section, I will explore how Vico's text also sketches that tradition.

The New Science is intended, says Vico, to be a 'rational civil theology of divine providence' (NS 342). In contemplating 'infinite and eternal providence,' the foreknowing, beneficent care and government of God, *The New Science* arrives at 'certain divine proofs' (343). By carefully considering these divine proofs, the reader 'experiences' in 'his mortal body a divine pleasure' (NS 345). But how is this divine pleasure to be felt?

The pleasure experienced by the reader of *The New Science* becomes divine in three stages. The first stage is simply that of the pleasure of creation. Or, as Vico puts it, 'he who meditates this Science narrates to himself this ideal eternal history so far as he makes it for himself' (NS 349). This remaking of the ideal eternal history of mankind is possible because the 'world of nations has certainly been made by men, and it must therefore be found within the modification of our own human mind' (NS 349). The fact that the human mind is responsible for the ideal eternal history of nations means that this history – unlike nature, which is made only by God and therefore only knowable by him – is completely knowable by the human mind. This constitutes the well-known Vichian principle of *verum-factum*, or 'the made is the true,' where the produced object is completely known and knowable by its maker. Made from scratch by the human mind, ideal eternal history is produced by Vichian man, who acts without imitating anything. He is therefore something of an analogue to Mallarmé's Mime, who is told 'to imitate nothing that in any way preexists his operation: neither an act (*"the scene illustrates but the idea, not any actual action"*) nor a word (*"stilled ode ... mute soliloquy that the phantom, white as a yet unwritten page, holds in both face and gesture at full length to his soul"*)' (D 198). Vichian man, like the Mime, 'ought only to write himself on the white page he is; he must *himself* inscribe *himself* through gestures and plays of facial expression' (198). This is why Vico states that 'speech was born in mute times as mental [or sign] language, which Strabo in a golden passage [1.2.6] says existed before vocal or articulate language.' The signs man produces in this mute 'first language' were, says Vico, composed of 'gestures or physical objects' (NS 401). The Vichian Mime therefore makes himself 'understood by gestures' (NS 225) before the meaningfully articulated language of the voice. In this way, he 'produces' his own meaning in the performance of these gestures. And because Vichian man is a Mime, he, like Pierrot, 'produces' his own meaning, his own self, in the absence of a prior Platonic *eidos* or voice.

But there is an added complication to this scene of mimicry, which, if read in conjunction with Derrida's analysis of Mallarmé's Mime, makes it possible to see the Vichian mime as purely textual. This complication comes to *The New Science* in the form of providence. Providence is that which acts 'without human discernment or counsel, and often against the designs of men' (NS 343), in order to make the history of nations as well. Since the reader of *The New Science* must also contemplate what 'providence has wrought in history,' it is this divine providence that must be met by the human mind if it is to know divine pleasure. But how is providence to be met by the human mind? What happens when the mind's contemplative fabrication of providence's work in history rises to meet (providence) itself in the second stage in the reader's experience of divine pleasure? It might also seem that providence precedes man and his mime. In preceding man and his mime, providence would constitute a sort of eidetic content for Vico's thought, because God, as divine creator, pre-exists all things human. However, the apparent eidetic content of providence is reinscribed by the very form of the meeting of the human mind and providence that Vico says is necessary in order to experience divine pleasure. This is because Vico sets up his meeting in such a way that it does not take the form of an event or an encounter.

This apparent paradox can be read in the following manner. If the mind can know completely the ideal eternal history, as Vico claims it does, it can do so only on the basis of knowing that which it has made. This is the previously mentioned *verum-factum* principle, according to which only the maker of an object can know that object completely and utterly. The principle of 'the made is the known' also applies, first and foremost, to God, since 'in God knowledge and creation are one and the same thing' (NS 349). Since both providence and the human mind 'make' human history, God and the human mind meet in its 'production.' In this history, the human mind produces in the exact same way as providence, and it may therefore contemplate the ideal eternal history of nations as if it were (the) divine. In other words, if creation is for God *ex nihilo*, then the reader who is to experience the divine pleasure of creation must also experience *creatio ex nihilo*.

How does this happen? The reader can only experience *creatio ex nihilo* if s/he discovers her/himself as its mime, as its productive writer who writes from scratch. Only then can the reader experience the divine pleasure of God, who creates from nothing. God himself no longer creates from an *eidos*. Even though God creates without model, he offers himself to man as the model for creation. However, in offering himself as the model of creation that does without a model, God withdraws as a model insofar as he presents the model of imitation or production without model. In effect God tells man to contemplate as he does, without a model. In offering that model, he withdraws as model of imitation, and this leaves man free to experience the divine model of creation without model, *ex nihilo*. Vichian man is therefore once again put in the position of the Mime in Derrida's examination of Mallarmé: 'What Mallarmé *read*, then, in this little book is a prescription that *effaces itself through its very existence*, the order given to the Mime to imitate nothing that in any way preexists his operation' (D198). God's withdrawal of himself as model even as man goes to meet him in imitation means that the meeting of God and man does not take place. God's model therefore withdraws itself in the textual manner discussed in the previous subsection. The event of the meeting never happens precisely because God effaces himself as model. For Vico, the first stage in the making of history without model is that of taking the auspices: the observation of bird flight in divination. In chapters 2 and 3 I will explore in depth the *Wake*an analogue to this Vichian making without model: the detailed staging of the scene of writing that composes the hen's letter in I.5. This detailed staging of the Vichian origins of man as writing allows *Finnegans Wake* to both participate in and reinscribe Vico's productive method.

II

Immargination: Différance, *Doubling, Laughter*

The Vichian-Joycean mode of imaginary writing is a mimicked performance in that the model or *eidos* to be imitated withdraws from, or effaces itself as, presence. Because of this, mimicry can be understood as *différantial* in the sense Derrida gives to the word. *Différance* is a French neologism coined by Derrida to convey the sort of differentiation in time and space that disrupts simple punctual presence. By recognizing *différance* at work in the mimicry of Vichian-Joycean imaginary writing, the remaining section of this chapter moves closer to sketching an imaginative framework that will enable the reader to negotiate an expanded conception of Joyce-Derrida intertextuality. As I will argue here, *différance* acts as a sort of bridge that makes it possible to bring Joycean-Vichian imaginative writing into contact with the thought of Heidegger and Hegel. Read in this way, the theoretical potential of Vichian-Joycean imaginary writing is also made clearer.

The first subsection to follow explores how *différance* exposes imaginary textual production in Joyce's text to the difficult relationship that *différance* has with Heidegger's thought. Because these difficulties play themselves out in relation to Heidegger's analyses of the imagination in Kant, it becomes possible to make use of the *différantial* resources of Heidegger's analyses of the imagination in order to develop further the exploration of the non-eidetic Joycean imaginary framework begun in the first section of this chapter. The next subsection traces an interesting effect that arises from reading the catachrestic writing of Joycean-Vichian imaginative textual production in conjunction with *différance*. This effect has primarily to do with how *différance* can be read as shorthand for relating the known (that is, the *eidos* as philosophical presence, knowledge, meaning, etc.) to the unknown (non-presence, text, writing, etc.). As has been suggested so far, this relation takes the forms of the disruption, catachresis, reinscription, and so on, of presence. However, by itself, the relation of the known to the unknown remains within the enclosure bounded by the speculative philosophy of Hegel, a form of Platonism (D 194). As Derrida says, Hegelianism 'complet[es] itself' by 'includ[ing] and anticipat[ing] all the figures of its beyond, all the forms and resources of its exterior' (WD 252). Understood in this way, Hegelianism bears a structural resemblance to what Derrida has analysed as the 'yes' and 'hypermnesic' laughter of Joyce (AL 281 and PSJ 147). Their structural resemblance would consist in the watchful vigil these structures constantly keep over all their 'others' in order to appropriate them to themselves. Thus, if this study is to avoid making the catach-restic and imaginary writing discussed above seem like a mere moment to be appropriated by Hegelianism, Platonism, or the hypermnesic laughter of Joyce, then a comparison of *Finnegans Wake* to the Hegelian project is methodologically necessary.[44] In other words, this compari-son must be attuned to a Hegelian equivalent[45] of the other laughter of the *yes, yes* if the present study's analysis of imaginary writing is to be developed into a theoretical framework that will enable the reader of Joyce and/or Derrida to negotiate and theorize an expanded concept of Joyce-Derrida intertextuality. In order to fulfil these requirements, this study will carry out a sustained comparison of *Finnegans Wake* and Der-rida's most engaged deconstruction of the Hegelian project: *Glas*. When carried out in this manner, this comparison will also serve to test the general applicability and flexibility of the imaginative framework that I am attempting to develop here by using it to identify, isolate, and theorize the remarkable correspondence between the key figures and textual strategies of *Glas* and *Finnegans Wake*.

'Unconsciousness' and Imagination

The Vichian structure of the always deferred (non)event of the meeting of human and divine mind discussed in the last section opens Vichian history as one that is written in the absence of an eidetic model. This history is therefore not one that is constrained by events that actually 'occur' as its content. Instead history, as Vico conceives of it, can be considered as a place where '[e]verything happens *as if*' according to a mythopoetic structure that Derrida analyses in relation to the Freudian 'event' of the paternal slaughter that gives rise to law:

Nobody would have encountered [the Freudian event of paternal slaugh-
ter] in its proper place of happening, nobody would have faced it in its
taking place. Event without event, pure event where nothing happens,
the eventiality of an event which both demands and annuls the relation in
its fiction ... However, this pure and purely presumed event nevertheless
marks an invisible rent in history. It resembles a fiction, a myth, or a fable,
and its relation is so structured that all questions as to Freud's intentions
are at once inevitable and pointless ('Did he believe it or not? Did he
maintain that it came down to a real and historical murder?' and so on).
The structure of this event is such that one is compelled neither to believe
nor disbelieve it ... Demanding and denying the story, this quasi-event
bears the mark of fictive narrativity (fiction *of* narration as well as fiction
as narration: fictive as the simulacrum of the narration and not only as the
narration of an imaginary history). It is the origin of literature at the same
time as the origin of law. (AL 199)[46]

The importance of Vichian or Freudian historiography lies not in its
factual accuracy, but rather in what Derrida calls the 'the invisible rent'
this historiography makes in 'factual history.' This rent is the condition
for the possibility (and impossibility) for history insofar as it 'demands
and denies' a (hi)story. The (real, eidetic) event never actually takes
place in this historiography that ceaselessly defers the event according
to the spatio-temporal delay that Derrida names *différance*.[47]
   In the previous quote Derrida notes in passing the relation the his-
toric non-event has with the imagination, a relation that Vico in *The
New Science* generalizes as he discusses the first men's creation of their
world through their imagination: '[T]he first men ... created things
according to their own ideas ... by virtue of a wholly corporeal imagination. And because it was corporeal, they did it with marvellous sublimity; a sublimity so great that it excessively perturbed the very
persons who by imagining did the creating, for they were called
"poets," which is Greek for "creators"' (NS 376; see also 185). Here, the
imaginative ideas – and not rational ideas, something I will return to
momentarily – 'make' the entire world of the first men. Through the
imagination the first men create their world in a process that does
without the 'objective reality' of the world. The law takes shape in the
poet's imaginative creation of the world that perturbs to excess in
order to 'teach the vulgar to act virtuously' (376). Derrida also notes
this frightening aspect of the law even if one connects it to the workings of the imagination:

> Whether or not it has arisen from the imagination, even the transcendental imagination, and whether it states or silences the origin of fantasy, this in no way diminishes the imperious necessity of what it tells, its law. This law is even more frightening and fantastic, *unheimlich* or uncanny, than if it emanated from pure reason, unless precisely the latter be linked to an unconscious fantastic. As of 1897, let me repeat, Freud stated his 'certain insight that there are no indications of reality in the unconscious, so that one cannot distinguish between truth and fiction that has been cathected with affect.' (AL 199)

Derrida's caution regarding the imaginative origin of the law is entirely understandable if it is assumed that the imagination merely reproduces the presence of a prior *eidos*, meaning, or referent. Against this imagination, another imagination 'produces' according to the mode of catachrestic non-presence that I have argued is at work in the *Wake*'s conception of the 'immargination' or in Vico's conception of how the reader makes or writes *The New Science* for himself. This imaginative mode straddles the distinction between the fictive or f/actual, and can be understood in terms of an 'unconsciousness' where 'one cannot distinguish between truth and fiction.'

If the imagination comes together with 'unconsciousness' in the non-event of imaginative 'production' and historiography, that is because it structurally resembles the unconscious that is 'definitively exempt from every process of presentation by means of which we could call upon it to show itself in person. In this context, and beneath this guise, the unconscious is not, as we know, a hidden, virtual, or potential self-presence. It differs from, and defers, itself; which doubtless means that it is woven of differences ... [T]he "unconscious" is no more a "thing" than it is any other thing' (M 20–1). In the 'unconscious imagination' there is no longer any opposition between consciousness and unconsciousness because it is completely consumed by *différance*, to differ and defer: 'This radical alterity as concerns every possible mode of presence is marked by the irreducibility of the aftereffect, the delay. In order to describe [these] traces, in order to read the traces of 'unconscious' traces (there are no 'conscious' traces), the language of presence and absence, the metaphysical discourse of phenomenology is inadequate' (M 20–1). *Différance* saturates what I am nicknaming here the 'unconscious imagination' and opens it to the play of temporalization:

The structure of delay (*Nachträglichkeit*) in effect forbids that one make of temporalization (temporization) a simple dialectical complication of the living present as an originary and unceasing synthesis – a synthesis directed back on itself, gathered in on itself and gathering – of retentional traces and protentional openings. The alterity of the 'unconscious' makes us concerned not with horizons of modified – past or future – presents, but with a 'past' that has never been present, and which will never be, whose future to come will never be a *production* or a reproduction in the form of presence. Therefore the concept of trace is incompatible with the concept of retention, of the becoming-past of what has been present. One cannot think the trace – and therefore, *différance* – on the basis of the present, or of the present of the present. (M 21)

The temporalization and delay that composes the *différantial* of the unconscious imagination 'comes to solicit' 'the domination of beings,' understood as present 'objects' (SP 62ff.): '[I]t is the determination of Being as presence or as beingness that is interrogated by the thought of *différance*. Such a question could not emerge and be understood unless the difference between Being and beings were somewhere to be broached' (M 21). As is well known, this question is the very one that sets in motion Heidegger's philosophical corpus from *Being and Time* up to the late texts on Trakl. Catching a glimpse of this difference – which Heidegger calls the ontological difference – makes it easier to sketch *différance*. To this limited extent, therefore, Heidegger's philosophy is indispensable for the thought of *différance*.

But *différance* also goes beyond Heidegger's thought. *Différance* surpasses Heidegger's thought to the extent that it is held fast by the fascination with the '*meaning* or *truth* of Being,' and remains 'intra-metaphysical' (22). As was discussed above, *différance* flips around the intrametaphysical meaning and truth of Being, and asks us to think an 'unheard-of thought': 'that the history of Being, whose thought engages the Greco-Western *logos* such as it is produced via the ontological difference, is but an epoch of the *diapherein*.' This occurs because Being dissimulates 'itself in beings, then *différance*, in a certain and very strange way, (is) 'older' than the ontological difference or than the truth of Being.' *Différance* is the 'play of a trace which no longer belongs to the horizon of Being' and which 'has no meaning and is not' (M 22). Thus, on the one hand, Heidegger's thought is indispensable for thinking about *différance* because it tries to disrupt the metaphysical thinking about beings that sees them as being simply present; on the other, because Heidegger still seeks the meaning or truth of Being, *différance* exceeds his thought and (catachrestically) reinscribes it within the temporalization of delay in *différance*. Since *différance* is both due to and reinscribes Heidegger's thought, its temporalizing delay can also be understood to mark the point at which Heidegger's thought exceeds itself. Such a point would therefore mark the necessity of considering Heidegger's discourse in the context of this study's expanded conception of Joyce-Derrida intertextuality even as that intertextuality overtakes it. This consideration must take into account the fascinating relationship that *différance* has with Heidegger's thought through what Derrida calls the 'incumbency' of 'auto-affection' (SP 83). Auto-affection derives from Heidegger's analysis of the imagination in *Kant and the Problem of Metaphysics*.[48] According to Heidegger, the imagination gives time according to the structure of self- or auto-affection. In Derrida's hands, the temporality of auto-affection simultaneously makes possible and destroys presence in all its forms by introducing a pure difference into it, which doubles the self as other:[49]

> The process by which the living now, produced by spontaneous genera-
> tion, must, in order to be a now and retained in another now, ... is indeed
> a pure auto-affection in which the same is the same only in being affected
> by the other, only by becoming the other of the same ... [This] pure differ-
> ence, which constitutes the self-presence of the living present, introduces
> into self-presence from the beginning all the impurity putatively excluded
> from it. The living present springs forth out of its nonidentity with itself
> and from the possibility of a retentional trace. It is always already a trace.
> (SP 85)

Since 'auto-affection' thus reinscribed can be said to specifically name the operation of *différance* in/as the imagination, the imagination can therefore be regarded as the site where the 'incumbency' of Heidegger's thought for *différance* plays itself out. Because of this, the recourse to *différance* in order to explore Vichian and Joycean text also opens onto Heidegger's analysis of the imagination. If Heidegger's imagination can, through the structure of auto-affection, be thought in a non-eidetic sense, then it becomes necessary to utilize certain aspects of the Heideggerian analysis of the imagination in order to give intellectual rigour to this study's analysis of the workings of the *différantial* imagination in Derrida, *Finnegans Wake*, and Vico. In chapters 2, 3, and 4

I will also make use of the Vichian-Joycean-Derridean-Heideggerian nexus to fully develop this imaginative framework so as to enable the reader to negotiate the expanded conception of Joyce-Derrida inter-textuality.

The Case of Hegel: Finnegans Wake *and* Glas

As was discussed below, Western philosophy – whether it be in its Pla-tonic, Cartesian, or Hegelian forms – is always a matter of imitating an *eidos* or idea, whether it is a figure of the thing itself, as in Plato, or of both the thing itself and a subjective representation, as in Hegel (D 194). This structure of philosophical imitation remains intact wherever it is a matter of expressing, describing, representing, illustrating an *eidos*. In contrast to this philosophical schema of eidetic imitation, I have suggested that *Finnegans Wake* instead proposes an imagination that imitates nothing, that displaces and reinscribes the mimetic schema of Western philosophy. I have also argued that this imaginative reinscription shares an affinity with certain key textual strategies found in the work of Jacques Derrida. Since these strategies are found in texts that are, to a certain degree, 'outside' what is taken to be the 'usual' terrain of Joyce-Derrida intertextuality – that is to say, 'outside' of the texts where Derrida either explicitly writes on Joyce or mentions him by name – they suggest that there is an expanded zone of Joycean-Derridean intertextuality that stands in need of exploration by readers with an interest in the work of both these authors. However, arguing that the *Wake* may be understood as a sort of 'proto-deconstruction' that shares much with Derrida's careful tracing of the disruption of presence and philosophical mimesis poses a theoretical problem for readers of Joyce and Derrida. This theoretical problem, which has to do with the manner in which these philosophies attempt to appropriate their every beyond or exterior to themselves, can be clarified by con-sidering both Plato's and Hegel's eidetic philosophies and how they relate to what is at stake in this study's engagement with *Finnegans Wake*.

The role Hegel's philosophy plays in Derrida's writing is central to grasping this problem because it is the privileged heading under which 'the very project of philosophy' is 'displaced and reinscribed' (M19). The privilege accorded to Hegel by Derrida not only makes the detour through Hegelianism indispensable for this analysis, but it also has the effect of putting Hegel on the menu for a reader of Joyce and Derrida. Hegelian philosophy is constantly preoccupied by its 'beyond' or 'exterior,' which it seeks to anticipate and incorporate:

> The slumber of reason is not, perhaps, reason put to sleep, but slumber in the form of reason, the vigilance of the Hegelian *logos*. Reason keeps watch over a deep slumber in which it has an interest ... [At] the far reaches of this night something was contrived, blindly, I mean in a discourse, by means of which philosophy, in completing itself, could both include within itself and anticipate all the figures of its beyond, all the forms and resources of its exterior; and could do so in order to keep these forms and resources close by itself by simply taking hold of their enunciation. (WD 252)

There is nothing – even slumber – it would seem, that the empire of Hegelian *logos*, or reason, cannot use to further itself. But how does this Hegelian *logos* relate to the *eidos* as it has been discussed so far? This matter can be clarified by returning briefly to Mallarmé's Mime, whose mimicry disrupts the self-present *logos* that is 'shaped according to the model of the [Platonic] *eidos*' (D 188) by simulating, or doubling, it. In this simulated double space, therefore, both the *eidos* and the *logos* it shapes are displaced by a simulated double that imitates nothing. For Hegel, however, matters are slightly different, because the *eidos* or idea is both a subjective representation *and* the thing in itself (D 194). The Hegelian *logos* is therefore shaped by an *eidos* that is no longer separable from 'reality' or 'actuality,' since through it ontology becomes absolute logic, melding the subjective and objective, sensible and intelligible 'realms.'[50] But despite these differences, the Hegelian *eidos* still remains caught within the schema of imitation, because Hegel's project is to express or illustrate the pre-existent presence of its meaning or truth.[51] This project is indissociable from the desire to illustrate how philosophy overcomes the perilous passage through meaning's 'beyond' or 'exterior' – that is, the gap between philosophy and its non-philosophical 'others' – and it is the reason that Hegelian philosophy tries to anticipate those 'others' in order to (re)appropriate them (to itself). Since Hegel's philosophy includes and anticipates all the figures, forms, and resources of its exterior, it can be understood to provide the framework for Derrida's formulation of what he calls the 'Ulyssean circle of *self-sending*' and 'yes-laughter': 'I will say in conclusion that the Ulyssean circle of *self-sending* commands a reactive yes-laughter, the manipulatory operation of hypermnesic reappropriation'

(AL 304). Like Hegel's philosophy, the Ulyssean circle is allied with the 'yes-laughter' of 'hypermnesic' appropriation that 'takes joy in hyper-mnesic mastery' and forms a closed circuit wherein 'all the histories, stories, discourses, knowledges' would be prescribed in advance (292). For Derrida, the 'Hegelianism' of Joyce's *Ulysses*[52] makes it a sort of 'hypermnesic machine capable of storing in an immense epic work Western memory and virtually all the languages in the world *including traces of the future*' (AL 281, Derrida's emphasis). This hypermnesic laughter is no mere 'remembering' and is not confined to *Ulysses*, since it finds an even more powerful expression in the *Wake*, where the reader of Joyce is forced 'to be in his memory, to inhabit his memory, which is henceforth greater than all your finite memory can, in a single instant or a single vocable, gather up of cultures, mythologies, religions, philosophies, sciences, history of mind and of literatures' (PSJ 147). As a sort of 'hyper-memory,' the Joycean circle is a powerful variant of the circuit of reappropriative return to the *eidos* or *logos* as it is found in either Platonic 'anamnesis' or in Hegelian philosophy. The question of hypermnesia as it surfaces in Derrida's analyses of Joyce's text finds its roots in Derrida's consideration of Hegel's powerful elaboration of his eidetic philosophy. It is the manner in which the Hegelian and Joycean texts are concerned with their respective 'outsides' that puts Hegel on the agenda not only for a reader of Joyce and Derrida, but especially for the imaginative framework being developed here, since its explicit purpose is to theorize a broadened conception of Joyce-Derrida intertextuality.

It is with respect to this Joycean, or, to be more accurate, the Joycean variant of the Hegelian circle, then, that the relation between Joyce and Derrida is at its most complex, and such complexity demands a reconception of the textual relations of reading Joyce and Derrida together. If the reader of Joyce and Derrida is to avoid simply making Derrida's texts into mere 'moments' that are anticipated and appropriated in advance by either *Ulysses* or *Finnegans Wake*, account must be taken of the manner in which the Derridean texts negotiate this Hegelian circle. It would not be sufficient to invoke the *Wake*'s multiple languages as a way of 'stepping outside' that circle. This is because, as I mentioned in the Introduction, and as Derrida points out in 'Two Words for Joyce,' the Babelian motif of multiple languages is already a part of the Joycean hypermnesic circle. The hen's letter, her famous 'polyhedron of scripture' (107.8) written to try and clear her husband's name of wrongdoing, is an artefact composed in many different languages

(117.12–16). Not only that, but the *Wake* designates the letter's writing – and by extension its own 'lingo' – as that which is incommensurable with the 'practice' (116.29) of 'metaphysicians' (116.27). That is to say, the *Wake*'s idiomatic 'lingo,' 'however basically English' (116.25–6), is made up of a multiplicity of 'languoaths' (116.28) that disrupt the practice of metaphysicians. If the reader of Joyce cannot disrupt the underlying Hegelianism of the Joycean circle by citing the *Wake*'s multiplicity of languages, and if, since the Derridean 'project' is the deconstruction of metaphysics,[53] it appears that by taking multiple languages and the disruption of metaphysics into account in its hypermnesic circle, then the *Wake* has somehow already 'written' deconstruction in advance. This implies that when the reader of the *Wake* tries to find how 'deconstructive' Joyce's text is, s/he can only ever risk making Derrida's texts into a moment of the Hegelian-Joycean circle.

The attempt to avoid reducing these remarkable similarities to the simple anticipation of Derrida's texts by the Joycean circle engenders a corollary to the twofold approach outlined in the Introduction,[54] which involves the use of Derrida's disruptive strategies as a guide for disrupting hypermnesia itself. If Derrida's texts are not simply comprehended by Joyce's, then despite the similarities there must be a certain 'resistance' to the Joycean text by the Derridean text. It is precisely this relation of 'similar but resistant' that captures this study's reconception of the intertextual relation obtaining between the Joycean and Derridean texts in terms of the motif of doubleness, wherein each text resembles the other so closely that each runs the risk of being (mis)taken for the other. This doubled relation, not unlike Derrida's analysis of the relations at work in the '*yes, yes*,' is one where writing is 'self-penned to one's other, ... neverperfect everplanned' (489.33–4). It is this complex written double relationship therefore that forms the basis of this study's reconception of a broadened Joyce-Derrida intertextuality. Not only does this reconception of Joyce-Derrida intertextuality fit the criteria for avoiding the reductive conception of the similarities that Derrida's and Joyce's texts share to the 'pre-emptive' incorporation of Derrida's text by Joycean hypermnesia, but it also offers a necessary countervailing safeguard to the temptation to see Joyce's work as being 'subjected' to a Derridean reading that would have absolutely no regard for the specificity of *Finnegans Wake*.

On the face of it, the problematic of the double announced in the *yes, yes* would appear to be totally and 'pre-emptively' engulfed by the text of the *Wake*, not only in the form of the warring twins, Shem and Shaun (and their many avatars), or their sister Issy and her mirrored reflection, but also by the announcement of the general theme of doubling on the *Wake*'s 'first page' where things go 'doubling their mumper all the time' (3.8–9). It would appear, therefore, that at a cursory glance the very idea of doubling saturates the text of *Finnegans Wake* and focusing on it once more reduces Derridean deconstruction to a 'mere moment' of the appropriative Joycean circle. But doubling is also, as I have argued above, a spacing that 'passes the understanding as well as the hearing: a graphic or literal dimension, a muteness' that cannot be erased since the *Wake* 'could not be read without it.' The text 'must pass through acts of writing,' the 'spacing of its archive,' and 'would not take place without ... being put into letters and spacing' (PSJ 156). To the extent that the *yes, yes* is doubled and therefore spaced, it bears the same theoretical genealogy of the double that provided the chance for a 'break' with the Platonic *eidos* in the form of the Mallarméan 'idea.' But doubling can also be observed as the primal force that disrupts the eidetic Hegelianism that Derrida sees as underwriting Joycean hypermnesia. Doubling thereby opens the possibility of a reading of the *Wake* that also provides a context for the Derridean understanding of doubling and spacing and of the role it plays in the analysis of Joyce. It is to the doubling that not only constitutes Derrida's famous discussion of *différance* and its relation to Hegelian philosophy and laughter but that also sets the theoretical scene for the *yes*-laughter in Derrida's discussion of Joyce that I now turn.

For Derrida, it is *différance* that accounts for both the operation of the Hegelian *Aufhebung*[55] and the 'displacement and reinscription' of Hegelian thought that 'constrains' the *Aufhebung* 'into writing itself otherwise' (M 19). If *différance* disrupts the circle of Hegelian reappropriation, it does so by maintaining a problematic and difficult relationship with it. This is what Derrida calls 'the point of greatest obscurity, on the very enigma of *différance*, on precisely that which divides its very concept by means of a strange cleavage. We must not hasten to decide':

> How are we to think *simultaneously*, on the one hand[,] *différance* as an economic detour which, in the element of the same, always aims at coming back to the pleasure or the presence that have [*sic*] been deferred by (conscious or unconscious) calculation, and, on the other hand, *différance* as the relation to an impossible presence, as expenditure without reserve, as

the irreparable loss of presence, the irreversible use of energy, that is, as the death instinct, and as the entirely other relationship that disrupts every economy? It is evident – and this is the evident itself – that the economical and the noneconomical, the same and the entirely other, etc., cannot be thought *together*. If *différance* is unthinkable in this way, perhaps we should not hasten to make it evident, in the philosophical element of evidentiality which would make short work of dissipating the mirage and illogicalness of *différance* and would do so with the infallibility of calculations that we are well acquainted with, having precisely recognized their place, necessity and function in the structure of *différance*. Elsewhere, in a reading of Bataille, I have attempted to indicate what might come of a rigorous and, in a new sense, 'scientific' *relating* of the 'restricted economy' that takes no part in expenditure without reserve, death, opening itself to nonmeaning, etc., to a general economy that *takes into account* the nonreserve, that keeps in reserve the nonreserve, if it can be put thus. I am speaking of a relationship between a *différance* that can make a profit on its investment and a *différance* that misses its profit, the *investiture* of a presence that is pure and without loss here being confused with absolute loss, with death. (M 19)

Here, *différance* is doubled, cloven by its two forms: the one that aims to recover presence, pleasure, profit, meaning, and so on in a 'restricted economy' and the other that relates to the impossibility of presence, death, loss, non-meaning in a 'general economy' of 'expenditure without reserve.' The relation of both forms of *différance* is one of 'the economical and the noneconomical, the same and the entirely other,' which 'cannot be thought together' (ibid.). Relating both forms of *différance* is 'unthinkable' because they at the same time double for each other and are also entirely *différant*. I want to suggest here that even though this relation is 'unthinkable' – how can profit simultaneously be loss? – it bears a structural relation to the 'auto-affection' discussed above in connection with the imagination. In other words, 'auto-affective imagination' is the 'unthinkable' site where the same is simultaneously other. It is also the site where meaning is related to non-meaning, the known to the unknown, profit to loss. And it is this auto-affective imaginative relation that disturbs the 'very project of philosophy': 'Through such a relating of a restricted and a general economy, the very project of philosophy, under the privileged heading of Hegelianism, is displaced and reinscribed. The *Aufhebung – la relève –* is constrained into writing itself otherwise. Or perhaps simply into writing itself. Or, better, into taking account of its consumption of writing' (M 19). This project is closely related not only to the syntax and rhyme noted below, but also to the laughter that Derrida hears in the work of Bataille on Hegel, and it is key in forming a broader understanding of the status of laughter as it surfaces in Derrida's work on Joyce.

Derrida focuses on Bataille's discussion of sovereignty which disrupts the Hegelian concept of the lordship that emerges from the dialectic of master and slave. Briefly, elliptically, lordship consists in the master recognizing his 'truth,' his meaning within history, by becoming self-conscious (WD 254).[56] This process involves the master's coming to understand that he risks death in acquiring his 'property,' and realizing, at the same time, that he must maintain himself in the face of that death if he is to enjoy that property. Death, since it always threatens to overwhelm him, is therefore that which frees the master from being simply dependent upon life (ibid.). In trying to stay alive, in trying to maintain his life in the face of death, the master recognizes himself in the slave because the work of maintaining is carried out by the slave on the things that belong to the master. Because the slave does not own them, these things 'cannot be immediately negate[d] in pleasurable consumption,' so the slave can only 'work upon' or 'elaborate' them. Work and elaboration for the slave consist in 'inhibiting (*hemmen*) his desire, in delaying (*aufhalten*) the disappearance of the thing' (WD 255). Thus, it is in the work of maintaining himself in life – in being alive – that the master must recognize his truth, his meaning in history: 'To stay alive, to maintain oneself in life, to work, to defer pleasure, to limit the stakes, to have *respect* for death at the very moment when one looks directly at it – such is the servile condition of mastery and of the entire history it makes possible' (WD 255). Meaning and history in Hegel emerge therefore from the self-consciousness that faces death, but works to maintain itself in life.

Since the master must remain alive in the face of death, being dead would signify an absolute breakdown in the process that secures meaning in/as self-consciousness. To the non-meaning and 'abstract negativity' of death Hegel opposes 'the negation characteristic of consciousness, which cancels in such a way that it preserves and maintains what is sublated, and thereby survives its being sublated. In this experience self-consciousness becomes aware that life is as essential to it as pure self-consciousness.'[57] There are a number of shifts that must be followed closely here. 'Simple' death – absolute non-meaning – ends the process of meaning, cutting it off before it emerges through the process of constantly maintaining itself alive by confronting death. Since lordship or mastery 'is not tied up with life' (WD 254), because it constantly risks death, Hegel must conceive of a different form of life for self-consciousness:

> This life is not natural life, the biological existence put at stake in lordship, but an essential life that is welded to the first one, holding it back, making it work for the constitution of self-consciousness, truth and meaning. Such is the truth of life. Through this recourse to the *Aufhebung*, which conserves the stakes, remains in control of the play, limiting and elaborating it by giving it form and meaning (*Die Arbeit ... bildet*), this economy of life restricts itself to conservation, to circulation and self-reproduction as the reproduction of meaning; henceforth, everything covered by the name lordship collapses into comedy. (WD 255–6)

This 'life' takes the form of what survives when it is negated by consciousness: being conscious of something does not destroy or consume it, but rather negates it simply as an object outside of the subject's consciousness of it. This elicits a '[b]urst of laughter from Bataille' (ibid.). Instead of reading the emergence of meaning and self-consciousness from death in a pious manner, Bataille laughs not only at the so-called independent self-consciousness of lordship that 'liberates itself by enslaving itself,' but also at its attempt to draw meaning from the non-meaning of death (256). In other words, Bataille laughs at that in the Hegelian dialectic which attempts to recover meaning from the absolute non-meaning of death.

To laugh at this 'new life,' which looks at death and finds meaning in it (but still does not die), is also to renounce meaning insofar as laughter laughs at the attempt to secure meaning in/from death. This, says Derrida, is the Bataillian laughter of the 'sovereign' that exceeds dialectics:

> Laughter alone exceeds dialectics and the dialectician: it bursts out only on the basis of an absolute renunciation of meaning, an absolute risking of death, what Hegel calls abstract negativity. A negativity that never takes place, that never presents itself, because in doing so, it would start to work again. A laughter that literally never appears, because it exceeds phenomenality in general, the absolute possibility of meaning. And the word 'laughter' itself must be read in a burst, as its nucleus of meaning bursts in the direction of the *system* of sovereign operation ('drunkenness, erotic effusion, sacrificial effusion, poetic heroic behaviour, anger, absur-

dity [...]'). This burst of laughter makes the difference between lordship and sovereignty shine, without *showing* it however and, above all, without saying it ... Simultaneously more and less than a lordship, sovereignty is totally other. Bataille pulls it out of dialectics. He withdraws it from the horizon of meaning and knowledge ... Resembling a phenomenological figure, trait for trait, sovereignty is the absolute alteration of all of them ... Far from being an abstract negativity, sovereignty (the absolute degree of putting at stake), rather, must make the seriousness of meaning appear as an abstraction inscribed in play. Laughter, which constitutes sovereignty in its relation to death, is not a negativity. (Ibid.)

Laughter erupts from the renunciation of meaning, and since death is without 'present' meaning, it separates lordship – which is horrified by death and non-meaning – from sovereignty – which laughs. Sovereignty is 'totally other' than lordship – which it nevertheless resembles 'trait for trait' – by virtue of this burst of laughter at the life that tries to make death mean something. Lordship and sovereignty so closely resemble each other that their difference – laughter – has no meaning. Non-meaning, the blind spot of the Hegelian dialectic, is no laughing matter.

Unlike sovereign laughter, which renounces meaning, Hegelian dialectics submits that which is 'laughable' to the imperative 'that there must be meaning, that nothing must be definitely lost in death, or further, that death should receive the signification of "abstract negativity," that a work must always be possible which, because it defers enjoyment, confers meaning and truth upon the "putting at stake"' (WD 256–7). The Hegelian *Aufhebung* seeks to profit from death by giving it meaning:

[The *Aufhebung*] is laughable because it signifies the *busying* of a discourse losing its breath as it reappropriates all negativity for itself, as it works the 'putting at stake' into an *investment*, as it *amortizes* absolute expenditure; and as it gives meaning to death, thereby simultaneously blinding itself to the baselessness of the nonmeaning from which the basis of meaning is drawn, and in which this basis of meaning is exhausted. To be indifferent to the comedy of the *Aufhebung*, as was Hegel, is to blind oneself to the experience of the sacred, the heedless sacrifice of presence and meaning. (WD 257)

Laughter, insofar as it has to do with the sovereign relation to the non-meaning of death that precedes the *Aufhebung* and from which it tries to draw meaning, makes 'the seriousness of meaning appear as an abstraction inscribed in play' (WD 256).

Sovereignty, as was discussed above, is separated from Hegelian lordship only by the burst of non-meaningful laughter in relation to death. This difference means nothing because laughter has no meaning, but it takes the form of what Bataille calls the 'custom of the wake':

> I will cite a paradoxical example of a gay reaction before the work of death. The Irish and Welsh custom of the wake is little known, but was still observed at the end of the last century. It is the subject of Joyce's last work, *Finnegan's* [sic] *Wake*, Finnegan's funeral vigil (but the reading of this famous novel is uneasy). In Wales, the coffin was placed *open* and upright in the place of honour in the house. The dead person was dressed in his Sunday best and top hat. His family invited all his friends, who increasingly drank stronger toasts to his health. In question is the death of an *other*, but in such cases the death of the other is always the image of one's own death. No one could enjoy themselves thus, if he did not accept one condition: the dead man, who is an other, is assumed to be in agreement, and thus the dead man that the drinker will become, in turn, will have no other meaning than the first one.[58]

Glas is one of Derrida's most sustained attempts to dislocate and reinscribe the Hegelian speculative *eidos*. Insofar as *Glas* 'is also a sort of wake' (PSJ 150), it is laughter in the face of securing meaning in death. Its laughter is a laughter of non-meaning. (I will return to this momentarily.) The feast of the wake, the gaiety shown before death, puts one far from Hegel, and also very close: 'This gaiety is not part of the economy of life, does not correspond "to the desire to deny the existence of death," although it is as close to this desire as possible' (WD 258). In the wake-structure of gaiety and laughter before death, 'destruction, suppression, death and sacrifice constitute so irreversible an expenditure so radical a negativity – here we would have to say an expenditure *without reserve* – that they can no longer be determined as negativity in a process or a system' (WD 259, Derrida's emphasis). The utter destruction of meaning – absolute death – is the point of no return, the 'instance of an expenditure without reserve which no longer leaves us the resources with which to think of this expenditure as negativity' (ibid.). It is no longer of the order of the negativity that allows the Hegelian system to negate absolute death by becoming conscious of it and giving it meaning. As non-meaning, absolute death, this negativity absorbs Hegelian negativity and unhinges it to the point where it 'literally can no longer *labour* and let itself be interrogated as the "work of the negative"' (WD 260): 'In naming the without-reserve of absolute expenditure "abstract negativity," Hegel, through *precipitation*, blinded himself to what he had laid bare under the rubric of negativity. And did so through precipitation toward the seriousness of meaning and the security of knowledge' (WD 259, Derrida's emphasis). Here, Hegel's negativity in the service of work, self-consciousness, knowledge, meaning, history, and so on, is but a minor version of the general negativity he saw in the expenditure of absolute death.

Sovereignty, insofar as it follows Hegel closely, consists in 'agreeing with Hegel against himself' in a 'simulated repetition of Hegelian discourse' that produces the 'barely perceptible displacement' of 'doubling': 'In *doubling* lordship, sovereignty does not *escape* dialectics ... Far from suppressing the dialectical synthesis, it inscribes this synthesis and makes it function in the sacrifice of meaning' (260–1, Derrida's emphasis). Doubling therefore describes the complex relation of meaning to non-meaning, which can only take place in what Derrida calls 'significative discourse': '[T]here is only one discourse [and] it is significative' (261). Non-meaning – the 'unspeakable' – must be said in the servile language of meaning (262). Sovereignty is that 'in every discourse which can open itself to nonmeaning, of un-knowledge or of play, to the swoon from which it is awakened by the throw of a dice' (261). But what separates it from a discourse that would try to find meaning in non-meaning (and thus restart the Hegelian dialectic) is the 'affirmation of sovereignty' that provides 'the commentary on its absence of meaning' (WD 261). This affirmation of non-meaning is another modulation of the laughter discussed above: the other thing that separates meaningful discourse from sovereignty is the affirmation of that which has no meaning, in a doubling whose difference is both very slight and enormous but that has no meaning. By way of illustration, Derrida retraces Bataille's consideration of the word 'silence,' a word that 'silences itself, not as silence, but as speech,' and, in so doing, '*says* nonmeaning' (WD 262). Sovereignty is 'foreign to difference as the source of signification' because it is the experience of 'absolute difference, of a difference that would no longer be the one that Hegel had conceived more profoundly than anyone else: the difference in the service of presence, at work for (the) history (of meaning) the difference between Hegel and Bataille is the difference between these two' (263). The difference between differences is not only the difference between Hegel and Bataille, but also the difference between two *différances* mentioned above. These differences/*différances* are also the difference between two forms of writing, and constitute what Derrida terms the 'space of writing' (266). Sovereignty lends itself to writing rather than speech not only because it is 'unspeakable' and 'silent,' but also because it must be said. The impossibility of sovereignty can only be set down in a writing, the 'tissue of differences' that *'exceeds* the *logos.'*[59] In such writing, Hegel's 'concepts, apparently unchanged in themselves, will be subject to a mutation of meaning, or rather will be struck by (even though they are indifferent), the loss of sense toward which they slide, thereby ruining themselves immeasurably' (WD 267). Writing overflows or exceeds meaning by putting meaning into a doubled (and thus 'absolutely different') relation to 'the moment of sovereignty, to the absolute loss of meaning, to expenditure without reserve.' In this new relation meaning comes into contact with 'a nonmeaning which is beyond absolute meaning,' beyond the closure or 'the horizons of absolute knowledge' (268). The 'strategic twist ... imprinted upon language' catachrestically doubles meaningful discourse 'in order to relate its syntax and its lexicon to major silence' (264), and because it is a *relation* to non-meaning, it is not simply non-meaning (270):

> The writing of sovereignty *is neither sovereignty in its operation nor current scientific discourse.* This latter has as its *meaning* (as its discursive content and direction) the relation oriented from the unknown to the known or knowable, to the always already known or to anticipated knowledge. Although general writing also has a meaning, *since it is only a relation* to nonmeaning this order is reversed within it. And the relation to the absolute possibility of knowledge is suspended within it. The known is related to the unknown, meaning to nonmeaning. (WD 270–1)

Sovereignty, which reverses the relation of eidetic philosophy and mimesis to the known *eidos*, also, insofar as it 'dissolves the values of meaning, truth and a *grasp-of-the-thing-itself'* dissolves itself (270). It is the relation of the known to the unknown in sovereign writing that is at issue here. It reverses the Platonic-Hegelian movement towards the known, towards the *eidos*.

In *Ulysses* the relation of the known to the unknown is also at issue. In following this 'method,' the reader of Joyce can mime the Joycean circle by tracing the contours of the laughter of the 'unthinkable' (M 19) relation of meaning and non-meaning in Derrida's analysis of Hegel. It emerges during Mr Bloom's late night catechism on the 'heaventree of stars' with Stephen Dedalus in the 'Ithaca' episode of *Ulysses*. Mr Bloom has just finished depressing himself about the difficulties of self-improvement in the face of life's uncertainties and difficulties. The text then asks:

Did Stephen participate in [Bloom's] dejection?

He affirmed his significance as a conscious rational animal proceeding syllogistically from the known to the unknown and a conscious rational re-agent between a micro and a macrocosm ineluctably constructed upon the incertitude of the void. (17.1011–15)

Stephen's procedure in the uncertain void is the movement, just like *différance*, from the known to the unknown. Mr Bloom initially does not grasp this trajectory, and comforts himself with the thought that he has 'proceeded energetically from the unknown to the known' (17.1019–20) by jumping over the railings at the back of his house (17.1016–20). Later, however, Mr Bloom reconsiders this in the light of his contemplation of the divisibility of the universe and concludes that 'if the process were carried far enough, nought nowhere was ever reached' (17.1068–9). At first this may seem to be Mr Bloom's explicit rejection of Stephen's syllogistic procedure on the basis of divisions that literally arrive at nothing – 'nought.' However, on closer inspection it seems that Mr Bloom is in fact 'substantively' (17.1018) enacting the trajectory of *différance* – Stephen's 'syllogism.' Mr Bloom finds that in trying to arrive at the method of the known to the unknown, he gets caught up in an infinity of divisibility that ends up at an unknown 'nought nowhere was ever reached.' Further, he finds that even trying to think in terms of moving from the known to the unknown is unknowable, since he accepts that there is 'no known method from the known to the unknown' (17.1140–1). Mr Bloom in fact extends the realm of the unknown by including the method of relating the known to the unknown in the quotient of the unknown. This procedure, itself a version of the imaginative of Vico's and the *Wake*'s imaginative historiography insofar as the known is related to an unknowable lost presence, is non-eidetic insofar as it reverses the meaningful flow of discourse that, as Derrida points out, moves from the 'unknown to the known or knowable, to the always already known or anticipated knowledge' (WD 270). Thus, within the Platonic-Hegelian tradition of knowledge it is always a question of a progression towards a pre-existent *eidos*. By contrast, Mr Bloom's consideration of the stars and divisibility is non-eidetic in that it turns about the impossible method of going from the known to the unknown.

It is therefore not only Hegel's eidetic philosophy that underlies the Derridean conception of the Joycean hypermnesic circle, but also a complex engagement of Bataille with Hegel's philosophy that is necessary for grasping what is at stake in the laughter that Derrida finds at work in Joyce. That is, if the reader of Joyce and Derrida is to come to grips with what is at issue in Derrida's analysis of the *yes*-laughter in Joyce, it is first necessary to understand this laughter in terms of the sovereign laughter that Derrida finds in reading Bataille's analysis of Hegelian philosophy. In this laughter, 'the relation to the absolute possibility of knowledge is suspended,' the 'known is related to the unknown' (WD 270–1), meaning comes into relation with non-meaning, and Hegel's philosophy becomes inscribed in the general economy of non-meaning that comes before it and makes it possible. This laughter, which is also the gay anguish of the wake, is the laughter that resounds through *Glas* and is responsible for making it into 'a sort of wake' (PSJ 150). In the following chapters, I will perform a comparative study of the sites where this laughter is heard in both *Glas* and *Finnegans Wake*. Since these sites, as I hope to make clear, bear the hallmarks of the auto-affective imagination, they are of critical importance to this study's elaboration of a non-eidetic imaginative framework that, by considering that which is at stake in their shared laughter, will enable readers of Joyce and Derrida to theorize and negotiate a broadened conception of Joyce-Derrida intertextuality.

2 Following the Hen: Applied 'Epistlemadethemology'

I 'Lead, kindly fowl.'

In this chapter I wish to consider in some detail how Vico's *The New Science* offers the chance of reading *Finnegans Wake* non-eidetically through what Vico calls *auspicium*, or augury. In particular, I will consider how *auspicium* encapsulates the paradox inherent in the non-eidetic scene of imaginary 'production,' where the model presented withdraws itself as model. I will also explore this scene of imaginary 'production' as it relates to section I.5 of *Finnegans Wake*, which presents this mode as a scene of writing in which a hen leaves behind a letter to be read (and imitated, written, etc.) by the reader. Section II of this chapter considers the ways in which a letter written by a hen can be understood in terms of the *différantial* 'relation to the absolute possibility of knowledge,' where the 'known is related to the unknown' (WD 270–1; U17.1011–17). In order to do this, I will discuss in detail how the differential reinscription of the *eidos* can be given both theoretical and systematic rigour by utilizing the resources of Martin Heidegger's analyses of temporal self- or auto-affection and their relation to the imagination in Kant.[1] Finally, in section III I will examine how the actual marks that make up the text of the letter – the 'X's – figure the auto-affective discussed in section II. As such, these Xs are also to be found in Derrida's *Glas*, where they function as *différantial* icons or figures for an entirely non-eidetic strategy for reading-and-writing *Glas*.

In order to come to grips with what Vico understands by *auspicium*, it is necessary to return to what he sees as the forgotten origins of human civility and society. Vico attaches considerable theoretical weight to the origins of human civility and society, which, he says, took shape 'when the first men began to think humanly' (NS 347). The precise time of the origin of humanity in society is all too often ignored by other thinkers of the origins of human society. By behaving in this manner, these other thinkers violate the principle that 'the sciences [of man's origins] must begin where their subject matters began' (NS 347). According to the *New Science*, the first men began to think humanly with the birth of religion (NS 8). Such thinking began, says Vico, when 'heaven must have thundered and lightened.' The thunder and lightning terrified the first men, and their fear caused them to attribute the sky's fury to the first god, Jove. Each culture had its own Jove, and from 'the thunder and lightning of its Jove each nation began to take auspices, and taking the auspices' – which date from the first appearance of Jove as the sky – constitutes 'the first divine institution' (NS 9). For Vico, the observation of the sky while taking the auspices included the observation of birds or augury. Augury is a cognate of the word 'auspice,' itself from the Latin *auspex*, 'observer of birds' (*avis/specere*). Through the auspices it became possible to divine – from *divinari*, to foretell – what the gods had in store for mankind (NS 8), and human history was born, inaugurated by the observation of birds. Augury, the observation of birds in a wish to know what the gods had in store for men, is then the first flush of divine pleasure on the cheeks of the first men and women who make history. As such, augury must be the first withdrawn order of God who commands man to mime without model.

To the extent that the text of *Finnegans Wake* presents a scene of augury, it may be understood to take part in the same tradition of 'production' without model that Vico's text finds itself part of. In the *Wake*, the scene of augury takes a textual turn in I.5, when the reader is placed in the position of a child-like auspex who 'observes' 'a cold fowl behaviourising strangely on that fatal midden' (110.24–5):

Lead, kindly fowl! They always did: ask the ages. What bird
has done yesterday man may do next year, be it fly, be it moult,
be it hatch, be it agreement in the nest. (112.9–11)

The mode of reading the letter in I.5 is then augury: 'Let us auspice it!' (112.18). The reader-auspex follows the movements of the bird ('what bird has done yesterday'), which reveal the wisdom of the oracles to man ('man may do next year'). However, because the observation of the bird is the first step in Vichian man's non-eidetic writing of himself, the reader must be understood to mimic the actions and processes of the bird.

The parallels between Vichian writing and the hen's writing can be made clearer by considering the way in which the hen writes without a prior eidetic model. The hen, in short, starts from 'scratch':

> And then. Be
> old. The next thing is. We are once amore as babes awondering
> in a wold made fresh where with the hen in the storyaboot we
> start from scratch. (336.15–18; see also 369.23–70.14)

Later in the text, the act of scratching is connected with the act or scene of writing, as the instrument of writing. It is the 'pen [that] is upt to scratch, to compound quite the makings of a verdigrease savingsbook in the form of a pair of capri sheep boxing gloves' (412.32–6), as well as the 'hairpin slatepencil for Elsie Oram to scratch her toby, doing her best with her volgar fractions' (211.12–13).

Writing from scratch not only names the hen's style, but also links the letter's augury to Vico's assertion that the reader of the *New Science* makes the ideal eternal history for him/herself. If the hen makes these marks (from scratch) in the text, she can be understood to 'produce' without model. In other words, her model of 'production' – again, the word scarcely seems adequte – has no model, and because this scene of textual augury is without model, it can be understood to be pregnant with the structure of Vichian divine pleasure. If the reader imitates the hen's example of imitation without model, the reader can also be understood to imitate a model of writing without model. This is possible only because the hen presents a model for writing without model, and she can only efface herself in a scene of writing (and signing) the text without model. In other words, the hen withdraws from the text in much the same manner as God withdraws from the reader's rewriting of Vico's ideal eternal history. Thus, to follow is to imitate a model that withdraws itself in writing.

It is difficult to contain the effects of the hen's withdrawal within the letter. This is because the process by which the reader writes the text through the Vichian device of mime without model, marks everything that *Finnegans Wake* presents. It is only on the ground (if it is still possible to say 'ground' as it withdraws) of withdrawal of the pre-existent object or model that it becomes possible to imagine the figures at the *Wake*. This can be explained in the following manner.

First, the withdrawal of the object does away with the ability to make a constative statement about that object. This situation plays itself out around the quasi-biblical fall that loses Finnegan in I.1. Finnegan's fall imbues him with a certain amount of guilt. If there is guilt associated with a fall, then there must be a crime. Thus, I.1 sets about trying to reconstruct a primordial crime scene. This scene is related by Kate in the well-known 'Museyroom' exhibit of I.1. The Museyroom presents the crime scene in terms of a battle that was waged in the Phoenix Park. In this battle, Finnegan, in the guise of 'the Willingdone' appears 'on his same white harse, the Cokenhape.' Ranged opposite the Willingdone 'is the three lipoleum boyne grouching down in the living detch.' Also on the field are the female 'jinnies,' who show off 'their legahorns [while] feinting to read in their handmade's book of stralegy while making their war.' As the jinnies read their book of strategy, they 'make war' and 'make water,' or urinate. At the same time, the Willingdone spies 'on [their] flanks' with his 'big Willingdone mormorial tallowscoop Wounderworker.' As he watches, he 'git[s] the band up [French *bander*, to band, to get an erection].' But while erect, the Willingdone provocatively presents 'a profusely fine birdeye view from beauhind this park' (564.7–8) to the three soldiers in the ditch (8.9–36). Because the Phoenix Park in Dublin was famous as a site for the procurement of gay sex, it is easy to see how such a gesture puts in question the 'facts' of the Willingdone's 'municipal sin business' in the park (5.14). The scene remains hopelessly overdetermined, and it is impossible to say whether or not the Willingdone is guilty of a heterosexual voyeurism or a homosexual exhibitionism.[2] All this overdetermination marks the absence of the truth, of facts, of an eidetic model:

> Thus the unfacts, did we possess them, are too imprecisely
> few to warrant our certitude, the evidencegivers by legpoll too
> untrustworthily irreperible where his adjugers are semmingly
> freak threes but his judicandees plainly minus twos. Neverthe-
> less Madam's Toshowus waxes largely more lifeliked (entrance,
> one kudos; exits, free) and our notional gullery is now com-
> pletely complacent, an exegious monument, aerily perennious.
> (57.16–22)

Second, these 'unfacts' give all the exhibits at the *Wake*, and the reader is forced to occupy the space of what Vico calls 'rumour':

120 Because of the indefinite nature of the human mind, wherever it is lost in ignorance man makes himself the measure of all things.

121 This axiom explains those two common human traits, on the one hand that rumor grows in its course, on the other that rumor is deflated by presence [of the thing itself]. In the long course that rumor has run from the beginning of the world, it has been the perennial source of all the exaggerated opinions which have hitherto been held concerning remote antiquities unknown to us by virtue of that property of the human mind noted by Tacitus in his *Life of Agricola*, where he says that the unknown is always magnified.

The seat of this 'magnification' is precisely the imagination, a sort of childish, overly vivid memory run amok: '211 In children memory is most vigorous, and imagination is therefore excessively vivid, for imagination is nothing but extended or compounded memory.' Thus, if the exhibits at the *Wake* are undecidable, it is because the *Wake* is only concerned with the difficulties and aporias of 'production' without *eidos* – in the sense of a fully present thing-in-itself – that would put an end to wild imaginings. This why there can be no consensus arrived at regarding the alleged crime, and why there is so much textual time devoted in books I and III to the pursuit of the withdrawing HCE (Here Comes Everybody) in the apparent hope of getting at the truth surrounding his crime and disappearance.

The imaginary dimensions of this scene of writing become even clearer when the Museyroom scene is compared to a similar scene as it is explicitly imagined at the pub in II.3, where the customers discuss the circumstances surrounding the alleged crime of HCE (an avatar of Finnegan) and the various rumours regarding his guilt:

> what matter what all his
> freudzay or who holds his hat to harm him, let hutch just keep
> on under at being a vanished consinent and let annapal livibel
> prettily prattle a lude all her own. And be that semeliminal
> salmon solemonly angled,ingate and outgate. A truce to lovecalls,
> dulled in warclothes, maleybags, things and bleakhusen. Leave
> the letter that never begins to go find the latter that ever comes
> to end, written in smoke and blurred by mist and signed of
> solitude, sealed at night.
>   Simply. As says the mug in the middle, nay brian nay noel,
> ney billy ney boney. Imagine twee cweamy wosen. Suppwose
> you get a beautiful thought and cull them sylvias sub silence.

Then inmaggin a stotterer. Suppoutre him to been one bigger-
master Omnibil. Then lustily (tutu the font and tritt on the boks-
woods like gay feeters's dance) immengine up to three longly
lurking lobstarts. Fair instents the Will Woolsley Wellaslayers.
Pet her, pink him, play pranks with them. She will nod ampro-
perly smile. He may seem to appraisiate it. They are as piractical
jukersmen sure to paltipsypote. Feel the wollies drippeling out
of your fingathumbs. Says to youssilves (floweers have ears,
heahear!) solowly: So these ease Budlim! How do, dainty dau-
limbs? So peached to pick on you in this way, prue and simple,
pritt and spry! Heyday too, Malster Faunagon, and hopes your
hahititahiti licks the mankey nuts! And oodlum hoodlum dood-
lum to yes, Donn, Teague and Hurleg, who the bullocks brought
you here and how the hillocks are ye? (337.6–31)

In this imaginative rendering of the scene of the sin in the park, the factual decidability of either HCE's guilt or innocence and the true nature
of his crime are not very important. What does it matter what 'his
freudzay'? It only matters that he is 'gone,' a 'vanished continent.' So,
in his absence, why not let his wife, Anna Livia, 'prettily prattle a lude
all her own'? In other words, it is Anna Livia's prattling prelude – the
letter that is written in HCE's absence – that offers the self-effacing
model for imaginative writing without model.

  This complex structure encapsulates the paradox inherent in the
non-eidetic mode of imaginative writing. Even if the hen effaces
herself, she nonetheless leaves behind a letter to be read (and imitated, written) by the reader. The letter she writes from scratch
marks her withdrawal as model and presents it to be read. The letter offers the model of imaginative writing without model. It is
therefore the peculiar model of the letter, 'the letter that never begins
to go find the latter that ever comes to end,' that must now be
accounted for in a process of writing that claims to be one of writing without model.

Towards the Textual 'eidos'

But, as the reader might expect by now, nothing in the *Wake* is ever
simple, and this might be said to go double for the letter. The complexity of the letter asserts itself when the reader realizes that it does not
simply ignore the structural quest for truth:

[S]he who shuttered him after
his fall and waked him widowt sparing and gave him keen and
made him able and held adazillahs to each arche of his noes, she
who will not rast her from her running to seek him till, with the
help of the okeamic, some such time that she shall have been after
hiding the crumbends of his enormousness in the areyou looking-
for Pearlfar sea, (ur, uri, uria!) stood forth, burnzburn the gorg-
gony old danworld, in gogor's name, for gagar's sake, dragging
the countryside in her train, finickin here and funickin there,
with her louisequean's brogues and her culunder buzzle and her
little bolero boa and all and two times twenty curlicornies for her
headdress, specks on her eyeux, and spudds on horeilles and a
circusfix riding her Parisienne's cockneze, a vaunt her straddle
from Equerry Egon, when Tinktink in the churchclose clinked
Steploajazzyma Sunday, Sola, with pawns, prelates and pookas
pelotting in her piecebag, for Handiman the Chomp, Esquoro,
biskbask, to crush the slander's head. (102.1–17)

The wife's letter, now revealed as a site of imaginative writing, remains
concerned with justice and the desire to crush the slanderous rumours
that have been spreading like wildfire since HCE's fall and disappearance. This desire to find and present the truth about the crime and disappearance also structures the letter plot of *Finnegans Wake*. In this
plot, the hen, HCE's wife, ALP, composes the letter in order to clear her
husband's name. The trajectory of the letter is summed up neatly as
follows: 'Letter, carried of Shaun, son of Hek, written of Shem, brother
of Shaun, uttered for Alp, mother of Shem, for Hek, father of Shaun.
Initialled. Gee. Gone' (420.17–19). The letter is addressed to a 'Maggy's
tea, or your majesty' (116.24), an extremely enigmatic figure in the text
who still holds out the possibility, the promise, of truth. The letter
offers the chance for the hen to prove, for once and for all, that her husband is innocent of all the charges and allegations made against him.
To this extent, the letter can be understood to circulate in the quasi-
Hegelian space sketched out above, where 'meaning' relates to 'non-
meaning' in the form of 'evidential truth,' the 'what actually happened' (M 19). It is this relation that forces the letter into what Derrida
calls a certain complicity with Hegel. This complicity 'accompanies
Hegelian discourse, "takes it seriously" up to the end, without an
objection in philosophical form, while however, a certain burst of
laughter exceeds it and destroys its sense, or signals, in any event, the

extreme point of "experience" that makes Hegelian discourse dislocate *itself*; and this can only be done through close scrutiny and full knowledge of what one is laughing at' (WD 253). The essence of taking Hegel seriously lies in taking the mimetic structure of the philosophical *eidos* – which always searches for truth and meaning – seriously. This is because, as Derrida points out in *Dissemination*, philosophical Platonism, even in its Cartesian and Hegelian manifestations, is always a 'matter of imitating (expressing, describing, representing, illustrating) an *eidos* or idea, whether it is a figure of the thing itself, as in Plato, a subjective representation, as in Descartes, or both, as in Hegel' (194).

I want to suggest that the letter inscribes the relation of meaning, truth, and non-meaning, truth, as the letter itself. This is a complicated process, but it begins simply enough with seeing the letter as presenting the truth about HCE. The hen writes the letter because 'all schwants (schwrites) is to tell the cock's trootabout him' (113.11–12). Thus, the letter is designed to be 'very truthful' (113.17–18), and, to this extent, can be understood to play with the nature of philosophical evidence. As such, the letter points back to the truth of past event, a reality. It points to the significance of the truth of the matter, to the extent that it is designed to 'crush the slander's head.' At the same time, however, the letter also concerns itself with the distortion of that truth:

> Well, almost any photoist worth his chemicots will tip anyone
> asking him the teaser that if a negative of a horse happens to melt
> enough while drying, well, what you do get is, well, a positively
> grotesquely distorted macromass of all sorts of horsehappy values
> and masses of meltwhile horse. Tip. Well, this freely is what
> must have occurred to our missive (there's a sod of a turb for
> you! please wisp off the grass!) unfilthed from the boucher by
> the sagacity of a lookmelittle likemelong hen. Heated residence
> in the heart of the orangeflavoured mudmound had partly ob-
> literated the negative to start with, causing some features pal-
> pably nearer your pecker to be swollen up most grossly while
> the farther back we manage to wiggle the more we need the loan
> of a lens to see as much as the hen saw. Tip. (111.26–12.2)

Here, the text offers a 'tip' to the reader, one that pushes him/her in the direction of the Platonic *eidos*. But the eidetic evidence of the letter found by the hen has been distorted by the amount of time it has spent underground, and the *eidos* it presents is far from pristine. It is described by the text as 'a positively grotesquely distorted macromass of all sorts of horsehappy values and masses of meltwhile horse,' which is itself a distortion of the hippic *eidos* that puts in an appearance in the library of U 9.84: 'Unsheathe your dagger definitions. Horseness is the whatness of allhorse.' Nevertheless, it is temporal and thermal distortion of the text of the letter that brings it into contact with the (distorted) Platonic *eidos*. There is no pristine Platonic *eidos* in the letter; there is only distortion, and this distortion is what brings the (distorted) *eidos* into contact with the letter. All of this distortion takes place in/as the text of the letter (itself).

This distortion causes the reader to lose his/her sense of direction and become lost in the bushy undergrowth of a 'jumble of words':

> You is feeling like you was lost in the bush, boy? You says:
> It is a puling sample jungle of woods. You most shouts out:
> Bethicket me for a stump of a beech if I have the poultriest no-
> tions what the farest he all means. Gee up, girly! The quad gos-
> pellers may own the targum but any of the Zingari shoolerim
> may pick a peck of kindlings yet from the sack of auld hensyne.
> (111.3–8)

If the distortion is experienced as the 'puling sample jungle of woods,' then words can be understood as being the only possible medium in which the Platonic *eidos* can come to the text of the letter. But the jumble of words also names the letter itself. Therefore, the Platonic *eidos* can only take place in the *Wake* as the distortion of text. It therefore undergoes rewriting in the letter, and emerges as a literal or textual 'jumble of words.' In being rewritten, the *eidos* is not simply lost. Rewriting redirects all questions about the *eidos* towards text.

This text cannot be read with the naked eye, and its reader stands in need of 'the loan of a lens to see as much as the hen saw' (112.1–2). The presence of the hen suggests that the reinscription of the *eidos* has something to do with the scene of avian composition, which, as I argued above, does without a prior *eidos*. This suggestion also implies that the jumble of words can also be understood to do without prior meaning or signified. It is because (the) text displaces eidetic meaning that it disrupts the eidetic mode of reading. The reader who insists on searching for a prior meaning in the text ends up feeling like s/he is 'lost in the bush.' This is because a (Platonic) reader continues to seek a pre-existent meaning/signified/referent in the text *à la* the Platonic *eidos*. S/he tries to anticipate (the) meaning before the jungle/jumble of words, the state of nature, which can be returned to. For such a reader, words will always serve to uncover pre-existent meaning in the text. However, the text of the letter disorients such a reader, and does not allow the return to any pre-existent meaning in the text.

The text of the letter disorients because eidetic meaning is reconfigured as a textual 'jumble of words.' But this disorientation also impels the reader to struggle with the wordy text of this jungle-book. Instead of simply feeling 'lost in the bush' due to the dislocation of sense, which watches over the reader like a parent, the reader is invited to struggle against the tangled underbrush of words, in a manner similar to the scatological struggle in Vico's primaeval forest:

> Mothers like beasts, must merely have nursed their babies, let them wallow naked in their own filth. And these children, who had to wallow in their own filth, whose nitrous salts richly fertilized the fields, and who had to exert themselves to penetrate the great forest, would flex and contract their muscles in these exertions, and thus absorb nitrous salts into their bodies in greater abundance. They would be quite without fear of gods, fathers, and teachers which chills and benumbs even the most exuberant in childhood. They must therefore have grown up robust, vigorous, excessively big in brawn and bone, to the point of becoming giants. (NS 369)

Shit is something that finds its way into the text in a scene of motherly abandonment. The mother merely offers her breast, and then recedes or withdraws from the child. Her withdrawal causes her to neglect her other maternal duties towards the child, such as cleaning and toilet-training. This Vichian mother corresponds to the hen, who also effaces herself in the scene of non-eidetic writing. Without its mother, the reader-child defecates anywhere, and thus fertilizes the thick forest of the text.

The thickness of the bush in Vico's forest is also responsible for the multiplicity of languages in the world because it 'shut [the many different nations] off from each other' (NS 198), and each nation gave birth to its own language. This is why the struggle against the bush of the letter-text's 'lingo,' 'however basically English' (116.25–6), does not take place in just one language:

> It is told in sounds in utter that, in
> signs so adds to, in universal, in polygluttural, in each auxiliary

neutral idiom, sordomutics, florilingua, sheltafocal, flayflutter, a
con's cubane, a pro's tutute, strassarab, ereperse and anythongue
athall. (117.12–16)

For Vico, the bushiness of the forest is responsible for polyglottism,
a situation that demands translation and the construction of the
'common mental language' of *The New Science*:

> 161 There must in the nature of human institutions be a mental language
> common to all nations, which uniformly grasps the substance of things
> feasible in human social life and expresses it with as many diverse modifi-
> cations as these same things have diverse aspects. A proof of this is
> afforded by proverbs or maxims of vulgar wisdom, in which substantially
> the same meanings find as many diverse expressions as there are nations
> ancient and modern.
>
> 162 This common mental language is proper to our Science, by whose
> light linguistic scholars will be enabled to construct a mental vocabulary
> common to all the various articulate languages living and dead. We gave a
> particular example of this in the first edition of the *New Science*. There we
> proved that the names of the first family fathers, in a great number of dead
> and living languages, were given them because of the various properties
> which they had in the state of the families and in that of the first common-
> wealths, at the time when the nations were forming their languages.

Finnegans Wake, however, radicalizes Vico's procedure of 'construct[ing] a mental vocabulary common to all the various articulate
languages living or dead,' by juxtaposing the forested origin of nations
in response to the thunder of the gods with a particular scene of
Hebrew writing, or 'Soferim Bebel' (118.18). This scene of Hebrew
writing does not imply that the letter is somehow written in Hebrew
(the mere appearance of the text would defeat such a claim). Rather,
the scene of the letter's writing should be thought of as the product of
Hebrew writers (Hebrew, *Soferim*) who write in the shadow of Babel
('Bebel').[3] The written Babel motif casts it shadow across the scene of
the fall from the tower and the famous thunder-word that accompanies
it: 'The fall (bababadalgharaghtakamminarronnkonnbronntonnerronntuonnthunntrovarrhounawnskawntoohoohoordenenthurnuk!) of a
once wallstrait oldparr is retaled early in bed and later on life down
through all christian minstrelsy' (3.15–18). Here, insofar as the thunder-word is composed of the word for thunder in many different lan-

guages, it recalls what Vico calls the common sense of the different peoples who were separated by the primeval forest.[4] But Joyce includes the Babel motif in Vico's forest in order to use its story of the confusion of languages to shatter any remnants of the philosophical *eidos* that would have guided the construction of the tower to completion. In the storm of different tongues that is Babel, Joyce implies that the multiplicity of languages displaces the eidetic model. In this way the Babelian motif of the confused *eidos* may be understood to mirror the operation of the hen's letter insofar as it displaces the *eidos* with letter-text. It also disrupts the Vichian distinction between the gentes and the Hebrews: both races must struggle through the jungle of woods / jumble of words.[5]

If the absence or loss of the *eidos* in imaginative writing can be understood as being the same as its dislocation by a purely textual, or written *eidos*, then the letter offers yet another instance of what was analysed in chapter 1 in terms of the catachresis of Finnegan's imaginary 'buildung' of the tower. Because the textual *eidos* necessitates the loss or absence of the *eidos*, both catachrestic scenes offer the chance for understanding some of the ways in which imaginary writing disrupts (the) presence (of the *eidos*). But what has yet to be discussed is how the imaginary is itself structured so that it rigorously disrupts/dislocates presence, which always takes the form of privileging the present form of the now (SP 63). In order to show how all presence (signified, referential, etc.) rests on imaginary reinscription, I will explore in the next section of this chapter how the dislocation of the presence of the *eidos* is structurally given over to non-presence. I will also examine the various ways in which this non-presence is radicalized by *Finnegans Wake*.

II Imagination and Auto-affection

[The dominance of the now] designates the locus of a problem in which phenomenology confronts every position centered on nonconsciousness that can approach what is ultimately at stake, what is at bottom decisive: the concept of time. (SP 63)

Mark Time's Finist Joke. Putting Allspace in a Notshall. (455.29)

To the extent that the hen's letter reinscribes the purely Platonic '*eidos*' in a textual manner, it may be understood to *exceed* the realm of the philosophy of presence and the Platonist order of appearance that is rooted in it. But if the *eidos* is textually reinscribed in the hen's letter, one may ask how this letter relates to the *Wake*an 'immarginative' framework broached in chapter 1. How is the reader to grasp the letter 'immarg-inatively'? In the present section I will argue that the excess of the hen's textual *eidos* is, in fact, rooted in the operation of the imagination.

This, of course, is tantamount to reinscribing philosophy in the imagination, and there have been many texts that have attempted to do just that. As I have argued in chapter 1, the text of the *Wake* places the task of 'picturing' the never present Finnegan firmly on the imagi-nation. At the same time, however, the text also entrusts the task of preparing the way for Finnegan's eventual return to his *family*: to put it in its most brutally reductive form, the mother-hen dictates a letter to her writer-son, Shem the Penman, who then gives the letter to his brother, Shaun the Postman, to deliver it to the authorities who will then drop all charges against the missing giant, so he can once again take his place in the family. However, since Finnegan is structurally unable to 'return' in the text because he was never present to begin with, the peculiarly difficult task that the text charges the family with demands further consideration. I want to consider the possibility that the family's task in the text provides a clue for the operation of the non-present (non-eidetic) imagination in the text. In order to do this, I will focus particularly on the relations that obtain between the mother and her two sons. These sons are also legendarily bitter rivals who are perpetually at odds with each other. Their rivalry in book I is well known to readers of the *Wake*, and perhaps the most celebrated form their rivalry takes is also one of the first: I.6's war between time (Shem) and space (Shaun). I want to suggest that I.6's staging of their rivalry in terms of space and time serves, on the reading I am proposing here, to connect the operation of the imagination in the text to the very prob-lematic relation of space and time. Further, since a comparative analy-sis of *Finnegans Wake* and *Glas* is the primary goal of this book, this consideration of space, time, and the imagination should ideally also offer a way of opening Joyce's text onto Derrida's texts.

Fortunately, there is a text that meets a number of these seemingly unfulfillable criteria: Heidegger's *Kant and the Problem of Metaphysics*. I will also, but to a lesser extent, have recourse to his *The Basic Concepts of Phenomenology*.[6] Heidegger's texts suggest themselves because (a) BP reconsiders the philosophical *eidos* in terms of a re-evaluation of the bonds between the *eidos* and the scene of the imagination, or *phantasia*; (b) KPM is Heidegger's analysis of the operation of the imagination in

Kant; and (c) Heidegger's discussion of the imagination lends a systematic and theoretical rigour to this study's attempt to forumlate the imaginative framework broached in chapter 1. In particular, I will focus the discussion on the motifs of time, synthesis, and auto- or self-affection in Heidegger's analysis. That being said, Heidegger's analysis in KPM remains of limited use in analysing the war of time *and* space in the *Wake* to the extent that he privileges *pure* temporality in the operation of the imagination. For this reason, it is not possible to treat auto- or self-affection in exactly the same manner as Heidegger does. The imagination in the *Wake* calls for a gesture that is remarkably similar to Derrida's reconfiguration of the purely temporal imagination and auto-affection in the spatio-temporal light of *différance*. To aid me in my reconfiguration of the Heideggerian analysis of self- or auto-affection, I will draw on two texts of Derrida in particular: 'Ousia and Grammē' and *Speech and Phenomena*. I will use 'Ousia and Grammē' to explore Derrida's conception of spatio-temporality in order to connect it to his conception of *différance* and *Speech and Phenomena* in order to expand spatio-temporality in the direction of the body. My goal in doing this is to show how it is possible to map the fraternal war of space and time in *Finnegans Wake* onto the reconfigured role that the mechanism of auto-affection plays in the bodily imagination derived from this reading of Heidegger and Derrida. I will then go on to consider the brothers' relationship with their mother in terms of her letter-writing activity. I will conclude this section by suggesting that it is both the letter – the site of the imaginative (and thus non-present) reinscription of the Platonist *eidos* – and imaginative bodily temporality that form key passages through which the texts of both *Finnegans Wake* and Derrida's *Glas* open onto each other.

Imagination, Time, and Space

Heidegger, in *The Basic Concepts of Phenomenology*, sets about uncovering the schema that underlies the metaphysical interpretation of both perception and what is commonly understood to be the *eidos*. In its place, Heidegger proposes a reinterpretation of that schema 'with a view to production' and, more importantly, for my purposes, the operation of the imagination:

> If we take a being as encountered in perception, then we have to say that the look of something is based on its characteristic form ... For *Greek ontol-*

ogy, however, ... [the] look is not grounded in the form but the form, the morphe, is grounded in the look ... But, if the relationship between the look and the form is reversed in ancient thought, the guiding clue for their interpretation cannot be the order of perception and perception itself. We must rather interpret them *with a view to production*. What is formed is, as we can also say, a shaped product. The potter forms a vase out of clay. All forming of shaped products is effected by using an image, in the sense of a model, as guide and standard. The thing is produced by shaping, forming. It is this anticipated look of the thing, sighted beforehand, that the Greeks mean ontologically by eidos, idea. The shaped product, which is shaped in conformity with the model, is as such the exact likeness of the model ... The anticipated look, the proto-typical image, shows the thing as what it was before the production and how it is supposed to look as a product. The anticipated look has not yet been externalized as something formed, actual, but is the image of the imagination, of fantasy, phantasia, as the Greeks say – that which forming first brings freely to sight, that which is sighted. It is no accident that Kant, for whom the concepts of form and matter, morphe and hule, play a fundamental epistemological role, conjointly assigns to imagination a distinctive function in explaining the objectivity of knowledge. The eidos as the look, anticipated in imagination, of what is to be formed gives the thing with regard to what the thing already was and is before all actualization. Therefore the anticipated look, the eidos, is also called to ti en einai, that which a being already was ... The eidos, that which a thing already was beforehand, gives the kind of thing, its kin and descent, its genos. Therefore, thingness [or reality, *Sachheit*] is also identical with genos, which should be translated as stock, family, generation ... The determination of phusis also points toward the same direction of interpretation of the what. Phuein means to let grow, procreate, engender, produce, primarily to produce its own self. What again makes products or the produced product possible (producible) is again the look of what the product is supposed to become and be. The actual thing arises out of phusis, the nature of the thing. Everything earlier than what is actualized is still free from the imperfection, one-sidedness, and sensibilization given necessarily with all actualization ... The look, eidos, and the form, morphe, each encloses in itself that which belongs to a thing. As enclosing, it constitutes the limiting boundary of what determines the thing as finished, complete. The look, as enclosing the belongingness of all the real determinations, is also conceived as constituting the finishedness, the completedness, of a being. Scholasticism says perfectio; in Greek it is the teleion. This boundedness

of the thing, which is distinctively characterized by its finishedness, is at
the same time the possible object for an expressly embracing delimitation
of the thing, for the horismos, the definition, the concept that comprehends the boundaries containing the reality of what has been formed.
(BP 106–8; Heidegger's emphasis)

The reinterpretation of the *eidos* in terms of production that Heidegger
proposes here must be understood in the context of his larger project of
uncovering the meaning of Being through the destruction of the sterile
metaphysics of the present-to-hand begun in *Being and Time*.[7] Thus,
Heidegger is not interested in the Platonist 'order of perception' or
'perception itself,' which would see an eternal form/*morphē* as that
which determines the 'look' of something in advance. On the contrary,
Heidegger's reinterpretation of 'perception' uncovers the fact that
since the times of ancient Greek philosophy the entire theatre of
perception has been organized by the metaphor of making; he then
proposes going 'beyond' perception as it has been determined by the
metaphor of production by considering the 'look.' Instead of concerning himself with the Platonic 'idea,' Heidegger's reinterpretation of the
order of perception and the *eidos* uncovers the 'look' that he connects
with the 'image' (*Bild*). On this reading, the *eidos* is no longer an eternal
form that governs perception or something that is produced: rather, it
is now that which *precedes* perception and production. These 'looks'
that are prior to production are themselves given by what Heidegger
calls *phantasia*, or the 'imag-ination.' The *eidos* is a look or an image that
cannot be understood as a mere present-at-hand object or a pre-existent idea or presence that structures the order of perception – either
understanding or reason: the look or image can only be properly
understood by considering it as part of the 'imag-ination' that is 'older'
than *both* perception and production. For this reason the look/image
cannot be determined on the basis of ontotheological perception. What
Heidegger proposes, therefore, is the displacement of the ontotheological *eidos* and the ontotheologico-metaphysical order of perception
along with the metaphor of production that determines it.

There are three aspects of Heidegger's imag-inative reinscription of
the *eidos* that resonate with the previous chapter's discussion of catachresis, (non)production, and the allusion of mimicry. (1) Heidegger's
reinscription of the *eidos* also serves to bring it close to catachresis. If
we are no longer dealing with an eternal present in the *eidos*, then we
are no longer simply in the realm of the Platonic Forms: and, insofar as

the potter 'sees,' the 'look' here comes closer to its empirical roots in the *word 'eidō'* (Greek, 'to see'). At the same time, however, such 'seeing' retains a catachrestic kernel: the potter does not literally 'see'*any-thing*.[8] (2) Heidegger's reinscription of the *eidos* can also be connected to Derrida's indication of a textual 'practice' beyond the opposition of production/non-production, which I have already cited above (page 30). This (non)production is legible in the operation of the imagination, which occupies the space between the idea and the actual thing.[9] To the extent that it does not 'produce' anything, the operation of the Heideggerian imag-ination may then be read in terms of the previous chapter's discussion of the supplement and the general economy that does not turn a profit. (3) However, to say that there is *no product* in the Heideggerian imagination is not to suggest that the imagination is exhausted by an absolute *non*-production: on the contrary, there remains a certain *allusion* to the product as it will be. The allusion to the product may be usefully read in terms of the 'perpetual allusion' which 'mimes reference' that Derrida sees in Mallarmé's 'Mimique.' Allusion, on this reading, is an act that plays out 'without a referent' (D 219) because 'the signifying allusion does not go through the looking-glass' (D 210). Caught in the play of the mirror, without breaking through to 'reality,' this allusion mimes the spacing of reference and signification, without which there would only be presence. Thus, within allusion, there is no longer any way of deciding in the last instance on the absolute 'exteriority or anteriority, the independence, of the imitated, the signified, or the thing' (ibid.). When reread in conjunction with the Mime's allusion that does not break the mirror, Heidegger's imagination becomes an 'undecidable' space that is also *différantial*: presence and absence are originarily confused there; further, since there is only reference,[10] there is only the double of reflection without any 'original.' Once it is reread in the light of these motifs, Heidegger's imagination becomes catachrestic, a secondary origin, a 'between': what the imagination (non)produces, or better, practices – 'looks' – are neither simply sensory/actual nor simply intelligible/spiritual. What Heidegger gives in his comments on the imagination can be reinscribed as a practical, catachrestic imagination that both displaces and reinscribes all 'Platonisms.' It is precisely this non-Platonic imagination that I will consider in some detail in the remainder of this chapter. In many ways, this reinscription of the imagination constitutes one of the major theoretical frameworks in this study, not just because it guides my reading of Heidegger's *Kant and the Problem of Metaphys-*

ics, but also because it provides a locus for coming imaginatively to grips with the interplay of space and time in both *Finnegans Wake* and Derrida's 'concept' of *différance*.

Put in the most reductive terms, it might be said that Heidegger understands the imagination as a faculty that is both prior to knowledge and intimately bound up with the issue of time. This is most easily seen in his *Kant and the Problem of Metaphysics*, which is also a reading of the role the imagination plays in Kant's *Critique of Pure Reason*.[11] For the Kant of CPR, knowledge in general is composed of intuition and conception. Intuition is essentially sensible, and takes the forms of time and space. Concepts are the products of the understanding, and they unify the stuff of empirical, or sensible, intuition. Before there can be something like knowledge, then, both intuitions and concepts must be brought together. The imagination is the synthesizing power that binds intuitions and concepts, and it therefore precedes knowledge: 'Synthesis in general ... is the mere result of *imagination*, a blind but indispensable function of the soul, without which we should have no knowledge whatsoever but of which we are scarcely ever conscious' (KPM 62–3, citing Kant, CPR A73/B105). Further, since the imagination forms 'the horizon of objects' (KPM 97), it is not itself an 'object.' It nevertheless leaves its marks on the objects it forms, even before they become the logical or present objects of knowledge. The imagination is the uncosncious, synthetic space where objects and present beings come to stand.

Even though the imagination constitutes for Heidegger a sort of originary unity, it is nevertheless composed of two heterogeneous parts: intuition and conception. The imagination uses its two heterogeneous parts to form what Heidegger calls the 'looks' or images that precede knowledge or the present object. Heidegger begins his reading of Kant with a consideration of the Kantian pure intuitions of space and time that, he says, are prior to the experience of something present (KPM 31). These intuitions are not (re)presented in the (re)presenting of an object (32), but they are necessary if an object is to be experienced. They are also older than presence because they are the '"within which" what is at hand [or merely present] can first be encountered' (32). Thus, they 'give' 'what is intuited immediately' 'as a whole' (32). This intuition is 'original' intuition in that it lets something 'spring forth' (99). By reading in this way, Heidegger sets about dislocating the metaphysical conception of Being and .beings as eternally present-to-hand from his discourse.[12] This sort of presence in its turn derives from a conception of time: the temporal 'present-now.' Within philosophy, Derrida observes that 'there is no possible objection concerning this privilege to the present-now; it defines the very element of philosophical thought, it is *evidence* itself, conscious thought itself, it governs every possible concept of truth and sense.' Once the 'present-now' is put into question, the questioner falls 'outside' philosophy and good sense because such questioning 'remove[s] every possible *security* and *ground* from discourse' (SP 62). Reading in this way, one can easily see that the imagination in Heidegger's discourse can be aligned with a questioning that is no longer simply bound by the concerns of Western philosophy.

With respect to the originary springing forth of intuition, it is to the intuition of time that Heidegger grants a certain pre-eminence on the grounds that 'space gives in advance merely the totality of those relations according to which what is encountered in the external senses would be ordered' (KPM 34). The beauty of time is that it is not confined, unlike space, to the external senses: 'At the same time, however, we find givens of the "inner sense" which indicate no spatial shape and no spatial references. Instead, they show themselves as a succession of states of our mind (representations, drives, moods). What we look at in advance in the experience of these appearances, although unobjective and unthematic, is pure succession' (34).[13] And if it is the 'transcendental power of the imagination' that is the origin of pure sensibility as intuition, then the imagination must in some way be productive of time (121). Since 'intuition means the taking-in-stride of what gives itself' (122), intuition must also take in its stride the 'flow' of time, which it intuits as 'the succession of a sequence of nows,' (121) because 'it is not possible to intuit a single now insofar as it has an essentially continuous extension in its having-just-arrived and its coming-at-any-minute. The taking-in-stride of pure intuition must in itself give the look [image] of the now, so that indeed it looks ahead to its coming-at-any-minute and looks back on its having just arrived.' For this reason, intuition 'cannot be the taking-in-stride of a "present moment"' (122). In the place of this present-moment Heidegger substitutes the flow, the self- or auto-affection of time:

> Time is only pure intuition to the extent that it prepares the look of succession from out of itself, and it *clutches* this as such *to itself* as the formative taking-in-stride. This pure intuition activates itself with the intuited which was formed in it, i.e., which was formed without the aid of experience. According to its essence, time is pure affection of itself. Further-

more, it is precisely what in general forms something like the 'from-out-of-itself-toward-there ...,' so that the upon which [*das Worauf-zu*] looks back and into the previously named toward there ...' (KPM 132; Heidegger's ellipses)

Time, then, is given in the imagination, where it 'flows' by 'affecting itself,' clutching and binding itself to itself according to the structure of self- or auto-affection, and it shapes in general whatever is formed in the imagination.

It can easily be seen how a consideration of the imagination and time in a manner that does not conform to the 'present-now' is attractive for a study that is interested in the non-present as it functions in both Joyce's and Derrida's work. However, it is precisely his treatment of time as 'pre-eminent' (34), that would, on the face of it, limit the usefulness of Heidegger's analysis of the imagination for a reading of either *Finnegans Wake*, which considers time in conjunction with space, or Derrida's conception of *différance*, in terms of 'the becoming-time of space and the becoming space of time' (M 8; cf. P27) discussed in chapter 1. However, as I mentioned above, Heidegger cannot be said to simply ignore spatial intuition in his consideration of the imagination (KPM 34). Nor can it be said that Heidegger is not interested in the 'space,' as a quick perusal of the network of reference that constitutes *Dasein*'s world in *Being and Time* would confirm.[14] Nevertheless, it must be said that Heidegger does not develop this aspect of the imagination in KPM. Thus, if his analysis of the imagination is to remain of use for the present study's attempt to read both *Finnegans Wake* and *Glas*, it will be necessary to rework Heidegger's understanding of self- or auto-affection in the light of spatial considerations. To do this requires that one read the Heideggerian text beyond the constraints it has imposed on itself. A *différantial* reconsideration of time is therefore in order.

'hevnly buddhy time'

The question and necessity of reworking the Heideggerian analysis of the imagination is of immense importance for this study. In this section, I want to consider how the purely temporal succession of inner sense in the imagination may be reinscribed in a manner that will allow it to remain of use for this study's consideration of the *Wake*an war of time and space and the spatio-temporality of Derrida's conception of *différance*. In particular, I am interested in exploring how considerations of *différance* may be used to supplement Heidegger's discussion of the imagination. I will also consider how this reinscription of the imagination in terms of spatio-temporality opens onto a bodily conception of time. This bodily conception of time will play a crucial role in the next chapter's consideration of how the imagination bridges both *Finnegans Wake* and *Glas*. These issues – the germs of what I am calling the bodily conception of time, the *différantial* recasting of the operation of the imagination – can be examined in the context of a discussion of Derrida's consideration of the question of auto-affection and the pure temporality of philosophical sense in *Speech and Phenomena*. A discussion of this text will also make clear how a consideration of imagination must displace an understanding of meaning or sense that is based on pure temporality.

In *Speech and Phenomena*, a text devoted to an examination of Husserl's theory of signs, Derrida has occasion to consider one of the texts to which Heidegger's discussion of auto-affection in *Kant and the Problem of Metaphysics* is arguably most indebted: Husserl's *The Phenomenology of Internal Time-Consciousness*.[15] For Derrida, it is precisely the motif of auto-affection that permits '"time" to be conceived anew on the basis ... of difference within auto-affection, on the basis of identifying identity and nonidentity within the "sameness" of the *im selben Augenblick*' (68). When approached from this angle, 'time' is opened up to the difference of auto-affection, an opening that, I will argue below, can be understood to inscribe spaced-time within the operation of the imagination.

The opening of time to auto-affection is first glimpsed through Husserl's attempts to maintain what he calls 'the actual *now* [which] is necessarily something punctual and remains so, *a form that persists through continuous change of matter*' (SP 63, citing Husserl's *Ideas*, § 81; Husserl's italics). The difficulty arises, says Derrida, once it is understood that 'the presence of the perceived present can appear as such only inasmuch as it is *continuously compounded* with a nonpresence and nonperception, with primary memory and expectation (retention and protention)' (SP 64, Derrida's italics). Memory and expectation are not present: they are 'not-nows,' 'nonperceptions,' that are 'neither added to, nor do they *occasionally* accompany, the actually perceived now; they are essentially and indispensably involved in its possibility' (ibid). In extending the 'actual *now*' into the persistent form of presence, perception can readily be seen to be composed of two 'non-perceptual' 'non-presences': 'As soon as we admit this continuity of the now and the not-now, perception and non-perception, in the zone of primordiality common to primordial impression and primordial retention, we admit the other into the self-identity of the *Augenblick*; nonpresence and nonevidence are admitted into the *blink of the instant*. There is the duration of the blink, and it closes the eye' (65). This alterity, Derrida continues, 'is in fact the condition for presence, presentation' in general. And 'the difference between retention and reproduction, between primary and secondary memory, is not the radical difference Husserl wanted it to be; it is rather a difference between two modifications of nonperception' (65). In other words, memory and expectation compound and split the 'now' with 'not-now' and repetition, without which it would not be possible for Husserl to extend his 'actual *now*' into a 'form.'

Understood thus, the auto-affection plays with reproduction, memory, expectation, and otherness in a manner that is neither controlled by presence nor reliant on a prior present *eidos*, precisely because it is 'spontaneously generative': 'The process by which the living now, produced by spontaneous generation, must, in order to be a now and to be retained in another now, affect itself without recourse to anything empirical but with a new primordial actuality in which it would become a non-now, a past now – this process is indeed a pure auto-affection in which the same is the same only in being affected by the other, only by becoming the other of the same' (SP 85). This 'other of the same' opens out onto the *différantial* 'trace':

> The living present springs forth out of its nonidentity with itself and from the possibility of a retential trace. It is always already a trace. This trace cannot be thought out on the basis of a simple present whose life would be in itself; the self of the living present is primordially a trace ... [Sense] is never simply present; it is always already engaged in the movement of the trace, that is in the order of 'signification.' It has always already issued forth from itself into the 'expressive stratum' of lived experience. Since the trace is the intimate relation of the living present with its outside, the openness upon exteriority in general, upon the sphere of what is not 'one's own,' etc., *the temporalization of sense is, from the outset, a 'spacing.'* As soon as we admit spacing both as 'interval' or difference and as openness upon the outside, there can no longer be any absolute inside, for the 'outside' has insinuated itself into the movement by which the inside of the nonspatial, which is called 'time,' appears, is constituted, is 'presented.'

Space is 'in' time; it is time's pure leaving-itself; it is the 'outside-itself' as the self-relation of time. The externality of space, externality as space, does not overtake time; rather it opens as pure 'outside' 'within' the movement of temporalization. If we recall now that the pure inwardness of phonic auto-affection supposed the purely temporal nature of the 'expressive' process, we see that the theme of a pure inwardness of speech, or of the 'hearing oneself speak,' is radically contradicted by 'time' itself. The going-forth 'into the world' is also primordially implied in the movement of temporalization. (86)

Repetition, 'the bending back of a return' (SP 68), constitutes the 'trace in its most universal form.' This repeatability in turn constitutes the 'ideality of the form (*Form*) of presence itself [and] implies that it be infinitely re-peatable' (67). The 're-peatable' trace in auto-affection is the non-present origin of presence. And, to the extent that the auto-affection generates with no recourse to presence, it describes the scenes of writing and imaginary production discussed in chapter 1, where production takes place without the need for presence. The 'simple self-identity' of the present is thus 'radically destroy[ed]' (SP 66). Derrida implies that this not-now comes into contact with the 'after-effect' (*Nachträglichkeit*) in Freud, which is also a past that was never present (OG 66–7; WD 203):

> Now B would be as such constituted by the retention of Now A and the protention of Now C; in spite of all the play that would follow from it, from the fact that each one of the three Now-s reproduces that structure in itself, this model would prohibit a Now X from taking the place of Now A, for example, and would prohibit that, by a delay that is inadmissible to consciousness, an experience to be determined, in its very present, by a present that would not have preceded it immediately but would be con-siderably 'anterior' to it. (OG 67)

This conception of the unconscious delay disrupts the 'linear, objective, and mundane model' of successive time, replacing it with a non-linear understanding of time, where 'pastness' 'remain[s] as it were, to come – come from the future, from the *to come*' (Mem 58). On this reading, then, the 'not-nows' mark *both* spatio-temporal postponement *and* deferral.

It is precisely this temporal model that Derrida associates with the play of the supplement and which he explicitly associates with Vichian

time: 'This play of the supplement, the always open possibility of a catastrophic regression and the annulment of progress, recalls not only
Vico's *ricorsi* ... it makes history escape an infinite teleology of the
Hegelian type. In a certain way ... history can always interrupt its own
progress, (and must even progress in regression), (re)turn behind itself'
(OG 298). The Derridean reinscription of time I am considering here is
therefore *Vichian*. This is why this conception of time as auto-affection
can open so easily onto the text of *Finnegans Wake*. In fact, it is isomor-
phic with the strange temporality of the *Wake*an scene of non-present
imaginative 'buildung' discussed in chapter 1. I want to suggest that it
is only through this spatial-temporal or auto-affective displacement of
the present that the Vichian temporality of the *Wake* may be grasped.
Vichian 'time' displaces the present, inscribing it within a chain where
'ancients link with presents as the human chain extends, have done, do
and will again' (254.8–9). In other words, the 'presents'/presence no
longer control(s) the extension of the auto-affective chain: 'ancients'
always come to synthetically compound ('link') 'presents.' Furthermore, because these compounded extensions cannot be guided or
gathered by a presence that lies either in a past (present) or future
(present), they can be understood to displace and reinscribe both
Platonic *anamnesis* and Hegelian teleological anticipation.[16]

I want to compare Derrida's reworking of 'time' to the treatment of
temporality in the *Wake* in more detail. As is well known to readers of
Finnegans Wake, 'time' is most often associated with the feminized
flow[17] of the maternal River Liffey or Anna Livia Plurabelle (ALP),
which flows through the centre of Dublin City. On closer inspection,
however, ALP's flow is revealed to be not entirely smooth: it is punctuated by textual spaces and places (the 'B(r)ook of Life'). It is in these
textual spaces that the text recommends its readers 'sojournemus':

> Horn
> of Heatthen, highbrowed! Brook of Life, back-
> frish! Amnios amnium, fluminiculum flami-
> nulinorum! We seek the Blessed One, the
> Harbourer-cum-Enheritance. Even Canaan
> the Hateful. Ever a-going, ever a-coming.
> Between a stare and a sough. Fossilisation, all
> branches. Wherefore Petra sware unto Ulma:
> By the mortals' frost! And Ulma sware unto
> Petra: On my veiny life!

> In these places sojournemus, where Eblinn
> Water, leased of carr and fen, leaving amont her
> Shoals and salmen browses, whom inshore
> breezes woo with freshets, windeth to her
> broads. (264.5–19)

In these watery-textual places, these 'betweens,' time stops flowing altogether. The flow stagnates in a 'sough' or a bog ('carr') that opens the interplay of time (in the guise of a tree: *Ulma*, Latin, elm) and space (in the guise of a stone: *petra*, Latin, stone).[18] ALP's temporal 'flow' is therefore punctuated by intervals of space that produce a rhythmic 'ever a-going,' and 'ever a-coming.' These spaces, which are big enough for the 'Blessed One' to fall into and get lost, hold out the possibility of recovering the missing 'Harbourer-cum-Enheritance,' HCE. In other words, the river's spatio-temporal comings and goings play with the possibility of revealing/concealing the missing giant. On this reading, the 'flow' of the river echoes the *différance* that affects Finnegan/HCE with the peculiar sort of 'absence' discussed in chapter 1.[19] Elsewhere, the jerky flow of the river is explicitly associated with a Vichian model of time:

> Teems of
> times and happy returns. The seim anew. Ordovico or viricordo.
> Anna was, Livia is, Plurabelle's to be. (215.22–4)

On this reading it can easily be seen that 'time' in the *Wake* fits rather neatly with those texts of Derrida's that recast 'time' in terms of spatio-temporal *différance* and Vichian *ricorsi*.

The intervallic exteriority of the trace in auto-affection opens the intimacy of the subject and speech up (even as it forms them), and opens the relation between the signifier and signified to a reading that is simultaneously motivated and arbitrary because it plays with a certain proximity to the signified:

> Ideally, in the teleological essence of speech, it would be possible for the signifier to be in absolute proximity to the signified aimed at in intuition and governing the meaning. The signifier would become perfectly diaphanous due to the absolute proximity to the signified. This proximity is broken when, instead of hearing myself speak, I see myself write or gesture.

This absolute proximity of the signifier to the signified, and its effacement in immediate presence, is the condition for Husserl's being able to
consider the medium of expression as 'unproductive' and 'reflective.' (SP
80)

This recalls the 'sensory kernel' that lies at the heart of metaphor
(M 250) discussed in chapter 1.[20] In tracing the underlying figures of
philosophy and rhetoric – the catachrestic, or non-true metaphors –
the reader once again comes into contact with the deep structures of
philosophy and rhetoric wherein 'the body furnishes the vehicle for all
the nominal examples in the physical order' (256). This 'proximity' is
what prevents, for example, the analyses in 'White Mythology' from
treating the 'historical or genealogical (let us not say etymological) tie
of a signified concept to its signifier (to language) [as] a reducible contingency' (253). However, given all that has been said relating to the
proper noun of reference, whether it be the thing-in-itself or the signified *eidos*, the body, the sensory kernel must escape from the structure
of eidetic reference. It escapes because it is (self-)affect, and opens the
field of (re)motivation where the body forms an outside, even a world,
that is represented as constantly coming under the sway of time.[21] In
this way – as auto-affective surface – the body offers itself as a *différantial* exterior: 'I see myself, either because I gaze upon a limited region
of my body or because it is reflected in a mirror.' In these cases, 'what is
outside the sphere of "my own" has already entered the field of this
auto-affection, with the result that it is no longer pure' (SP 82). This
means that 'auto-affection supposed that a pure difference comes to
divide self-presence. In this pure difference is rooted the possibility of
everything we think we can exclude from auto-affection: space, the
outside, the world, the body, etc' (82).

It is the intrusion of the world, and particularly the body, into the
purely temporal auto-affective sphere of 'my own' in Derrida's text that
I want to focus on here. In particular, I want to suggest that this body –
whose intrusions forever prevent auto-affection from being pure – also
forms a bridging mechanism to the understanding of the body in *Finnegans Wake*. Just as the body in Derrida's text intrudes into pure auto-
affection via the spatial interval of the *Augenblick*, the *Wake*, too, explores
a corporeal temporality in the guise of what it calls the 'hevnly buddhy
time' (234.13–14). This 'body time' is explicitly associated with another
instance of the *Augenblick*: the fluttering eyelids that constitute the wink
made by 'dem dandypanies,' the flora-girls, who know 'de play of de

eyelids' (234.16). The seductive play of the girls' eyelids produces a
scene of ejaculatory ecstasy in the one winked at, who becomes
immersed in 'his gamecox spurts and his smile likequid glue' (234.17).
In this way, the wink comes together in the text with the rhythmic spurts
of ejaculation. Thus, the body-time of the *Wake* makes itself felt in the
text as the rhythmic contraction and release of orgasm: 'coming.'[22]

But, despite what would appear to be the obvious presence of the
seminal fluid in the 'likequid glue,' the orgasmic eruption is not
exhausted by being coded as male. In fact this entire scene works very
hard to prevent any such simple sexual coding. For example, the girls'
winking eyelids do not only evoke the contraction of the vaginal mus-
cles during orgasm, they also recall the eyelids of their brother, Yawn,
whose eyelids flutter as he yawns: 'ripely rippling, unfilleted, those
lashbetasselled lids on the verge of closing time' (474.7–8). Thus, 'de
play of de eyelids' is neither purely male nor purely female: in fact it
suggests a play wherein the sexes are no longer easily distinguished.
Yawn's eyelids mimic his sisters' eyelids which, through their fluttering, merge the ecstatic moment of orgasm with the moment of falling
asleep. In this state, the eyelids flutter – open and close repeatedly –
and as they do so, they are always playing, says the text, on the 'verge
of closing.' Here the 'feminine' action of contracting and relaxing the
eyelids is associated with the 'verge,' which, as the text of *Glas* is
always quick to remind its reader, is also a rod, a phallus, a prick. What
the *Wake* offers the reader through the 'hevnly buddhy time' is a
glimpse of a body neither male nor female, a body that fuses spatio-
temporality with the physical action of contraction and release. Further, it is the relation that this bodily time shares with the operation of
the imagination that constitutes the next of this study's theoretical
frameworks for comparing the texts of *Finnegans Wake* and *Glas*. I will
return to this bodily time in the next chapter.

The War of Space-Time in the Wake

'Flow' never runs smooth in *Finnegans Wake*. This is especially true of
the uneasy flow of time that is both staged and radicalized in the text
when spatio-temporal auto-affection (or *différance*) takes a downright
antagonistic turn during its transposition into the 'dime-cash' problematic of I.6. In this dime-cash problematic time and space become the
twin brothers – Shem and Shaun – who perpetually fight with each
other throughout the book. Their intuitive battle interrupts the letter

plot of book I. Section I.5 deals with the document/text of the letter, and I.7 deals with the author of the letter whom 125.23 identifies as 'Shem the Penman.' As the interval between the letter's examination (I.5) and its invention of the author (I.7), I.6's discussion of these forms of intuitions must, in some way, be important for the analysis of the letter in terms of imagination.

On its most basic level, the eleventh question of I.6 is an argument against time. Shaun is asked if he would help a poor beggar (Shem) who might ask him for food (for thought), or 'thomethinks to eath' (149.3). 'No, blank ye!' he roars, and he goes on in a highly indignant fashion to give exhaustive reasons as to why he won't:

> So you think I have impulsivism? Did
> they tell you I am one of the fortysixths? And I suppose you
> heard I had a wag on my ears? And I suppose they told you too
> that my roll of life is not natural? But before proceeding to con-
> clusively confute this begging question it would be far fitter for
> you, if you dare! to hasitate to consult with and consequentially
> attempt at my disposale of the same dime-cash problem elsewhere
> naturalistically of course, from the blinkpoint of so eminent a
> spatialist. (149.11–19)

The intuitive and imaginative problematic – that of space and time – here undergoes *Wake*an transformation and emerges as 'the same dime-cash problem' because 'time,' as the old adage has it, 'is money.'[23] Shaun is therefore placed in a somewhat ironic position as he denigrates time, his begging brother, 'from the blinkpoint of so eminent a spatialist.' But because the 'blinkpoint' involves seeing time, as I have suggested above, as productive spacing, a 'spatialist,' who sees nothing but space, will dismiss time as something that is a lie, something not to be trusted. For a spatialist, the two markers of time's treachery are (a) its exchangeability (it is also money) and (b) its transferability (it can also be given as charity to beggars). As such, it can only 'beg questions' without answering them. Shaun cites several authorities to back up his overdetermined 'blinkpoint' on time and the beggar's plea for help, before finally settling on Professor Bryllar's research to sum up his objections to his beggar-brother:

> But, on Professor Llewellys ap
> Bryllars, F.D., Ph. Dr's showings, the plea, if he pleads,

is all posh and robbage on a melodeontic scale since his man's
when is no otherman's *quandour* (Mine, dank you?) while, for
aught I care for the contrary, the all is *where* in love as war and
the plane where me arts soar you'd aisy rouse a thunder from and
where I cling true'tis there I climb tree and where Innocent looks
best (pick!) there's holly in his ives. (151.32–52.3)

The formulation offered by Shaun here is incredibly slippery, but it
arguably comes down to this: space, the where, is superior, says Shaun,
because it is 'the all,' whereas the when is 'no otherman's *quandour*
[Latin *quando*, when].'

In other words, Shaun's objection to his brother – who is now clearly
identified with time[24] – hinges on a view contrary to the one he held
earlier. Time, he now insists, is non-transferable because one man's
when [*quando*] is his own alone, and presumably inaccessible to anyone but him. For Shaun, time is idiomatic, whereas space ('the all is
where') is the universal element. Shaun's formulations on space may
here be connected with Heidegger's examination of the synecdochal
everywhere of space: 'The unity of space is not that of a concept, but
rather the unity of something which in itself is a unique one ... The
many spaces are only limitation of the one, unique space ... The unified, unique space is wholly itself in each of its parts' (KPM 32). The
*Wake*an equivalent of this 'unified and unique' space is the 'Eins within
a space and a wearywide space' in the tale of the 'Mookse and the
Gripes' as it is told in I.6. Space needs to be only once (Eins), and its
'oneness' (Eins) is everywhere. Individual spaces are limitations of
purely intuitive (and therefore non-eidetic) space.

Space gets its fullest systematic exposition later on in the same
chapter:

My heeders will recoil with a great leisure how at the out-
break before trespassing on the space question where even
michelangelines have fooled to dread I proved to mindself as to
your sotisfiction how his abject all through (the *quickquid* of Professor Ciondolone's too frequently hypothecated *Bettlermensch*)
is nothing so much more than a mere cashdime however genteel
he may want ours, if we please (I am speaking to us in the second
person), for to this graded intellecktuals dime *is* cash and the
cash system (you must not be allowed to forget that this is all
contained, I mean the system, in the dogmarks of origen on

spurios) means that I cannot now have or nothave a piece of
cheeps in your pocket at the same time and with the same man-
ners as you can now nothalf or half the cheek apiece I've in mind
unless Burrus and Caseous have not or not have seemaultaneously sysentangled themselves, selldear to soldthere, once in the
dairy days of buy and buy. (160.35–61.14)

On the face of it, the space system – the 'cash' system – as it is presented here, is locked into the logic of non-contradiction wherein one
person cannot occupy the space of another. In the exposition offered by
Shaun, this is translated into not being able to have (or not have) the
same 'piece of cheeps' that another has in his trouser pockets. However, Burrus and Caseous (or Butter and Cheese) can only chase the
(same) piece of cheese if they 'have seemoultaneously sysentangled
themselves' at a specific time in the past, designated as 'once in the
dairy days of buy and buy.' If the two brothers have been intertwined
in the past, this also means that both brothers are forevermore capable
of being 'seemoultaneously sysentangled.' Further, the extent to which
they come together implies a temporalizing wrinkle in the 'dogmarks'
– as it were, a disruptive marking of the dogma – of non-contradiction
inherent in Shaun's outline of the spatial system. Temporalization is
denigrated by Shaun because it is inherently contradictory. It is idiomatic yet transferable. It can permit two different things to occupy the
same space as well as the same things to occupy two different spaces
by virtue of the simple fact that it is always flowing past. This flow
scandalizes non-contradiction because it facilitates the relation of one
man's idiomatic time to another's by allowing them occupy the same
space, but it does not translate those idioms for each other. Rather, time
maintains their untranslatability even as it makes them available to be
read. This has an effect that is similar to the one analysed above relating to the impossible translation of philosophy and *différance*: each
idiom loses sense, but remains, to a degree legible in the absence of
total sense or meaning. Both men's times simply regard each other,
exchange looks with each other, in less-than-perfect comprehension.
But because each time is so different, time can be as baffled by itself as
space. In this way, the idioms of time and space only relate to each
other as other, flowing together according to the dynamics of *différance*.

These *différantial* dynamics are laid out in I.4, where the fusion of the
spatio-temporal twins is figured as the fusion of tree and stone (148.32–
68.14; also 215.31–16.6). Insofar as the tree is temporal, and the stone

spatial (*Annotations*, 213), time and space may be understood to come together in an auto-affective manner in the synthetic figure of 'Tree-stone' (113.19), or 'Tristan.' The 'symphysis' that tree and stone undergo does not remove all the differences between the two:

> cumjustled as neatly
> with the tristitone of the Wet Pinter's as were they *isce* et *ille*
> equals of opposites, evolved by a onesame power of nature or of
> spirit, iste, as the sole condition and means of its himundher
> manifestation and polarised for reunion by the symphysis of
> their antipathies. Distinctly different were their duasdestinies. (92.6–11)

Thus, even though the twins are a 'symphysis' – a 'cumjustled' synthe-sis – of tree and stone, they remain 'distinctly different.' Both are fused in a 'cum' that recalls the rhythms of corporeal ejaculation mentioned above and explicitly imprints the fusion of both twins with one of the distinctive marks of the imagination: synthesis. Read in terms of this 'come,' Treestone figures the becoming time of space and becoming space of time. Understood thus, Treestone figures *différance* in his many appearances throughout the book.[25] The *différantial* Tristan crosses himself because he/it can never simply be him-/itself, and always relates to him-/itself as (br)other. This is why he can also be under-stood to not just figure, but also allegorize, *différance*. Because *différance* is itself allegorical, to the extent that allegory literally means 'to speak (*agoria*) otherwise (*allos*),' the auto-affective fusion of the twins in Tristan *différantially* figures *différance*, the relationship where the same relates to itself as other (SP 85). I will return to this reflexive structure in the next chapter.

The *différantial* structure that fuses the twins returns again and again in the *Wake*, and each time it does, it reveals itself as feminine. This culmi-nates in the womanly 'O' of ALP, a figure for both the womb and the vagina as the *site* where the antagonistic twins (Shem and Shaun, now Nike and Mike) are brought together as *différance*: 'You may spin on youthlit's bike and multiplease your Mike and Nike with your kick-shoes on the algebrars, but volve the virgil page, the O of woman is long' (270.22–6). The 'O of woman,' the bicycle, is where the brothers pass into each other incessantly. It is to this 'O' that I want to turn now. Specifically, I want to consider how the 'fusion' of time and space in the O cannot be understood as 'unity' in any simple sense precisely because the female figures in the text are not themselves unified. I also want to explore how contemplating these disjunctive feminine figures makes it impossible to consider time in the absence of space or space in the absence of time. I will try to show that in *Finnegans Wake* the feminine is the *différantial* site of *différance*. To this end, I now return to I.6, the site of the fraternal war between time and space.

If the O of woman can be understood to function as the site of brotherly fusion in the text, its fusion is not simply a peaceful space where the differences between time and space are resolved in a dialectic of perfect unity or harmony. Perhaps the most obvious reason for this is that the female figures in the *Wake*an text are not unified:

> Every admirer has seen my goulache of Marge (she is so like the sister, you don't know, and they both dress A L I K E !) which I titled *The Very Picture of a Needlesswoman* which in the presence ornates our national cruetstand. This genre of portraiture of changes of mind in order to be truly torse should evoke the bush soul of females so I am leaving it to the experienced victim to complete the general suggestion by the mental addition of a wallopy bound or, should the zulugical zealot prefer it, a congorool teal. The hatboxes which composed Rhomba, lady Trabezond (Marge in her *excelsis*), also comprised the climactogram up which B and C may fondly be imagined ascending and are suggestive of gentlemen's spring modes, these modes carrying us back to the superimposed claylayers of eocene and pleastoseen formation and the gradual morphological changes in our body politic which Professor Ebahi-Ahuri of Philadespoinis (Ill) whose bluebutterbust I have just given his coupe de grass to neatly names a *boîte à surprises*. (165.13–30)

Through these 'changes of mind' the text recasts the temporalized 'inner sense' discussed above in terms of Marge's 'changes of mind.' These changes 'space' the self across a series of different, and yet similar, states of mind – drives, moods, etc. – to produce woman's 'fickleness.'[26] This fickle mode of self-affection is, according to the Shaun-like professor's commentary, characteristic of the 'bush soul of females.' Woman's hatboxes and changes of mind allegorize temporization in which her self can only relate to itself as another in different moods. Each 'mood-box' is one in a long line of '*boîte[s] à surprises*' that never settles down to form a predictable pattern. As such, this surprising box recalls the *Now* X discussed in the previous section that comes to absurdly and unconsciously disrupt linear time (*Now* A, B, C, etc.). This tangled bush-box of others-selves problematizes simple space in that it permits two different things – self/other – to occupy the same space, a temporal proposition that the professor/Shaun has already found to be scandalous (160.35–61.14). Driven by the need to keep things cleanly separate in space, the professor/Shaun tries to (re)theorize the boxy 'bush soul of females' as the site of the clean separation called birth ('proper parturience'). However, his attempts to clean-up the female box are all the while magnetized by the slang for a vagina, 'box.' This is why Shaun's reconsideration of female boxes quickly becomes his rumination on the vagina which gives rise to the proper birth that separates mother from son, which is then to be reinforced by proper toilet training. In a world without time, clean space would properly separate the son from the mother in a successful parturition. The cleanliness of this separation is finally figured in the successful completion of toilet training. But the cleanly operating O is distracted by the other, unpredictable O, the series of 'boxes,' which is also the site of scandalous fusion: 'My solotions for the proper parturience of matres and the education of micturious mites must stand over from the moment till I tackle this tickler hussy for occupying my uttentions' (166.27–9). It is the O-□ that both provides and removes the ground for the professor's/Shaun's spatial argument. The O-□ intrudes on both sides of Shaun's spatial analyses as the condition for proper separation as well as the site of contamination. As such, it relates to itself always as other.

This play of the O-□ in Shaun's mind puts his discourse squarely in the problematic of the spatial difficulties caused by temporality's ability to permit different things to occupy the same space. He tries to escape the problem once again by making an example of a female figure (yet another self-lubricating woman), Margareena. This time, however, the professor's/Shaun's meditations on space become an alphabetical consideration of Margareena's promiscuity with Antonius, Burrus, and Caseous. Through his consideration of her promiscuity, the professor/Shaun gropes towards the same place that can be occupied by another:

> Margareena she's very fond of Burrus but, alick and alack!
> she velly fond of chee. (The important influence exercised on

everything by this eastasian import has not been till now fully
flavoured though we can comfortably taste it in this case. I shall
come back for a little more say farther on.) A cleopatrician in
her own right she at once complicates the position while Burrus
and Caseous are contending for her misstery by implicating herself with an elusive Antonius, a wop who would appear to hug
a personal interest in refined chees of all chades at the same time
as he wags an antomine art of being rude like the boor. This
Antonius-Burrus-Caseous grouptriad may be said to equate
the *qualis* equivalent with the older socalled *talis* on *talis* one
just as quantly as in the hyperchemical economantarchy the tan-
tum ergons irruminate the quantum urge so that eggs is to whey
as whay is to zeed like your golfchild's abe boob caddy. (166.30–67.8)

The professor/Shaun is fascinated by Margareena's ability to accommo-
date three male figures – Antonius-Burrus-Caseous – all at once. To the
extent that Margareena can peform this trick, she becomes a promiscuous space that once again disrupts the smooth sequence of A-B-C by taking them on as 'grouptriad' wherein all three lose their identity: X-Y-Z
flow into each other and into A-B-C: 'eggs is to whey as whay is to zeed
like your golfchild's abe boob caddy.' Understood thus, Margareena's
promiscuous space is therefore also aligned with time: she introduces
herself as the sort of time where different objects can occupy the same
space into the professor's/Shaun's ruminations on space.

The professor/Shaun, however, is unable to control his fascination
or desire for the promiscuous spatio-temporality, and he tries to dis-
tract himself by rounding on his beggar-brother, Shem, who has asked
him for aid. He tries to hide his attraction for Margareena by accusing
Shem of being the one who is led astray by promiscuous intuition:

> And this
> is why any simple philadolphus of a fool you like to dress, an
> athemisthued lowtownian, exlegged phatrisight, may be awfully
> green to one side of him and fruitfully blue on the other which
> will not screen him however from appealing to my gropesarch-
> ing eyes, through the strongholes of my acropoll, as a boosted
> blasted bleating blatant bloaten blasphorus blesphorous idiot
> who kennot tail a bomb from a painapple when he steals one
> and wannot psing his psalmen with the cong in our gregational
> pompoms with the canting crew. (167.8–17)

The promiscuity of intuition leads, in Shaun's opinion, to idiocy, a condition that is tantamount to being two colours at once and to being unable to distinguish things that look alike, for example, a bomb and a pineapple.

The irony here, of course, is that the inability to distinguish has already attached itself to Shaun's portrait of Margareena and leads him to say that 'she is *so* like the sister, you don't know, and they both dress ALIKE!' (165.14–15). Thus, Shaun's attempts to displace his weakness onto his brother make it clear that each accusation Shaun directs at his brother is also directed at himself: it is his own fascination that he accuses. This becomes clearer later still in I.6 when Shaun's fascination with Margareena's promiscuity starts, at the end of his exposition of the pre-eminence of space, to fuse him with his brother, Shem:

> She that will not feel my ful-
> moon let her peel to thee as the hoyden and the impudent! That
> mon that hoth no moses in his sole nor is not awed by conquists
> of word's law, who never with humself was fed and leaves
> his soil to lave his head, when his hope's in his highlows from
> whisking his woe, if he came to my preach, a proud pursebroken
> ranger, when the heavens were welling the spite of their spout,
> to beg for a bite in our bark *Noisdanger*, would meself and Mac
> Jeffet, four-in-hand, foot him out? ay! were he my own
> breastbrother, my doubled withd love and my singlebiassed hate,
> were we bread by the same fire and signed with the same salt,
> had we tapped from the same master and robbed the same till,
> were we tucked in the one bed and bit by the one flea, homo-
> gallant and hemycapnoise, bum and dingo, jack by churl, though
> it broke my heart to pray it, still I'd fear I'd hate to say! (167.35–68.12)

But it is not until the final question and answer of the chapter, number twelve, that this fusion is itself expressed in its most condensed form:

12. *Sacer esto?*
Answer: *Semus sumus!* (168.13–14)

The reference here is to the Law of the Twelve Tables, VIII.21: '*Patronus si clienti fraudem fecerit, sacer esto*' (If the patron abuses the client, let him be accursed)[27] (*Annotations*). Originally, this was a penalty where the offender was made a sacrifice (*sacer*). But later, as Rome became more civilized, the *sacer* penalty became one of disgrace. Thus the questioner, Shem, follows through on Shaun's indictment of Shem, by asking him if the beggar – Shem – should be sacrificed/disgraced – '*Sacer esto?*' Interestingly, Shaun's response to this question becomes *temporal* despite itself. His answer, '*Semus sumus*,' means both 'We (*sumus*) are the same,' or 'We are Shem.' In both ways then, temporalization gets the last word as both brothers – despite themselves – double for each other and come to occupy the 'same' space: Shem the Penman, the figure of the author-forger-son in the text, and the subject of the next chapter (I.7) in the book.

But it is not until the 'Nightlessons' chapter of the *Wake* (II.2), when the children are doing their homework, that the O-□ of the woman in the form of 'youthlit's bike' (270.23) is both illustrated and explicitly named as the site where time-space is characterized as 'interplay' (293.L1–4):

Uteralterance or
the Interplay of
Bones in the
Womb.

It is thus the womb, the 'O of woman,' that the text identifies as the site where the twin-bones of time and space are given together. Since this 'O' is also that of the mother-hen, Anna Livia Plurabelle (ALP), the O of woman is also the site of flowing-together in the water (*eau*). *Eau*/O marks the originary production of the twins of space and time: one cannot be given without the other. The O/*Eau* of the mother-river exceeds 'Professor Llewellys ap Bryllars'' conclusion that one 'man's *when* is no otherman's *quandor*' (151.35) precisely because it is where Shaun and Shem have formerly 'seemoultaneously sysentangled themselves' together, where they have previously occupied each other's spatio-temporality. The complexity of this *Eau*/O-space is marked by the in-fighting that takes place there: it is the site of the '*Uteralterance or the Interplay of Bones*.' But even though the womb allows the brothers to flow together, it does not allow them to simply meld into each other with absolutely nothing left over. In this way, the womb preserves the proverb 'how one once meet melts in tother wants poignings [one man's meat is another's poison]' (143.18–19). In other words, occupying another's place/time does not mean that either one has to adopt the other's idiomatic constitutional preferences, since the

Eau/O of the womb preserves differences even as it brings together. The womb is therefore the site of spatio-temporal *différance*, and this is also why its peculiar mode of bringing together is called 'Putting truth and untruth together' (168.8–10).

Since the intuitions of 'time' and 'space' are given by the imagination (KPM 121), it now becomes possible to see the woman's *Eau*/O as imagination. It is the site of the non-eidetic 'heliotropical noughttime' in II.3 that produces the fusion of the two brothers (now in the guise of Bull and Taff/Batt and Tuff) It brings them together to form a non-Platonic *eidos* – what the text of the *Wake* terms an 'idolon,' a false image, which etymologically derives from the same stock as the philosophical *eidos*:

> In the heliotropical noughttime following a fade of trans-
> formed Tuff and, pending its viseversion, a metenergic reglow
> of beaming Batt, the bairdboard bombardment screen, if taste-
> fully taut guranium satin, tends to teleframe and step up to
> the charge of a light barricade. Down the photoslope in syncopanc
> pulses, with the bitts bugtwug their teffs, the missledhropes,
> glitteraglatteraglutt, borne by their carnier walve. Spraygun
> rakes and splits them from a double focus: grenadite, damny-
> mite, alextronite, nichilite: and the scanning firespot of the
> sgunners traverses the rutilanced illustred sunksundered lines.
> Shlossh! A gaspel truce leaks out over the caeseine coatings.
> Amid a fluorescence of spectracular mephiticism there caoculates
> through the inconoscope stealdily a still, the figure of a fellow-
> chap in the wohly ghast, Popey O'Donoshough, the jesuneral
> of the russuates. The idolon exhibisces the seals of his orders:
> the starre of the Son of Heaven, the girtel of Izodella the Calot-
> tica, the cross of Michelides Apaleogos, the latchet of Jan of
> Nepomuk, the puffpuff and pompom of Powther and Pall, the
> great belt, band and bucklings of the Martyrology of Gorman.
> It is for the castomercies mudwake surveice. The victar. (349.6–25)

Here the televised image of the idolon can be understood to mark the excessive decomposition of the philosophical idiom's unity,[28] that is to say, the unity of the Platonic *eidos*. This *eidos* is only legible in the text of the *Wake* as an 'idolon,' a ghost, a false image, a simulacrum of the *eidos*. This once more seems to suggest that the philosophical idiom loses sense within the bounds of the *Wake* and it decomposes into its

non-philosophical double, the idol, the false image. The unity of the
(Platonic/philosophical) *eidos* is here ruptured, and it starts to affect
itself with its non-philosophical double, its *différantial*, spectral, and
imaginative other. Once again, this rupture does not happen to any
'prior unity': 'prior unity' is revealed to be an 'idolon' that is possible
only on the grounds of an 'older' *différantial* relation wherein the twin
brothers affect each other (as other). In other words, the idolon interrupts the punctual presence of the Platonic/philosophical *eidos* by
opening it up along the lines of *différantial* temporization in a manner
analogous to the expectation and retention that disrupt present perception. This means that in the *Wake* there is only a (non)philosophical
eidos, and it is always already fractured, doubled, by *différance*. In the
next chapter, I will explore this site of bringing together in terms of
the hen's 'ygathering' (010.32), which I will argue may be read as the
parodic doubling of the philosophical *logos*.

It should be apparent that the structure of *différantial* temporization
is of major importance for this study: it sketches 'the locus of a problem
in which phenomenology confronts every position centered on nonconsciousness that can approach what is ultimately at stake, what is at
bottom decisive: the concept of time' (SP 63). This locus is also the
locus of what chapter 1 calls reinscriptive *différance*, the relation the
'restricted economy' – the desire for eidetic presence, meaning, etc. –
has to the 'general economy' of 'expenditure without reserve,' 'death,'
and 'nonmeaning' (WD 19), the known to the unknown. And it is the
imaginary production of 'time' as *différance* that best sketches the relation the known has with the unknown for texts – such as Derrida's
and Joyce's – that explore forms of writing that have little to do with
presence.

III X: The *Wake* Glosses *Glas*

From Signature to Text

The letter, which, as I argued above, is a site of productive or imaginative textual augury in *Finnegans Wake*, can also be understood as the
maternal womb, yet another site of productive imagination. But this
observation does not yet confront what the hen writes in/as the letter.
To do that, the reader-writer as auspex should pay due care and attention to the marks she leaves behind. This also means that the reader-
writer is placed in the position of the son who, regardless of gender,

follows the maternal writing in /as text. In this section, I will argue that this maternal bond is figured in the Xs the hen writes in the letter. Because they are non-eidetic, these Xs can also be understood to mark the 'absurd' spatio-temporality where 'nows' from pasts that were never present unconsciously recur. Thus, they can be read as the iconic analogues for the type of *différantial*, or spatio-temporal production discussed in the previous sections of this chapter.

Thus, and once again, the reader must return to the scene of the hen's textual dance as she scratches about on the midden heap in I.5:

> The bird in the case was Belinda of the Dorans, a more than
> quinquegintarian (Terziis prize with Serni medal, Cheepalizzy's
> Hane Exposition) and what she was scratching at the hour of
> klokking twelve looked for all this zogzag world like a goodish-
> sized sheet of letterpaper originating by transhipt from Boston
> (Mass.) of the last of the first ... (111.5–10)

That this dance is textual is underlined by the fact that the hen uncovers what the text calls a 'goodishsized sheet of letterpaper' – the letter itself. As she uncovers this sheet of paper, she also 'writes' (upon) it and the midden-heap. The text guides the reader to the figure she traces at line 7, by associating her 'scratching' with the word 'zogzag.' The 'zogzag' or zig-zag scratches cross in a repetitive change of direction, and trace out, on the midden and in the body of the letter, the reiterated scratches of the 'four crosskisses' found in the letter at 111.17:

> Dear whom it proceded to
> mention Maggy well & allathome's health well only the hate
> turned the mild on *the van* Houtens and the general's elections
> with a *lovely* face of some born gentleman with a beautiful present
> of wedding cakes for dear thankyou Chriesty and with grand
> funferall of poor Father Michael don't forget unto life's & Muggy
> well how are you Maggy & hopes soon to hear well & must now
> close it with fondest to the twoinns with four crosskisses for holy
> paul holey comer holipoli whollyisland pee ess from (locust may
> eat all but this sign shall they never) affectionate largelooking
> tache of tch. (111.10–20)

Further, these Xs, which trace the 'Axe on thwacks on thracks, axenwise' (19.20), also sign the letter, in much the same way as the X that is traced across the printer's backside in Joyce's poem 'Gas from a Burner':

> Who was it said: Resist not evil?
> I'll burn that book, so help me devil.
> I'll sing a psalm as I watch it burn
> And the ashes I'll keep in a one-handled urn.
> I'll penance do with farts and groans
> Kneeling upon my marrowbones.
> This very next lent I will unbare
> My penitent buttocks to the air
> And sobbing beside my printing press
> My awful sin I will confess.
> My Irish foreman from Bannockburn
> Shall dip his right hand in the urn
> And sign crisscross with reverent thumb
> *Memento homo* upon my bum.[29]

The hen's zig-zag marks also recall Joyce's method of crossing out the material he incorporated and reincorporated from his notebooks into the drafts of the *Wake*.[30]

But these Xs do not sign or mark the letter-writer's identity in any simple sense: they also cross out identity, giving it over to the forces that can blur any simple identity. It is precisely this blurring of identity that is illustrated by the letter insofar as it is understood to be written by an amalgamation of mother and son through a sort of 'dictation' (420.17–19). Read in this manner, the 'Tiberiast duplex' (123.30), which elsewhere denotes the writer of the letter, is composed of mother and son. This du/plex immediately cleaves the writer, marking 'him' as a lack of unity. In other words, du/plicity affects the writer through the model-less model of production discussed above. The model – here, the mother-hen – withdraws, or effaces herself in the productions of the reader-son, which she nevertheless gives to him in the form of what the text calls 'uttering.' This uttering should not be regarded as the originary speech that constitutes the full import of the letter because it too remains an uttering for her, from elsewhere (420.18).

The duplicity that affects the writer is perhaps most interesting here because it can also be read as offering a complex *Wake*an analogue to the non-phenomenological imaginary of auto-affection discussed in the previous section of this chapter. The hen's withdrawal affects the writer with a lack of unity, which is marked in the text as the split between the ear and the eye, 'mikealls or nicholists,' or 'browned or nolensed':

> Let us now, weather, health, dangers, public orders and other
> circumstances permitting, of perfectly convenient, if you police,
> after you, policepolice, pardoning mein, ich beam so fresch, bey?
> drop this jiggerypokery and talk straight turkey meet to mate, for
> while the ear, be we mikealls or nicholists, may sometimes be in-
> clined to believe others the eye, whether browned or nolensed,
> find it devilish hard now and again even to believe itself. (113.23–9)

Her withdrawal may therefore be understood to set in train a series of tensions that mark the letter-text's disruption of the simple unity of the reader-writer by calling two reading figures to the fore. These figures are as antagonistic as the auto-affective twins in that they are prone to fight with each other because they cannot see eye to eye:

> I am a worker, a tombstone mason, anxious to pleace avery-
> buries and jully glad when Christmas comes his once ayear. You
> are a poorjoist, unctuous to polise nopebobbies and tunnibelly
> soully when 'tis thime took o'er home, gin. We cannot say aye
> to aye. We cannot smile noes from noes. Still. One cannot help
> noticing that rather more than half of the lines run north-south
> in the Nemzes and Bukarahast directions while the others go
> west-east in search from Maliziies with Bulgarad for, tiny tot
> though it looks when schtschupnistling alongside other incuna-
> bula,it has its cardinal points for all that. (113.34–14.7)

These two auto-affective readers can only squint at each other in a text wherein they are figured as two lines that cross each other – one running 'north-south,' and the other running 'west-east.' The crossed text splits the reader who becomes cross-eyed (in a way) by following the Xs left in the text by the hen as she withdraws in criss-crossing the mound.

The zig-zagging that signs the letter with 'four crosskisses' (111.17) is also a form of writing. But the Xs do not figure the letter's writing icon-ically simply because they sign the hen's writing. The Xs that sign the letter are capable of expansion insofar as they also figure the auto-affective antagonistic criss-crossing of two reader-writers as the actual writing of the letter, which is itself scripted 'boustrephodontically,'[31] by a 'writing' that travels 'thithaways end to end and turning, turning and end to end hithaways writing and with lines of litters slittering up and louds of latters slettering down, the old semetomyplace and jupet-backagain from tham Let Rise till Hum Lit' (114.16–19). The zig-zagging Xs thus also show the hen's crossed style of writing. It is this crossed writing that is mimicked by a reader in a theatre of production without model, and subjects him/her as a writer to the auto-affective split. In this complex scene of writing, the reader-writer of the text is constantly disrupted by the influences of a mother and a rival.[32]

The scene of letter-writing in *Finnegans Wake* can be seen as a writing that repeatedly criss-crosses itself, constituting the reader as the site where two antagonistic textual forces pull him/her in two directions at once: the textual lines that run north-south and east-west. It is these lines that repeatedly cross in (as) the letter-text. Understood thus, the hen's writing cannot be said to be 'linear' in any simple sense. Further, since she writes by criss-crossing and zig-zagging across the rubbish tip, the hen's writing is not imitative: it is of the order of Mallarmé's mime discussed in chapter 1. And since her non-linear writing marks both the mound and the letter, it cannot be contained by the usual concept of (phonetic) writing. The hen is therefore a Derridean writer.[33]

The Auto-Affective X

In marking any potential reader-writer with the auto-affective split, auto- or self-affection, *Finnegans Wake* opens its reader-writer to what Heidegger calls their finitude, their death: '[Self-affection] forms the essence of something like self-activating. However, if it belongs to the essence of the finite subject to be able to be activated as a self, then time as pure self-affection forms the essential structure of subjectivity' (KPM 132). In other words, a subject who is subject to finitude is subject to death and temporality. Violent death and temporality also await the reader who both reads and mimics the hen's letter-writing: following the hen also requires coming to terms with the 'numerous stabs and foliated gashes' (124.2) in her text.

It is precisely this violent and fatal aspect of textual auto-affection that is explored at the end of I.5. On closer inspection, the letter-text reveals itself as something dangerous, its surface studded with all manner of sharp edges:

> Yet on holding the verso against a lit rush this
> new book of Morses responded most remarkably to the silent
> query of our world's oldest light and its recto let out the piquant
> fact that it was but pierced butnot punctured (in the university
> sense of the term) by numerous stabs and foliated gashes made
> by a pronged instrument. These paper wounds, four in type,
> were gradually and correctly understood to mean stop, please
> stop, do please stop, and O do please stop respectively, and
> following up their one true clue, the circumflexuous wall of a
> singleminded men's asylum, accentuated by bi tso fb rok engl
> a ssan dspl itch ina — Yard inquiries pointed out → that they
> ad bîn "provoked" ay ∧ fork, of à grave Brofèsor; àth é's Brèak
> — fast — table;   ; acùtely profèššionally *piquéd*, to=introdùce a ·
> notion of time [ùpon à plane (?) sù ' ' fàç'e'] by pùnct! ingh oles
> (sic) in iSpace?! (123.34–24.12)

Here, the text of the letter is doubled: not only is it 'wounded,' its surface marred by numerous stabs and gashes – it also *wounds*. Its text
forms the wall of a 'singleminded men's asylum' (124.7), topped off
with 'bi tso fb rok engl a ssan dspl itch ina' (124.7–8). Now, since the
text splits the reader, it cannot remain a tranquil asylum for a singleminded reader: its textuality exceeds such a reader. Thus, the letter-
reader is forced to scale 'the circumflexuous wall' (6–7) and be cut by
the shards of broken glass and English that line its top lip. In other
words, the reader of the letter-text cannot remain a traditional reading
subject, searching for sense and meaning, protected inside the asylum
of the text. All these 'bi tso fb rok engl a ssan dspl itch ina' can therefore be brought together with the lines of letter-text in that they both
exceed the 'singleminded man' by cutting 'him' up or pulling 'him'
into two directions at once. Once the *Wake*an reader of the letter-text
scales the wall of the text, s/he becomes an 'outlex' (169.3), at large in
the text.[34] This in turn aligns the reader with the co-writer of the letter,
the hen's/ALP's son, Shem: once associated with Shem the reader-
writer loses his/her 'respectable stemming' and becomes a notorious
bastard (169.3–8).

However, this cutting and splitting of the reader-writer should not be
taken as the text's desire to debilitate or silence its reader; on the contrary, the cutting/splitting of the singleminded man here constitutes the
'one true clue' (124.6) for reading the letter's criss-crossed text: the let-

ter's 'wounds, four in type' (124.3). Thus, it is wounds that are of central importance in reading this letter. These wounds are not only the marks of spatio-temporal auto-affection in that they 'introdùce a notion of time [ùpon à plane (?) sù ' ' fàç'e'] by pùnct! ingh oles (sic) in iSpace?!' (124.10–12), they also form the basis on which the letter-text comes together with the letter-reader: the wounded text has sharp textual edges that exceed the singleminded reader by fatally carving him/her up into antagonistic finite readers who can no longer see eye to eye with each other because they are strangers to each other. Understood along these lines, the sharp edges of the letter-text crucify the reader-writer, becoming both the cross and nails that stretch, split, and wound the him/her, marking him/her with the stigmata of the 'stabs and foliated gashes' (124.2) that also mark the body of the letter-text. In other words, the reader who wishes to read-write the letter-text well must submit to a scene wherein s/he is split and pulled in two directions and receives four wounds. This is perhaps appropriate: only a cut-up and doubled reader-writer can follow a cut-up and doubled text. This textual stigmata also performs a double service: it offers the reader his or her place in the text as one of sacrifice by crucifixion, and permits the reader to think of his or her outlaw body in the same *différantial* or textual terms as the body of the letter-text in a scene of non-eidetic genealogy.

These fairly complex reader–writer–text relations can be made clearer by considering the special kinship the letter-text shares with one text in particular, a text that is suggested by the 'one true clue' of the 'wounds, four in type': the Irish ninth-century illuminated gospel manuscript, the Book of Kells. I would like to consider this kinship by returning to the Xs as they appear in the hen's letter. As I argued in the previous section, the hen's 'four crosskisses' (111.17) do not just sign the letter; they also sketch the very form of its writing. These Xs therefore open a sort of textual abyss: the part can metonymically stand for the whole and vice versa. But that is not all: the 'four crosskisses' also become, over the course of I.5's consideration of the letter, the four obeli – † – that call attention to redundancy in its text:

> all those red raddled obeli cayennepep-
> percast over the text, calling unnecessary attention to errors,
> omissions, repetitions and misalignments: (120.14–16)

Understood thus, the Xs not only mark both part and whole of the letter, they also mark those errors that are unintentionally introduced into the letter. It is these Xs or †s that put the hen's letter into direct contact with Sir Edward Sullivan's description of the Book of Kells in a paragraph that could pass for a description of the text of *Finnegans Wake* itself:

> There are a considerable number of errors in orthography in the pages of the Irish manuscript, many of which have never been corrected. One important instance of correction is to be found on fol. 219 R., where the text of the preceding page, fol 218 V., has been erroneously repeated. Attention is drawn to the error by four obeli in red, running down the middle of the page between the lines, and others around the margins, and red lines around the corners. Peculiar spellings of words occur also.[35]

In both *Finnegans Wake* and the Book of Kells, the red obeli mark the occasions of scribal oversight and error. According to *Finnegans Wake*, the obeli-kisses in both the Book of Kells and the letter also recall the large cruciform 'X' of the so-called *Tunc* page (f. 124r):[36]

> the cruciform
> postscript from which three basia or shorter and smaller oscula
> have been overcarefully scraped away, plainly inspiring the tene-
> brous Tunc page of the Book of Kells (and then it need not be
> lost sight of that there are exactly three squads of candidates for
> the crucian rose awaiting their turn in the marginal panels of
> Columkiller, chugged in their three ballotboxes, then set apart for
> such hanging committees, where two was enough for anyone,
> starting with old Matthew himself, as he with great distinction
> said then just as since then people speaking have fallen into the
> custom, when speaking to a person, of saying two is company
> when the third person is the person darkly spoken of, and then
> that last labiolingual basium might be read as a suavium if who-
> ever the embracer then was wrote with a tongue in his (or per-
> haps her) cheek as the case may have been then) and the fatal
> droopadwindle slope of the blamed scrawl, a sure sign of imper-
> fectible moral blindness; (122.20–36)

Here, the letter aligns itself with the *Tunc* page on the basis of the shared †-Xs, which are also kisses (*basium*). The letter even goes so far as to suggest that it 'plainly inspir[ed] the tenebrous *Tunc* page of the Book of Kells.' It is this mysterious filiation of the *Tunc* page and the letter that offers a way of reading the strangely doubled 'tunc's dimis-sage' (298.7) that exceeds the presence of a pre-existent and meaningful philosophical *eidos*. This can be understood as follows.

In the Book of Kells, the *Tunc* page illustrates the text of the crucifixion of Christ and the two thieves – '*Tunc crucifixerant XPI cum eo duos latrones*' (Then were there two thieves crucified with him) – from Mat-thew 27:38 in a decorative line of script that itself takes the shape of a cross.[37] This textual figure, called a rebus, is a 'structural device in Irish art which Joyce shares with the Book of Kells.'[38] On the *Tunc* page, the X takes up the crossed lines of letter-text to form a visual pun on the scene of crucifixion where 'the "X" of the text (the cipher of Christ)' figures 'the cross of Christ's death' (126). In this pun-structure, text dispenses with the need for a 'referent' (here, for example, the 'cross' of Christ's death, and Christ 'himself'), precisely because that referent appears itself in a decorative textual form. Because the rebus is a figure that embodies both literal and visual puns, a physical object can stand in for a name, and 'speak.' Such speaking objects constitute what Vico calls heraldry, the 'official' language of the heroic age. Heraldic speech is therefore speech expressed in 'symbolic' form by utilizing 'signs and ... heroic devices' (NS 140). These devices are also known as 'canting arms':

> In *The Books at the Wake*, James Atherton gives close attention to the num-ber of heraldic motifs in FW. He first identifies heraldry as the language of Vico's second, heroic age, and cites Vico's description from the *New Sci-ence*: 'The second [language] was by blazonings with which arms are made to speak' (Atherton 32). This idea of arms 'made to speak' is espe-cially evocative of the canting arms which occupy so prominent a position in Joycean heraldry (cf. the French expression for canting arms, 'armes parlantes'). (JJH 92)

In *Finnegans Wake*, the rebus structure of signification is played out in the crossings of the letter-text's obeli-crosskisses that draw the reader's attention both towards and away from a particular part of the letter, contaminating the part with its whole. In this way, the X of the obelus or kiss, each of which is only one small part of the letter, communicates with the entire letter itself, which, as I mentioned above, can itself be understood as one large cross:

> One cannot help
> noticing that rather more than half of the lines run north-south

in the Nemzes and Bukarahast directions while the others go
west-east in search from Maliziies with Bulgarad for, tiny tot
though it looks when schtschupnistling alongside other incuna-
bula, it has its cardinal points for all that. (114.2–7)

Understood thus, the *Wake*an X plays abyssally with size and doubling
through the figurative or decorative substitution of a part of the text
for the whole of the text. Because the rebus structure of signification
employs a visual pun – the figurative 'X' on the '*Tunc*' page of the Book
of Kells or the crosskisses of the letter – its structure of signification can
no longer be regarded as simply 'representing' a 'meaning' that could
be 'found elsewhere.' This is because in the rebus form, content, and
referent all come to double for each other in a manner that is remarkably similar to Nietzsche's strategy of what Derrida calls *mettre-en-
abyme*. In the *abyme* 'metaphoricity' is generalized 'by putting into
abyme one determined metaphor' (M 262), an operation that risks the
contamination of the non-metaphoric language (scientific, conceptual,
etc.) by metaphor (M 263). If one regards the rebus along similar lines,
then the rebus outlined in Vico, the *Wake*, and the Book of Kells constitutes a mode of signification that is no longer subjected to the metaphysics of the classical oppositions (signifier/signified, sign/referent,
etc.), but rather one that thrives on the doubleness that comes to ruin
(*abîmer*)[39] those oppositions.

A certain death also becomes legible in the doubled form of signification of the X, because the rebus of the 'tunc's dimissage' plays with
crosses and death in a scene of crucifixion. It is precisely to the extent
that death and crucifixion may be read in the letter's iconic Xs that the
scene of readerly production parodies Christ's crucifixion. In this parody, it is the reader who mimes the death of Christ by being erected
and killed on the cross of the text. This occurs because if it is the task of
the reader is to follow the textual auspices of the hen as she criss-
crosses the midden, then s/he must allow him/herself to be pulled in
the two directions indicated by the topic of the criss-crosses in the text.
In following the hen and making both the text and him/herself, the
quasi-Vichian reader of the *Wake* therefore not only makes the cross-
text of the letter in a scene that does without meaning understood in
the eidetic or referential sense, but also puts him/herself to death.

In crucifixion, the cross operates by stretching and erecting the victim across its frame, squeezing the spirit out of him/her, in much the
same way that the letter draws the reader in two directions at once

across the lines of the letter-text. In *Finnegans Wake*, death of the Christ-reader can be understood as being held in place by overdetermined points in the letter that also coincide with 'wounds, four in type' (124.3). These points mark where the lines of text running east–west and north–south cross at 'cardinal' and 'doubtful points' (112.7–9). But these points set up a play that proceeds 'by crossing out predicates or by practising a contradictory superimpression that then exceeds the logic of philosophy' (WD 259), because as 'points' they are also 'crosses,' in that the 'points' are composed of 'points' where lines 'cross' and the 'crosses' are 'crosses' only insofar as they are 'lines' that cross at specific 'points.' The play of contradictory superimpression here takes the form of a quasi-metonymic relation that violates logic by not only inscribing the described in the description, but also cease-lessly putting into question the possibility of ever making a positive identification of either a cross or a point, or vice versa.

These cross-points are figured in the obeli-daggers (†) insofar as they are precisely 'cross-points.' At 120.14–16 these cross-points merely dis-rupted the letter's penmanship by drawing the reader's attention to the 'errors, omissions, repetitions and misalignments' in its text; now they puncture the body of the letter, as I noted above. But the †s do not just fragment the text with all manner of punctuation marks, diacritical marks, accents, and other icons: they also mark the points where, just like the 'bi tso fb rok engl a ssan dspl itch ina,' 'time' is given as a num-ber of coexistent holes punched in 'space': they are spatio-temporal. To the extent that these 'points' configure the spatio-temporality dis-cussed above, they are traces: the 'holes' made by these points erase themselves *as holes*. Understood thus, these cross-points mark the site of the reader's (Christic) death as one that is inextricably bound up with the *différantial* temporalization and auto-affection that is born of a multiplicity of maintained 'now-points.' These spatio-temporal points make it possible to understand *Wake*an auto-affection in terms of 'cubist historiography,' wherein history is no longer seen as 'a plotted narrative toward resolution, but as a cubist painting whose elements maintain' an 'aestheticized structure of interrelations to each other.'[40]

The obeli, insofar as they mark both the non-eidetic model of the hen's writing and temporalized interrelations of the text of the *Wake*, are doubly inassimilable to the presence of philosophical meaning. However, since the reader's corpse becomes textual through being affected with the spaced-time of these cross-points, they also serve to cross the body of the (Christic) reader together with the body of the text of the letter, inscribing each in one another through the mark of doubling temporalized auto-affection. Thus, the death of the reader cannot have any meaning as presence that would once more amount to a desire 'to deny the existence of death' (WD 259). Bataille, as I argued in chapter 1, offers an alternative to this death in what he calls the 'gay anguish, anguished gaiety' in the face of death. Such gaiety, which is as close as possible to the desire to deny death, 'present[s] me with "absolute rending" in an aspic in which it is my joy that finally rends me asunder, but in which abatement would follow if I was totally torn apart, without measure' (ibid.). This type of gay death takes place, for example, at 'Finnegan's Wake [sic]' and insofar as it does not look for meaning, forms the 'blind spot of Hegelianism, *around* which can be organized the representation of meaning.' It is 'the *point* at which destruction, suppression, death and sacrifice constitute so irreversible an expenditure, so radical a negativity – here we should have to say an expenditure and a negativity *without reserve* – that they can no longer be determined as negativity in a process or a system.' This point wherein lies the gay death 'cannot be inscribed in discourse, except by crossing out predicates or by practising a contradictory superimpression that then exceeds the logic of philosophy' (ibid.). However, the death of the reader should not be understood as a finite death in the face of an empirically infinite richness of the text; on the contrary, the death of the reader should be understood as the play-ful dislocation of the reader as the centre of meaning in the text.

The death of the reader is also a sacrifice. The contours of this sacrifice can be made clearer by reconsidering the auto-affective points of spaced-time in the letter. Further examination of which reveals

> that the fourleaved
> shamrock or quadrifoil jab was more recurrent wherever the
> script was clear and the term terse and that these two were the
> selfsame spots naturally selected for her perforations by Dame
> Partlet on her dungheap ... (124.20–4)

If the reader's death is a parody of Christ's, then his or her bond with the hen's text may be said to suggest a sort of familial bond between reader and text that must be considered further.[41] Since the mortal stigmata-punctuation marks turn out to be holes put there by the hen, in the guise of 'Dame Partlet' from Chaucer's The Nun's Priest's Tale, it is therefore the 'mother-hen' – the one who makes her 'son,' the reader-writer who makes him/herself – who also sacrifices that son, inflicting the four wounds of the stigmata on him/her with her obelus-beak. Since the shape of the weapon and the wounds themselves cross in the auto-affective Xs that also write and sign the letter, this implies that in the hen's non-eidetic scene of writing where the reader-writer 'makes' him/herself, the reader-writer's death has always already been a necessary part of that 'making.' Understood in this way, the auto-affection in the *Wake*'s letter inscribes finitude as a gay death given by the 'mother'-text to her reader-'son.'

The Quasi-Rabbinical Jesus: Finnegans Wake *Regards* Glas

> According to the X (The chiasmus) (which can be considered a quick thematic diagram of dissemination), the preface, as *semen*, is just as likely to be left out, to well up and get lost as seminal *différance*, as it is to be reappropriated into the sublimity of the father. (D 44, translation slightly modified)

The auto-affective sacrificial death of the *Wake*an reader-writer split by crucifixion provides an indispenable context for coming to grips with the figure of the Jesus, who shows up in *Glas* only so that he 'breaks in two and flees.'[42] The figure of 'Jesus' in *Glas* functions in a way that is remarkably similar to the X in letter-text in the *Wake*, where he acts as a *différantial* icon or figure for *Glas*'s reading of Hegel. As the above citation from *Dissemination* indicates, the mark of dissemination also recalls the mark of Jesus – the 'χ' recalls the chrismon. Jesus-χ, insofar as he breaks in two and flees, can be understood to erase himself. As such, Jesus, and thus the dead reader of *Finnegans Wake*, would no longer be the 'son of God' to the extent that they instead experience the loss of his/her self under the spatio-temporal mark of Jesus (χ-X) in the text. This formulation is consistent with Derrida's consideration of the trace towards the end of 'Freud and the Scene of Writing.'[43] 'The trace is the erasure of selfhood, of one's own presence, and is constituted by the threat or anguish of its irremediable disappearance, of the disappearance of its disappearance. An unerasable trace is not a trace, it is a full presence, an immobile and uncorruptable substance, a son of God, a sign of parousia and not a seed, that is a mortal germ' (WD 230). Since this 'erasure is death itself' (ibid.), the reader of the *Wake*, in being inscribed under the sign of Jesus as a mortal trace that would no longer have the ability to appear in presence, is also inscribed as a disseminative seed/semen. To the extent that they bear the traces of a mortal seed, it is perhaps easy to see how both the reader and Jesus can take their place in the *Wake*an spatio-temporal/ejaculatory system of the *cum*/come, trace, *différance*, spatio-temporality, auto-affection, mortality, and so on, outlined above.

This system also links χ-Jesus to what Derrida calls 'the *restance*': 'a sort of writing' (D 7), a textual remains or remainder that cannot be reduced to the 'effects of meaning, content, thesis or theme' (8). Textual remains – prefaces, forewords, introductions, preludes, preliminaries, and so on – 'have always been written, it seems, in view of their own self-effacement.' This effacement also constitutes a 'residue' to the extent that it 'remains anterior and exterior to the development of the [philosophico-speculative] content it announces.' Text is therefore that which is considered secondary – an excessive or superfluous 'form,' an 'empty husk' (9) – to the meaningful 'content' that it announces. However, since 'the route which has been covered must cancel itself out,' this 'subtraction leaves a mark of erasure, a *remainder* which is added to the subsequent text and which cannot be summed up in it' (ibid.). Hegel, says Derrida in the context of a discussion of *The Phenomenology of Spirit*,[44] disqualifies the preface from speculative philosophy on the grounds that 'philosophical exposition has as its essence the capacity and even the duty to do without a preface' (ibid.). To the extent that the Jesus-reader is a mortal germ, s/he is also revealed as something of a textual preface, a 'material'[45] husk (or, as I will suggest in chapter 3, an envelope), the written remainder that speculative dialectics cannot, but ought to have been able to, do without. For the remainder of this chapter, I will sketch what is at stake for a reading of *Glas* that considers the figure of Jesus as mortal germ and textual preface. This reading, which will provide important context for understanding the non-dialectical role the siglum X-χ plays in the spatio-temporal/ejaculatory system of both *Glas* and *Finnegans Wake*, will be of increasing importance for the remainder of the present study.

Because the figure of Jesus 'splits,' and is 'broken in two,' he plays two similar but different roles in *Glas*. On the one hand, he is properly eidetic, and as such plays an absolutely central role in speculative philosophy insofar as Hegel sees him as occupying a seminal position with respect to the Spiritual *Aufhebung* of the father's filiation with his son. This seminal reading would correspond to that part of χ which is to be 'reappropriated into the sublimity of the father' (D 44). χ would therefore occupy a crucial place in Hegelian philosophy because the *Aufhebung*-Jesus radicalizes philosophical difference (that is, difference determined as opposition) and the abstract, veiled, universal form of the Jewish God who cannot 'manifest the concrete spirit' precisely because 'he has no acknowledged son' (31a). God cannot be a father without his son. Thus, it is Jesus, the acknowledged son of the Christian God, who allows his father to manifest (himself) in/as concrete spirit. The Christian God manifests himself by 'dividing himself in his seed that is *his* [proper] other, or rather that is himself as the object for himself, the other for him and that returns to him, in which he returns to himself: his son [*fils*]' (31a). In other words, the father is the son, the son is the father.

The filiation of father and son names the very structure and trajectory of that which Hegel's philosophy pursues through all history, art, and religion: spirit. However, spirit, in its most radical formulation is thoroughly philosophical, which is to say that it surpasses even the Christian religion. Nevertheless, it is Christian filiation that best figures the heavily eidetic self-conscious return of spirit to itself, for 'spirit is neither the father nor the son, but filiation, the relation of father to son, of son to father, of father to father through the mediation of the son, of the son to the son through the mediation of the father. The spirit is the element of the *Aufhebung* in which the seed returns to the father' (31a). This the immortal Jesus alluded to in *Dissemination*.

On the other hand, there is another (piece of) Jesus, one who is to be read as a catachresis of the Jesus who 'has departed; leaving his disciples without present, leaving them suspended between memory and hope, he has separated himself from the world' (91a). In leaving, in losing presence, this Jesus becomes suspended between memory and hope. It is memory and hope, or, what I have already analysed above in terms of the auto-affective non-perceptual extension of a present that extends this Jesus' presence. This other Jesus cannot be simply present, and any presence that he may have had is suspended (precisely) between two modifications of non-presence and non-perception. Jesus does not simply leave behind or forget his body as his spirit departs. The body is not present when the tomb is opened.

Jesus splits, and Christianity 'repeats, a little higher up, the Jewish cutting [*coupure*]; the disciples remained as sheep without a shepherd; the name [Jesus] has not yet been recognized. The check [*échec*, also 'failure'] of filiation, of the family, of the city, hypocrisy, calculus, violence, appropriation. Stones/Peters [*Pierres*]' (92a). Here, the name 'Jesus' has not yet been recognized dialectically because Jesus is (not yet) himself. If 'Jesus' remains a little too Jewish (i.e., is not yet Christian), that is perhaps because he (is) split(s): that is, he repeats the medium of Jewish thought and its relation to the law. Jesus becomes Jewish (again) because his split (re)cuts (across) the surface and figure of Christianity in their entirety. Christianity is therefore doubled, and along with it 'the structure of the relief, too' (92a). The cut articulates the relief, doubling it as two reliefs (*Aufhebung*). In being 'split,' Jesus also repeats (himself) as two (rival) Jesuses who relate to each other according to the Jewish conception of justice, where 'both Xs must ... take account of one another, [and] reflect, record and inscribe themselves equally in one another' (59a), according to the law of 'an eye for an eye.' As cut and repetition, Jesus is once again allied with the *différantial* trace, the 'bending-back of a return,' the 'movement of repetition' that is older than presence (SP 68). He is perhaps best marked by the crossed legs of χ.

To read Jesus thus – as auto-affectively doubled – is to 'risk' what the text of *Glas* calls 'Jewish reading' (84a). Performing a Jewish reading of Jesus necessarily involves disrupting (the) Hegelian (priority of) sense, because Jesus operates according to the Jewish economy of justice and the law that understands the mirroring rivalry of two Xs who are at odds with each other. The Jewish risk involves reading the doubleness that simultaneously offers Jesus auto-affectively (i.e., *différantially*) and under Jewish law. This means that the reader-writer of Jesus in the text must become familiar with, and follow closely, Hegel's description of the objective structures of rabbinical law to the extent that they can be read as the inassimilable remains of the *Aufhebung*. But these remains do not simply have nothing to do with the *Aufhebung* to the extent that they are the text that speculation cannot do without.

Hegel's main difficulty with the Jews lies in their 'unintelligible' relation to the law (47a). This is because the Judaic (moral) order is one of what he calls 'abstract right and duty, of the objective law, the duty of fidelity, fidelity as duty' (35a). This duty does not forbid the desire for, say, infidelity, and as such remains objective. Thus, Jesus preaches the interiorization of the interdict through love in marriage, where desire is no longer other than the interdiction of infidelity (35a). I am freer because I am no longer subject to an outside interdiction. The Jewish relation to the law therefore remains without love and as such is mired in unfree abstract objectivity. It is caught in an economy of 'violence and slavery' (36a) that can be traced back to the Jew's being 'cut off from' nature after the aggression of the flood. The Jew is cut off from nature because he vows vengeance against nature; this then leads to the contract with God, who promises Noah 'to place the elements [and nature] at his service' in return for his obedience (38a).

With Abraham, the cut is repeated: Abraham wants to tear apart 'the [natural] communal bonds of life,' the bonds of family. Thus, he 'breache[s]/broache[s] his history and engender[s] the history of the Jewish people.' Abraham can therefore be understood to write himself outside the bonds of love and family, and as a result his lineage 'never touches the earth' (40a). But this cut only retains that which is cut from it: Abraham cuts the bonds of family 'only in order to become the stronger father of a more determinate family. What remains of/from the cut becomes stronger.' As a result, the 'Jew arranges himself so that the cut part [le coupé] remains attached to the cut. Jewish errance limited by the adherence and the countercut. The Jew is cutting only in order to treat thus, to contract the cut with itself' (41a). Abraham behaves like a master over his family, but is in fact a slave (42a, 44a): he is subject to the contract of obedience to God, which prohibits him from loving anything, even his own son, Isaac. Because he cannot love, he can only feel 'fear' and cause it in others (42a). The Jew therefore does not understand anything of life; he 'kills, transforms to dead, that is materializes everything he touches and everything not his own ... He petrifies, makes everything ugly, transforms everything into matter' (44a). It is this relation, where the master remains a slave, that remains for Hegel the 'unintelligible' aspect of the Jewish relation to the law (47a). The unintelligibility of the Jews has everything to do with the imagination. The Jew is caught at the level of the imagination that marks an 'impossible adequation,' because it does not incarnate itself, does not attain adequate actuality. Thus, Jewish appeal to the imagination 'remains abstract, disordered, artificial' (48a), and makes Hebrew poetry a poetry 'of the *negative* sublime: an impotent, crushed, overwhelmed effort for expressing the infinite in ... phenomenal representation' (48a). In other words, Jews are 'incapable of seeing ... the invisible in the visible, the sensible in the insensible, of letting themselves be affected by their unity.' This is why idols remain 'just stone and wood to them; it sees not, it hears not, it hears not, etc. – with this litany they fancy themselves wonderfully wise; they despise the idol because it does not manage them, and they have no inkling of its deification (*Vergöttlichung*) in the enjoyment of its beauty or in the intuition of love' (49a).

This sensitivity to empty signifiers leads to the structure of the tabernacle:

> The tabernacle gives its name and its place to the Jewish family dwelling. That establishes the Jewish nation. The Jewish nation settles in the tabernacle, adores therein the sign of God and his covenant. At least such would be believed.
>
> Now the tabernacle (texture of 'bands' whose excess we must continually reuse, Exodus 26) remains a signifier without signified. The Jewish hearth forms an empty house. Certainly, sensible to the absence of all sensible form, the Jews have tried to produce an object that gave in some way rise, place, and figure to the infinite. But this place and this figure have a singular structure: the structure encloses its void within itself, shelters only its own proper interiorized desert, opens onto nothing, confines nothing, contains as its treasure only nothingness: a hole, an empty spacing, a death. A death or a dead person, because according to Hegel space is death and because this space is also an absolute emptiness. Nothing behind [derrière] the curtains. Hence the ingenuous surprise of a non-Jew when he opens, is allowed to open, or violates the tabernacle, when he enters the dwelling or the temple, and after so many ritual detours to gain access to the secret center, he discovers nothing – only nothingness.
>
> No center, no heart, an empty space, nothing.
>
> One undoes the bands, displaces the tissues, pulls off the veils, parts [écarte] the curtains: nothing but a black hole or a deep regard, without color, form, and life. (49a)

This emptiness, the Jewish hearth in which one looks for a centre 'under a sensible cover [enveloppe] – the tent of the tabernacle, the stone of the temple, the raiment shrouding the text of the covenant – is finally discovered as an empty room, is not uncovered, never ends being uncovered, as it has nothing to show' (50a). Because it is empty of all proper content, its 'vacant center would signify that the Jewish essence is totally alienated. Its ownness, its property would be infinitely foreign to itself' (50a).

So the alienated Jew has no properness, and because he is the slave 'of an invisible sovereign,' his relation to that law is one of the letter, since the spirit is absent:

> So the Jews are all slaves of an invisible sovereign: between them and their sovereign, no legal and rational mediation, only heads of tribes appearing

or disappearing according to the state of forces. The powers are real, not juridical. There are indeed empiric powers, officials or 'scribes (*Schreiber*).' But the scribes are not guided by the spirit of the law. They obey rules, precepts, and commandments (*Befehle*). Their writing is heteronomic. And as this literality remains empiric, the prescription can always be violated when the situation of forces permits or requires it. (53a)

Jewish law remains external, written without spirit because the 'Jewish tongue [*langue*] speaks without yet knowing how to speak, without being able to develop fully the sperm of the [Christian] *logos*. It is the childhood of the tongue' (73a). To raise this mortal germ, this 'Pharisaic letter' would involve the literal body of the letter's being 'animated, aerated, roused lifted up, benumbed by the spiritual intention.' In this way, the letter would become Christian speech (54a). Lacking *logos*, and speaking childishly, the Jew cannot fly like the conceptual eagle, and so he falls. The Jew falls because his logic 'remain(s) the stone's' (55a). The Jew 'holds back, pulls the *Aufhebung* towards the earth. The case of the Jew does not refer to a past event. He indicates the system of a figure in the synchrony of the spirit. He is even what as such resists history' (55a).

But, by breaking in two and fleeing, Jesus also splits (irremediably) the religion of Christianity, and this gap or 'cleavage stays in absolute religion; and it stays for all time and all the figures of Christianity' (55a). Christ's split both gives Absolute Religion – Christianity – to be read and splits it for once and forever. As a result, Christianity 'cannot resolve in this world the painful opposition between the living and the dead, the divine and the real' (91a). The Christic corpse is the rem(a)inder of this split: 'They have often lived emigrating, in waiting, in the sign. Everything happens around a sepulcher. No doubt the memory of the rotting body was first effaced in the intuition of the glory, but it has returned, was insistent, to the very extent the split continued its work' (91a). In the (split) Christian religion the (split) God is suspended between heaven and earth, weighted down by his corpse: 'A kind of weight "draw[s]" it "down to earth (*ihn zur Erde zieht*)," and the "God is thus supposed to hover (*schweben*) midway between heaven's infinity, where there are no limits, and earth, this gathering together of plain restrictions"' (91a). Unable to simply depart for Heaven because he is weighed down by his corpse, Jesus remains behind: 'In his wandering and his teaching, the Christ stays nailed down or rotting: "monstrous connection (*ungeheure Verbindung*)"' (92a). Filiation, the return of Christ (to the father), is prevented.

The other Jesus therefore disrupts filiation with (return to) the eidetic father. In the place of this filiation, *Glas* offers a *'regard'* that (forcefully) reinscribes (catachrestically) the 'new testament' of son returning to father through the maternal bond:

> In painting, a *regard* is the disposition of two figures who see one another. Example from Littré: 'He has a *regard* of a Christ and a Virgin in his collection.' The *regard* is also the opening of a hole through which one watches over water drainage.
> Double regard. Cross-eyed [*bigle*: bi-gl] reading. While keeping an eye on the corner column [*la colonne d'angle*] (the contraband), read this as a new testament. (113bi)

The regarding bond reinscribes filiation by letting mother and child, Christ and Virgin, watch each other as the 'contraband' of columns. The contraband, or illegal, filiation of the *regard* halts the simple passage of the father through the mother. It opens up a strange contraband of regarding columns wherein mother and son resemble each other in a way that is different from filiation. This resemblance means that they relate to each other (according to the form of Jewish economical law) as two 'Xs [that] must ... take account of one another, [and] reflect, record and inscribe themselves equally in one another' (59a). Mother and son are rival columns that exchange regards in a scene of non-filiation. The X names the general shape of this contraband filiation, and reveals that each rival column is already crossed by the look of the other, is already doubled.[46]

The *regard* of columns can also be read as a description of a page of *Glas*. Each page in the book is composed of two columns of text. Column (a), on the right, pursues a reading of Hegelian philosophy, and column (b), on the left, pursues a reading of the texts of Jean Genet. Each column is disrupted by smaller insertion of text (i) (also called a 'judas' [113bi]) that comments on the content of the column in which it appears. However, the content of each column is reflected (and distorted) in the other, and the scene of the Immaculate contraband or catachresis can be read as a paradigm for reading-writing *Glas*.

Since the X of the *regard* is also a hole, it opens up two figures to each other according to the maternal bond, which reinscribes the guaranteed filiation of father and son. Because the X is also a hole, it (re)opens the play of contradictory superimpression that takes the form of a quasi-metonymic relation that violates logic by not only inscribing the described in the description, but also by ceaselessly erasing the possibility of ever positively identifying the obelus as either a cross or a point (or vice versa). This crossed-hole also disrupts each figure's individuality by inscribing the one in the other with difference. As such, the *regard* is also a figure for *différance*, which is also figured in the text as an 'X': 'X, an almost perfect chiasm(us), more than perfect, of two texts, each sets facing [*en regard*] the other: a gallery and a graphy that guard one another and disappear from view' (43–44b). This 'X' is also the 'χ' that traces what Derrida elsewhere calls 'the general intersection of *Glas*, of its beginnings or ends in twisted and spaced-out bands' (*The Truth in Painting* 166).[47] These (maternal) bands form the tabernacle that encloses nothing, which is empty and has no proper content. For this reason this bond is treacherous: the hole that opens up one text to another is also a '*judas*' (113bi). This judas is the other Jesus that betrays the smooth operation of the Hegelian *Aufhebung* even as he plays with it. Jesus plays at double-cross.

In this way the 'duplex' of the X can be understood to mark the general structure of the crossed style of writing that is found in both the letter-text of *Finnegans Wake* and *Glas* to the extent that the X marks the auto-affective loss of meaning. This X is always written because 'everything' 'passes through [its] chiasmus, all writing is caught in it – frequents it.' The written dislocation of meaning names 'the form of the chiasmus, the χ, ... not as the symbol of the unknown but because there is here a sort of fork (the series *quadrifircum*, grid, grill, key, etc.) which is moreover unequal, one of its points extending its scope [*porteé*] further than the other, a figure of the double gesture and the crossing' (TP 166, citing *Positions*). And because this X writes the entire text of *Glas* in a metonymic fashion, it also conforms to the general structure of the X in the *Wake* that marks both part and whole of the letter. The X turns the letter into a sort of tabernacle around which bands (O) are also contracted (IOUs):

> Tubbernacul in tipherairy, sons, travel-
> lers in company and their carriageable tochters, tanks tight anne
> thynne for her contractations tugowards his personeel. Echo,
> choree chorecho! O I you O you me! (584.31–4)

On this reading, the X-χ sketches an essential textual opening or site that inscribes each text in the other, figuring both *Finnegans Wake* and *Glas* in terms of columns that *regard* each other 'without end' (43b). But the regard also sketches a mode of reading these texts together that disrupts the activity of reading understood as the quest for meaning. The

X opens the spatio-temporal relation of one idiomatic text to another. As such, the regarding X does not translate those idioms for each other, but rather retains them in their untranslatability for each other. But because these texts can still read each other badly, which is to say, in the absence of complete sense, such reading is always incomplete. Both texts simply regard each other, exchange looks with each other, in less-than-perfect comprehension.

As such, it is the X figure that allows the reader to imagine *Glas* and *Finnegans Wake* together according to the 'gallery and the graphy' of (any) two texts that read each other, badly, that is, with imperfect sense. Both texts therefore usher the crossed style of writing figured in the X or χ centre stage, where it flourishes as an iconic figure for reading-writing both texts. And because it functions as both content and form, the X is also subject to the structured rebus-like play that loses meaning because it denotes both form and content prior to their separation. But the X, in both *Finnegans Wake* and *Glas*, always comes back to an odd relationship with the mother. It is this complex relationship – that of the maternal bond – that disrupts filiation by offering itself as a non-eidetic, textual model to be imitated by a reader-writer. In this writing from scratch, as I have argued above, the reader steps into the topos of a cross that the mother-hen prepares for him/her. But as the hen makes, she mars: in crossing out and puncturing the letter-reader, the hen's writing inflicts a spatio-temporality upon the plane surface of the reader-letter by punching holes in it. The womb, which is also the site of imaginative production, fuses with the letter, and letter-writing becomes womb-writing. This writing fuses the rival twins, Mick and Nick, who cross in the letter, but cannot see eye to eye. In so doing, the womb/letter-writing also fuses the rival twins in I.6, where they take the form of the intuitions of time and space, in auto-affection. As such auto-affective fusion, the X can also be read as the iconic ana-logue of *différance* that opens the economy of the *regard* wherein one idiomatic text reads another without perfect sense. All this fusive writ-ing can be understood as the 'ygathering' (10.32) of a 'parody's bird' (11.09) that offers an alternative to the 'gathering' of the philosophical *logos*. In the following chapter I will explore the ways in which the 'gathering' of this 'parody's bird,' as she scratches about on the mound, imaginatively parodies the very idea of a pre-existent *logos*.

3 *To Hen*: The 'parody's bird' of *Logos*

[O]ne might say that between memory of being and memory of the other there is perhaps the disjunction of allegory.

Derrida, *Mémoires: for Paul de Man* 79[1]

But we will analyze the metaphysical exchange, the circular complicity of the metaphor of the eye and the ear. (M xiii)

As I argued in the previous chapter, both the 'presence of the present' and 'self-presence' is only possible through 'the movement of a repetition' and the 'bending-back of a return' reflection (SP 67–8). This repetition and spacing is 'undermined ... by "time" to be conceived anew on the basis now of difference with identity, on the basis of identifying identity and non-identity' within 'sameness' (68). This spacing, tracing, repetition, *différance*, and writing correspond with the mortal seed of dissemination and writing as remains/remainder of the textual preface that Hegelian philosophy wishes to do without (D 8–10). The *wake* also concerns itself with those *différantial* remains in the examination of its scene of letter-writing: 'let us see all there may remain to be seen' (113.32–3). Reflection means 'to bend back or reflect,' and designates the process of reflection or its product, the reflected image. Reflection also means to consider, and can relate to either the subject or the object. On this reading, philosophical reflection is saturated by this (prefatory) text: 'The preface would thus occupy the entire *location* and *duration* of the book' (D 11). As a result, 'the outlines of the preface and of the "main" text are blurred' (39).

On the one hand, Hegel, perhaps more than any other writer, is caught in text, since reflection performs an incredibly rich function in his dialectics. For Hegel, the object is a *schein*, the reflected shine of an appearance that in turn reflects its underlying essence (its 'meaning').[2] Essence is thus reflected in the appearance, and since reflected light is also always reflected back towards its source, the appearance reflects back upon the object's essence to make it the particular object it is.[3] In its turn, the subject's reflection on the object mirrors the object's immanent reflection as appearance/essence, and since the subject's reflection on the object is immanent to the subject, the essence of the subject is reflected in the back and forth between the object and the subject.[4] Self-consciousness in the subject comes about when the subject recognizes that, since they mirror each other, there is no real difference between the process of reflection immanent in the object and the subject's process of reflection.[5] It is therefore a combination of these types of reflection that plot the path of the Hegelian *logos* and define its relation to its *eidos*. This combination also means that the Hegelian system cannot be disrupted by a criticism that would naively insist on a simple distinction between 'ideas' and 'reality' or 'subject' and 'object.'[6]

However, if Hegelian dialectics is shot through with this reflective bending-back of text, it is nevertheless the most powerful expression of an attempt to control the repetition, spacing, *différance*, and so on, of 'bending-back' 'by saturating the text with meaning': 'The signifying *pre-cipitation*, which pushes the preface to the front, makes it seem like an empty form still deprived of what it wants to say; but since it is ahead of itself, it finds itself predetermined, in its text, by a semantic *after-effect*' (D 20). Meaning, like presence with respect to the trace, is an 'after-effect' – it comes after the text. The Hegelian *logos* (as fully present meaning, speech, reason, account, discourse, etc., derived from the Greek word *legein*, to gather, collect) is perhaps the most powerful formulation of anticipatory meaning to the extent that it fuses these oppositions, 'gathers' these reflections, all these movements of 'bending back,' into the movement of a return to the already 'known' – the meaningful *eidos* – as self-consciousness. In other words, 'by *teleologically* equating [text] with its *conceptual tenor*, by reducing all absolute dehiscence between writing and wanting-to-say,' Hegel erases the 'break between *anticipation* and *recapitulation*' (ibid.). In seeking to close the gap, cut, or split between, the dialectical scene of meaning is therefore always a scene of conceptual gathering into the presence of self-consciousness, where meaning always comes back to itself.

Finnegans Wake presents its own version of the scene of gathering. However, the scene of gathering in the *Wake* does not try to reduce the repetition, spacing, and tracing of the *différantial* text. In the *Wake*an version, the gathering of the *logos*, is aped in the actions of the hen, who, as a 'parody's bird' (11.9), scuttles about on the midden 'ygathering' (10.32) bits of rubbish to put in her sack. In order to indicate what is at issue in this parody of the gathering of *logos*, it is necessary to examine the hen's gathering in relation to the immarginative reading of the *Wake* proposed so far. If, as I have been suggesting, the text of the *Wake* functions as a theatre of mimicry in which the hen is to be 'imitated' by the reader-auspex of *Finnegans Wake*, and she withdraws, then, to the extent that she withdraws, the hen's scene of writing can be understood as a scene of imaginary writing. In this theatre the object that the reader imitates withdraws, as I argued in the previous chapter, and, as it does so, reflects the reader who imitates it. I also suggested in chapter 2 that imaginary writing can be read in terms of auto-affection, even though auto-affection is for Heidegger just one component of the imagination on the basis that auto-affection can be seen as a synecdochal figuration of the entire mechanism of the imagination. In this chapter, then, I will argue that the hen's 'ygathering' writes a text – the letter – that *both* parodies *and* imaginatively reinscribes the *logos* of speculative dialectics. In other words, what the hen writes can be read as a mark of the *Wake*'s preoccupation with that 'remainder' which every speculative dialectics believes it can do without but which it cannot dominate.

In order to take stock of the hen's gathering, it is necessary to revisit the spatio-temporality of the auto-affective twins discussed in the previous chapter. The reason for this can be seen if it is remembered that auto-affection cannot fully account for the hen's gathering to the extent that, as I suggested in passing, she is the principle that brings about the fusion of the rival twins in her womb (293.L1–4). In other words, she would appear to be that which the fusion that plays itself out as auto-affection in the twins' interactions in questions 11 and 12 of the 'Questions and Answers' chapter (I.6) requires. As I have argued above, in the course of these twenty pages of this catechism, the twins, who are figured as the twin intuitions of time and space, play out the spatio-temporal fusion of auto-affection (148.33–68.14). Because the *Wake* associates auto-affection with being generated in the womb, the action of the womb must be taken into account when trying to come to terms with a parodic gathering that points to the 'unity' of spatio-temporality.

To the extent that it somehow seems to 'unite' *différantial* spatio-tempo-rality, it is possible to reread Heidegger's understanding of the imagi-nation as a synthesizing power in the light of the hen's 'womb.' On this reading, the hen is perhaps the most fitting way of rereading that other component of the imagination that Heidegger calls 'conception.'

Conception, says Heidegger, is a 'gathering' (KPM 36). The imagina-tion is the site prior to knowledge that synthesizes the components of knowledge – intuition and conception. In the imagination both intu-ition and conception are not yet knowledge and are allied to imaginary writing or (non)production. The imagination is, strictly speaking, an unknown synthesis of intuition and conception. Because it is a site of unknowing synthesis, conception must bear the traces of the intuition in the form of temporal auto-affection, and vice versa. Thus, the entire synthesizing power of the imagination must then be affected by auto-affection, which relates the same *différantially* to its non-philosophical other. In this way it remains possible to mark the difference between intuition and conception, even if they are no longer opposed to each other and no longer really very different from each other because they can be synthesized. If the relation between the two components of the imagination is one of auto-affection, then the entire imagination is auto-affective. The imagination can only affect itself as the imagination through the auto-affection of intuition and conception. Because the auto-affective relation between the two components of the imagination cuts into both auto-affective intuition and conceptual gathering, con-centrating on the hen's mode of gathering makes it possible to see how auto-affection might be understood, paradoxically, to 'gather.' How-ever, since it can only 'gather' auto-affectively, the hen's 'conception' cannot be of the order of the philosophical *eidos* that would attempt to gather itself into self-present meaning or knowledge. Thus, even though the hen's conception 'gathers' or 'unites,' it cannot ever over-come the auto-affective *différance* that prevents what she gathers from being perfectly gathered into present meaning, even as it suggests a mode of gathering. 'Ygathering' would therefore be a 'non-gathering,' nameable only via a catachresis. Further, since 'ygathering' cannot be easily distinguished from 'auto-affection,' this suggests that the hen's imaginative parody of gathering is, in a curious twist, itself constituted by the auto-affection that disrupts identity wherein the same relates to itself as other (SP 85): imaginative gathering can therefore be under-stood to allegorize itself since allegory (Greek '*allos*,' other, and '*-agoria*,' speaking) literally always 'speaks otherwise.'

In this chapter, then, I will reread the auto-affective other of imaginary intuition, conception, in the light of the hen's parodic 'ygathering.' However, it should be noted here that even though Heidegger's analysis of the imagination can be reread in order to isolate the process of allegorization in auto-affection, he never explores it as such. This, I will argue in the latter sections of this chapter, opens a gap between Heidegger's analysis of the imagination and the text of *Finnegans Wake*. *Finnegans Wake* exceeds the Heideggerian imagination precisely because it radicalizes the operation of the auto-affective imaginary by allegorizing that operation in the complex scene of writing that draws together brother/brother/mother, intuition and conception. I will also discuss how this radical allegory of imaginary writing creates the textual horizon, or the conditions for the possibility and impossibility, of that which is written in the text of *Finnegans Wake*. Finally, this chapter will explore the ways in which the hen's parodic allegorization of the auto-affective imaginary relates to the text of *Glas*. This relation insistently makes a certain 'body' legible. It is perhaps not surprising that this body will be wholly obscene and parodic, for it is the body, as Georges Bataille deliriously illustrates in 'The Solar Anus,' that obscenely parodies and mimics the 'effort at total identification' that is always concerned with proper meaning in 'brains devoted to [philosophical] reflection' (*Visions of Excess* 9).[7] That the body acts as a site that parodies philosophical reflection would appear to account for the obscenity that erupts uncontrollably through both the hen's 'ygathering' in *Finnegans Wake* and the obessive motif of 'zig-zagging' in *Glas*. This 'body' can never become an underlying 'identity' because, as I argued in chapter 2, it is the body that permits the 'self' to be seen as 'other.' On this reading, the eruption of bodily obscenity can be understood as a general index of the spatio-temporality of the trace. And this body that displaces and reinscribes 'pure' auto-affection through the interval of its spacing is also a mortal seed insofar as it is dissemination: 'Dissemination generalizes the theory and practice of the *graft* without a body proper' (D 11). Indeed, the fact that such an auto-affective 'body' lacks 'properness' prevents it from being either human or animal, since it asks us to reckon with the impossible locus or topic of a hen's womb. The lack of 'identity' of this parodic body also acts as the site that opens the possibility of developing further the present analysis of both *Finnegans Wake* and *Glas*. Its lack of identity will only be given added force through its being described as 'cross-eyed' (113bi) and 'Dufblin' ('deaf' and 'blind,' 447.23) and through its indissociabil-

ity from the sexual undecidability of fetishism in both texts. Since to
maintain this body is also to maintain the auto-affective text, both text
and body corresponds to what Derrida calls 'the critical gap between
the logical or scientific [that is, Hegelian] development of philosophy
and its empiricist or formalist lag. This, indeed, is a lesson of Hegel's to
be maintained, if possible, beyond Hegelianism: the essential complicity between empiricism and formalism' (D 11). The body as text, the
textual body – as both body and text – which I began to sketch in the
previous chapter as the Christ-like reader-χ of *Finnegans Wake* would,
to the extent that it preceeds philosophical meaning, both mark and
maintain that complicity beyond dialectics. And it is this very strange
body, the contours of which I will endeavour to sketch in this chapter,
that will provide the basis for my consideration of the body in Vico and
Nietzsche in chapter 4.

'*ygathering*': '*bi tso fb rok engl a ssan dspl itch ina*'

As I argued in chapters 1 and 2, the reader of the letter in *Finnegans
Wake* is placed in a reading position that divides him/her as reader-
writer. The reader-writer's division is registered in the letter as the
incompatibility of (at least) two modes of interpretation:

> There was a time when naif alphabetters would have written it
> down the tracing of a purely deliquescent recidivist, possibly
> ambidextrous, snubnosed probably and presenting a strangely
> profound rainbowl in his (or her) occiput. To the hardily curio-
> sing entomophilust then it has shown a very sexmosaic of nym-
> phosis in which the eternal chimerahunter Oriolopos, now frond
> of sugars, then lief of saults, the sensory crowd in his belly
> coupled with an eye for the goods trooth bewilderblissed by
> their night effluvia with guns like drums and fondlers like forceps
> persequestellates his vanessas from flore to flore. (107.9–18)

In other words, the letter, a 'polyhedron of scripture' (107.8), does not
settle down to provide one possible interpretation since it can be read
from two different points of view – that of a quasi-phrenologist or that
of an entomologist. Nevertheless, these two very different modes of
interpretation share a common trait. They both search for an author:
'Say, baroun lousadoor, who in hallhagal wrote the durn thing any-
how?' (107.36–108.1). The search for the author of the letter (which pro-

duces multiple interpretive strategies) is here represented as a quasi-Hegelian ('hallhagal') search for meaning.

But the search for a unified author is also frustrated by the darkness and distance of time:

> All's so herou from us him in a kitchernott
> darkness, by hasard and worn rolls arered, we must grope on till
> Zerogh hour like pou owl giaours as we are would we salve aught
> of moments for our aysore today. (107.20–3)

Our author is difficult to see because s/he is in the distance, far off (Armenian, *herou*, far) from us readers. Since s/he is 'worn' away by a thousand (Armenian, *hasard*) and 'worn' (one) 'rolls,' it is perhaps not surprising that the search for the author comes up with nought because it could take until 'Zerogh hour.' However, the lack of an author is intolerable to the Four Old Men (the Mamalujo) who read it in I.5, and they devise a strategy that should permit the reader to overcome the distance that separates him/her from the author who remains in the shadows: what the reader needs to do is to 'stoop' down to its text. Once in this pose the reader is in a better position to 'inspect' the text:

> Closer
> inspection of the *bordereau* would reveal a multiplicity of person-
> alities inflicted on the documents or document and some prevision
> of virtual crime or crimes might be made by anyone unwary
> enough before any suitable occasion for it or them had so far
> managed to happen along. In fact, under the closed eyes of the in-
> spectors the traits featuring the *chiaroscuro* coalesce, their con-
> trarieties eliminated, in one stable somebody similarly as by the
> providential warring of heartshaker with housebreaker and of
> dramdrinker against freethinker our social something bowls along
> bumpily, experiencing a jolting series of prearranged disappoint-
> ments, down the long lane of (it's as semper as oxhousehumper!)
> generations, more generations and still more generations. (107.23–35)

Closer inspection of the text is the key to overcoming the appearance of a multiplicity of personalities inflicted on the documents, and revealing the identity of the author. Under the 'closed eyes' of the reader-inspectors, the traits of multiplicity 'coalesce' into the 'one stable somebody' of a recognizable author. 'Close inspection' has the power to unite the dispersed author(s), and it can be understood as corresponding to the X-structure that unites and separates the writers and readers of the letter who cannot see eye to eye (113.34–14.20). Since this X is also the X that the hen traces as the letter, and the X with which she signs it, closer inspection of the letter's writing brings together the author. Further, because the scene of letter-writing is also that of imaginative writing or (non)production, the X is also the sign that the reader imitates as s/he writes him/herself. In other words, the X fuses the reader-writer together as the writer(s) of the letter's 'document or documents' into 'one stable somebody.'

In bringing together, the X performs the same function as the hen-mother's womb in that it is the site for the auto-affective fusion of the rival brothers (293.L1–4; cf. 148.33–68.14, and 349.6–20). The function of the written X of the hen's tracing/writing on the mound is also characterized by the text as 'gathering.' When the reader first meets the hen in book I.1, she is a 'parody's bird' who scratches about on the midden after a holocaustic battle between the father, the 'Willing-done,' and his sons, the 'Lipoleums,' which has reduced the world to rubble:

> there's that
> gnarlybird ygathering, a runalittle, doalittle, preealittle, pouralittle,
> wipealittle, kicksalittle,severalittle,eatalittle,whinealittle,kenalittle,
> helfalittle,pelfalittle gnarlybird. A verytableland of bleakbardfields!
> Under his seven wrothschields lies one, Lumproar. His glav toside
> him. Skud ontorsed. Our pigeons pair are flewn for northcliffs.
> The three of crows have flapped it southenly, kraaking of de
> baccle to the kvarters of that sky whence triboos answer; Wail,
> 'tis well! She niver comes out when Thon's on shower or when
> Thon's flash with his Nixy girls or when Thon's blowing toom-
> cracks down the gaels of Thon. No nubo no! Neblas on you liv!
> Her would be too moochy afreet. Of Burymeleg and Bindme-
> rollingeyes and all the deed in the woe. Fe fo fom! She jist does
> hopes till byes will be byes. Here, and it goes on to appear now,
> she comes, a peacefugle, a parody's bird, a peri potmother,
> a pringlpik in the ilandiskippy, with peewee and powwows
> in beggybaggy on her bickybacky and a flick flask fleckflinging
> its pixylighting pacts' huemeramybows, picking here, pecking
> there, pussypussy plunderpussy. (10.31–11.13)

The hen crosses the battlefield-midden 'ygathering' the debris of 'the spoiled goods' of battle, which then 'go into her nabsack' (11.18–19). As she gathers, she does so literally from scratch, next to nothing, just as Finnegan builds imaginatively from next to nothing (4.18–5.4). In this way, the hen's gathering can be read as a reinscription of Finnegan's theatre of imaginative buildung without the benefit of the *eidos*. By gathering without the benefit of a present model, her 'ygathering' parodies the gathering of the logos, which, as Vico points out, is itself a 'gathering' that can be traced through the Latin word for 'law,' *lex* (NS 240). Instead of (re)producing present meaning, the hen's gathering comes closer to the gathering Vico isolates that 'collect[s] [*lex*] letters, and mak[es], as it were, a sheaf of them for each word, [and is] called *legere*, reading' (NS 240). However, this gathering in which letters are collected does not settle down into a present meaning.

Although the hen gathers in a scene of imaginary writing, her 'ygathering' cannot be fully grasped in terms of the analysis of auto-affection carried out in the previous chapter. The rival twins represent time and space in I.6.11, which are always gathered by a female principle such as the womb (293.L1–4), or Margareena and Nuvoletta (148.32–68.14). It is this female gathering that gives spatio-temporal auto-affection. Three aspects of what I am calling here 'female gathering' can now be outlined with reference to auto-affection. First, insofar as female gathering gives auto-affection, it cannot be understood to (re)produce present meaning. Second, gathering gives the auto-affection that is subject to a certain amount of sway by the female principle of non-present unity in the text. Finally, if I grant a certain privilege to the hen's gathering here among all the different examples of the female principle of non-present unity, it is because she explicitly gathers gathering into one insofar as her name parodies the fully present gathering of the neo-Platonic *logos*, the One, or, in Greek, *to hen* (110.22).

Since the hen gathers and writes imaginatively, which cannot be simply grasped in terms of auto-affection insofar as she gives rise to it, she can be understood to correspond to the other aspect of the imagination as it is analysed by Heidegger, conception. As I mentioned in the previous chapter, the isolated elements of 'pure knowledge' are 'time as universal, pure intuition' and the 'concepts,' or 'notions,' which are 'thought in pure thinking' (KPM 41). Under the heading of the Veritative Synthesis, Heidegger examines the interdependency of these two parts of knowledge. In this synthesis, 'pure intuition is offered in its own right ... in the direction of pure thinking' (44). This

'offering' is called by Heidegger 'affecting.' This 'affection' is not simply that of being affected through the senses. Rather, intuition (as time)
affects thinking, and Heidegger says that 'our pure thinking always
stands before the time which approaches it' (44). But it is also the case
that this intuition must fit with the conceptual determining that is
called thinking:

> This reciprocal preparing-themselves-for-each-other takes place in that
> act which Kant generally calls synthesis. In it, both pure elements come
> together from themselves from time to time; it joins together the seams
> allotted to each, and so it constitutes the essential unity of pure knowl-
> edge.
>
> This synthesis is neither a matter of intuition nor of thinking. Mediating
> 'between' both, so to speak, it is related to both. Thus in general it must
> share the basic character of the two elements, i.e., it must be a represent-
> ing. (KPM 44)

Both intuition and conception, or reflection, are 'synthetic.' This is to
say that they 'gather' together 'dispersion' (KPM 43–4). Intuition is a
'synopsis' that gathers together the 'manifold,' or that which is subject
to intuition. Reflection is that which gathers the many into the one.
These 'representations' are themselves unified by something Kant calls
'synthesis in general,' which 'is the mere result of the *power of the imagination*, a blind but indispensable function of the soul without which
we would have no knowledge whatever, but of which we are seldom
conscious even once' (KPM 44, citing CPR A78/B103; cited italics are
Heidegger's). Once Heidegger has identified the imagination's power
as the unity of both intuition and concept, he concludes saying that
'everything about synthetic structures in general' involved in knowledge 'is brought about through the power of imagination' (44).

Reflection, or conception, takes 'the object of an intuition, which is
always a particular' and determines it as '"such and such" in a "universal representation," i.e., in the concept' (KPM 36). Because it is synthetic, it is an imaginary structure, and as synthesis, it drives towards
'unity':

> In the representing of a linden, a beech or a fir as a tree, for example, the
> particular which is intuited as such and such a thing is determined on the
> basis of a reference to the sort of thing which 'applies for many.' Indeed,
> this applicability to many [instances] characterizes a representation as

concept, but nevertheless it does not hit upon its original essence. For its part, then, this applicability to many instances as a derivative character is grounded in the fact that represented in the concept is the one [*das Eine*] in which several objects agree. Conceptual representing is the allowing of agreement of many in this one. The oneness of this one must be anticipatively kept in view in conceptual representing, therefore, and it must allow for all assertions concerning the many which are determinative. This preliminary keeping in view of the one within which the many should be able to agree is the basic act of the forming of a concept. (KPM 37)

But this unity is still caught in the understanding of Being as presence in that it makes reference to a tree, which can still be construed by metaphysics as a present being. In order to remove this residue of presentness, Heidegger invokes what he calls 'pure conception,' which is the conceptual equivalent of the pure non-present intuition of time as auto-affection. These pure concepts are to be found, says Heidegger, in the understanding. There 'pure concepts,' unlike the example of the concept 'tree' used above, would have their content given a priori – a '*conceptus dati a priori*' (KPM 38). However, such concepts are difficult to put one's finger on. They must form the determinate concepts such as the concept of a tree. Since everybody knows what a tree is, the a priori concepts must be comprehended already in the example of the tree. The clue for the existence of these concepts lies in the 'basic act of concept-formation as such, in reflection' (38). The 'basic act' of reflection is a 'gathering,' and it is the 'essence of [conceptual] understanding':

> The representations of the guiding unity lie already prepared in the structure of the act of understanding as representing unification. These represented unities are the content [*Inhalt*] of the pure concepts. The content [*Wasgehalt*] of these concepts is the unity which in each case makes unification possible. The representing of these unities is in itself already conceptual a priori on the grounds of its specific content [*Inhalts*]. The pure concept no longer needs to be endowed with a conceptual form; it is itself this form in an original sense. (38)

The content of non-present conception is already given in the non-present, or pure, concepts. In other words, non-present conception is reflected (37) in the non-present concepts. However, this reflection is no longer of the order of the philosophical reflection mentioned at the outset of this chapter precisely because it is no longer governed by the value of presence or presentness. To the extent that conceptual gathering fuses the manifold of intuition into one, it can be said to perform the same function as the hen's writing, which, as I have argued, brings together the rival twins, who in I.6 correspond to space and time, in a gathering that cannot be present.

However, this pure non-present a priori is difficult to grasp. As an a priori, it is in the past in that it comes before any present object, such as the tree in Heidegger's example of unity. The tree is not a priori because it can be construed as a metaphysically present object of cognition. The a priori in which no object is present does not present itself either. It is therefore in a past that was never present. This a priori also gives what Heidegger calls the 'anticipated look, the proto-typical image, [which] shows the thing as what it was before production and how it is supposed to look as a product' (BP 106, 107). In other words, the a priori is also oriented towards the future, where it promises the look of a certain (present) object even though it itself never becomes present in that future. The a priori is therefore both a non-present past gathering, which never becomes present and offers a future glimpse of an object without ever becoming present in the future itself. This form of conception comes very close to what Derrida calls the 'memory' of allegory. Memory, says Derrida,

> is not essentially oriented toward the past, toward a past present deemed to have really and previously existed. Memory stays with traces, in order to 'preserve' them but traces of a past that has never been present, traces which themselves never occupy the form of presence and always remain, as it were, to come – come from the future, from the *to come*. Resurrection, which is always the formal element of 'truth,' a recurrent difference between a present and its presence, does not resuscitate a past which had been present; it engages the future ... [O]ne could say ... there is only memory but, strictly speaking, the past does not exist. It will never have existed in the present, never been present, as Mallarmé says of the present itself: 'un présent n'existe pas.' The allegation of its supposed 'anterior' presence *is* memory, and this is the origin of all allegories. (Mem 58–9)

The *différantial* allegory 'memory of the future,' insofar as it is concerned with the future and the past, but without ever becoming present itself, can now be understood to correspond to what Heidegger calls conception in its relation to the imagination. It is conception, then, that develops the allegorizing thrust of the imagination that is also found in the reincryption of auto-affection as temporalization.

'ygathering': Agglutination: Come/cum

The actions of the hen, as I have been suggesting, follow a zig-zag pattern that gathers the 'multiple personalities' of the writers of the letter into 'one stable somebody.' However, unity is in part imaginary, and it is riven with what might be described as conceptual *différance*. This zig-zag technique is inscribed in I.5 as another zig-zag letter, 'W.' In the letter manuscript, the 'doubleyous' as they are called, mark the *différance* of same and other as being 'of an early muddy terranean origin whether man chooses to damn them agglutinatively' (120.29–30). The *différantial* 'doubleyou' originates through a process of a reiterated agglutinative gluing that unites the many different scraps of letters – such as the 'Vs' to generate 'Ws' and 'Xs' – scratched up/out after the holocaust of battle on the midden heap (10.25–11.28), in order to compose the Xed-out writing of the letter as the 'With Kiss. Kiss Criss. Cross Criss. Kiss Cross.' (11.27).

The hen's zig-zag mode of gathering mimics the textual procedure of *Glas*. *Glas*'s text 'induces by agglutinating rather than demonstrating, by coupling and decoupling, gluing and ungluing rather than by exhibiting the continuous, and analogical, instructive, suffocating necessity of a discursive rhetoric' (75b). The heuristic isomorphism of *Finnegans Wake* and *Glas* is carried further if the reader considers the textual kinetics of *Glas*'s textual mechanics:

> What always remains irresoluble, impracticable, nonnormal, or nonnormalizable is what interests and constrains us here. Without paralyzing us but while forcing us on the *course* [*démarche*]. Zig-zagging, oblique to boot, jostled by the bank [*rive*] to be avoided, like a machine during a difficult maneuver. (5a)

It is in this agglutination that the reader of the *Wake* and *Glas* may hear a parodic doubling of Hegel's 'Preface' to *The Phenomenology of Mind*, where he argues for a conception of the Absolute as something that manifests itself through the appearance of phenomena. Hegel may thus be said to be remarking the necessary initial attachment of the 'Absolute' – derived from the Latin *absolutus*, meaning loosened, detached, and complete – to appearances. To begin with, the Absolute can only ever appear as the 'self-origination of the wealth of detail, and a self-determining distinction of shapes and forms' (cf. *Phenomenology of Mind* §§ 15–16). Eventually the Absolute frees itself of these shapes, forms, and details to become the Absolute proper. Instead of charting the course of the Absolute's emergence, *Finnegans Wake* and *Glas* parody the Absolute's desire for a pure and decisive detachment through what I have just suggested may be gathered under the headings of agglutination and 'irresolubility.' As both *Glas* and *Finnegans Wake* make clear, the dynamics of reading 'agglutinatively' are figured in 'zig-zagging,' which instals the problematic of both textuality and writing at the origin of the Absolute. Not only does this introduce a disruptive shuddering into Hegel's unfurling of the Absolute in *The Phenomenology of Mind*, it also prevents any 'Absolute' from emerging. 'Zig-zagging' marks a textuality that is from its very inception multiple or written in that 'it' 're-crosses' 'itself.' *Finnegans Wake* and *Glas* offer the X (43–4b) as the textual emblem of both the 'zig-zagging' wherein it is always a matter of at least two texts *regarding* each other and the 'cross-eyed' reader required to read such double-texts (113bi).

The motifs of 'zig-zagging' and being 'cross-eyed' reintroduce the problematic spacing and binds it to the 'body' of the reader confronted with the texts of *Finnegans Wake* and *Glas*. The reader's body is represented as becoming modified by the text insofar as s/he become cross-eyed in following the zig-zags. The effects of this 'zig-zagging' will be felt not only in the problems caused for the eyes and ears, but, as I will indicate later, also for sexual decidability. However, for the moment, it is enough to note that these effects are not just confined to the reader, but also extend to the author. This is why *Glas* goes on to consider how exchanging looks in the *regard* also brings about a confusion of signatories, which it thematizes as the tolling of a *glas*, or death-knell:

> The *glas* [death-knell] also has to do with a war for the signature [*seing*], a war to the death – the only one possible – in view of the text. Then [*donc*] (ding-dong), that finally, obsequently, remains no-one's. *Glas* is written neither one way nor the other ... *Glas* strikes between the two. The place the clapper will, necessarily, have taken up, let us name it *colpos*. In Greek, *colpos* is the mother's [*de la mère*], but also the nurse's breast [*sein*], as well as the fold [*pli*] of garment, the trough of the sea [*repli de la mer*] between two waves, the valley pushing down into the breast [*sein*] of the earth. (71bi)

Here, the signatories of texts become confused with each other in much the same way that the signatoriies of the readers and writers in the theatre of *Wake*an letter-writing do. For the text of *Glas*, lost signatures and property are cast as the *colpos*, the clapper moving between (at least) two identities: the (authentic) breast of the mother can always be the (less authentic) breast of the nurse. The *colpos*, or breast (French, *sein*; in German *Sein* is being), is also, according to a process of a homophonous ringing, the signature (*seing*) of the mother (*mère*) and the sea (*mer*). The ringing of the French is underlined by the *donc*/ding-dong of the clapper-breast. The clapper/*colpos*, is, according to *Glas*, the mother's *sein(g)* resounding over the text(s), confounding the structure of a signature that might claim to be the sole author of a text. Such is the fascination with the signature (X, *sein(g)*) of the mother in both *Finnegans Wake* and *Glas*: she allegorically and imaginarily gathers (the) writer(s) together in an impossible unity that promises wholeness and identity even as she confounds it.

The mother-hen's agglutinative (W, X) writing – the gluing together of the broken pieces of the wor(l)d – disrupts what Derrida calls 'the metaphysical exchange, the circular complicity of the metaphors of the eye and the ear' (M xiii) because in its X reader-writer(s) can no longer believe their eyes or their ears:

for
while the ear, be we mikealls or nicholists, may sometimes be inclined to believe others the eye, whether browned or nolensed,
find it devilish hard now and again even to believe itself. *Habes
aures et num videbis? Habes oculos ac mannepalpabuat?* Tip! Drawing nearer to take our slant at it (since after all it has met with
misfortune while all underground), let us see all there may remain
to be seen.
   I am a worker, a tombstone mason, anxious to pleace avery-
buries and jully glad when Christmas comes his once ayear. You
are a poorjoist, unctuous to polise nopebobbies and tunnibelly
soully when 'tis thime took o'er home, gin. We cannot say aye
to aye. We cannot smile noes from noes. Still. One cannot help
noticing that rather more than half of the lines run north-south
in the Nemzes and Bukarahast directions while the others go
west-east in search from Maliziies with Bulgarad for, tiny tot
though it looks when schtschupnistling alongside other incuna-
bula,it has its cardinal points for all that. (113.24–14.7)

Here, the eye can no longer say or hear its 'aye,' its affirmation of self-present identity with itself. Instead, it can only hear itself in a non-present fashion in the 'aye.' This confusion of the eye and ear elsewhere attaches to the brothers in the guise of the Mookse and the Gripes:

> The Mookse had sound eyes right but he could not
> all hear. The Gripes had light ears left yet he could but ill see.
> (158.12–13)

The *différantial* X of the letter, to the extent that it fuses the brothers, interferes in the easy recognition of a proper signatory by agglutinating the ear to the eye. In agglutinating the eye to the ear, the eye or ear can no longer hear or see each other outside of *différance*. The *Wake* goes on to trace this complicity[8] to a site of originary theft:

> The prouts who will invent a writing there ultimately is the
> poeta, still more learned, who discovered the raiding there origin-
> ally. That's the point of eschatology our book of kills reaches
> for now in soandso many counterpoint words. What can't be
> coded can be decorded if an ear aye sieze what no eye ere grieved
> for. (482.31–6)

The writing of the letter-text (con)fuses the eye with the ear, playing with the ease of the circular complicity of metaphors of the eye and ear. This (con)fusion is then situated as the stolen site of an invented fatal writing that, nevertheless, allows itself to be read ('raiding'). The mother's writing, insofar as it is an auto-affective gathering X that confuses identities by robbing the real author of his or her rights, is also a fatal confusion of the eye and ear. It takes them over, and makes their meaning, their *eidos*, dull. The *eidos* therefore becomes a mere 'eyedull' (351.23), something that the Jew in *Glas* would see as merely empty (49a).

The eye that is always an eye-ear, is made dull through the introduction of an 'earwaker' (351.23). For this reason the more radical effects of the mother's agglutinative disruption of the metaphysical complicity of the eye and ear can be traced by considering how the written (con)fusion of the eye/ear attaches to the main figure in the text, the lost builder-giant Finnegan. Finnegan, as I read him, is essentially ventriloquized by the mother's writing through the twists and turns of the long implicit sentence that results from the loss of his presence, name, reference, and so on. However, one clause of that implicit sentence is particularly interesting because it speculates on how he came by his 'occupational agnomen' 'Earwicker' (30.3–31.3).

Earwicker, the reader is told, was originally a gardener who spent his days trying to keep earwigs out of his garden. One day, while he is at work, a king passes by and asks him what he is up to. Earwicker's response is that he is 'cotchin on thon bluggy earwuggers' (31.10–11). This pleases the king, who then bestows the name 'earwicker' on him (3.27–8). This act of bestowing begins the text's long and complex association of Earwicker the earwig catcher with the organ the ear,[9] with him eventually becoming 'Earwicker, that patternmind, that paradigmatic ear, recepto-retentive as his of Dionysius' (70.35–6). In the *Wake*, then, the paradigm for hearing is explicitly associated with the Dionysian ear, an echoing prison chamber in the palace of Dionysus that amplified any sounds that were made there. Earwicker's ear is also always 'Earopean' (598.15), making it into a sort of multilingual amplifying echo-chamber for the sounds of all the European languages in the *Wake*. But Earwicker's status as the paradigm for hearing in the text is also merged with his paradigmatic ability to see. This can be elliptically grasped in the name the king bestows on him insofar as it derives from the Anglo-Saxon *Euerwaar* or Ever-waker, meaning 'watchman.'[10] Earwicker's eye is therefore always open and he 'sees' by hearing:

> (I am sure that tiring chabelshovel-
> ler with the mujikal chocolat box, Miry Mitchel, is listening) I
> say, the remains of the outworn gravemure where used to be
> blurried the Ptollmens of the Incabus. Used we? (He is only pre-
> tendant to be stugging at the jubalee harp from a second existed
> lishener, Fiery Farrelly.) It is well known. Lokk for himself and
> see the old butte new. Dbln. W. K. O. O. Hear? By the mauso-
> lime wall. Fimfim fimfim. With a grand funferall. Fumfum fum-
> fum. 'Tis optophone which ontophanes. List! Wheatstone's
> magic lyer. They will be tuggling foriver. They will be lichening
> for allof. They will be pretumbling forover. The harpsdischord
> shall be theirs for ollaves. (13.8–19)

Here, the four old men in Book I arrive in Dublin looking for the fabled giant HCE/Finnegan after his fall. In order to see him, they just have to look for him in the old but new. In looking for the old but new, it is the 'optophone which ontophanes.' An optophone is a machine that converts light into sound, and can help the blind read print. The optophone, when it 'ontophanes,' brings 'what is' (Greek, *ta onta*, existing things) to light (and sound) (*phaino*, to bring to light, to make appear). The optophone is therefore a paradigmatic way of reading the text that converts light into sounds. On this reading, being in *Finnegans Wake* asserts itself as the rumbling 'phonemanon' of thunder:

> For the Clearer of the Air from on high has spoken in tumbul-
> dum tambaldam to his tembledim tombaldoom worrild and, mogu-
> phonoised by that phonemanon, the unhappitents of the earth
> have terrerumbled from fimament unto fundament and from
> tweedledeedumms down to twiddledeedees. (258.20–4)

This roll of thunder recalls/anticipates Vico's roll of thunder that first scares men into the caves and gets the human world under way. Through the ear of 'phonemanology,' it is possible to hear the sounds of things never seen, never witnessed by the blind eyes of the optophonist. However, this 'phonemanology' should not be taken as the simple relationship of the blind to a fully present phenomenology of sound. Somewhat paradoxically, the phenomenology of sound is first displaced by the 'phonemanology' of optophonic technique in that it implies that Earwicker's ever-watchful paradigmatic ear-eye is to some extent 'blind.' For example, eyes go black (16.29), the blind author sees only through the 'undeleted glete [with] glass eyes for an eye' (183.36). Elsewhere, the eyes are 'irismaimed' (489.31) and can therefore only see imperfectly with 'eyewitless foggus' (515.30). Since the text goes to great lengths to fuse the eye and the ear, the eye's impairment must point to the ear's impairment. Once impaired, seeing and hearing are only possible through the delay or interposition of a device (an 'eyetrompit') that simultaneously helps and impairs vision. Because the eyetrompit fuses the more traditional ear-trumpet with a prosthesis for the eye, it is the perfect instrument for a bad ear-eye in that it functions something like the optophone that reads light as sound: 'He knows for he's seen it in black and white through his eye-trompit' (247.32–3).

The reason for Earwicker's disrupted hearing is suggested by the text as having to do with the scene of his being named. Because of the way Earwicker acquires his name, he is also, to a certain extent, that

which he catches, an earwig. In 'Earopean' (598.15) folklore, earwigs
are associated with the penetrating disruption of hearing. For example,
in Old English the earwig is *earwicga*, or 'ear-worm'; in French the earwig is *'perce-oreille,'* an ear-piercer, and the ballad of HCE/Finnegan in
I.2 is called 'The Ballad of Persse O'Reilly'; German *Ohrwurm*, ear-
worm, and so on. In the following passage the ear is supplemented by
an elaborate technology that makes it epic: its purpose is to listen for
Finnegan in history in order to 'serve him up':

> Whyfor had they, it is Hiberio-Miletians and Argloe-Noremen,
> donated him, birth of an otion that was breeder to sweatoslaves,
> as mysterbolder, forced in their waste, and as for Ibdullin what of
> Himana, that their tolvtubular high fidelity daildialler, as modern
> as tomorrow afternoon and in appearance up to the minute (hear-
> ing that anybody in that ruad duchy of Wollinstown schemed 16
> to halve the wrong type of date) equipped with supershielded um-
> brella antennas for distance getting and connected by the magnetic
> links of a Bellini-Tosti coupling system with a vitaltone speaker,
> capable of capturing skybuddies, harbour craft emittences, key
> clickings, vaticum cleaners, due to woman formed mobile or
> man made static and bawling the whowle hamshack and wobble
> down in an eliminium sounds pound so as to serve him up a mele-
> goturny marygoraumd, eclectrically filtered for allirish earths and
> ohmes. This harmonic condenser enginium (the Mole) they
> caused to be worked from a magazine battery (called the Mimmim
> Bimbim patent number 1132, Thorpetersen and Synds, Joms-
> borg, Selverbergen) which was tuned up by twintriodic singul-
> valvulous pipelines (lackslipping along as if their liffing deepunded
> on it) with a howdrocephalous enlargement, a gain control of
> circumcentric megacycles ranging from the antidulibnium onto
> the serostaatarean. They finally caused,or most leastways brung
> it about somehows (that) the pip of the lin (to) pinnatrate inthro
> an auricular forfickle (known as the Vakingfar sleeper, mono-
> fractured by Piaras UaRhuamhaighaudhlug, tympan founder
> Eustache Straight, Bauliaughacleeagh) a meatous conch culpable
> of cunduncing Naul and Santry and the forty routs of Corthy
> with the concertiums of the Brythyc Symmonds Guild, the
> Ropemakers Reunion, the Variagated Peddlars Barringoy Bni-
> brthirhd, the Askold Olegsonder Crowds of the O'Keef-Rosses
> and Rhosso-Keevers of Zastwoking, the Ligue of Yahooth o.s.v.

so as to lall the bygone dozed they arborised around, up his
corpular fruent and down his reuctionary buckling, hummer,
enville and cstorrap (the man of Iren, thore's Curlymane for
you!), lill the lubberendth of his otological life. (309.11–10.21)

Even though the 'tolvtubular high fidelity daildialler' is supposed to
hark back to Finnegan in history, the signals it hears subject to 'static'
and 'mobile' (309.21–2) interference. The machine strives to overcome
this interference by attempting to 'pinnatrate inthro an auricular forfickle' (310.9–10: the pinna is the 'wing' of the ear, the broad upper part
of the external ear, and can also be applied to the whole external ear; the
'auricular forfickle' evokes both the taxonomic Latin for the earwig, *For-
ficula Auricularia*, and the auricula, another word for the external ear).
The 'harmonic condenser enginium' may thus be understood to follow
the penetrative path of the earwig – the *'Bug of the Deaf'* (134.36) – as it
penetrates Percy O'Reilly/HCE's ear. The dynamics of this scene follow
a path that should be familiar by now: Finnegan is both that which penetrates – 'Piaras UaRhuamhaighaudhlug' (310.11: Irish, Piers O'Reilly) –
and that which is penetrated. This is a scene of (non)production, and it
is not surprising that the machine's attempt to hear becomes that which
disrupts hearing insofar as it punctures the eardrum: deafness accumu-
lates in the attempt to hear. This, in turn, causes the parts of the ear to be
audible in a way that makes them harder to recognize: the three bones
in the ear, the hammer, the anvil, and the stirrup, become 'hummer,
enville and cstorrap' (310.19–20). The ear itself is marked with deafness
from the very outset because of its penetration by the earwig. This deafness, however, is not paralysing: on the contrary, the penetrating passage through the ear allows Earwicker (who penetrates himself) to
organize – 'arborize' (310.18) – the sounds of the past in his Dionysian
ear, 'the lubberendth of his otological life' (310.21), in which an ontology
of present sound is displaced by indistinctly hearing a non-present
amplified echo. The earwig's penetration therefore pierces and deafens
present hearing, submerging it in a labyrinth of deafness that stands in
need of a prosthesis that ironically creates the condition it was supposed
to remedy. This is why Earwicker, the 'paradigmatic ear' (70.36) in the
text, is variously alluded to as 'Taubling' (7.6; German, *Taub*, deaf), in a
political state of 'sorestate hearing' (242.1), 'as daff as you're erse'
(268.L4), and can only speak in what the *Wake* calls 'sordomutics'
(117.14; Spanish, *sordo*, deaf; Latin, *mutus*, dumb).
Just as Earwicker cannot become the present model for truth in the

text, his paradigmatic ear-eye is disrupted and he is afflicted with what the text calls 'Fickleyes and Futilears' (176.13). He is a 'Dufblin' (447.23), who can only speak a redubbed dialect of Irish since he has 'learned to speak from hand to mouth till he could talk earish with his eyes shut' (130.18–19). His lack of presence afflicts his eyes and ears, which can never gather sight/sound into present-ness. His Dionysian ear can only hear present sounds in the form of amplification and echoes. As such he cannot be said to experience (in a present sense) sound. His 'fickleyes' need an 'eyetrompit,' which both delays and mediates the present-ness of a look or sight to his eyes. He figures the irremediable disruption of the 'the metaphysical exchange, the circular complicity of the metaphors of the eye and the ear' (M xiii). However, insofar as it disrupts this complicity of the eye and ear, the *Wake* does not simply oppose it or confront it as being 'wrong.' Rather, the *Wake* exploits this complicity to the fullest as it tampers with its (proper) functioning.

The agglutinative writing of the *Wake* disrupts the circular complicity of the eye and ear of metaphysics by piercing the ear so that it can no longer hear present sight/sound, but only fragmented amplified echoes. Jacques Derrida's *Margins of Philosophy* tries to reinscribe these piercings as a way to puncture what he calls the philosopher's tympanum:

> Can one violently penetrate philosophy's field of listening without its imme-
> diately – even pretending in advance, by hearing what is said of it, by
> decoding the statement – making the penetration resonate within itself,
> appropriating the emission for itself, familiarly communicating it to itself
> between the inner and middle ear, following the path of a tube or inner
> opening, be it round or oval? In other words, can one puncture the tympa-
> num of a philosopher and still be heard and understood by him?
>
> To philosophize with a hammer. Zarathustra begins by asking himself if
> he will have to puncture them, batter their ears (*Muss man ihren erst die
> Ohren zerschlagen*), with the sound of cymbals or tympani, the instruments,
> always, of some Dionysianism. In order to teach them 'to hear with their
> eyes' too. (M xii–xiii)

Puncturing the philosopher's ear is not simple, however. The philosopher, who is always aware of the edges of his discourse, tries to absorb
this sound as his proper other, his opposite. Opposition always 'risks

permitting the noisiest discourse to participate in the most serene, least disturbed, best served economy of philosophical irony' (xiii). In other words, the crashing cacophony of sounds and noise is always in danger of becoming a mere footnote to the type of reflective or speculative philosophy that watches over its borders. Thus, in order to penetrate his ear in a way that the philosopher cannot appropriate, the noise must make itself heard in a way that is other than (philosophical) opposition.

As I argued above, *Wake*an ear-piercing, instead of opposing the domain of philosophy's hearing, disrupts it (better) by taking a less confrontational approach to it. It is the less confrontational, more oblique approach to philosophy that keeps the *Wake*an exploitation of philosophical metaphor on the margins of philosophy by rewriting it according to the mode of non-opposition, which, for philosophy, is a non-relation:

> Certainly, except by writing this relationship following the mode of a non-relationship about which it would be demonstrated simultaneously or *obliquely* – on the philosophical surface of the discourse – that no philosopheme will ever have been prepared to conform to it or translate it. This can only be written according to a deformation of the philosophical tympanum. This is also, thematically, the route of *Dissemination*. We know that the membrane of the tympanum, a thin and transparent partition separating the auditory canal from the middle ear (the *cavity*), is stretched obliquely (*loxos*) ... The tympanum squints.
>
> Consequently, to luxate the philosophical ear, to set the *loxos* in the *logos* to work, is to avoid frontal and symmetrical protest, opposition in all the forms of *anti-*, or in any case to inscribe *antism* and overturning, domestic denegation, in an entirely other form of ambush, of *lokhos*, of textual maneuvers. (M xiv–xv)

But because the other tympanum squints, this does not mean that it hears better. Hearing that is perfect wants to bring sound into full (self-)presence. Its essence wants to converse or correspond with only itself. But 'How,' Derrida asks, 'to block this correspondence destined to weaken, muffle, forbid the blows from the outside, the other hammer? The "hammer that speaks" to him "who has the third ear" (*der das dritte Ohr hat*)' (xvi). There is, therefore 'another tympanum' (xviii), one that 'sees' so badly that it must squint. It relates non-philosophically, which is to say, non-oppositionally, to the philosophical tympanum as its deformation. This other tympanum is not opposed to the philosophical tympanum. Further, in remaining a tympanum, this other tympanum bears a doubled relationship with the philosophical tympanum. This points to a 'multiplicity of these tympanums' about which 'philosophy, being situated, inscribed, and included within it, has never been able to reason' (xxvii).

The doubling of the tympanum therefore marks a non-oppositional or oblique difference between the philosophy and its non-dialecticiz- able other. However, because the limit that runs between the tympa- num and itself is auto-affective, or obliquely non-philosophical, there is no limit, no opposition, to philosophy that could guarantee its proper domain: 'Therefore, what legal question is to be relied upon if the limit in general, and not only the limit of what is believed to be one very particular thing among others, the tympanum, is structurally oblique? If, therefore, there is no limit *in general*, that is, a straight and regular form of the limit? Like every *limus*, the *limes*, the short cut, sig- nifies the oblique' (M xvii). So, what might such a badly heard passage that obliquely (and therefore non-philosophically) overflows the limits of philosophy sound like?

An answer to this question is sketched by the text of *Dissemination* that discovers Plato in the back room of his pharmacy, where he is try- ing to separate the 'good' *pharmakon* (Greek, poison, cure), the Platonic remedy or cure for sophism, from that which it protects against, pre- cisely, the 'bad' *pharmakon*, the sophistic poison. Plato quickly realizes that the *pharmakon*, which is both cure and poison, marks the originary contamination wherein the 'good' *pharmakon* is irremediably tainted by the 'bad' *pharmakon*:

> Holding the *pharmakon* in one hand, the calamus in the other, Plato mut- ters as he transcribes the play of formulas. In the enclosed space of the pharmacy, the reverberations of the monologue are immeasurably ampli- fied. The walled-in voice strikes against the rafters, the words come apart, bits and pieces of sentences are separated, disarticulated parts begin to circulate through the corridors, become fixed for a round or two, translate each other, become rejoined, bounce off each other, contradict each other, make trouble, tell on each other, come back like answers, organize their exchanges, protect each other, institute an internal commerce, take them- selves for a dialogue. Full of meaning. A whole story. An entire history. All of philosophy ...
>
> In this stammering buzz of voices, as some philological sequence or

other floats by, one can sort of make this out, but it is hard to hear: *logos* beds itself [*le logos s'aime lui-même* = logos loves itself; *s'aime* is a homonym for *sème*: to sow, as in in a flower bed – trans.] ... *pharmakon* means *coup* ... 'so that *pharmakon* will have meant: that which pertains to an attack of demoniac possession [*un coup démoniaque*] or is used as a curative *against* such an attack' ... an armed enforcement of order [*un coup de force*] ... a shot fired [*un coup tiré*] ... a planned overthrow [*un coup monté*] ... but to no avail [*un coup pour rien*] ... like cutting through water [*un coup dans l'eau*] ... *en udati grapsei* ... and a stroke of fate [*un coup de sort*] ... Theuth who invented writing ... the calendar ... dice ... *kubeia* ... the calendar trick [*le coup du calendrier*] ... the unexpected dramatic effect [*le coup de théâtre*] ... the writing trick [*le coup de l'écriture*] ... the dice-throw [*le coup de dés*] ... two in one blow [*le coup double*] ... *kolaphos* ... *gluph* ... *colpus* ... *coup* ... glyph ... scalpel ... scalp ... *khrusos* ... *chrysolite* ... *chrysology* ...
  Plato gags his ears ... (D 169–70)

These blows that echo about Plato's pharmacy drum a different sort of rhythm to that of eidetic philosophy. They cannot form philosophy's (proper) other, the one that philosophy usually dialecticizes and interiorizes, nor can they be stopped from parasiting philosophy in order to overflow it and derange the ear of the philosopher. Plato, in desperation, tries to plug his ears against the onslaught. He is unsuccessful because in trying to isolate his good *pharmakon*, he has already heard the *pharmakon*'s multiplicity, insofar as it has given him his remedy.

This non-philosophical drumming game is also expertly played by the *Wake*, which, as I have been arguing, drums according to the rhythmic beat of the Dionysian ear, the amplification and echoing that dislocates the hold of present-ness on sight and sound. The *Wake* also frames the paradigmatic ear as the paradigmatic constitution of identity insofar as it is stuttered: 'I am amp amp amplify' (533.33). This amplified rumble recalls the rumble of thunder that sounds at the beginning of the book when HCE/Finnegan falls from his ladder in all the languages of Babel – '(bababadalgharaghtakamminarronnkonnbronntonnerronntuonnthunntrovarrhounawnskawntoohoohoordenenthurnuk!)' (3.15–18) – which is then recalled by Mutt's stuttered attempt to recover from something 'hauhauhauhaudibble':

Jute. – But you are not jeffmute?
Mutt. – Noho. Only an utterer.
Jute. – Whoa? Whoat is the mutter with you?

Mutt. – I became a stun a stummer.
Jute. – What a hauhauhauhaudibble thing, to be cause! How,
Mutt?
Mutt. – Aput the buttle, surd.
Jute. – Whose poddle? Wherein?
Mutt. – The Inns of Dungtarf where Used awe to be he.
Jute. – You that side your voise are almost inedible to me.
Become a bitskin more wiseable, as if I were
you.
Mutt. – Has? Has at? Hasatency? Urp, Boohooru! Booru
Usurp! I trumple from rath in mine mines when I
rimimirim ! (16.14–28)

Mutt's response to the 'amp, amp , amplified' roar of the fall, of battle,
and of thunder is to remember, through an amp, amp, amplification of
his own, the roar of thunderous battle ('buttle'; 'poddle') and the rang-
ing of a strong male figure: 'Urp, Boohooru! Booru Usurp! I trumple
from rath in mine mines when I rimimirim!' Mutt both stutters and
shudders ('trumples') at the mere image of this thunderer conjured by
his 'mines I.' Because the (re)imagined scene was so traumatic, even its
retelling causes the text to stutter: 'a stun a stummer'; 'Has? Has at?
Hasatency?'; 'I trumple from rath in mine mines when I rimimirim!'
and so forth. But perhaps what is most interesting about this scene of
doubling is that it calls the scene of the 'original trauma' into question
because the original shock is 'itself' 'reproduced' in/as memory. Memory therefore (re)produces the sound that causes the shock in such a
way as to double (for) it insofar as the reproduction reproduces both
the shocking yell as well as the reaction to it, the stammer. As a result,
the obsessively recurrent textual motif in the *Wake* that denotes all
those things that go 'doublin their mumper all the time' (3.21–2), can
be read as being no longer motivated by the recovery of originals. In
this way the text marks the loss of this original presence, which can
never recover/reproduce an original model. Such a model is lost from
the outset, 'amp, amp, amplified,' and not subject to presence.

The loss of the original is explicitly underlined in another scene in
I.1. This time, the rhythmic roll of the thunder heard in more than one
language rocks the 'cubehouse' of I.1 as it rolls across the sky:

> Our cubehouse still rocks as earwitness
> to the thunder of his arafatas but we hear also through successive
> ages that shebby choruysh of unkalified muzzlenimiissilehims that

would blackguardise the whitestone ever hurtleturtled out of
heaven. (5.14–18)

However, from the very outset, the multi-lingual roll of thunder is lost,
'amp, amp, amplif[ied]' 'through successive ages' as a 'shebby cho-
ruysh.' Shabbiness, in other words, contaminates the original thundering fall. Finnegan's idiomatic stutter, which marks his speech
everywhere throughout the book, is amplified so that it is to be heard
(badly) everywhere. His echoing reiterations are no longer 'his' in that
they do not point to a property that would be Finnegan's alone. In
other words, Finnegan's Dionysian ear is the paradigm for hearing in a
text that everywhere explores the loss of presence, the *eidos* or the
model. Its ear plays with what *Glas* calls the '*glas*' effect:

No absolute idiom, no signature. The idiom or signature effect does nothing but restart – reverberate – the *glas*.

There is – always – already more than one – *glas*.

Glas must be read as a singular plural ... It has its breaking in itself. It affects
itself and immediately resounds with this literal damage. (149bi–50bi)

The loss of the signature returns the reader-writer to the scene of X-
writing in which the mother-son(s) write(s). Section I.7 reinscribes I.1's
'earwitness/eyewitless' to the thunder that rocks 'our cubehouse' in a
much more complex scene of amplified echoing. In this scene, the
mother-hen's agglutinative writing that fills her 'culdee sacco of wabbash' (210.1), becomes the son's scene of writing in yet another echoing
'cell,' Shem's little 'haunted inkbottle' house (182.30–2).
    In this (reinscribed) scene of reinscriptive writing, Shem sits in 'con-
dign satisfaction' (172.29), surrounded by the echoing fragments and
'delicate tippits' (172.32) of 'every crumb of trektalk' (172.30). In this
scene of writing, the writer is 'covetous of his neighbour's word'
(172.30). In other words, he only creates by agglutinatively amplifying
the echoes of the words of others in order to form a 'stinksome inkenstink, quite puzzonal to the wrottel':

The house O'Shea or O'Shame, Quivapieno, known as the
Haunted Inkbottle, no number Brimstone Walk, Asia in Ireland,
as it was infested with the raps, with his penname SHUT sepia-

scraped on the doorplate and a blind of black sailcloth over its
wan phwinshogue, in which the soulcontracted son of the secret
cell groped through life at the expense of the taxpayers, dejected
into day and night with jesuit bark and bitter bite, calico-
hydrants of zolfor and scoppialamina by full and forty Queasi-
sanos, every day in everyone's way more exceeding in violent
abuse of self and others, was the worst, it is hoped, even in our
western playboyish world for pure mousefarm filth. You brag
of your brass castle or your tyled house in ballyfermont? Niggs,
niggs and niggs again. For this was a stinksome inkenstink, quite
puzzonal to the wrottel. Smatterafact, Angles aftanon browsing
there thought not Edam reeked more rare. My wud ! ...

                                            ... to

which, if one has the stomach to add the breakages, upheavals
distortions, inversions of all this chambermade music one stands,
given a grain of goodwill, a fair chance of actually seeing the
whirling dervish, Tumult, son of Thunder, self exiled in upon
his ego,a nightlong a shaking betwixtween white or reddr haw-
rors, noondayterrorised to skin and bone by an ineluctable phantom (may the Shaper have mercery on him!) writing the mystery
of himsel in furniture. (182.30–84.10)

Shem creates a stink in a scene of composition that mimics and recalls
that of Stephen Dedalus in the first chapter of *Ulysses*, or Dolph in his
cot in II.2. The 'chambermade music' that surrounds Shem recalls and
anticipates, amplifies and echoes, through non-present sounds, the
overheard conversations of his neighbours, which, in his chamber,
become indistinguishable from the roll of 'Thunder' (184.6). In this
writing chamber, the originality of the thunder is lost in overheard café
chatter. This music composes the 'basically English' 'lingo' (116.26, 25)
of the letter by 'traduc[ing it] into the jinglish janglage' (275.F6).

But this form of composition is shot through with theft. Shaun says
that it is a low form of 'bardic memory' (172.28): it steals away the originality of his work, which in turn steals away the original thunder by
losing it in café chatter. This type of theft is one of the main reasons,
Shaun tells the four old men, why he would like to 'squelch' Shem and
cut (off) him with 'Ex. Ex. Ex. Ex.' (424.6, 13). Even the letter that Shaun
carries is only written because of Shem's thievery:

Every dimmed letter in it is a copy and not a few of the
silbils and wholly words I can show you in my Kingdom of

Heaven. The lowquacity of him! With his threestar monothong!
Thaw! The last word in stolentelling! And what's more right-
down lowbrown schisthematic robblemint! (424.17–36)

Shem's writing mirrors the mother-hen's writing because it steals
words away from their proper owners. The mother steals because, as
Glas puts it, she 'is a thief and a beggar. She appropriates everything,
but because she has nothing that is properly hers' (150bi). Because she
is improper, she and her son are therefore reinscriptions of Hegel's Jew
in Glas who is also left without property. S/he cannot even be said to
be the mother in any simple sense. However, this stolen writing should
not be understood as holding out the promise of another, more proper
meaning that somehow lies behind the appropriated meaning of the
text. The point would not be to restitute the truth of this writing,
assuming that this were still possible at the site of an origin that only
comes about as a theft. Reading the crossed X of the mother-hen's writing is not an attempt to expose the folly of the father-figure's meaning
by coming to rest on the mother's:

But the mother? Above all the mother who dispenses with the father?
May one not hope for a pure genealogy from her, purely singular, immediately idiomatic? Isn't the proper finally from the mother?

No more than the glas [death knell] she sets ringing [met en branle]. (150bi)

The mother-hen's agglutinative writing may therefore be understood to
exploit the metaphysical complicity of the eye/ear, without taking it on
confrontationally, oppositionally. As it does so, the ears parasite the
eyes, and one 'hears with [the] eyes' as Nietzsche puts it. And yet the
eyes puncture the ears, and one can only hear, through a Dionysian ear,
the non-present sounds that baffle philosophy. But, as I have argued
above, the mother-hen's agglutinative writing never finishes reinscribing philosophy non-philosophically. In the next subsection of this chapter, I will explore the manner in which the hen fabricates and dislocates
both the truth and the phallus by reinscribing them otherwise in a tangle
of fetishistic writing that remains attached to the auto-affective body.

Fetish Writing

The hen's writing, as I suggested in chapter 2, gathers the rival twins
into an 'idolon,' an idol that can be taken for 'a still, the figure of a fel-

lowchap in the wohly ghast' (349.18–19). This 'still,' Clive Hart argues, has its roots in spiritualism, and the fusion of textual fragments may be understood to form a whole through the theory of 'psychic cross-corre- spondences.' This theory 'concerns the approximately simultaneous transcription by widely separated "sensitives" of "messages" purport- ing to come from a single departed spirit who is attempting to estab- lish his survival in the next world. In the simplest case, the two messages are closely related by some common word, phrase or image' (S&M 155). By way of illustration, Hart lets the nineteenth-century psychic researcher Alice Johnston speak:

> The characteristic of these cases – or at least some of them – is that we do not get in the writing of one automatist anything like a mechanical verba- tim reproduction of phrases in the other; we do not even get the same idea expressed in different ways, – as might result from direct telepathy between them. What we get is a fragmentary utterance in one script, which seems to have no particular point or meaning, and another frag- mentary utterance in the other, of an equally pointless character; but when we put the two together, we see that they supplement one another, and there is one coherent idea underlying both, but only partially expressed in each. (S&M 155)

I have already alluded to the observation of the hen's zig-zagging or weaving about on the midden heap. If this activity is borne in mind, then Hart's meditation on the writings of Alice Johnston will serve to bring the hen's cross-weaving into line with the operations of psychi- cal weaving:

> '[In the spirit messages] ... repeated injunctions are to be found for the application of processes described as *destringere* [to unsheathe], *nexere* [to weave or bind together], *superponere* [to superpose], to the words of the script; in particular, it is constantly urged that if some words were taken, *sume,* and some process of superposition were then applied, *superponere,* sense would be seen where now there is apparent nonsense. But no defi- nite directions have ever been given as to the process of this superposi- tion.' (Cf. 299.8: 'a superpbosition! Quoint a quincidence!') (S&M 156; initial bracketed text is Hart's insertion)

Hart then lists the injunctions to 'weave' and 'superpose' as he finds them in Johnston's text:

'What you have done is always dissociated; improve it by denying folds;
weave together, weave togther always.'
'To one superposing certain things on certain things, everything is clear.'
'Why do you not superpose all in a bundle and perceive the truth?'
'Twofold is the toil, but whole ... In mysteries I weave riddles for you and
certain others for whom it is right.' (S&M 156)

The weaving process of superposition leads Hart to identify the technique of the leitmotif: 'Motifs are often comprehensible only when all
their occurrences are related together, a part of one version combining
with a part of another to build up the sense. As Joyce puts it: "let every
crisscouple be so crosscomplimentary" (613.10)' (S&M 156–7).

All of these exhortations to weave together and superpose are found
already in the by now familiar *topos* of the crossed lines of the letter-
text:

> One cannot help
> noticing that rather more than half of the lines run north-south
> in the Nemzes and Bukarahast directions while the others go
> west-east in search from Maliziies with Bulgarad for, tiny tot
> though it looks when schtschupnistling alongside other incuna-
> bula,it has its cardinal points for all that. (114.2–7)

In following what I have called the different directions of a split reading, the reader who wishes to read the letter-text well must submit to
being pulled in two separate directions, which results in the split per-
sonality of the reader who follows the hen as she weaves about on the
midden. But because the shape being discussed here is a cross, the
lines cannot help but sketch out the 'cardinal points' of 112.7, or the
'doubtful points' of 112.9 where the textual lines cross in the letter. At
these points, the reader following the hen crossing the midden brings
together the east-west and north-south lines that cross in (as) the text.
These cardinal/doubtful points also form crossed knots that knot the
two tensile reading directions together, and form the textual wound-
holes mentioned above.

These crossed readings coincide in the figure of the four 'crosskisses.' Their coincidence means that the cross can be understood both
as the medium of unity, the knotting or weaving mentioned above,
where its two axes cross, as well as the medium of splitting and cutting
of the body/mind of the 'singleminded' reader when it takes the form

of the dagger-obelus (†). The cross therefore gives a figure for a textual weaving where two modes of reading cross running east–west and north–south with one trying to unify as the other tries to cut. Both modes cross (themselves) in the cross. The hopping between the two modes of reading in the cross can also be understood in terms of differences in metonymic scaling. Scaling permits the larger textual crosses to (re)produce smaller crosses (in the form of the obeli), which (re)produce in turn the larger textual crosses that cannot help but knot together the two modes of reading together in the form of the cross(es).

The connective power of such knotting is made clearer by recalling the importance Margaret Solomon attaches to the hen's 'reconstructive' activity: 'The hen, digging up the letter, is apparently rescuing something no longer reconstructable in its *original wholeness* – something which needs *her* for its recomposition, for its recovered ability to function in a way analogous to its former activity even though it must depend upon an adulterated form.'[11] Here, Solomon identifies how this reconstruction may be read as going, in a certain way, beyond what Hart says about spiritualist weaving insofar as it is caught completely in a web of fabrication. In other words, Solomon identifies a scene of manufacture without recourse to nature, or rather, its value as the original wholeness to be copied in an eidetic scene of imitation.

This shift from nature to something other than originary wholeness is most readily grasped in one of the titles for △'s 'untitled mamafesta' (104.4), '*How to Pull a Good Horuscoup even when Oldsire is Dead to the World*' (105.28–9),[12] referring to the Egyptian myth of Isis and Osiris. Osiris was one day attacked by Set, a god of the Egyptian underworld. Set's attack on Osiris was so ferocious that he tore Osiris to pieces and scattered him all over the cosmos. Isis, Osiris's sister and wife, set about retrieving what she could of her husband-brother. After finding what she could of Osiris's body, she put him back together again. The only piece of Osiris' body she could not find was his phallus. To supplement this, Isis modelled Osiris a new phallus out of clay, which she put in the place of the lost one. That done, she mounted the prosthetic phallus she had made, and conceived a son, whom she named Horus. Horus swore to avenge his father's death and, when he was grown, castrated Set.

If it is granted that the reader of the letter has been split up by the text, then following the Isis-hen makes it possible for the reader to recompose him/herself. S/he must be like Isis and fashion a prosthetic phallus that disrupts the possibility of recovering anything like a phallus again. As a replacement phallus, it also plays in the absence of both the 'cock's troot' (113.12) and the absent giant, HCE.

Weaving in the *Wake* takes place around the crossed figure of auto-affective X in the letter, the *topos* of the cross, discussed in chapter 2 above, and may be understood to gather both the prosthetic phallus and the figure of Christ or χ together. However, the 'Christ' I am referring to here is no longer the Jesus of filiation. He is the other Jesus, the risky Jewish one. Because he has no longer any proper content, this Jewish Jesus submits to reinscription under the uncertain value of the fetish that dislocates the presence of both the phallus and truth in *Finnegans Wake* and *Glas*.

Finnegans Wake begins this reinscriptive process by bringing Jesus, the Messiah, into contact with the fetish. In III.3 the reader follows the delivery route of the letter-text, which is now in hands of Shaun the Post, who is charged with the delivery of the letter. Shaun, who has been travelling for the first two chapters of book III, finds himself tired, so he decides to stretch out on a mound to rest. It is there that the Mamalujo catch up with him and put a long list of questions regarding the letter and HCE to him. They begin their inquisition with the letter itself:

> – Now, to come nearer zone; I would like to raise my
> deuterous point audibly touching this. There is this maggers.
> I am told by our interpreter, Hanner Esellus, that there are fully
> six hundred and six ragwords in your malherbal Magis lande-
> guage in which wald wand rimes alpman and there is resin in all
> roots for monarch but yav hace not one pronouncable teerm that
> blows in all the vallums of tartallaght to signify majestate, even
> provisionally, nor no rheda rhoda or torpentine path or halluci-
> nian via nor aurellian gape nor sunkin rut nor grossgrown trek
> nor crimeslaved cruxway and no moorhens cry or mooner's
> plankgang there to lead us to hopenhaven. Is such the *unde deri-*
> *vatur* casematter messio! Frankly. *Magis megis enerretur mynus*
> *hoc intelligow.* (478.6–18)

Shaun, on the other hand, seems confused by their bafflement, and tells them their pronunciation is at fault:

> – How? C'est mal prononsable, tartagliano, perfrances. Vous
> n'avez pas d'o dans votre boche provenciale, mousoo. Je m'in-

cline mais *Moy jay trouvay la clee dang les champs.* Hay sham nap
poddy velour, come on! (478.19–22)

The reason they cannot find the key to salvation in his language, he
says, has to do with the fact that they do not have water ('o'/*eau*) – or
the labial flexibility to form an 'o' – with/in their mouths. Shaun then
tells them in a different tongue that he has found the *clef* (French, key,
but also German, *Klee*, clover) in the fields. With this information, the
Mamalujo quickly discover the 'clee' to salvation:

  – Hep there! Commong, sa na pa de valure? Whu's teit dans
yur jambs? Whur's that inclining and talkin about the messiah
so cloover? A true's to your trefling! Whure yu! (478.23–5)

The associative structure that permits the clover/key that dangles
between Shaun's legs to fuse with Messiah/Christ is the 'erection.'[13]
The erection permits the Messiah and the phallus-clover to come
together because they both have the potential to rise (again). Thus, the
Christ-body becomes phallic according to a metonymy of erection in
which both body and phallus play with their erections according to a
reinscription of the crucifixion scene where HCE experiences the
'rouserection of his bogey' (499.1).[14] This play of erections must take
place around the *topos* of the cross to which the phallic Messiah is
attached.

Dangling between his legs, the shamrock-clover covers up – in
much the same way that the prosthetic clay phallus of Isis did – the
presence/absence of the phallus-god, Christ, beneath the undecidable
logic of what *Glas* calls 'the argument of the *girdle*, the *sheath* [gaine]':

In very subtle cases both the disavowal and the affirmation of the castration have found their way into the construction of the fetish itself. This
was so in the case of a man whose fetish was an athletic support-girdle
which could also be worn as bathing drawers. This piece of clothing covered up the genitals entirely and concealed the distinction between them.
Analysis showed that it signified that women were castrated and that
they were not castrated; and it also allowed of the hypothesis that men
were castrated, for all these possibilities could equally well (*gleich gut*) be
concealed behind the girdle – the earliest rudiment of which in his childhood had been the fig-leaf on a statue. A fetish of this sort, doubly
derived from contrary ideas, is of course especially solid. (211ai)

With the loss of the 'real' Christ, a generalized field of fetishism is prompted. As a fetish, a supplement, the phallus-c functions badly as a key to meaning in the text insofar as it denotes its own limits as key by becoming embroiled in sexual undecidability. But the field of generalized fetishism cannot be the simple and triumphant denial of castration understood as sexual difference (210ai). Rather, the loss of sexual identity gives rise to a construction of the fetish that

> rests *at once* on the denial and on the affirmation (*Behauptung*), the assertion and the assumption of castration. This at-once, the in the same-stroke, the *du-même-coup* of the two contraries, of the two opposite operations, prohibits cutting through to a decision within the undecideable ... There is an economic *speculation* on the undecideable. This speculation is not dialectical, but plays with the dialectical. The feint consists in pretending to lose, to castrate oneself, to kill oneself in order to cut [*couper*] death off. But the feint does not cut it off. One loses on both sides, in both registers, in knowing how to play all sides [*sur les deux tableaux*]. On this condition does the economy become general. (210ai)

The fetish, says Derrida, is 'before' castration, which is to be understood here as the traditional marker of sexual difference understood as sexual opposition. Since it is prior to castration, the fetish 'is more powerful than the truth' because it is also 'the subtle case' of the girdle, the medium within which the truth of sexual difference would be decided:

> The very subtle case ... of an athletic support-girdle (*Schamgürtel*) that absolutely concealed the genital organs ... This allowed supposing *besides* 'that women were castrated and that they were not castrated' and *what is more* (*überdies*) permitted the supposition (*Annahme*) of the man's castration ... If the fetish is all the more solid, has all the more consistency and economic resistance as it is doubly bound to contraries, the law is indicated in the very subtle case and in the appendix ... The fetish's consistency, resistance, remnance [*restance*], is in proportion to its undecideable bond to contraries. Thus the fetish – in general – begins to exist only insofar as it begins to bind itself to contraries. So this double bond, this double ligament, defines its subtlest structure. All the consequences of this must be drawn. The economy of the fetish is more powerful than that of the truth – decidable – of the thing itself or than the deciding discourse of castration (*pro aut contra*). The fetish is not opposable.

It oscillates like the clapper of a truth that rings awry. (226–7b)

In *Glas*, the undecidability of the fetish marks the site wherein castration is inscribed within what the text calls antherection and prosthesis:

> The logic of antherection must not be simplified. It (*Ça*) does not erect *against* or *in spite of* castration, *despite* the wound or the infirmity, by castrating castration. It (*Ça*) bands erect, castration. Infirmity itself bandages itself [*se panse*] by banding erect. Infirmity is what, as they still say in the old language, *produces* erection: a prosthesis that no castration event will have preceded. The structure of prosthesis belongs to intumescence. Nothing stands upright otherwise. (138b)

The logic of antherection relates to the undecidability of the fetish because it bears the marks of sexual difference without ever deciding on either one. This undecidability is what the 'double bond' (227b) of *bander* refers to here: 'Double postulation. Contradiction in (it)self of two irreconcilable desires. Here I give it, accused in my own tongue, the title DOUBLE BAND(S), putting it (them) into play practically. A text laces [*sangle*] in two directions. Twice girt. Band contra band' (66bi). *Bander* is, as I have mentioned, the French slang for 'to get an erection,' as well as meaning to band(age) around. Its coinage serves to mark the undecidability of the fetish. The erection, or rather, antherection of the fetish, is not, therefore, a scene 'of what should be compensated, the member missing, but of the prosthesis that bands erect all alone. The stance, the stanza, of the peg, as of a stony colossus, no longer knows repose; dispenses with the subject, survives the wearer, and shelters him from any failure; stays awake when he sleeps' (139b). In *Finnegans Wake* the prosthetic antherection takes place as the X in the text of the letter. This X is the auto-affective *topos* into which the Christ-reader(s) step(s) in the text. Since it is auto-affective, this *topos* can only ever mark multiple *topics*, and this multiplicity irremediably disrupts Christ's 'authenticity' insofar as any reader(s) may step into any of the places marked by the X, χ, or †. Further, each X is already haunted by its other forms, and it/they cannot be boiled down to a simple present. The X(s) outlast(s) the reader(s), and get(s) erect all alone to the extent that it/they dispense(s) with its reader's subjectivity, marking its finitude by opening it up to itself serially as other in the *différance* of auto-affection, which cannot help but be disruptive of the traditional reader's 'singleminded men's asylum.'

Glas's 'golden fleece' brings together the double bands of the fetish and the logic of antherection. Its upsurge derails any appeal to an authentic, or true, bisexuality or phallus. The fleece 'surrounds the neck, the cunt, the verge,' becoming 'the apparition or appearance of a hole in erection, of a hole and an erection at once, of an erection in the hole or a hole in the erection: the fleece surrounds a volcano' (66b). As the fleece erects itself, it traces and weaves a sort of fetish-writing:

> Around the spitting gulf, the inexhaustible eructation of letters in fusion, the fleece (ερυον), the fleece *pubienne* weaves, braids, preens, *tricks out* its writing. Within it everything is sewn [*se coud*], fit out with, makes way, on the borders for all flowers. The gulf hides its borders there. In the weaving of this dissimulation, the erection is produced only in *abyme*.

> The tangled tracing of its filial filaments assures *at once* (impossible castration decision) sewing *and* overlap cutting again [*la couture* et *la recoupe*]: of the mass of flowers as a phallic upsurging *and* a vaginal concavity ... , intact virginity *and* bleeding castration, *taille* (clipping and size) of a rose, of 'the red rose of monstrous size and beauty' that will soon open up into a 'shadowy pit.'

> The *erion* – fabric of writing and pubic fleece – is the maddening, a topical place of the *verily*: more or less (*than the*) truth, more or less than the veil. The erion derides everything said in the name of truth or the phallus, sports the erection in its down being [*l'être à poil*] of its writing. (67–9b)

This fetishistic writing that sports holes in its woven erection traces the general style of *Glas*, the entire surface of which is articulated by so many peep-holes or judases: 'Looking more closely, you see the columns [of the text] are not intact, smooth. Bits and pieces in another style, bits and pieces from one word to many pages, seem carved in each column' (*Glassary*, 32c). In a similar manner, this fetishistic weaving can be understood to characterize the hen's writing of the letter. The letter is woven from Xs and is 'holey' to the extent that it is also a crucifixion scene. This scene brings together the disruptive value of the fetish with the stigmatic wounds inflicted on the prosthetic phallus. That is to say, the phallus-Messiah-reader-body-letter is riddled with holes. Its entire surface is 'pierced but not punctured' by 'all those red raddled obeli cayennepeppercast over the text,' Dame Partlett's beak, and 'bi tso fb rok engl a ssan dspl itch ina' in I.5:

> Yet on holding the verso against a lit rush this
> new book of Morses responded most remarkably to the silent
> query of our world's oldest light and its recto let out the piquant
> fact that it was but pierced butnot punctured (in the university
> sense of the term) by numerous stabs and foliated gashes made
> by a pronged instrument. These paper wounds, four in type,
> were gradually and correctly understood to mean stop, please
> stop, do please stop, and O do please stop respectively, and
> following up their one true clue, the circumflexuous wall of a
> singleminded men's asylum, accentuated by bi tso fb rok engl
> a ssan dspl itch ina, — Yard inquiries pointed out → that they
> ad bîn 'provoked' ay ∧ fork, of à grave Brofèsor; àth é's Brèak
> — fast — table;   ; acùtely profèššionally *piquéd*, to=introdùce a
> notion of time [ùpon à plane (?) sù ' ' fàç'e'] by pùnct! ingh oles
> (sic) in iSpace?! (123.34–24.12)

The letter is covered with these wounds and gashes that etch both time
and the signifiers of both sexes, and as such, it is reinscribed as a fetish
that plays with both the phallus and the vagina in the piercings/carv-
ings that mark all these texts-columns-bodies-letters-phallus-vaginas,
etc., with both sexes.

The 'Nightlessons' chapter of the *Wake* explores this particular reinscription of the letter. The children settle down to their homework after
their evening fun and games. Their homework consists of proving
Euclid's first proposition concerning the construction of an equilateral
triangle (293.15–95.27). The figure they construct comprises two inter-
penetrating circles that overlap to form an ovoid figure known as the
Vesica Piscis, or fish's bladder. William Stirling's *The Canon* is used by
Roland McHugh to explain the background of the Vesica Piscis in his
The Sigla of Finnegans Wake:

> It is well known both to freemasons and architects that the mystical figure
> called the Vesica Piscis, so popular in the middle ages, and generally
> placed as the first proposition of Euclid, was a symbol applied by the
> masons in the planning of their temples ... [T]he Vesica was also regarded
> as a baneful object under the name of the 'Evil Eye,' and the charm most
> generally empoyed to avert the dread effects of its fascination was the
> Phallus ... In the East the Vesica was used as a symbol of the womb ... To
> every Christian the Vesica is familiar from its constant use in early art, for
> not only was it an attribute of the Virgin and the feminine aspect of the

Saviour as symbolized by the *wound* in his side, but it commonly surrounds the figure of Christ, as his Throne when seated in glory. (*Sigla* 68,
citing Stirling, 11–14)

The feminized phallic figure of Osiris-Christ thus bears a pudendum in
the form of the wound in his side, a figure that toys with castration as
the marker of sexual opposition. But the Vesica is most interesting here
because it binds the fetishistic writing that is not motivated by the
presence of the phallus or truth, once again to the relation of the
mother and son in the scene of writing. Thus does the fetish writing
recall the X of *Glas's regard* of Virgin and child, as well as the traced X
of both the hen's writing and the reader-writer who mimics her. The X
also marks the sons gathered into auto-affection, as well as the mother
who gathers them there. To this extent the X marks the *différantial*
synthesis of the components of knowledge in the imagination as it is
analysed by Heidegger.

To the extent that the X also holds out the possibility of arriving at
the 'one stable somebody' responsible for the letter it may be regarded
as allegorical in the sense discussed above, which retains the traces of
the past – its being written – while holding out the promise of 'establishing the identities in the writer complexus (for if the hand was one,
the minds of active and agitated were more then so)' (114.32–5). In
other words, it sketches the 'formal element of "truth,"' as a 'future resurrection' that 'does not resuscitate a past which had been present'
(Mem 59). The past present of a stable somebody is relentlessly
deferred by the X that indefatigably confuses and steals the signatures
of those who enter into its scene of writing. Whoever the 'one stable
somebody' that is promised to come is, s/he cannot ever arrive into
presence because s/he will be marked by the X of internal division that
separates/joins the brother-sons to/from each other. In this complicated, fully imaginary structure, classical sexual difference is repeatedly undone by the auto-affective structure that relates the brother-
sons to each other and the mother as the same who/which is also
(an)other. The brother is another mother and the mother another
brother.

All of this points to the X-ed letter as the site where, or the horizon
within which, auto-affective time (intuition/sons) is gathered into the
one (conception/hen) and united. As such a site, the letter assumes the
power of the imagination in much the same way as Heidegger analyses it in Kant:

[T]he pure power of imagination carries out the forming of the look of the horizon. But then it does not just 'form' ['*bildet*'] the intuitable perceivability of the horizon in that it 'creates' [this horizon] as a free turning-toward. Although it is formative in this first sense, it is so in yet a second sense as well, namely, in the sense that it provides for something like an 'image' ['*Bild*']. (KPM 64)

Thus, the Joycean imaginary may be said to hinge on the letter's writing, which itself creates the non-present horizon of the images that are formed in *Finnegans Wake* as postal correspondence.

II Allegorizing the Imagination

Image as Correspondence: The Postal Technique of the Textual 'eidos'

I have already indicated how the imagination (as it is analysed by Heidegger) precedes knowledge in that it is the synthesizing power that fuses the components of knowledge – intuition (time) and concept (unity) – in advance of their becoming knowledge. This means that these components of knowledge are already found in the imagination, where they are inseparable from each other. As such, they are different but contiguous, and this concatenation marks the very structure of the imagination. At the end of the previous subsection, I suggested that the letter in *Finnegans Wake* may be read as the site of this prior inseparability of intuition and conception. This unity takes the form of the letter's style of writing, an X that *différantially* unites both brother to brother and mother to son.

In this subsection, I want to explore in more detail what I called above the postal horizon the letter offers for reading-writing *Finnegans Wake*. This will involve discussing how the term image can be understood to be in keeping with the non-eidetic and non-philosophical examination of the text so far. In order to do this, I will discuss how the letter can be read as an allegorization of the traits of 'correspondence' inherent in Heidegger's analysis of the image and as an image of *Finnegans Wake* itself. I will then explore how the postal horizon of the letter-image in *Finnegans Wake* radicalizes those aspects of Heidegger's analysis that uncover the auto-affective allegorization inherent in imaginary buildung or writing. The form this allegory takes is, I will suggest, sketched in large part by the strange interaction that is locatable by the fault line that divides the close of I.7 from the beginning of

I.8. This fault line marks the place where the workings of the 'postal' imagination are radically allegorized as the rhythmic interaction of the intuition of time in the form of the hybrid author-forger-son, Shem, with unity, the mother-hen. The rhythm of this allegory for the imagination is, I will suggest, composed of arrest, or constriction, followed by an outflow. I will then explore how the allegorical rhythm of the postal imaginary reinscribes the crossed fetishistic writing style of both *Finnegans Wake* and *Glas*.

The postal horizon of *Finnegans Wake* is sketched, in a preliminary manner, by the insight that the letter offers an image of the entire book. This insight is not new to *Wake*an studies,[15] and perhaps one of the best descriptions of how the letter may be read as literal image of the book is offered by Clive Hart in *Structure and Motif in 'Finnegans Wake'*:

> [The] wonderfully rich and expressive motif-complex which makes up the Letter must rank first among the many 'expanding symbols' in *Finnegans Wake*. Significantly, it begins with the word 'Reverend' (615.12) – pronounced in popular Irish speech almost exactly like 'riverrun' [the first word of the book itself] – and it goes on to treat every theme in *Finnegans Wake*, so that it quickly comes to stand for the book itself. Detailed correspondences proliferate in all directions as the Letter is developed in all conceivable contexts. (S&M 200)

It can easily be seen that Hart's comments regarding the letter centre on a version of it other than the one at I.5. The version Hart refers to is found in book IV of the text, but there are so many other versions of the same letter that it rapidly becomes impossible to say which version is to be regarded as the most important.[16] All these versions of the letter also conspire to make sure that it is rarely itself from one place in the text to another.

The odd nature of the letter can be made clearer by placing some different versions of the letter alongside each other, and trying to discover some of the structures that allow them to be discussed as versions of the 'same' letter:

(a)

Dear whom it proceded to
mention Maggy well & allathome's health well only the hate

turned the mild on the van Houtens and the general's elections
with a lovely face of some born gentleman with a beautiful present
of wedding cakes for dear thankyou Chriesty and with grand
funferall of poor Father Michael don't forget unto life's & Muggy
well how are you Maggy & hopes soon to hear well & must now
close it with fondest to the twoinns with four crosskisses for holy
paul holey comer holipoli whollyisland pee ess from (locust may
eat all but this sign shall they never) affectionate largelooking
tache of tch. (111.10–20)

(b)
Mesdaims, Marmouselles, Mescerfs! Silvapais! All
schwants (schwrites) ischt tell the cock's trootabout him. Ka-
pak kapuk. No minzies matter. He had to see life foully the
plak and the smut, (schwrites). There were three men in him
(schwrites). Dancings (schwrites) was his only ttoo feebles.
With apple harlottes. And a little mollvogels. Spissially (schwrites)
when they peaches. Honeys wore camelia paints. Yours very
truthful. Add dapple inn. (113.11–18)

(c)
(Dear (name of desired subject, A.N.),
well, and I go on to. Shlicksher. I and we
(tender condolences for happy funeral, one
if) so sorry to (mention person suppressed for
the moment, F.M.). Well (enquiries after all-
healths) how are you (question maggy). A
lovely (introduce to domestic circles) pershan
of cates. Shrubsher. Those pothooks mostly
she hawks from Poppa Vere Foster but these
curly mequeues are of Mippa's moulding.
Shrubsheruthr. (Wave gently in the ere turning ptover.) Well, mabby (consolation of
shopes) to soon air. With best from cinder
Christinette if prints chumming, can be when
desires Soldi, for asamples, backfronted or,
if all, peethrolio or Get my Prize, using her
flower or perfume or, if veryveryvery chumming, in otherwards, who she supposed adeal,
kissists my exits. Shlicksheruthr. From Auburn
chenlemagne. (280.9–28)

These three examples of the letter – two from I.5, and one from II.2 – obviously are not intended to present exhaustively the versions of letters in the *Wake*. Rather, the examples chosen are intended to indicate how it is the same letter that is at issue in each instance. This sameness comes to view in the following manner: version (a) mentions 'Father Michael' and his 'grand funferall.' The funeral is not mentioned in version (b), but it does crop up again in version (c) – Issy's homework exercise – as the 'happy funeral' for the 'person suppressed for the moment, F.M.' Version (a) is signed by the 'affectionate largelooking tache of tch,' or teastain, whereas version (b) is signed by the phrase 'add dapple inn,' or A-N-N, the mother. The A-N-N is echoed in Issy's version in the phrase 'must close it now with fondest to the twoinns,' meaning both the twins, Shem and Shaun, as well as the two N's of Ann's name. Issy actually signs her version of the letter with 'From auburn chenlemagne,' which recalls her redheaded mother-hen. Further, Issy's version (c) has the kisses of version (a), but this time they invite the reader to 'kissits my exits,' or her arse. Lastly, the letters share the 'beautiful present of wedding cakes' found in version (a), which becomes, in version (b), an apple charlotte (113.16) before finally reverting in version (c) to a 'lovely (introduce to domestic circles) pershan of cates' (280.15–16).

When Heidegger turns to grapple with the question of what different images share, he takes the image of a house as his example. A house carries more information than just its being a particular house. This is because a house 'shows how a house in general appears.' In being somehow 'general,' a house must therefore show 'what we represent in the concept house.' He continues:

> In what way does the look of this house show the 'how' of the appearing of a house in general? Indeed, the house itself offers this determinate look, and yet we are not preoccupied with this in order to experience how precisely this house appears. Rather, this house shows itself exactly in such a way that, in order to be a house, it must not necessarily appear as it does. It shows us 'only' the 'as ... ' in terms of which a house can appear ... A house could so appear ... What we have perceived is the range of possible appearing as such, or, more precisely, we have perceived that which cultivates this range, that which regulates and marks out how something in general must appear in order to be able, as a house, to offer the appropriate look. (KPM 67)

Grasped in this way, it is easy to see why the letter never appears in the same form twice: the letter appears in the text in order to give a general look of what a letter is. The letter itself gives the general range or image for what a letter is. Such a letter must then give the general criteria for the appearing of what may be seen as a letter, a rule that is itself laid down in and by the letter of I.5 as taking the auspices by following the textual prescriptions in the form of the hen. The letter thus presents, by virtue of its being a letter, a postal image. Thus, the letter represents the 'rule ... in the "how" of its regulating.' This performative rule that promises what a letter will look like through the 'how' of its regulating in its regulation, is, says Heidegger, the 'free "imaging" ["*Bilden*"] of a making-sensible as the providing of an image ... which is not bound to something [present] at hand' (KPM 68). The general image overflows itself because it is an image 'of which no [present] uniqueness can be demanded': 'The concept of a dog signifies a rule according to which my power of imagination can specify the form [*Gestalt*] of a four-footed animal in general, without being limited to any particular form which experience offers to me, or also any possible image which I can present *in concreto*' (KPM 69, citing CPR, A141/B180). The performative rule offered here for the appearance of something has nothing to do with any present experience (and hence has nothing to do with experience that is always understood in terms of a present that has been experienced) or present object. Even so, its look can only become available through the structure Heidegger calls 'correspondence.' Correspondence is the 'turning-toward ... which lets-[something]-stand in opposition.' This 'turning-toward' is the 'original turning-toward [which] the finite creature first allows a space for play [*Spielraum*] within which something can "correspond" to it. To hold oneself in advance in such a play-space, to form it originally, is none other than the transcendence which marks all finite comportment to beings' (KPM 50). Since correspondence is a non-present mode of turning-towards, the value of its opposition must be reinscribed. It can no longer be understood in terms of a subject standing opposite an object, since neither subject nor object can take shape without the value of presence. The opposition of correspondence is rather one in which the 'finite being' which is not yet a subject 'relate[s] itself to a being which it itself is not, and which it has not created' (50). The turning-towards does not create the present-ness of that which is turned towards; rather, 'correspondence' between a 'finite knowing creature' and 'a being which it itself is not' cannot be 'ontically creative' because it does not 'give [present] exist-

ence' to the being. Because 'something' is not made there, correspondence is, says Heidegger, 'a nothing' (51). For Heidegger, the
'nothing' where a 'not-nothing' (or being) shows itself forms the
horizon as the 'empty play-space' where beings come to show themselves.

The importance of the look lies in the relation it has to the horizon of
correspondence: 'In order for the horizon of letting-stand-against as
such to function, however, ... it needs a certain perceivability' (KPM
63). To be perceivable, says Heidegger, 'means: immediately capable of
being taken in stride in intuition' (63) In other words, it is intuition
that forms the auto-affective framework for perceivability. This type of
perceivability 'present[s] itself in a preliminary way and constantly as
a pure look [*Anblick*]' (63). The perceivability of the horizon is therefore
pure because it is never presently perceived. It is worked over by *différance* that protentively/retentively extends the '*Blick*' into a constant
look. The auto-affection of intuition 'guides and sustains' the conception that is the work of the 'pure understanding' (63), and because it
'stands in an essential relation to pure synthesis,' the 'pure power of
the imagination,' it also 'carries out the forming of the look of the horizon' (64): 'But then it does not just "form" ["*Bildet*"] the intuitable perceivability of the horizon in that it creates [this horizon] as a free
turning-toward. Although it is formative in this first sense, it is also yet
in a second sense as well, namely, in the sense that in general it provides for something like an "image" ["*Bild*"]' (64). But in originarily
creating and giving the image of the horizon within which (ontic)
beings come to stand, the imagination cannot be ontically creative.
This is why Heidegger offers the example of an image based on the
'look' offered by the 'landscape' or a 'collection' of paintings in a gallery (64). In neither case can the landscape or the collection of paintings
be understood as the ontic creation of the one forming their look.'
Thus, the landscape can be seen to be equivalent to the text of the hen,
letter, Vico, and so on: the look formed by correspondence corresponds
to the situation of the reader-writer in Vico, Joyce, or Derrida, who imitates the almost nothing of (a) text in a reinscription of the scene of
mimesis without a (present) model or *eidos*. Heidegger goes on to indicate how this look 'makes sensible' pure concepts:

> In the occurrence of this double forming (the creating of the look), the
> ground for the possibility of transcendence is first visible, and the neces-
> sary look-character of its preliminary essence, which stands against and

offers, is first understandable. Now, transcendence, however, is finitude, so to speak. If in letting-stand-against, the horizon which is formed therein is to be made intuitable (and again, finite intuition is called sensibility), then the offering of a look can only be the making-sensible of the horizon. The horizon of transcendence can be formed only in making-sensible.

The letting-stand-against [correspondence], seen from the standpoint of pure reason, is a representing of unities as such which regulate all unification (pure concepts). Hence, transcendence is formed in the making-sensible of pure concepts. Because it is a preliminary turning-towards, this making-sensible must likewise be pure.

The pure making-sensible occurs as a 'Schematism.' The pure power of the imagination gives schema-forming in advance the look ('image') of the horizon of transcendence. (KPM 64)

Correspondence is a pure, that is, non-present, 'making-sensible' of pure conception in a non-present image.

The letter, as I argued above, can be understood to offer the rule for the forming of an image or look that disrupts any attempt to simply link it to any particular present object in *Finnegans Wake*. However, because it is a letter, it also offers itself as the structure of correspondence that forms the look of the horizon as turning-toward that forms the look or image of something in that it is 'self-penned to one's other' (489.33–4). The look of the letter always turns towards another. This, in turn, makes the letter purely allegorical in that it opens the same to its other.

The letter is also allegorical insofar as it captures the workings of the imagination allegorically as the trajectory of a letter offered in the imagination. However, because the *Wake*an letter is textual, and therefore not a present being, its appearance in the imagination may also be understood to radicalize Heidegger's analysis of the imagination to the extent that the non-present horizon wherein present beings might once have shown themselves now only shows a non-present being, a written text. As a result, present-ness, just like Finnegan, is completely lost, sent off on a long implicit sentence without proper reference, meaning or name. In sending presence away, the letter, as apparent content of the imagination, can double for the form or structure of the imagination itself, wherein the letter reflects only upon itself.

The letter presents itself in the corresponding imaginary in a non-present fashion, and opens the way for other non-present images to allegorize the operation of the imagination precisely to the extent that they, too, are non-present. In remaining non-present, they do not allow 'present-ness' into the pure imagination, which seems to have been Heidegger's main reason for not discussing imagery in his texts on the imagination. The *Wake*'s allegorical radicalization also subjects these non-present correspondence images to constant reinscription precisely because they are always speaking otherwise according to the mode of auto-affection already examined. This generalized allegorization generates a more general network of postality that is itself built up through the expanding series of reinscribed correspondences, and that, in referring to each other, lead the reader-writer on his/her zigzag route across the text of the book.

But the look of these correspondences does not simply attach to a perception where something is seen. The letter, as I argued above, is also the site of writing that confuses eyes/ears: 'for while the ear, be we mikealls or nicholists, may sometimes be inclined to believe others the eye, whether browned or nolensed, find it devilish hard now and again even to believe itself. *Habes aures et num videbis? Habes oculos ac mannepalpabuat?*' (113.26–30). In other words, the pure look of correspondence without presence is, to the extent that it is formed by the letter, also a pure, non-present sound. Understood in this manner, seeking correspondences 'produces' (or better, (non)produces) in a manner that cannot be understood as ontically creative in that it only works with the 'almost nothing' of text. Further, the letter, insofar as it offers an intuitive image (in the sense discussed above) of the conceptual gathering of the hen, becomes the site where intuition and conception come together to schematize the imaginary horizon of the text of *Finnegans Wake* as correspondence.

Fetish Writing II: The Agglutinative Rhythm of the Postal Imagination

At the end of I.7 the two brothers who fuse together at the end of I.6 start to fight again. Their argument results in their being polarized as Mercius and Justius, who once again figure the multiplicity of personalities within the one writer-reader who is given at the end of I.5 and the outset of I.7 as the hybrid figure of Shem (125.23; 169.1–9). Justius, an avatar of Shaun, builds up to his final pronouncement on Mercius's (Shem's) morbid condition before he tries to silence him:

> That a
> cross may crush me if I refuse to believe in it. That I may rock
> anchor through the ages if I hope it's not true. That the host

may choke me if I beneighbour you without my charity! Sh!
Shem, you are. Sh! You are mad!
    He points the deathbone and the quick are still. *Insomnia,*
somnia somniorum. Awmawm. (193.24–30)

Justius, who appears here under the sign of a cross that can crush,
thinks Mercius is mad, and he tries to silence him with the death-bone,
a magical tool designed to still the quick. The imagery Justius uses –
crushing, choking, being anchored – forms a vocabulary of constriction
and restriction that results in death. Justius seeks to crush and squeeze
the life out of his brother-rival, himself.

    Mercius's response to his brother's squeezing, constrictive desire for
his death is, by contrast, to concern himself with the 'acoming' 'flow' of
their river-mother:

our turfbrown mummy is acoming, alpilla, beltilla, ciltilla,
deltilla, running with her tidings, old the news of the great big
world, sonnies had a scrap, woewoewoe! Bab's baby walks at
seven months, waywayway! Bride leaves her raid at Punchestime,
stud stoned before a racecourseful, two belles that make the
one appeal, dry yanks will visit old sod, and fourtiered skirts
are up, mesdames, while Parimiknie wears popular short legs,
and twelve hows to mix a tipsy wake, did ye hear, colt Cooney?
Did ye ever, filly Fortescue? With a beck, with a spring, all her
rillringlets shaking, rocks drops in her tachie, tramtokens in
her hair, all waived to a point and then all inuendation, little
oldfashioned mummy, little wonderful mummy, ducking under
bridges, bellhopping the weirs, dodging by a bit of bog, rapid-
shooting round the bends, by Tallaght's green hills and the
pools of the phooka and a place they call it Blessington and
slipping sly by Sallynoggin, as happy as the day is wet, bab-
bling, bubbling, chattering to herself, deloothering the fields on
their elbows leaning with the sloothering slide of her, giddy-
gaddy, grannyma, gossipaceous Anna Livia. (194.22–95.4)

Mercius's joyful description of the flow of the mother then responds to
the death-bone of Justius by lifting his 'lifewand' that causes words
for the dead to spurt forth in order to bring them back to life:

He lifts the lifewand and the dumb speak.
– Quoiquoiquoiquoiquoiquoiquoiq! (195.5–6)

The ejaculatory response to the restriction of the other brother may also be read in terms of the structure of the apotrope, or the attempt to ward off an evil influence or bad luck. Ejaculation, Mercius's response to the squeezing constriction of his brother, is an apotropaic response to being literally crushed, choked, and 'squeezed' to death in the text.

This fraternal squeezing and overflow at the end of I.7 is almost straightaway typographically figured as a constrictive maternal 'O' or '△' through which the text of I.8 is poured:

> O
> tell me all about
> Anna Livia! I want to hear all
> about Anna Livia. Well, you know Anna Livia? Yes, of course,
> we all know Anna Livia. Tell me all. Tell me now. You'll die
> when you hear. (196.1–6)

The 'O,' which stands at the top of the textual pyramid in the centre of the page, unleashes a flow of water (*eau*) text that expands and spreads out as a typographic delta, which eventually fills the width of the entire page. This O is also the delta (△), or estuary, through which the Liffey flows into the Irish Sea:[17]

> *Only for my short Brittas bed made's as snug as it smells it's*
> *out I'd lep and off with me to the slobs della Tolka or the plage au*
> *Clontarf to feale the gay aire of my salt troublin bay and the race*
> *of the saywint up me ambushure.* (201.17–20)

The river-mouth is also the vagina, the deltic pubic 'bush' of the river's 'ambushure' through which she feels the 'race of saywint.' The O (△) thus recalls the 'deep *regard* of a judas' in the text of *Glas*:

> In painting, a *regard* is the disposition of two figures who see one another. Example from Littré: 'He has a *regard* of a Christ and a Virgin in his collection.' The *regard* is also the opening of a hole through which one watches over water drainage.
> Double regard. Cross-eyed [*bigle*: bi-gl] reading. While keeping an eye on the corner column [*la colonne d'angle*] (the contraband), read this as a new testament. (113bi)

The maternal 'O' restricts a flow of water, and allows it to be watched over. Even though the hole is a constriction, it is also a perforation, a puncture through which something (a liquid) flows.

This rhythmic theatre of squeezing and flowing figures the imaginary interaction between the brothers and their mother according to the same kind of auto-affective oscillation discussed above wherein the mother can function as the other (rival) of the brother, and vice versa. This is why Justius's cross that threatens to squeeze the life out of Shem can trade places with the hen's beak that punctures holes in the letter according to the strange metonymic structure discussed in chapter 2 where the obeli double for circular punch-holes in the letter's fleecy writing. Constriction is almost indistinguishable from the hen's beak that punctures holes in the text in order 'to=introdùce a notion of time [ùpon à plane (?) sù ' ' fàç'e'] by pùnct! Ingh oles (sic) in iSpace?!' (124.10–12). These puncture holes, insofar as they inflict time on space, are auto-affective, but they also figure Shem, who is allied to time in the text as a series of puncture holes. As a sort of an 'O,' Shem can flow in response to his brother-mother squeezing him, just like his mother, who flows through her own typographically constrictive 'O' at the start of I.8. Each figure in this rhythmic theatre is subject to auto-affective substitution, and the play of constriction and flow can be understood to reinscribe allegorically the imaginary interaction of conception (the hen) with intuition or time (the author-forger son, Shem) in the rhythmic interaction of a squeezing constriction followed by an outflow. Because this rhythmic theatre is essentially auto-affective, it can only ever relate to 'itself' as 'other.' This auto-affective otherwise affects the rhythm of the imagination as allegorical and opens it up to constant reinscription. As a result, the contractual rhythm of the postal imaginary shears away from the mother-son(s) bond(s) into the brother-sister bond in the so-called Games chapter (II.1). The reinscription of the rhythm through the brother-sister bond develops further the sexual allegorization of the imaginary and its rhythmic flow.

The imaginary allegory of mother-son(s), which is itself allegorized in the rhythm of constriction and flow, is reinscribed by the heliotropic maggies as they open and turn themselves 'towooerds [Shaun] in heliolatry' (237.1), listening in ecstasy to his fertlizing sun-words:

> Just so stylled with the nattes are their flowerheads now and
> each of all has a lovestalk onto herself and the tot of all the tits of
> their understamens is as open as he can posably she and is tourne-
> soled straightcut or sidewaist, accourdant to the coursets of
> things feminite, towooerds him in heliolatry, so they may catch-
> cup in their calyzettes, alls they go troping, those parryshoots

from his muscalone pistil, for he can eyespy through them, to
their selfcolours, nevertheleast their tissue peepers, (meaning
Mullabury mesh, the time of appling flowers, a guarded figure
of speech, a variety of perfume, a bridawl, seamist inso one) as
leichtly as see saw (O my goodmiss! O my greatmess! O my
prizelestly preshoes!) while, dewyfully as dimb dumbelles, all
alisten to his elixir. Lovelyt! (236.33–37.9)

The maggies, insofar as they turn toward, enact the correspondence
that lies at the heart of the imagination as I examined it above. This
turning-toward is here allegorized as the play of rings and erections.
The ring the maggies form is a constricting 'courset' that tightens
around their brother Shaun as they go troping about him. The corset-
ring they wend around Shaun is woven of a 'Mulberry mesh,' a
'bridawl [bridal/bridle]' of 'tissue peepers' all 'seamist inso one.' This
woven ring of corsetry tightens around Shaun and finally causes him
to pour forth a 'greatmess' of his 'elixir' that ejaculates in 'parryshoots
from his muscalone pistil.'

The play of corsets and ejaculations takes various forms throughout
the course of the book. Each new instance of it serves to make even
more explicit the mechanics of what might be called the ringing allegory of the imagination. In this sort of 'ringing,' a tightening band
squeezes the other and gives rise to an erection/ejaculation. In being
passed around the other, the band erects the other-one by applying the
pressure of a certain pleasurable grip around him, just as it does
Shaun. As the ring of the dancing maggies grips him, it once again provokes the erection of the 'stud,' brings his postal speech to a head, in
the rhythmic 'spurts' of his 'likequid glue,' his semen-words (234.10–
29).[18]

However, 'ringing' does not just give rise to Shaun's erection; the
band and erection are also figured in the number ten, where the
fatherly 'Ainsoph' is made into 'this upright one,' by 'that noughty
besighed him zeroine' (261.23–4). Shaun's brother, Shem, is also subject
to the play of bands and erections when he is seduced by his sisters
during the game of 'Colours.' As is well known, the object of the game
of 'Colours' the children play is for Shem to guess the colour of the
girls' (the maggies') knickers. The correct or 'winning word' (249.4) is
the colour of knickers chosen by the maggies/Issy. Shem gets three
chances to guess the word, and each of his guesses is in turn preceded
by a sort of tempting flower dance by the girls that lures him to them.

When he gets close enough, they form a ring around him just as they did Shaun:

> With a ring ding dong, they raise clasped hands and advance
> more steps to retire to the saum. Curtsey one, curtsey two, with
> arms akimbo, devotees.
> Irrelevance.
> All sing:
> – I rose up one maypole morning and saw in my glass how
> nobody loves me but you. Ugh. Ugh.
> All point in the shem direction as if to shun.
> – My name is Misha Misha but call me Toffey Tough. I
> mean Mettenchough. It was her, boy the boy that was loft in the
> larch. Ogh! Ogh!
> Her reverence.
> All laugh.
> They pretend to helf while they simply shauted at him sauce to
> make hims prich. And ith ith noth cricquette, Sally Lums. Not
> by ever such a lot. Twentynines of bloomers gegging een man
> arose. Avis was there and trilled her about it. She's her sex, for
> certain. So to celebrate the occasion:
> – Willest thou rossy banders havind?
> He simules to be tight in ribbings round his rumpffkorpff.
> – Are you Swarthants that's hit on a shorn stile?
> He makes semblant to be swiping their chimbleys.
> – Can you ajew ajew fro' Sheidam?
> He finges to be cutting up with a pair of sissers and to be buy-
> tings of their maidens and spitting their heads into their facepails.
> Spickspuk! Spoken. (249.22–50.10)

Here, the circular 'corsetry' that was earlier wrapped around Shaun becomes 'rossy banders,' or the red knickers of an impudent woman (Anglo-Irish, rossy). As such, they both figure and explicitly re-elaborate the constrictive ring-play of corsetry as a scene of *bander*. It is these bands that encircle Shem, binding him 'tight in ribbings round his rumpffkorpff.' As a result of the constriction of these bands, Shem's erection springs up as the prophetic 'burning would' of *Macbeth* (250.16).[19]

But even though Shem gets erect just like Shaun through being bound, these scenes of fraternal erection are not identical. The scene of

Shem's *bander* complicates Shaun's scene by inverting the heliotropic turning-toward that in turn provokes a catachrestic 'female erection.' As the maggies lure Shem to them, they 'rise' up the phallic maypole, which they also ring around. As the top of their erection around the maypole, the 'puke' with a 'roohish' (250.11) 'shaut[s]' their own 'sauce' at Shem and 'make hims prich.' In other words, as the maggies 'erect' Shem in order to 'make hims prich [*sprich*, the German word for speech, as well as a 'prick'],' they *bander* in a way that is caught up in the bands of their 'rossy banders' (250.3). These 'rossy banders' erect by constricting and binding the other in 'tight in ribbings round his rumpffkorpff,' which *band* Shem with ribbons in order to 'make hims sprich.'

The 'rossy banders' therefore generate the same (con)fusion of male and female as the antherection of the fetish, but their catachrestic erection/ejaculation does not allow the *bander* to settle down into a simple erection. The unusual nature of their ejaculate is sketched a little earlier in the text:

> In the house of breathings lies that word, all fairness. The walls
> are of rubinen and the glittergates of elfinbone. The roof herof is
> of massicious jasper and a canopy of Tyrian awning rises and
> still descends to it. A grape cluster of lights hangs therebeneath
> and all the house is filled with the breathings of her fairness, the
> fairness of fondance and the fairness of milk and rhubarb and the
> fairness of roasted meats and uniomargrits and the fairness of
> promise with consonantia and avowals. There lies her word, you
> reder! The height herup exalts it and the lowness her down aba-
> seth it. It vibroverberates upon the tegmen and prosplodes from
> pomoeria. A window, a hedge, a prong, a hand, an eye, a sign, a
> head and keep your other augur on her paypaypay. And you have
> it, old Sem, pat as ah be seated! And Sunny, my gander, he's
> coming to land her. The boy which she now adores. She dores.
> Oh backed von dem zug! Make weg for their tug! (249.6–20)

The scene is here set in the mouth of Issy/the maggies. Its description outlines the parts of the allegorized mouth – teeth, lips, uvula, and so on. However, it is in the (female) 'ejaculation' of their 'sauce' in the form of 'that word' that the girls mimic the postal scene of Shaun's semen-worded sermonizing in the jerky arrest of a 'viboverberation' that gushes forth in the form of a 'prosplosion' that violates the 'pomoeria,' a sacred space that runs both inside and outside the boundary wall of a city.

The maggies' word gushes forth as the list of the English equivalents to the meanings of Hebrew letters understood as 'things':

Window = H
Hedge = E
Prong = L
Hand = I
Eye = O
Sign = T
Head = R
Eye = O
Mouth = P[20]

The 'sauce' of the 'winning word' is then revealed as the circular orbit of their turning-toward in heliotropic 'corsetry.' But the circular 'gush' (251.9) of correspondence quickly becomes through paradigmatic substitution the 'gash' of a 'fair ripecherry' (251.10) in an erection. They open a 'gape' in the 'pokestiff' they have given rise to, which they then bandage in the binding of a 'leash':

> I'll strip straight after devotions
> before his fondstare – and I mean it too, (thy gape to my gazing
> I'll bind and makeleash) and poke stiff under my isonbound with
> my soiedisante-chineknees cheeckchubby chambermate for the
> night's foreign males and your name of Shane will come forth
> between my shamefaced whesen with other lipth I nakest open
> my thight when just woken by his toccatootletoo my first morn-
> ing. (461.21–8)

In other words, the ejaculation of the word from the mouth of the maggies cuts vaginal gashes into the erection, which it then bandages and binds. These gashes mark the flowerlike 'shorn stile' (250.5) of an erection, which allows the reader to understand how an erection can be penetrated like a chimney by Shem (250.6–7). This gashed erection corresponds to the other female ejaculation that squirts the 'Anna Livia Plurabelle' chapter (I.8) through its typographic 'O,' which both punctures and gathers the fetish by putting the circular holes of an orifice – a mouth, a vagina, and so on – in it. It also figures the 'holey' fetish-writing of both *Glas* and the hen's letter, where the pubic fleece 'surrounds the neck, the cunt, the verge,' and becomes 'the apparition or appearance of a hole in erection, of a hole and an erection at once, of an erection in the hole or a hole in the erection' (66b).

The scene of the heliotrope-*bander*[21] plays out the allegory of the imagination in the elaborate ring-play of constriction and erection. This *bander* is also, as I mentioned above, extremely useful in reading what *Glas* describes as its 'double postulation': 'Double postulation. Contradiction in (it)self of two irreconcilable desires. Here I give it, accused in my own tongue, the title DOUBLE BAND(S), putting it (them) into play practically. A text laces [*sangle*] in two directions. Twice girt. Band contra band' (66bi). These double 'bands' sketch the horizon for the double look or 'double *regard*' (or chiasmatic X [43b]) that 'keep[s] an eye on the corner column,' 'the contraband' (113bi) that marks the general writing style of *Glas*: 'Two unequal columns, the say distyle [*disent-ils*], each of which – envelop(e)(s) or sheath(es), incalculably, reverses, turn inside out, replaces, remarks, overlaps [*recoupe*] the other' (1b). The immense scope of this horizon is registered in the 'enveloping' writing style of *Glas*, which 'propose[s] that one try to replace the verb *to be* with the verb *to band erect* [*bander*]' (133bi). In other words, *Glas* reinscribes all 'present being' in the 'double banded' antherection of the fetish-*bander* that 'incorporate[s] all sexes at once' in that it 'assumes the cutting [*coupure*] and the supplement within the double band. But as soon as there are two bands, by reason of the supplementary strewking, *coupture* (grafted flower), a double, undecideable sex activates itself sheathing father and mother all at once' (247–8b). In other words, the band plays with both sexual difference (understood as castration) and present being in a scene of *bander*.

In the *Wake* the 'sauce' of the 'gamecox spurts' of 'likequid glue' (234.18) can be put into anyone's mouth. These sticky words too find their way (almost intact) into *Glas*: 'Sperm, saliva, glair, curdled drool, tear of milk, gel of vomit – all these heavy and white substances are going to glide into one another, be agglutinated, agglomerated stretched out (*on*)*to the edge* of all the figures and pass through all canals' (139–40b). This form of writing that sees these sticky, gluey substances flow through canals and into one another figures the imaginary flow of the image that occurs at the end of I.7 and the beginning of I.8: 'Association is a sort of gluing contiguity, never a process of reasoning or a symbolic appeal; the glue of chance [*aléa*] makes sense, and progress is rhythmed by *little jerks*, grippings and suctions, patchwork tackling [*placage*] – in every sense and direction – and gliding penetration. In the embouchure or along the column' (142a). The image also conforms to this process because it is never itself: an image always seems to be composed of other bits (of itself) that adhere to it, come to it agglutinatively, from elsewhere.

This gluey gliding agglutinative flow of all the bodily substances in *Glas* can also be related to spatio-temporality and imagination. In order to illustrate this relation, I will briefly examine Derrida's 'Ousia and *Grammē*,' a text that predates *Glas*. In particular, I will focus on those aspects of Derrida's discussion of spatio-temporality that centre on the Latin '*cum*.' When read in this manner, the spatio-temporal *cum* of 'Ousia and *Grammē*' organizes the 'heavy and white substances' that 'glide into one another' in *Glas*. This spatio-temporal *cum* is also of particular interest here because it also touches upon the obeli-points discussed in chapter 2. Within the *cum*, nows can 'coexist' as points in space. This, of course, destroys the 'now' as time because it conceives time in spatial terms; as a result, this sort of 'time' can no longer simply be 'time' in the philosophical sense. In other words, the 'now' is exceeded through the impossible relations it has with itself as the point (*stigmē*) and the double:

> Time is distinguished from space in that it is not, as Leibniz will say, an 'order of coexistences,' but an 'order of successions.' The relationship of points between themselves cannot be the same as that of the nows between themselves. Points do not destroy each other reciprocally. But if the present now were not annulled by the following now, it would coexist with it, which is impossible ... A now cannot coexist, as a current and present now as such. Coexistence has *meaning* only in the unity of a single same now. This is *meaning*, sense itself, in what unites meaning to presence. One cannot even say that the coexistence of two different and equally present nows is impossible or unthinkable: the very signification of coexistence or of presence is constituted by this limit. Not to be able to coexist with an other (the same as itself), with an other now, is not a predicate of the now, but its essence as presence. The now, presence in the act of the present, is constituted as the impossibility of coexisting with another now, that is, with an other-the-same-as-itself. The now *is* (in the present indicative) the impossibility of coexisting *with itself*: with itself, that is, with an other self, an other now, an other same, a double. (M 54–5)

What is of importance here is the alignment of the now with the point. What is lurking behind the 'succession' of 'nows' that annihilate each other is a consideration of what might occur if nows were grasped *spatially* as 'points' that can coexist with each other in space. However, such a reconceptualization of time would be, Derrida points out, 'impossible,' and could not have any sense or meaning since 'the very signification of coexistence or of presence is constituted by this limit.' Nows that would somehow 'coexist' would no longer even be 'nows': the 'now *is* (in the present indicative) the impossibility of coexisting *with itself*: with itself, that is, with an other self, an other now, an other same, a double.' The 'nows' that would 'coexist' nevertheless occupy an odd space: whatever they are 'one cannot even say that the coexistence of two different and equally present nows is impossible or unthinkable.' This implies, of course, that the coexistence of two nows is neither purely impossible nor unthinkable. Once a now flirts with the possibility of coexisting, it ceases to be 'a current and present now as such': in other words, it loses its 'essence as presence.' Coexistent nows are neither present nor presence.

It is this possible impossibility or thinkable unthinkable spatio-temporality that I wish to grope towards here using the motif of the double as a guiding thread. The impossible, nonsensical, 'double' now always brings with it issues of sameness *and* difference:

> This impossibility [of a now coexisting with itself as a double] implies in its essence, in order to be what it is, that the other now, with which a now cannot coexist, is also in a certain way the same, is also a now as such, and that it coexists with that which cannot coexist with it. The impossibility of coexistence can be posited as such only on the basis of a certain coexistence, a certain *simultaneity* of the nonsimultaneous, in which the alterity and identity of the now are maintained together in the differentiated element of a certain same. To speak Latin, the *cum* or the *co-* of coexistence has meaning only on the basis of this impossibility, and vice versa. The impossible – the coexistence of two nows – appears only as a synthesis – taking this word neutrally, implying no position, no activity, no agent – let us say in a certain complicity or coimplication *maintaining* together several current nows [*maintenants*]. Time is a name for this impossible possibility.

> Conversely, the space of *possible coexistence*, precisely that which one believes is known by the name of space, the possibility of coexistence, is the space of the impossible coexistence. In effect, simultaneity can appear

as such, can be simultaneity, that is, a *relating* of two points, only in a synthesis, a *complicity*: temporally. One cannot say that a point is *with* another point; and a point, whether one says it or not, cannot *be with* another point, there cannot be another point with which, etc., without a temporalization. Which maintains together two different nows. The *with* of spatial coexistence arises only out of the with of temporalization. (M 55)

The synthesizing Latin '*cum*' here is the impossible medium of 'time' – the impossible possibility of the coexistence of two nows in 'a certain *simultaneity*' of alterity and identity that boils down to spatio-temporality. Within the space of this simultaneity, the complict synthesis of this Latin '*cum*,' any effort to treat time and space as being purely different is 'to remain naïve' since 'as Hegel and Heidegger remind us, one cannot treat space *and* time as two concepts or two themes'[22] (M 55). Thus, even if 'time' 'is a name for this impossible possibility,' time is always bound up with space. This is also why 'time' is always 'other' than 'itself': every 'now' is a 'point,' and vice versa. Furthermore, time in Aristotle's text, says Derrida, does not pass intact into a spatial representation if that representation is punctuated by points: '[I]f one uses the point and the line to represent movement [in space], one is manipulating a multiplicity of points which are both origin and limit, beginning and end; this multiplicity of immobilities, this series (if it can be called such) of successive arrests, *does not give time*' (Derrida's italics, M 59). These now-points that are supposed to represent time cause its flow to shudder to such an extent that what they represent – 'time' – 'does not give time': these points cross time out as they mark it. That which is no longer 'time' in the simple (present) sense is aligned with the now, which, 'if it is considered as limit (*peras*),' is both 'accidental' and 'outside time, foreign to time' because time 'is not thought on the basis of the now' (61). The now-limit-point would, on this reading, appear to be that which makes the philosophical concept of time shudder.[23]

All that remains is to consider how that which is related to time but is not time may be mapped onto Derrida's description of *différance*. Above I suggested that a now that flirts with the possibility of coexisting ceases to be 'a current and present now as such' and loses its 'essence as presence' (M 54–5). Coexistent nows are neither present nor presence and their coexistence is not 'a question of relating space *and* time' because 'each of the terms [space and time] *being* only what it is not' consists 'first of all, only of the *com*-parison itself' (56). As such,

they can be understood to be beyond the 'something' that bears a relation to time, but is not time 'that is to be thought beyond the determination of the Being as presence' (60). According to Derrida, Aristotle
himself, even though he gestured towards a time that is no longer
bound by the present (49), does not pursue this point (54, 56). Nevertheless, Derrida finds that Aristotle's text is articulated by the *'cum'*
discussed above:

> Now, if Aristotle gives himself the difference between time and space (for
> example, in the distinction between *nun* and *stigmē*) as a constituted dif-
> ference, the enigmatic articulation of this difference is lodged in his text,
> hidden, sheltered, but operating within complicity, within the complicity
> of the same and other, within the *with* or the *together*, with the *simul* in
> which Being-together is not a determination of Being, but the very pro-
> duction of Being. (56)

In Aristotle's text the 'enigmatic articulation' of the difference between
time and space is 'sheltered' – one notes that this is also the same word
Derrida uses to locate the erased trace in presence – takes the form of
the word *hama*: 'In Greek *hama* means "together," "all at once," both
together, *"at the same time."* This location is neither spatial not temporal. The duplicity of the *simul* to which it refers does not yet reassem-
ble, within itself, either points or nows, places or phases. It says the
complicity, the common origin of space and time, appearing together
[*com-paraître*] as the condition for all appearing of Being. In a certain
way, it says the dyad as the minimum' (56). Insofar as it inscribes the
complicity of time and space – that is, is neither simply temporal nor
spatial – the *hama* corresponds to *différance*, the 'temporalization and
spacing, the becoming-time of space and the becoming space of time,
the "originary constitution" of space and time' (8). *Hama*, like *différance*,
generates Being, is '"older" than Being itself' (26). The 'enigmatic
articulation of this difference,' the *'cum'* or synthesis is therefore the
'originary' contamination of time and space. It is the differing that is
'older' than both of them.[24]
   Once again, this should serve as a reminder to the reader that 'time'
as it appears in this study should, at the very least, be considered to
mark a catachresis,[25] that is, to mark the site where 'space' and 'time'
are irretrievably contaminated by each other, the site where the 'now'
has been originally and eternally infected with the 'point' (and vice
versa). *Différance*, auto-affection, spatio-temporality, and so forth, do

not mark 'time itself'; they are *related* to time.[26] It is important to note that this relation of relatedness that is bound up with the now-points and their shuddering spatio-temporality remains *a poor representation of time* that, as Derrida insists, *'does not give time.'* In other words, 'time' henceforth in this study must be read as that which remains related to time as spatio-temporality, but also remains exiled as a poor representation of time.[27]

As I mentioned above, the spatio-temporal come-together points form a 'multiplicity of immobilities,' a 'series (if it can be called such) of successive arrests,' which *'does not give time'* (Derrida's italics, M 59). It is precisely this spatio-temporal shuddering of 'non-time' that makes itself felt in the texts of *Glas* and *Finnegans Wake*. In *Glas*, Derrida cites Genet in order to detail the process of how one column agglutinatively flows into another:

'You did not move, you were not asleep, you were not dreaming, you were in flight, motionless and pale, frozen [*glacé*], straight, stretched out stiff on the flat bed ... while I, all attention, felt you flow into me, warm and white, in little continuous jerks. Perhaps you were playing at coming' ... In little continuous jerks, the sequences are enjoined, induced, glide in silence. No category outside the text should allow defining the form or the bearing [*allure*] of these passages, of these trances of writing ... Take into account the overlap-effects [*effets de recoupe*], and you will see that the tissue ceaselessly re-forms itself around the incision [*entaille*]. (24–5b)

Similar spurts or 'little continuous jerks' figure the general style of *Glas* as the typographic 'judases' or peep-holes (2bi–3bi) that are cut into the flanks of each textual column. The linkage between the judases and the jerky rhythm is made explicit but is itself nested in a judas. This judas cuts into the right column's description of its own course for reading Hegel as 'zigzagging, oblique to boot, jostled by the bank [*rive*] to be avoided, like a machine during a difficult maneuver' (4a). The judas works 'by *à-coups*, fits and starts, jolts, little successive jerks, while touching, tampering with the borders' (4ai). This zig-zag agglutinative rhythm also writes the *Wake*'s letter, which

... is not a miseffectual why-
acinthinous riot of blots and blurs and bars and balls and hoops
and wriggles and juxtaposed jottings linked by spurts of speed:
it only looks as like it as damn it; (118.28–31)

It is the fleecy look of the letter's writing that compels Shaun's description of Shem's cell and his writing in I.7 to proceed 'agglag-glomeratively' (186.7). In being forced to speak agglomeratively of Shem's writing, Shaun pieces and glues together the semi-digested and rotting fragments of the 'pure mousefarm filth' of the 'western playboyish world' (183.4) scattered about the cell. Such gluing takes the form of proceeding from the known to the unknown in that it *dif-férantially* 'put[s] truth and untruth together' so that 'a shot may be made at what this hybrid actually was like to look at' (169.8–10). Since 168.14 fuses the two brothers together under the 'same' name of a 'hybrid' Shem (*'Semus sumus'* [168.14]; a Latin neologism that can mean 'We are Shem / the same'), when Shaun pieces together the hybrid Shem, he too writes himself agglutinatively. As he glues himself together, he re-enacts the hen's zig-zagging trajectory across the rubbish-heap. Agglutination binds and glues the author's mode of writing with the writing of the one commenting on him to the point where they can (almost) be mistaken for each other. The agglutination of the hen that agglutinates the two brothers (con)fuses them, and they become (in following the hen's example) other 'parody's bird[s]' (11.9) who gather by picking over the traditions of the 'western playboyish world' and carrying it about in a 'culdee sacco of wabbash' (210.1). 'Flowey,' sticky, imaginary writing would therefore be composed of what *Glas* calls the 'glue of chance [*aléa*] [that] makes sense' (142a). However, this agglutinative scene is one of personal composition after the manner of Stephen Dedalus and Dolph, and it can produce 'a stink-some inkenstink, quite puzzonal to the wrottel' (183.6): one comes by one's own 'personal aroma' by digging about in rubbish heaps.

That such a jerky flow, which brings about the writing of both *Glas* and the *Wake*an letter of I.5, should have something to do with death is already familiar to readers of Joyce's *Ulysses*:

THE CROPPY BOY

(*the ropenoose around his neck, gripes in his issuing bowels with both hands*)

I bear no hate to a living thing,
But I love my country beyond the king.

RUMBOLD, DEMON BARBER

(*accompanied by two blackmasked assistants, advances with gladstone bag which he opens*) Ladies and gents, cleaver purchased by Mrs Pearcy to slay

Mogg. Knife with which Voisin dismembered the wife of a compatriot
and hid remains in a sheet in the cellar, the unfortunate female's throat
being cut from ear to ear. Phial containing arsenic retrieved from body of
Miss Barron which sent Seddon to the gallows.

*(He jerks the rope. The assistants leap at the victim's legs and drag him down-
ward, grunting. The croppy boy's tongue protrudes violently.)*

THE CROPPY BOY

Horhot ho hray hor hother's hest.

*(He gives up the ghost. A violent erection of the hanged sends gouts of sperm
spouting through his deathclothes on to the cobblestones. Mrs Bellingham, Mrs
Yelverton Barry and the Honourable Mrs Mervyn Talboys rush forward with
their handkerchiefs to sop it up.)*

RUMBOLD

I'm near it myself. *(he undoes the noose)* Rope which hanged the awful
rebel. Ten shillings a time. As applied to Her Royal Highness. *(he plunges
his head into the gaping belly of the hanged and draws his head out again clotted
with coiled and smoking entrails)* My painful duty has been done. God save
the king! (U 15.4531–58)

Here, an Irish rebel, the croppy boy, is put to death by hanging in a
phantasmatic scene from *Ulysses* 15. As the text makes clear, his death
on the gallows recalls the death of χ as he 'gives up the ghost' on the
cross. The scene may thus be taken to fuse the erection of the phallus-
tongue with the erection of the Christic-body in the manner discussed
in section I above (pp. 148–63). Once again, the erection is a fetish
because the hanged erection is slit open, gashed at the belly, and its
crucified erection is so violent that it empties itself in an ejaculation of
consciousness, tongue, blood, entrails, spirit, and sperm. The unconscious, mute, of uncertain lineage, hollow, unconscious matter, and
spent 'antherection' of the fetish nevertheless courts resurrection when
bound to the cross, even though it just hangs there like an idol that has
been emptied of all present content.

Such hollowed-out erection/resurrection scenes come as no surprise
to the reader of *Finnegans Wake*, where they have been a critical
commonplace since Campbell and Robinson's *Skeleton Key*. They are

numerous and take various forms, and may be said to sketch the general form of the Irish wake, where the unknown – death – enters into a
relation with the known – life. This relation is insisted upon each time
the text has recourse to the allegorical figures of arising again, such as
the phoenix, Tim Finnegan, Christ, Osiris, the sleeper stirring at the
end of book III and throughout book IV, Earwicker's experience of the
'rouseruction of his bogey' (499.1), and the rhythmic fall and rise of
various civilizations. All of these falls share something of the disrupted
phall-us:

> Phall if
> you but will, rise you must: and none so soon either shall the
> pharce for the nunce come to a setdown secular phoenish.
> (4.15–17)

The *Wake* multiplies these hollowed-out and cut phalluses to explore
an unending series of 'phalls' that are no longer simply phalluses but
fetishes, which play, like 'phoenixes,' with the rhythm of resurrection.
And as resurrections they both allegorize and play with what Derrida
in *Memoires* calls the 'formal element of "truth"' that

> is not essentially oriented toward the past, toward a past present deemed
> to have really and previously existed. Memory stays with traces, in order
> to 'preserve' them but traces of a past that has never been present, traces
> which themselves never occupy the form of presence and always remain,
> as it were, to come – come from the future, from the *to come*. Resurrection,
> which is always the formal element of 'truth,' a recurrent difference
> between a present and its presence, does not resuscitate a past which had
> been present; it engages the future ... [O]ne could say ... there is only
> memory but, strictly speaking, the past does not exist. It will never have
> existed in the present, never been present, as Mallarmé says of the
> present itself: 'un présent n'existe pas.' The allegation of its supposed
> 'anterior' presence *is* memory, and this is the origin of all allegories.
> (Mem 58–9)

As the traces of protentive and retentive allegorizing memory, or, what
I have been calling here imagination, these resurrections are mimed
insofar as they never come to rest in present consciousness, but remain
instead caught in an 'unconscious,' in the sense that Derrida gives to
the word:

In this context, and beneath this guise, the unconscious is not, as we know, a hidden, virtual, or potential self-presence. It differs from, and defers itself which doubtless means that it is woven of differences, and also that it sends out delegates, representatives, proxies; but without any chance that the giver of proxies might 'exist,' might be present, be 'itself,' somewhere, and with even less chance that it might become conscious. In this sense, contrary to the terms of an old debate full of the metaphysical investments that it has always assumed, the 'unconscious' is no more a 'thing' than it is any other thing, is no more a thing than it is a virtual or masked consciousness. This radical alterity as concerns every possible mode of presence is marked by the irreducibility of the aftereffect, the delay. In order to describe [these] traces, in order to read the traces of 'unconscious' traces (there are no 'conscious' traces), the language of presence and absence, the metaphysical discourse of phenomenology is inadequate. (M 20–1)

All the resurrected phall can ever do is defer and allegorize itself in its delegates, representatives, and proxies, 'without any chance that [it] might "exist,"' which is to say, become present or conscious, even as it holds out that (unfulfilled) promise. The *Wake* thus radicalizes the *Ulysse*an scene of the hollowed holey fetish by deferring and allegorizing it throughout its text. It can no longer be localized, and its potential to appear anywhere in the text is limitless. And if the text of *Finnegans Wake* is so caught in the constricting noose of its own making, then its text exercises precisely the same kind of power Derrida identifies in *Glas*:

> The rare force of the text is that you cannot catch it (and therefore limit it to) saying: *this is that*, or, what comes down to the same thing, this has a relation of apophantic or apocalyptic unveiling, a determinable semiotic or rhetorical relation with that, this is the same subject, this is not the subject, this is the same, this is the other, this text here, this corpus here. There is always some question of yet something else. Rare force. At the limit, null. One would have to say the text's power, its potence [*puissance*]. As one would speak of the musculature of the tongue. But also of a mathematical expansion. But also of the enveloping of that which remains potential [*en puissance*]. At the limit, null. Nonexistent from remaining infinitely potential. From being condemned to power and remaining there.

What I wanted to write is the text's GALLOWS [*POTENCE*].

> I expose myself to it, I tend toward it very much [*beaucoup*], I stretch
> much on it. (199b)

The constricting power of the text's gallows lies in the fact that no
present content (meaning, *eidos*, consciousness, etc.) can be revealed
there. Its 'null potentiality' displaces the present form of the 'is' that
says 'this' or 'that.' As such, it can be understood to correspond to
Heidegger's analysis of the schema-image. The schema-image is, as
mentioned in the previous subsection, 'nothing': as the turning-toward
that lets-stand-against, the 'premonition' 'cannot be a being.' 'But if not
a being, then just a nothing [*ein Nichts*]. Only if the letting-stand-
against of ... is a holding oneself in the nothing can the representing
allow a not-nothing [*ein nich-Nichts*], i.e., something like a being if such
a thing shows itself empirically, to be encountered instead of and
within the nothing' (KPM 51). If the image is 'null' – that is, has no
present content – then it is potential. It promises infinitely a content
that it can never deliver because the image cannot be '"limited to any
particular form which [present] experience offers to me, or also to any
possible image which I can present *in concreto*"' (KPM 69 citing CPR
A141/B180). The 'null potentiality' of the image takes place on the gallows that raises, suspends, kills, erects, promises, but never delivers
presence.

The gallows fits itself neatly onto the cross-points in the text of the
letter of I.5. The lines of text stretch the reader in two directions: east–
west and north–south on a large textual cross. This rhythm of the
crossed flow is also the flow of the two antagonistic readers of/in the
letter into each other. Neither can do without the other: each tries at all
times to keep his/her eye on the other, watching carefully over the
two-way flow into the other. The flow is momentarily arrested by the
pricking checks of the obeli (†), which call 'unnecessary attention to
errors, omissions, repetitions and misalignments' (120.15–16) in the
text. As the crossed reader(s) regard(s) the hen, s/he sees stereoscopically, like a bird.[28] To see stereoscopically also means:

> To see double. Two columns, two hills [*collines*], two breasts. It is impossi-
> ble. The *colpos*, between the one and the two. You divide yourself, you feel
> nauseated, you want to vomit, your head turns you around. You seem

more than alone, more alone than ever. Without me. But jealous of yourself, you erect yourself, if you still can. More than ever you want to.
(114bi)

To vomit is also to succumb to the rhythm of the arrest and the flow,
and the doubled erection-ejaculation that lends itself to this rhythm
that is at once a tightening and a projection, is the 'double posture' of
the 'DOUBLE BAND(S)' mentioned above.

The shared imagery of *Finnegans Wake* and *Glas* does not stop there,
however. In *Glas*, the fetish represents 'the mass of flowers as a phallic
upsurging *and* a vaginal concavity' (68b). Understood in this manner,
these flowers not only recall the Christ figure spoken of above, but
they also serve to reinscribe what may be called by now a commonplace of *Finnegans Wake*, the scene of fetishistic heliotrope, where the
flower-girls gush and rush (as heliotrope) towards the (wounded)
Christ (X) on the cross (†) (236.33–37.9), as those in *Glas* rush to surround erections, opening up the logic of what Derrida calls 'antherection,' a logic that *Finnegans Wake* explores as the Quinet sentence.

Quinet: The Grafted Flowers of History

The overlapping flow spoken of above in relation to the two columns
of *Glas* is, as I have been suggesting, neatly named by *Glas*'s coinage
of 'antherection.' The word 'antherection' is derived from *Glas*'s
consideration of Genet's *The Thief's Journal*. The word itself names
a prison scene, where the 'violence of [the murderer's] organ,' 'the
strongest, with a horn [*qui bandent*],' is veiled by the material of the
convict's garb, which 'evokes[,] both by its colors and roughness, certain flowers whose petals are slightly fuzzy.' Such flowers 'must signify sorrow, death. Thus I sought love as it pertained to the penal
colony' (129–30b). The flower that comes to cover the doomed murderer's phallus at the 'penal colony' names the structure of the antherection:

> As it pertained to the penal colony: this is the place of what we shall
> henceforth call *antherection*: the time of erection countered, overlapped
> [*recoupée*] by its contrary – the (the) place of the flower. Enanthiosis.
> The overlap goes over itself again indefinitely. Whence the effect of cap-
> italization, but also of the unlimited outpouring. If the erection is inhab-
> ited by contraband, by what produces it in cutting it off, if then it is in

advance, already, antherection, there can, there must be a castration of
castration, an antherection of antherection, and so on to infinity. (130b)

Antherection thus names the cut (anti-) as well as the erection: in this
way the antherection is also the fetishistic fleece of writing no longer
governed by the values of presence or truth (66b). Antherection therefore always 'assumes the cutting [*coupure*] and the supplement within
the double band. But as soon as there are two bands, by reason of the
supplementary strewking, *coupture* (grafted flower), a double, undecidable sex activates itself sheathing father and mother all at once'
(247–8b).

As I mentioned above, this image recalls the perforated fetish writing of the letter in *Finnegans Wake* that is itself 'pierced butnot punctured (in the university sense of the term) by numerous stabs and
foliated gashes made by a pronged instrument' (124.1–3), both a break-
fast fork and the hen in the guise of 'Dame Partlet on her dungheap'
(124.23–4). These are the tears and gashes made in the text's reader and
impart a notion of time (intuition) to 'iSpace!' (124.6–12). However,
these stigmatic puncture wounds that affect the text and the reader-
writer with time are immediately dressed by the 'fourleaved shamrock
or quadrifoil jab' that irrupts as it cuts (124.20–1). In other words, the
text's response to the piercing questions of authorship and authenticity
is the riddling graft of the shamrock-Shem:

> ... all put grown in waterung-
> spillfull Pratiland only and a playful fowl and musical me and
> not you in any case, two and two together, and, with a swarm
> of bisses honeyhunting after, a sigh for shyme (O, the petty-
> bonny rouge!) separated modest mouths. So be it. And it was.
> The lettermaking of the explots of Fjorgn Camhelsson when he
> was in the Kvinnes country with Soldru's men. (124.24–30)

Shem's name pokes through the text of this riddle as that which is
grown in 'Pratiland [Ireland] only': *S*hamrock; the playful fowl is the
*H*en; the 'musical me' is *E* in sol-fa ('mi'); 'not you' is *M*e; and –*US* is a
case ending. *Shemus*'s other signature irrupts just a few lines later at
125.1–2, where he/it 'shoots off in a hiss,' '*Sh*,' followed by a muddled
sound, '*em*,' both of which are gathered into his 'whole' name, which is
the same as that of Noah's eldest son, *Shem*.

Even though the Shem/shamrock grafts itself onto the text after it

has been cut and gashed, its irruptive graft cannot be taken as a resto-
ration or restitution of some prior state of plenitude or wholeness:
Shem and his shamrock are a 'sham.' Their sham status is underlined
by Shaun when he revisits Shem's posing of the 'first riddle of the universe,' 'When is a man not a man?' – which is answered by 'When he is
a sham.' In other words, whatever or whoever the author of the letter
may be, he is not a man, but a sham, a hoax, deception (170.5–26). He is
held out as the promise and possibility of authorial identity, but his
sham status can only ever recall him and promise him as the graft of a
'fourleaved shamrock.' The sham-rock, which Saint Patrick used as a
symbol to reveal the mystery of the Trinity to the native Irish pagans,
hides itself in a tangle of other 'shamrocks' and weaves the girdle of
'clover/klee' as it dangles between Shaun's legs as a sort of sham Messiah (478.19–30).

The literal graft of the sham-fetish of shamrock-clover is reinscribed
by the *Wake*'s use of Edgar Quinet's sentence from his *Introduction à la
philosophie de l'humanité* (*Oeuvres complètes*, volume 2, 367):

> *Aujourd'hui comme aux temps de Pline et de*
> *Columelle la jacinthe se plaît dans les Gaules,*
> *la pervenche en Illyrie, la marguerite sur les*
> *ruines de Numance et pendant qu'autour d'elles*
> *les villes ont changé de maîtres et de noms, que*
> *plusiers sont entrées dans le néant, que les*
> *civilisations se sont choquées et brisées, leurs*
> *paisibles générations ont traversé les âges et sont*
> *arrivées jusqu'à nous, fraîches et riantes comme*
> *aux jours des batailles.* (281.4–13)[29]

Through this sentence, the text reinscribes the shamrock graft as a flo-
ral graft that comes to dress the historical battle wounds of the 'phalls'
of names, masters, cities, and civilizations that have always been col-
liding and smashing into one another. Dressing the wound of cities
with flowers names what the text of *Glas* calls antherection, which also
names the sexual parts of a flower. The anther of a flower is that 'part
of the stamen containing the pollen or fertilizing dust, which when
mature is shed forth for the fertilization of the ovary; it is often sup-
ported on a slender pedicel called the filament' (OED). Interestingly, it
was Quinet's Roman historian, Pliny, who first applied the word 'stamen' to the part of a flower, the word originally having named the

warp of thread. The *Wake*an antherection of the Quinet sentence also offers the 'double band' of the sexes as a 'MUTUOMORPHOMUTA-TION' (281.L11–13),[30] wherein the male and female sexes are interchangeable. Although the sex-swap is not immediately apparent, it stands out if the whole Quinet sentence is compared with the 'Musey-room' episode's sketch of the incident in the park:

> This is the three
> lipoleum boyne grouching down in the living detch. This is an
> inimyskilling inglis, this is a scotcher grey, this is a davy, stoop-
> ing. This is the bog lipoleum mordering the lipoleum beg. A
> Gallawghurs argaumunt. This is the petty lipoleum boy that
> was nayther bag nor bug. Assaye, assaye! Touchole Fitz Tuo-
> mush. Dirty MacDyke. And Hairy O'Hurry. All of them
> arminus-varminus. This is Delian alps. This is Mont Tivel,
> this is Mont Tipsey, this is the Grand Mons Injun. This is the
> crimealine of the alps hooping to sheltershock the three lipoleums.
> This is the jinnies with their legahorns feinting to read in their
> handmade's book of stralegy while making their war undisides
> the Willingdone. The jinnies is a cooin her hand and the jinnies is
> a ravin her hair and the Willingdone git the band up. (8.21–34)

Here, the text indicates that there are three 'lipoleum boyne' and two 'jinnies' (one a dove, the other a raven). In response to the three boys' backsides and two urinating girls, the Willingdone 'git[s] the band up,' or an erection (*bander*). But when this scene is compared with the Quinet sentence, the shift in sex is grasped as the shift in number: the three male figures have become two historians – Pliny and Columella, while the two girls become three flowers – hyacinth, periwinkle, and daisy.

The close companionship of flowers and ruined cities is also underlined in *Glas's* reading of Genet: 'After the demolition of the shelter [*édicule*], the obsequent procession gets going, as did the convicts after the castration of Guiana. At the edge of the still smoking scar, the faggots come to place their flowers. The burial place is erected once more through the care of a delegation, a detachment of transvestites' (238b). The flowers left by the 'faggots' are 'roses, placed ... on the edge of a hole and on the vestigial site of a column' (243b). Here, too, flowers soothe and dress the wound, the place of death, revealing the 'movement of erection,' as I showed with χ, to be one of 'theatrical and funereal reversal' (232bi). The theatrical reversal of erection in the *Wake's* antherection of the Quinet sentence can now be understood to watch over the entire scene of heliotropic erection and ejaculatory 'irruption' of the heliotropic 'sauce' that the maggies shout/shoot at the sham Shem in order to 'make hims prich.' The shamrock-flowers come to dress and provoke 'erection,' antherecting it as the fetish, and their operation is the lesson that the hybrid author-forger-Shem must learn in the game of II.1.

The irruptive flow of flowers is once more reinscribed in the radical allegory of the imaginary. I will conclude this chapter by indicating how this reinscription recommences through the correspondence the Quinet sentence has to a sheet of paper in *Finnegans Wake*. This correspondence, which will in chapter 6 reinscribe writing as I have so far examined it, comes to the fore in one of Issy's footnotes to the Quinet sentence at 281, where she challenges the reader to 'Translout that gaswind into turfish, Teague, that's a good bog and you, Thady, poliss it off, there's nateswipe, on to your blottom pulper' (281.F2). In order to 'translout' the 'gaswind' of the Quinet sentence into the 'turfish' of the 'blottom pulper,' it is useful to recall the actions of the Russian general on the field of battle, as Butt does for Taff in II.3. Not surprisingly, the scene lets itself be reinscribed into yet another two ejaculations:

> For when meseemim, and tolfoklokken rolland
> allover ourloud's lande, beheaving up that sob of tunf for to
> claimhis, for to wollpimsolff, puddywhuck. Ay, and untuoning
> his culothone in an exitous erseroyal *Deo Jupto*. At that instullt
> to Igorladns! Prronto! I gave one dobblenotch and I ups with
> my crozzier. Mirrdo! With my how on armer and hits leg an
> arrow cockshock rockrogn. Sparro! (353.15–21)

The impressive Russian general, who ranges over the field of battle, is finally shot by Butt when he sees him wipe his backside with a 'sob of tunf' after defecating. The gesture after the evacuation is too much for Butt (in the guise of Buckley), who views this act as an 'instullt to Igorladns.' Incensed, he 'ups with [his] crozzier,' takes aim ('Mirrdo!' – Italian *miro*, I take aim; and French *Merde*), and fires ('Sparro!' – Italian *sparo*, I shoot, fire). Thus is Buckley's explosive shot – which is also his shit/ejaculate – fuelled by the explosive 'gaswind' of the sentence. The general's evacuation, which may also be read as a form of 'ejaculation,' heliotropically provokes Buckley's shit/shot/ejaculation. This scene of erection provoking erection is also another reinscription of the *bander* in the park in I.1 where HCE, in the guise of 'the Willingdone' 'git[s] the band up' (8.34) for the two jinnies, as he simultaneously shows his backside to the three fusiliers (9.23).

Given these explosive and effusive ejaculations of both semen and excrement, it is perhaps not surprising that Issy's footnote calls for something like Mrs Yelverton Barry's handerkerchief, to sop the mess up: 'poliss it off, there's nateswipe, on to your blottom pulper.' The turf therefore acts as a sheet of toilet and/or blotting paper. As turf-paper, these sheets correspond to the paper of the *Wake*an letter through Sheridan Le Fanu's *The House by the Churchyard*. In Le Fanu's book, a sod of turf 'so much as a good sized sheet of letter-paper might cover,' was 'trod and broken' by an intruder during an attempted break-in (224). Turf is always that which is ruined by an intruder, just as it was when the Russian general 'blotted' his backside with it. The national sod of turf, thus connected by Le Fanu's text to a letter, becomes the *Wake*'s 'goodish-sized sheet of letterpaper originating by transhipt from Boston (Mass.)' (111.8–10).

But what is Issy doing when she counsels the reader to 'translate' the gaswind of the Quinet sentence into a sod of turf-letter in order to wipe one's arse? The sod of turf-letter-paper that is itself ignited by the explosive 'gaswind' would seem to bring about the antagonistic and polemical war that destroys cities and calls for the graft of flowers. Behind the letter, there is a cycle of fire that is intimately bound up with the war of ejaculation/evacuation. Even more curious, perhaps, is the fact that after such a war, this writing, this letter survives to wipe up the mess, a utility that would seem to make it into yet another grafted flower. As such, the letter-turf of the Quinet sentence must be both before and after the war. I will return to this enigmatic ring of fire in detail in the last chapter of this analysis. Given all this, the letter offers itself as the long implicit sentence of an 'enigma' (M 243); but it is also an enigma that is bound up with excretion and ejaculation. As such, its rhythm is to be found in the pages of *Glas*, in the very 'gl' of its death-knell (*glas*):

> So the enigma is of the sphingtor, of what will have let the sphigma pass. To squeeze (the text) so that it (*ça*) secretes, repress it with an antileptic (g), the liquid antagonism floods [*écoule*] the coming [*jouissance*]. No

period after gl, a comma and yet, gl remains open, unstopped [*débouché*], ready for all concubinations, all collages. This is not an element; gl debouches toward what is called the element (an embouchure on the ocean [*la mer*], for example.

It is not a word – gl hoists the tongue but does not hold it and always lets the tongue fall back, does not belong to it – even less a name, and hardly a *pro – prénom*, a proper (before the first) name. (236b)

The text that empties itself through rhythmed squeezing draws attention to an important feature of the letter as it is discussed in I.5: its empty envelope. I will discuss this 'sphingtor' and related figures in the next chapter under the heading of the 'feelful thinkamalinks' (613.19) of the Vichian *topics*. These *topics*, I will argue, offer a powerful way to read the allegorization of the bodily rhythms of the imagination.

4 'Feelful thinkamalinks': Vichian Bodies, *Wake*an Bodies

I The Vicissitudes of Production: Discharge/Release

Both divine and human truth are made, but they differ in terms of the way each is made.

Donald Verene

[T]o see science under the optics of the artist, but art under the optics of life.

Nietzsche, preface to 1886 edition of The Birth of Tragedy

In this chapter I will explore how the bodily rhythms arrived at in the last chapter offer an opportunity to graft *Finnegans Wake* onto Vico's formulations of production and the topic. In so doing I will return to both Heidegger's examination of production and Derrida's consideration of metaphor in order to discuss how these formulations can be understood in the mode of non-presence. The textual body as I have been considering it thus far does not conform to the Hegelian operation that 'would suspend and sublate what is outside discourse, logos, the concept, or the idea,' since, as body-text, it '*affirms* the outside' and 'marks the limits of [the] speculative operation' by 'deconstruct[ing] and reduc[ing] to the status of "effects" all the predicates through which speculation appropriates the outside' (D 35). In fact, this body-text insistently announces and affirms the limits of the Hegelian dialectic. In grafting this non-dialectical body onto the processes of the imagination and invention in Vico's *The New Science*, I intend to explore in detail what these processes of this non-dialectical body share with the imagination and what Vico calls 'invention.' For Vico, the imagination would appear to be productive: it 'alters or recreates things.' Invention can either give things 'a new turn' or 'put them into proper arrangement and relationship' (NS 819).[1] As such, invention can mean 'perception, invention, and the faculty of discerning relations between things, which issues on the one hand in analogy, simile, metaphor, and on the other in scientific hypotheses' (Vico, *Autobiography* 216n141). However, it should be possible to both displace and reinscribe the productivity of both the Vichian imagination and invention – insofar as they can alter and give things a new turn – in terms of the scene of catachrestic writing explored by Derrida in his essay 'The White Mythology.' This reinscription and displacement can only take place through something like the intervening 'between-space' of a body: the body offers itself as the site of catachrestic writing and, for Vico, the site where both God and man meet in conatus. I will then go on to explore the 'formal' aspects of Joyce and Vico's bodily writing by considering the ways in which such writing 'empirically' displaces and reinscribes the teleological principles of consciousness and meaning by comparing it to Nietzsche's genealogies of bodily rhythm, pleasure, and 'unpleasure.'

According to Donald Verene, Vico at the beginning of *On the Ancient Wisdom of the Italians* (OAW) divides making into two: 'divine truth is a solid image of things, a kind of plastic art; human truth is a monogram, a flat image, a kind of painting' (*Vico's Science of Imagination* 37).[2] The difference between divine and human truth gives rise to metaphysics, which tries to learn about and understand this difference. But this difference is merely analogical; that is to say, when grasped by metaphysical speculation, human truth stands in a different but analogical relationship to divine truth:

> The divine has an inside relationship to what it makes. It makes the specific forms of nature. Humans are not the makers of these divine forms and we have only an outside relation to things of divine creation. In a world of images our truths are those of the plane. We are painters who through our ingenuity, our own genius, can more and more approximate the plastic through perspective, but our making is still that of the flat surface. To this flat making we have an inside relationship. It is this relationship that approximates the truth of our making to the divine. We must, like the Renaissance painter Paolo Uccello, spend our nights mastering perspective. (37)

The concepts of *verum* and *factum*, or truth and making, undergird these analogical types of making. Both these concepts have a reciprocal meaning, which can, according to Vico, be put in scholastic terms as *'verum et factum convertuntur'* (OAW 3). For Vico, then, God can be usefully grasped as a sculptor, a maker whose being comprehends or contains the things of his making. As the cause of the world, God is thus the knower of its truth; he has an immediate proximity to that which he makes, and it is this very proximity that provides the condition for his knowing the truth of what he has made. Thus, the relationship of the divine maker to what is made may be said to amount to a matter of the utmost intimacy.

It is in view of what I am calling this 'intimacy' that Vico casts about for a branch of human knowledge that might function as a human analogue to the intimacy of divine making; he finds it in mathematics:

> For Vico mathematics is a divine science, not because it discovers the principles by which God created nature, but because it imitates the divine act. In producing the science of geometry man makes his own truth. He creates the point, the line, and the plane out of his own mental ingenuity. The truths of geometry are truths because the mind is their maker, their cause. The mind creates such objects, Vico says, as if it created them from nothing, ex nihilo [OAW, ch. 1, sec. 2]. In mathematical thought something is true only if we can make it from the fundamentals or elements that are themselves directly made by the mind. (VSI 39)

It is for this reason that physics, which takes the divinely made world for its object, is markedly different from mathematics: physical objects lie outside the human sphere of production as material, whereas the mathematical object has no outside. What is of interest here in the intimacy of divine or mathematical making is the fact that its products remain, to a certain extent, 'unproduced,' in that they never become merely produced 'objects': they share the (non)productive space of the hen's writing, Mallarmé's mimic, and Finnegan's 'buildung.' This interest, in its turn, gives rise to a difficulty: at first glance, it might seem that the intimacy of divine making simply cannot open itself up to the sort of auto-affective outside examined in the previous chapters. However, this is not necessarily the case. A preliminary path to the opening up of divine making can be broken by a return to Heidegger's analysis of production carried out in *The Basic Problems of Phenomenology*.

Opening up the intimacy of the Vichian 'productive scene' as it has been laid out above begins with Heidegger's tackling the disruption of intimacy by considering the externality of the producer to the product. Although his analyses have in view the elucidation of the direction and apprehension peculiar to productive comportment of *Da-sein*, I will not pursue this angle here. Rather, I want to follow these analyses only in order to grapple with a certain aspect of 'production,' specifically 'that to which productive activity relates as something which, in and through the producing, is supposed to be extant as finished in *its own self*' (BP 113).

Heidegger interprets what he calls the 'intention' that guides production in terms of the 'absolution' of the product's relation to the producer:

> Not *contrary* to its intention but in *conformity* with it, it releases from this relation this being that is to be produced and that which has been produced. Productive comportment's understanding of the being of the being toward which it is behaving takes this being beforehand as one that is to be released for its own self so as to stand independently on its own account. The *being* [*Sein*] that is *understood in productive comportment* is exactly the *being-in-itself of the product*. (113)

The absolution of the product's relation to the producer marks production *from the outset* with a certain externality, an externality that is 'no longer bound to the productive relation.' This rupture is *already* at work in production; or better, it marks, like the 'look' discussed in chapters 2 and 3, that which is prior to production. It is this rupture, the pre-productive or pre-objective release, that interests me here: that which is marked by this 'finished in *its own self*' can be read as the marginal remains of production that give rise to production of an object without ever becoming produced 'itself.' If Vico's scene of divine production is reread in the light of Heidegger's analysis of production, it becomes possible to say that Vico's divine production must be caught in the space of this 'release': otherwise it would not be production. Even so, this does not alter the fact that in Vichian divine making nothing is released: the reading of divine Vichian making that emerges from its contact with Heidegger's analysis becomes *neither* simple release *nor* simple intimacy. It is this pre-productive rupturing 'release' that I wish to reread in terms of 'the remains' exhumed at the end of chapter 3.

Heidegger's analysis also makes it possible to graft Vichian divine making onto both auto-affection and the imagination through the mechanism of 'Discharge and release' (114). Discharge and release – that is, the action that discharges and releases, and which, as such, always retains a residue of attachment – relate to the non-present structures of auto-affection and correspondence examined above, to the extent that they mark the *'being-in-itself of the product'* without which no 'product' – divine or otherwise – could come to stand. Understood thus, discharge and release form the 'horizon' of what is produced as present product. Since the horizon of discharge and release generates (what is) (the) (present), it cannot itself be 'present,' for the same reasons that imagination cannot, as discussed in chapters 2 and 3. Further, since this 'horizon' is itself constituted as a point where presence relates to non-presence, it corresponds to the *différantial* 'passageway' where the self and other bear an auto-affective relation to each other (as other). Read thus, discharge and release may be understood to reinscribe the phenomenological circle of productive intentionality within a theatre of *différance* where the same can only relate to itself as an externalized other.

When man looks on his geometrically and mathematically produced objects, he becomes God-like precisely because he does not *properly* experience either release or discharge: the man-made products of geometry remain the products of their maker who, as their cause, knows them thoroughly because he knows them intimately. This sets the products of geometry and mathematics off from the products of experimental physics, where, as Verene points out, 'the convertibility of *verum* and *factum* is not possible' (VSI 40). Vico finds what may be termed a sort of 'double intimacy,' where the divine known-cause coincides with the human known-cause in the human world of *The New Science*, which constitutes a sort of middle term between the intimacy of divine making and the intimacy of human making (ibid.). In what follows, I want to suggest that the Vichian conception of divine making explored above can be read as being rooted in Vico's conception of the body as the site where God and man meet in 'conatus,' which 'hold[s] in check the motions impressed on the mind by the body' (NS 341). However, before coming to this body and conatus, one must pass through the Vichian 'topic.'

The point of contact between two concepts is, says Verene, the topic, which is metaphoric and preconceptual and pre-logical insofar as it is given by the imagination:

Topics is the art of locating the connecting link between concepts, the art of the 'middle term' [Vico, *Study Methods*, 15]. A mind trained in conceptual clarity is flat and inelegant because it lacks the perspective possible through metaphor ... Vico knows that any inference done by the mind at the conceptual level presupposes the powers of imagination and memory to create topics. In the widest sense this requires the creation of the *sensus communis*,[3] the ultimate context within which any piece of conceptual reasoning is meaningful. Logic does not create the meanings of its terms; it uses them. In the narrower sense this means that the 'middle term' of an inference through which the mind can pass from one proposition to another is created by something other than the mind's logical powers. A specific topic is necessary to support the conceptual connection. The mind must see a unity-in-difference, something it learns by the early metaphorical exercise of its powers of imagination and memory. The metaphor is always a unity-in-difference, which is different from an analogical combination of elements. On the conceptual level of thought the metaphor can be transformed into an analogy. But to make an inference and a process of reasoning that can follow from it, the mind must have the power to create the point where two concepts touch, their locus in a middle term. It must produce the *topos* as a concrete from which conceptual discretes can emerge as an inferential structure. (VSI 41)[4]

The 'middle term,' or 'topic,' as I mentioned above, is also that which opens the Vichian system onto Scholasticism:

In several pages of remarks on the meaning of the *verum-factum* principle, Fisch suggests that it is associated with the traditional notion of 'transcendentals' in metaphysics. *Verum* is one of the transcendentals in the medieval conception of metaphysics and is convertible with the others on the traditional list: *ens, unum, verum, bonum* – being, one, true, good. As Fisch points out, the transcendentals are above categories, apply to every category, and refer to the truth of things, not to propositions. Fisch claims *verum* means true in this sense of transcendentals and, more precisely, it means 'intelligible.' The reciprocal identification of *verum* and *factum* is not part of the traditional list, but it has a basis in the medieval doctrine of God as Maker. *Factum*, the made, enters the list because of its convertibility with *ens*, the *ens-factum* principle of God's being, and it follows that what is made is the true or intelligible. What is true or intelligible is intelligible to its maker. (45)

According to Verene and Bergin, Vico then uses the scholastic doctrine of 'God as Maker' to grasp the universe created by God as a sort of divine mathematics. What seems to be occurring however, is a sort of chiasmus: on the one hand, the residue of the divine mode of creation is found in man's mathematical and geometrical creations: this constitutes proof for the divine origins of man. On the other hand, it could be argued that man's mathematical creation becomes the model upon which God's mode of creation is modelled; Vico then, knowingly or unknowingly, exploits the work of the chiasmus to claim that man's mathematical creation shares traits with God's mode of creation. Both scenarios remain equally possible; what is most important here, however, is the fact that it is the imaginative and metaphorical topic as middle term, a sort of non-conceptual tissue, that originarily (con)fuses God's and man's creation: in other words, the imaginative and metaphorical topic is the site where the human and divine criss-cross each other without end. The *verum-factum* principle would seem to come *after* the topic's imaginative confusions. If this is the case, then one may already start to suspect that the topic fabricates an imaginary text that is 'older' than the truth or intelligibility of the concepts of either divine or human production: in the topic, God and man are no longer opposed to each other; with respect to what they make divinely, they are the same. In their topical 'sameness,' both God and man are originarily ruptured and are *already* flowing into each other. And since the scene of the postal imagination has, in chapters 2 and 3, been read in terms of an auto-affective flow where the one turns towards the other, the 'topic' of God and man can be understood to already flow together imaginatively. This also implies that a spontaneous opening has already inscribed the intimacy of God and man. Further, in order to flow into each other, they must also already have been subject to the process of release and discharge. In flowing together, neither has ever been simply 'pure': each already contains the residue of the other. I will try to sketch the rhythm of this opening below.

The topics, insofar as they mark the coming together of God and man, are also the site of Vichian productive writing that opens itself to divine pleasure:

349 Our Science therefore comes to describe at the same time an ideal eternal history traversed in time by the history of every nation in its rise, development, maturity, decline, and fall. Indeed, we make bold to affirm

that he who meditates this Science narrates to himself this ideal eternal history so far as he himself makes it for himself by that proof 'it had, has, and will have to be.' For the first indubitable principle posited above is that this world of nations has certainly been made by men, and its guise must therefore be found within the modifications of our own human mind. And history cannot be more certain than when he who creates the things also narrates them. Now, as geometry, when it constructs the world of quantity out of its elements, or contemplates that world, is creating it for itself, just so does our Science [create for itself the world of nations], but with a reality greater by just so much as the institutions having to do with human affairs are more real than points, lines, surfaces, and figures are. And this very fact is an argument, O reader, that these proofs are of a kind divine and should give thee a divine pleasure, since in God knowledge and creation are one and the same thing.

In the topics, the reader writes him/herself, in a writing without model, wherein writing acts as a sort of 'mathematical geometry.'[5] Similarly, the reader of the hen's letter writes his/her own letter – which is also the letter the hen writes – by going over the 'cardinal' or 'doubtful' 'points' (114.7, 9) where the hen's writing criss-crosses itself. These points not only 'gather' the reader-writer auto-affectively; they also mark the coming together of reader-writer and the hen: in the cardinal points the hen and reader-writer mime the Vichian topics where God and man are both intimate and ruptured. Elsewhere in *The New Science*, Vico recasts these topics in terms of the conatus that restrains human passions:

340 But these first men, who later became the princes of the gentile nations, must have done their thinking under the strong impulsion of violent passions, as beasts do. We must therefore proceed from a vulgar metaphysics [182], such as we shall find the theology of the poets to have been [366], and seek by its aid that frightful thought of some divinity which imposed form and measure on the bestial passions of these lost men and thus transformed them into human passions. From this thought must have sprung the conatus proper to the human will, to hold in check the motions impressed on the mind by the body, so as either to quiet them or altogether, as becomes the wise man, or at least to direct them to better use, as becomes the civil man. This control over the motions of their bodies is certainly an effect of the freedom of human choice, and thus of free will, which is the home seat of all the virtues, and among the others of jus-

tice. When informed by justice, the will is the fount of all that is just and of all the laws dictated by justice. But to impute conatus to bodies is as much as to impute to them freedom to regulate their motions, whereas all bodies are by nature necessary agents.

Conatus is therefore topical: it marks those 'points' where both the god/God[6] and man come together in the checking and restraining of bodily 'motions.' Understood thus, these 'conatus points' stand between humanity and divinity; they are 'real' (that is real according to the *verum-factum* principle) for both the god/God and man. In exercising control over his bodily motions, man meets the god/God in himself as a terrifying divinity. In the criss-cross chiasmus of the conatus point, man 'is' the god/God. The god/God becomes finite, man infinitely extended. Insofar as these conatus points humanize or civilize man, they are the topics that write the 'vulgar metaphysics' of the first founders of humanity as the sensory topics of the poetic genera: 'The first founders of humanity applied themselves to a sensory topics, by which they brought together those properties or qualities or relations of individuals and species which were, so to speak, concrete, and from these poetic genera' (NS 490).

The topics cannot amount to conceptual knowledge because they are both imaginative and sensory. This is remarkably similar to an observation Derrida makes in his examination of Aristotle's *Topics* V, 3, 131b20–30: sensory content always involves a loss of clear and certain knowledge:

> Every object of sensation, when it passes outside the range of sensation, becomes obscure; for it is not clear whether it still exists, because it is comprehended only by sensation. This will be true of such attributes as do not necessarily and always attend upon the subject. For example, he who has stated that it is a property of the sun to be 'the brightest star that moves above the earth' has employed in the property something of a kind which is comprehensible only by sensation, namely 'moving above the earth'; and so the property of the sun would not have been correctly assigned, for it will not be manifest, when the sun sets, whether it is still moving above the earth, because sensation then fails us. (M 250)

If the limitation of sensation always has something to do with the loss of an object's presence, sensation also loses the proper knowledge of something – here, the sun. This loss is what opens the passage between sensation and the loss and openness of metaphor, which is defined by Aristotle as 'giving the thing a name that belongs to something else' (M 231). Metaphor 'risks disrupting the semantic plenitude to which it should belong. Marking the moment of the turn or of the detour [*du tour ou du détour*] during which meaning might seem to venture forth alone, unloosed from the very thing it aims at however, from the truth which attunes it to its referent, metaphor also opens the wandering of the semantic. The sense of a noun, instead of designating the thing which the noun habitually must designate, carries itself elsewhere' (241).

If metaphor and sensation are always thus open, then they provide a clue for the further opening of the Vichian art of the topics. To the extent that the Vichian sensory topics bleed into the topical conatus points where the god/God and man meet, the conatus points can be considered as metaphoric in that they retain a sensory charge:

236 The human mind is naturally inclined by the senses to see itself externally in the body, and only with great difficulty does it come to understand itself by means of reflection.

237 This axiom gives us the universal principle of etymology in all languages: words are carried over from bodies and the properties of bodies to signify the institutions of mind and spirit.

Here Vico explicitly connects the sensory nature of imaginary poetic knowledge to the temporizing structure of auto-affection discussed above. The auto-affection *différance* is precisely the process whereby the 'the human mind' has no choice but to 'see itself externally in the body.' And it is within this auto-affection that disrupts philosophical 'reflection' that Vico's etymology sets about reinscribing the human body's relation to metaphor that has been erased by philosophical language:

405 It is noteworthy that in all languages the greater part of the expressions relating to inanimate things are formed by metaphor from the human body and its parts and from the human sense and passions. Thus, head for top or beginning; the eyes on needles and potatoes; mouth for any opening; the lip of a cup or pitcher; the teeth of a rake, a saw, a comb; the beard of wheat; the tongue of a shoe; the gorge of a river; a neck of land; an arm of the sea; the hands of a clock; heart for centre (the Latins used *umbilicus*, navel, in this sense); the belly of a sail; foot for end or bot-

tom; the flesh of fruits; a vein of rock or mineral; the blood of grapes for wine; the bowels of the earth. Heaven or the sea smiles; the wind whistles; the waves murmur; a body groans under a great weight. The farmers of Latium used to say the fields were thirsty, bore fruit, were swollen with grain; and our rustics speak of plants making love, vines going mad, resinous trees weeping. Innumerable other examples could be collected from all languages. All of which is a consequence of our axiom [120] that man in his ignorance makes himself the rule of the universe, for in the examples cited he has made of himself an entire world. So that, as rational metaphysics teaches that man becomes all things by understanding them (*homo intelligendo fit omnia*), this imaginative metaphysics shows that man becomes all things by *not* understanding them (*homo non intelligendo fit omnia*); and perhaps the latter proposition is truer than the former, for when man understands he extends his mind and takes in things, but when he does not understand he makes the things out of himself and becomes them by transforming himself into them.

Vico's axiom, 'that man in his ignorance makes himself the rule of the universe,' is similar to the extension of a signifier to an apparently unsignifying signified that Derrida finds at work in catachresis. Because Vico refuses the notion of extension on the grounds of his objections to the philosophical idea of the 'extension of the mind' (NS 405), extension must be taken as being bodily: man becomes the measure of all things through the catachrestic extension of his body.

The sensory charge that adheres to all felt or sensory data takes the form of 'poetic genera' (NS 495) through the power of 'invention.' Invention is a power of *memoria* that has the power to change things by giving things 'a new turn' or putting 'them into proper arrangement and relationship' (NS 819). As such, it is virtually indistinguishable from the operation of the Vichian imagination, which has the power to 'alter and recreate' things (ibid.). As I mentioned above, invention can also mean 'perception, invention, and the faculty of discerning relations between things, which issues on the one hand in analogy, simile, metaphor, and on the other in scientific hypotheses' (*Autobiography*, 216n141). Invention is therefore an inherently creative and descriptive way of processing the world, which structures the invention of the topics in an argument. In order for an argument to be persuasive, the orator must seek out 'something that will be generally accepted by a community of hearers. This element of general acceptance gives the argument a locus or place from which to work, without which no argument is meaningful' (VSI 168). Thus, the topic or place (*topos*) in Vico is an example of the '*sensus communis*.' Vichian and Aristotelian topics can therefore be said to be similar to the extent that both are sensory, and may be felt as a commonly held belief that can be kept in mind for the invention of probable arguments.[7] Most important, however, is the fact that the topics are invented by the orator with feeling. Since the topics are also the middle term between God and man in metaphysics, they are not merely the commonly felt points where God and man come together; they are also the site where the gods of the gentes blur with the Christian God. This can be easily seen in Vico's first example of such a middle term of conviction in the figure of Jove. Jove, says Verene, is also 'the first name and first place from which human thought brings itself forth' (168). Invention, which 'invents' the imaginary topic from scratch, then sets about extending the image of Jove outwards, subjecting it all the while to 'new turns' (NS 819). Each new turn extends the topic beyond its proper use by applying it to situations that it was not originally supposed to apply to. These extensions cannot be contained or controlled even by the god/God: he is caught in the random extension of invention's new turns through the very structure of the topic as the middle ground between the god/God and man.

Such a new twisting openness can read read as catachrestic to the extent that it 'concerns first the violent, forced, abusive inscription of a sign, the imposition of a sign upon a meaning which did not yet have its own proper sign in language. So much so that there is no substitution here, no transport of proper signs, but rather the irruptive extension of a sign proper to an idea, a meaning, deprived of their signifier' (M 255). If this mode of catachresis is borne in mind, then Vico's examination of how human thought brings itself forth through the topic and invention gives the slip to the way in which philosophy has, according to Derrida's *Margins*, traditionally interpreted catachresis as 'nontrue metaphor' (M 258). Invention's imaginary and auto-affective productions are incompatible with philosophical interpretation, which, says Derrida, traces the 'the twisting return toward the already-there of a meaning, *production* (of signs, or rather of values), but as *revelation*, unveiling, bringing to light, truth. This is why "forced metaphors" may be, must be "correct and natural"' (M 257). In other words, catachrestic invention begins to fall outside of the philosophically governed field of classical rhetoric and metaphor. Vico's thought would *remain* traditionally philosophical – which is to say rhetorical – if the 'correct and natural' order of forced metaphors were grasped simply as invention's ability to put nature into 'proper arrangement and relationship' (NS 819). That is to say, without a radicalized conception of the extension inherent in invention, the already-there would hang in the mind like a grid without a word.

For Vico, the conatus-topics are inherently generative in that they spin and weave every thread in the entire social and institutional fabric of humanity:

341 ... [M]an in the bestial state desires [*ama*] only his own welfare; having taken wife and begotten children, he desires [*ama*] his own welfare along with that of his family; having entered upon civil life, he desires [*ama*] his own welfare along with that of his city; when its rule is extended over several peoples, he desires (*ama*) his own welfare along with that of the nation; when the nations are united by wars, treaties of peace, alliances, and commerce, he desires [*ama*] his own welfare along with that of the entire human race. In all these circumstances man desires [*ama*] principally his own utility. Therefore it is only by divine providence that he can be held within these institutions to practice justice as a member of the society of family, of the city, and finally of mankind. Unable to attain all the utilities he wishes, he is constrained by these institutions to seek those which are his due; and this is called just. That which regulates all human justice is therefore divine justice, which is administered by divine providence to preserve human society.

Caught in a state of nature, man is consumed by a plain and simple concern with the self and the self's welfare. After a while, man makes the institutions of city, state, nation and eventually all of mankind itself. For Vico, men, even if they are always acting for private utility, end up, in the formation of institutions, observing their social nature. In so doing, they accomplish something other than what they intend (the pursuit of private utility), which (paradoxically) is also the accomplishment of what they intend (the pursuit of private utility). In this way, Vico, even if he does not destroy the value of intention in this theatre of production, at least disrupts it by introducing the mark of unintentionality into intention. Thus, when he makes in this fashion, man's productions give the intentional/unintentional binary the slip, and in pursuing what is natural (private utility), man pursues what is beyond the natural (but which is, nevertheless, still 'within' 'nature'). This structure makes it possible to see the Vichian commonplace 'that law exists in nature' (NS 2).[8]

As I argued above, the body is seen by Vico as the site of the conatus points where the god/God and man write human society, and this same conception is to be found in his conception of education:

> 520 The heroes apprehended with human senses those two truths which make up the whole of economic doctrine, and which were preserved in the two Latin verbs *educere* and *educare*. In the prevailing best usage the first of these applies to the education of the spirit and the second to that of the body. The first, by a learned metaphor, was transferred by the natural philosophers to the bringing forth of forms from matter. For heroic education began to bring forth in a certain way the form of the human soul which had been completely submerged in the huge bodies of the giants, and began likewise to bring forth the form of the human body itself in its just dimensions from the disproportionate giant bodies [524, 692].

Education 'brings forth' the ideals of the human body and soul as a sculptor might, using the sharpened cutting tools of religion and punishment (NS 522–4). As it brings forth human bodies, education leaves behind it a remains: the 'huge bodies of the giants.' These huge bodies remain trapped in their senses, passions, thoughts, and so on. This remainder is non-existence, falsehood, nothingness:

> 378 But the vulgar nature of our civilized minds is so detached from the senses, even in the vulgar, by abstractions corresponding to all the abstract terms our languages abound in, and so refined by the art of writing, and as it were spiritualized by the use of numbers, because even the vulgar know how to count and reckon, that it is naturally beyond our power to form the vast image of this mistress called 'Sympathetic Nature.' Men shape the phrase with their lips but have nothing in their minds; for what they have in mind is falsehood, which is nothing; and their imagination no longer avails to form a vast image. It is equally beyond our power to enter into the vast imagination of those first men, whose minds were not in the least abstract, refined, or spiritualized, because they were entirely immersed in the senses, buffeted by the passions, buried in the body. This is why we can scarcely understand, still less imagine, how those first men thought who first founded gentile humanity.

The origin of poetry lies locked within these vast bodily imaginations that gave rise to idolatry, divination, and sacrifice. And yet, Vico's text retains the traces of the remains of the 'false' giant imaginative bodies that are 'nothing': the remains of these bodies remain to be read in Vico's text. In other words, *The New Science* retains the remains *as* remains (falsehood, nothingness). As such, these bodily remains must also correspond to the imagination – residue as residue – that precedes the civilized and spiritual conceptual mind in that they still give themselves to be read – but only as remains. Not only that, but the residues of these giants cling to the margins of Vico's text all the while he is concerned with the process that 'draws forth' the ideal human body and the human mind. One does not seem to be possible without the other as other; this implies that Vico's text is thoroughly *différantial* since, in drawing the human body and mind forth, he simultaneously draws forth its inassimilable, total other – *as totally other*. Just like that which 'belongs to both the inside and to the outside of the concept,' Vico's *The New Science* is actually a writing that is a *double* science: as such, it 'must be assigned two locations and two sorts of scope' (D 11). Bodies would here also be bound up with the 'mask of empiricism' that Derrida speaks of in *Dissemination*; and that which is written under this mask prevents the sublation of the Hegelian dialectical operation (D 33). To the extent that the totally other remains 'nothing' in Vico, it cannot be said to be produced, or 'set free' as a present being; and it is in this sense that Vico's text becomes yet another scene of the (non)productive praxis discussed in chapter 1:

> What is to be said about this praxis? If to produce is to draw out of darkness, to bring to light, to unveil or to manifest, then this 'practice' does not content itself with the act of making or producing. It cannot be governed by the motif of truth whose very horizon it *frames*, for it is just as rigorously accountable for *non*production, for operations of nullification and deduction, and the working of a certain textual zero. (D 296; Derrida's italics)

Further, it is (non)productive praxis that pushes Vico's text in the direction of catachresis. To the extent that Vico's text is both (non)productive praxis and catachrestic, it is no longer comprehendable within the philosophical framework of metaphor that is governed by the teleological return of meaning.

The destruction of metaphor can also be seen at work in Vico's text particularly around the topic of *educ-ation*: poetic and imaginative praxis is also inherently educational because it is caught up in the play that 'brings or draws forth' the human mind and body (NS 376, 520–1).

At the same time, the process of drawing or bringing forth can be understood to characterize what Vico's text 'is' in that it expressly sets itself the task of drawing forth humanity, starting from 'when the first men began to think humanly' (NS 338, 347), by retracing the poetics of bodily conatus. In other words, drawing forth is the 'metaphor' that names *both* the *form and* the *content* of Vico's entire text. And it is here that the metaphor of education, or drawing forth, is destroyed, because, as Derrida reminds us, this type of generalization ruins metaphor by putting it into an abyss. What Derrida calls the *'abyme'* generalizes according to the form of the heraldic device of *mettre en abyme*, where a shield bears a replica of the whole as a smaller escutcheon on its surface. In French, *abyme* also recalls the verb *abîmer*, to ruin (M 262n73). In other words, this type of generalization ruins (the) metaphor (of drawing forth) because it is forcefully or catachrestically extended to cover the entire ground on which the metaphor itself once stood. Because the Vichian system can be understood to rely upon the figure of drawing forth, those points where it discusses drawing forth destroys the opposition of proper and figurative discourse (M 270–1). The ruined figure of drawing forth asserts its catachresis everywhere something is drawn forth. The conatus points, where *amore* ('desire') constitutes the *différantial* and supplemental middle ground that allows man and the god/God to touch, are the primary sites where such drawing forth takes place. In attempting to describe this imaginative remainder *as such*, Vico goes quite far in the direction of dislocating what Derrida calls the 'white, or anemic, mythology' of philosophy (M 213).

If desire or love (*amore*) is that which draws the body forth, then it may be usefully reread in terms of the *bander* discussed in the previous chapter. The *bander*, which, it will be recalled, is imaginative, postal, doubled, sexually undecidable, prosthetic, and fetishistic,[9] is both the band and the erection: it simultaneously names both the Maggies – the troop of the heliotrope girls who form a ring around Shaun in order to make him erect/ejaculate/speak: 'They pretend to helf while they simply shauted at him sauce to make hims prich' (249.34–5). To the extent that *amore* is both nature and its divine other (law), it may be said to correspond to what the text of *Finnegans Wake* calls the 'onesame power of nature or of spirit' (92.8). For all the reasons I have argued above, one should not be too hasty to see in this 'spirit' a speculative or dialectical formulation. Nature and the spirit of the law supplement each other in the Vichian system, where the wants of man supplement the wants of the god/God, and the course of the history of humanity can be tracked in the modifications of man's wants. *Finnegans Wake* develops this *amore* in the direction of the body when it explores the 'call' that calls the writer to write human history:

> Then, pious Eneas, conformant to the fulminant firman which enjoins on the tremylose terrian that, when the call comes, he shall produce nichthemerically from his unheavenly body a no uncertain quantity of obscene matter not protected by copriright in the United Stars of Ourania or bedeed and bedood and bedang and bedung to him, with this double dye, brought to blood heat, gallic acid on iron ore, through the bowels of his misery, flashly, faithly, nastily, appropriately, this Esuan Menschavik and the first till last alshemist wrote over every square inch of the only foolscap available, his own body, till by its corrosive sublimation one continuous present tense integument slowly unfolded all marryvoising moodmoulded cyclewheeling history (thereby, he said, reflecting from his own individual person-life unlivable, transaccidented through the slow fires of consciousness into a dividual chaos, perilous, potent, common to allflesh, human, only, mortal) but with each word that would not pass away the squidself which he had squirtscreened from the crystalline world waned chagreenold and doriangrayer in its dudhud. This exists that isits after having been said we know. (185.27–86.9)

In hearing the call of *amore* one writes; however, one does not simply write in the present. On the contrary, the scene of writing that Joyce presents here displaces and reinscribes presence – 'the continuous present tense integument' of all 'marryvoising moodmoulded cyclewheeling history' – in the play of the scene of writing. In this scene, Shem hears a 'call,' which, far from simply being something divine, is hard to distinguish from the digestive processes of an alchemical body – after all, ink is here produced 'nichthemerically from his unheavenly body' via the squeezing of the rhythmic contractions of sphincters. Once the ink of history is ready, the artist writes this cyclical and shitty history on the 'only foolscap available,' the skin of 'his own body' to produce what I earlier referred to as a 'cubist historiography.'[10] The scene of writing, therefore, is a scene of bodily writing: the body calls for writing, it produces the ink, and it writes on itself. It is impossible to dissociate the two in Joyce's scene of writing, and it recalls those scenes of auto-affective writing previously discussed in relation to the texts of both Vico and Derrida. The present, such as it is, only comes to pass after the space of a delay, *after* the body-text, after the digestive modifications of the artist's body that is itself the site of the 'corrosive sublimation' of time that eventually issues from the artist's bowels. Only after the textual body, the writing of rhythmic evacuation and *amore*, does there emerge the 'slow fires of consciousness' that, even when they appear, can only refer back to 'a dividual chaos' 'common to allflesh.'

To the extent that the mechanism of discharge and release is bound up with a praxis of (non)production, it opens the pathways between Vico's *The New Science* and both the rhythm of the *Wake*an postal imaginary examined in chapters 2 and 3 and the rhythm of the scene of writing in *Finnegans Wake*. This rhythmic mechanism also opens up a pathway between both Joyce's and Vico's text and 'the remains' that opens the right-hand column of *Glas*:

> Case and scrap [*recoupe*]. What remains of a signature? First case: the signature belongs to the inside of that (picture, relievo, discourse, and so on) which it is presumed to sign. It is in the text, no longer signs, operates as an effect within the object, plays as a piece in what it claims to appropriate or to lead back to its origin. The filiation is lost. The *seing* [signature] is defalcated.
>
> Second case: the signature holds itself, as is generally believed, outside the text. The signature emancipates as well the product that dispenses with the signature, with the name of the father or of the mother the product no longer needs to function. The filiation again gives itself up, is always betrayed by what remarks it.
>
> In this double case the secreted loss of the remain(s) overlaps itself. There would be only excrement. If one wanted to press, the whole text (for example, when it signs itself Genet) would gather itself in such a 'vertical coffin' (*Miracle of the Rose*) as the erection of a *seing*. The text re(ma*ins*) – falls (to the tomb), the signature re(ma*ins*) – falls (tombs) – the text. The signature remain(s) resides and falls (to the tomb). The text labors to give the signature up as lost [*au faire son deuil*]. And reciprocally. Unending overlap [*recoupe*] of noun and verb, of the proper name and the common noun in the case of the cast-off [*rebut*]. (4–5b)

Structurally speaking, the remains of the signature in *Glas* that breaks the 'filiation' of author and work (that is to say, the present-ness of being and phenomenological intentionality) is indissociable from the reading of the mechanism of the discharge and release in relation to the Vichian conception of divine making proposed above. Because the signature (*seing*) is both inside and outside the text, it is never *properly* detached even if filiation is lost, betrayed, and broken by what marks it. The signature's double attachment breaks/binds the affiliation of author/text, and since both 'cases' of the *seing* cross leaving nothing but excrement, the remains of both the signature and text are, from the very first pages of *Glas*, indissociable from excrement. The series of *seing*-excrement-text is that which engulfs presence (the '*is*') in the remains and tombs/falls (French, *tombe*) of the text: 'The text re(ma*ins*) – falls (to the tomb), the signature re(ma*ins*) – falls (tombs) – the text.'

In order to come to grips with what is taking place in *Glas* around the signature and the text with respect to both the fall/tomb and the remains, it is perhaps necessary to invoke once more what Derrida says in *Dissemination* regarding the relations that obtain between the remainder and the fall/tomb (*la tombée*) when he is discussing the written preface/prolegomenon and its relation with the mechanism whereby speculative dialectics sublates its outside in the service of the teleogical return of/to meaning:

> But if something were to remain of the prolegomenon once inscribed and interwoven, something that would not allow itself to be sublated [*relevé*] in the course of philosophical presentation, would that something necessarily take the form of that which *falls away* [*la tombée*]? And what about such a fall? Couldn't it be read otherwise than as the excrement of philosophical essentiality – not in order to sublate it back into the latter, of course, but in order to learn to take it differently into account? (D 11)

Here, the remains, the fall, and excrement all mark the disruption of speculative dialectics. At least part of the point here would involve not seeing excrement solely in terms of that which falls away – *la tombée* – the fall/tomb, which would once again make it into the outside of philosophy to be reappropriated. One must also see in that which the spincteral actions 'produces' – here, excrement – the remains: that which does not simply fall away, that which adheres, not unlike the doubled case of the signature. The remains remain that which *as text* '*affirms* the outside' and 'marks the limits of [the] speculative operation' (D 35). However, insofar as 'text re(ma*ins*) – falls (to the tomb), the signature re(ma*ins*) – falls (tombs) – the text,' the *seing* and text of

Glas are *both* remainder *and* tomb, they 'must be assigned two locations and two sorts of scope' since each 'belongs to both the inside and outside of the concept' (D 11). The text, like Vico's *The New Science*, is once again marked as the site of a double science.[11]

Like text, the excremental signature remains: this is why the text 'labors to give up the signature as lost' – the signature remains. Through the labour of the signature, the text displaces 'proper names,' reinscribing them in 'common nouns': this labour can readily be seen in both *Glas* where, for example, Derrida signs himself in 'the debris of [*débris de*]' (262b) (just as Genet's signature is read in the *genêt*),[12] and in *Finnegans Wake* where Joyce signs in the form of pleasure in 'joyicity' (414.23). The text of *Glas* binds the remains of the signature (*seing*) to an evocation of Heidegger's repeated question about the being (*Sein*) of the thing:[13]

> The great stake of literary discourse – I do say discourse: the patient, crafty, quasi animal or vegetable, untiring, monumental, derisory too, but on the whole holding itself up to derision, transformation of his proper name, *rebus*, into things, into the name of things ...
>
> Of what does the act of 'magnifying' nomination consist? Of giving the form of a common noun to a proper name? Or the inverse? In both cases one (un)names, but is this, in both cases, to appropriate, expropriate, reappropriate? What?
>
> What is a thing? What is the name of a thing? (5b)

Thus does the text of *Glas* set about reinscribing the theatre of production and filiation – in which the signature (*seing*) would always refer back to its bearer – within the scene of shit and discharge. This scene also displaces the theatre of being (*Sein*) in which the thing made would always refers back to the simple 'independence' of a thing as was intended by its maker. The propriety of the proper name – which means or names one thing only – is disrupted by opening it up to the name of things. In this way the author 'signs' the text in a manner that nevertheless breaks filiation. This 'production,' insofar as it does not properly 'release' the product from the producer, corresponds to the praxis discussed above. This praxis plays at discharge and production frames truth as its condition of possibility without getting caught in it. And, to the extent that there is no proper release, this praxis remains a (non)production that dislocates the productive intention and propriety of a language that guarantees the truth of a name or meaning.

The discharge and release of *Glas* hands present production and naming over to the excremental/textual remainder (4b), and the 'little continuous jerks' of 'warm and white' liquid (25b) that saturate the text of *Glas*. The problematic of discharge and release binds naming and 'production' to the rhythmic contraction of the 'sphingtor,' which in turn binds the *cum*/come to excrement: 'So the enigma is of the sphingtor, of what will have let the sphigma pass. To squeeze (the text) so that it (*ça*) secretes, repress it with an antileptic (g), the liquid antagonism floods [*écoule*] the coming [*jouissance*]' (236b). The sphincter is the 'muscular ring normally closing an orifice' (ODEE). It derives from the Greek word *sphigkter*, denoting a band of contractile muscle, which in turn derives from the Greek *sphiggein*, to bind tight.[14] The sphigma, that which the sphingtor 'lets pass,' itself derives from the Greek *sphugmos* or pulse, beat, throb (ODEE). Thus, one comes closer to the 'Remain(s) – to (be) know(n) – what causes shitting' (37b). In this remains, the sphincteral contractions do not only 'cause shitting' – they 'produce' the flood of all manner of (bodily) liquid – and are marked by the residue of that which they 'let pass.' Even though this residue does not *fall away* (D 11), these rhythmic remains (are) also 'flow.' The remains remain that which *as text* '*affirms* the outside' and 'marks the limits of [the] speculative operation' (D 35). The coming/flooding/ flow – somewhat paradoxically – 'remains' by affirming the 'outside,' in an action that does not simply become a 'fall' or a 'tomb': the contradictions here marked by the quotation marks serving to indicate the destruction of 'meaningful' discourse.

These forces converge to form the name of the text of *Glas* itself: 'g' referred to in the text of *Glas* corresponds to the arrest of the closed sphingtor, which must eventually give way to the sphigma, the flow of the letter 'l':

> gl tears the 'body,' 'sex,' 'voice' and 'writing' from the logic of consciousness and representation that guided those debates. While ever remaining a bit-effect (a death-effect) [*effet de mors*] among others, gl remarks in itself as well – whence the transcendental effect, always, of taking part – the angular slash [*coupure*] of the opposition, the differential schiz *and* the flowing [*coulant*] continuum of the couple, the distinction and the copulation unity (for example of the arbitrary and the motivated). It is one of, only one but as party to, the de-terminant sluices, open closed to a rereading of the *Cratylus*.
>
> Socrates feigns to take part. For example: 'And perceiving that the

tongue (*glōtta*) has a gliding movement (*olisthanei*) most in the pronunciation of l (*lambda*), he made the words (*onomase*) *leia* (level), *olisthanein*
(glide) itself, *liparon* (sleek), *kollōdes* (glutinous), and the like to conform
(*aphomoiōn*) to it. Where the gliding of the tongue (*olisthanousēs tēs glōttēs*)
is stopped by the power of g (*antilambanetai ē tou gamma dunamis*) he
reproduced (*apemimēsato*) the *gliskhron* (glutinous), *gluku* (sweet), and
gloiōdes (gluey).' (235–6b)

Together, the 'g' and the 'l' form the rhythm of the imaginary, a scene
that corresponds to that of the sphincter. The strangulation of the
sphincter opens the text to the 'other scene' of the '*Ich*,' or 'snatched
fish body' (TP 157), even as it forms the crossed lines of the *chi*asmatic
'X' discussed in the last two chapters. Thus can the 'X' become 'chi,' or
the Greek letter 'χ,' which can form 'the general intersection of *Glas*'
where 'two death drives cross.' These crossed lines also result in the
'asphyxia of the phallus extracted from the sea and ascending column'
(TP 161).

As such, this rhythm 'names' the *différance* of lifedeath. For Nietzsche, as for Freud, death is immanent in life. Thus, life 'itself' and
death 'itself' can be written only as 'lifedeath.' Derrida does not name
lifedeath until his text on Nietzsche, *Spurs*, but its structural rhythm is
already laid out in an earlier text:

> In *Beyond the Pleasure Principle* Freud writes: 'Under the influence of the
> ego's instincts of self-preservation, the pleasure principle is replaced by
> the reality principle. This latter principle does not abandon the intention
> of ultimately obtaining pleasure, but it nevertheless demands and carries
> into effect the postponement of satisfaction, the abandonment of a num-
> ber of possibilities of gaining satisfaction and the temporary satisfaction
> and the temporary toleration of unpleasure as a step on the long indirect
> road (*Aufschub*) to pleasure.'
>
> Here we are touching on the point of greatest obscurity, on the very
> enigma of *différance*, on precisely that which divides its very concept by
> means of a strange cleavage. (M 19)

The point, however, is not to hurry to a decision between pleasure/
presence/life and unpleasure/absence/death:

> How are we to think *simultaneously*, on the one hand, *différance* as the eco-
> nomic detour which, in the element of the same, always aims at coming

back to the pleasure or the presence that have been deferred by (conscious or unconscious) calculation, and, on the other hand, *différance* as the relation to an impossible presence, as expenditure without reserve, as the irreparable loss of presence, the irreversible use of energy, that is, as the death instinct, and as the entirely other relationship that apparently interrupts every economy? It is evident ... that the economical and noneconomical, the same and the entirely other, etc., cannot be thought *together*. If *différance* is unthinkable in this way, perhaps we should not hasten to make it evident, in the philosophical element of evidentiality which would make short work of dissipating the mirage of illogicalness of *différance* and would do so with the infallibility of calculations that we are all well acquainted with, having precisely recognized their place, necessity and function in the structure of *différance*. (M 19)

The structure of lifedeath where pleasure and unpleasure are intermixed recalls both the 'antherection' of *Glas* and the Quinet sentence in the *Wake*. Antherection is the 'overlap' of the erection' 'by its contrary – in the place of the flower' (130b).

II The Rhythmic Contractions of the *Topics*

In *The New Science*, Vico holds that the position of the *famuli* or *socii*, those in service to the first fathers, was a precarious one, since, at any moment they might be used as sacrificial victims or dismembered for a misunderstood word. Structurally speaking, both these possible results are problems of interpretation. Dismemberment and interpretation – both of which involve cutting – lead in their turn to Vico's continued engagement with birds and interpretation in the auspices. The auspices and their interpretation constitute yet another 'topic,' or conatus point where the problems of text, interpretation, communication, and obedience meet, and without which God and man would be unable to enter into a social and historical contract.

Vico surmises that the *famuli*'s unhappiness with living in constant danger of dismemberment must have led to a desire to overcome this constant peril. In order to try and overcome the danger of this cut, the *famuli* entered into a dispute with the fathers over the interpretation of the auspices. The right to intepret the auspices protected the power of the fathers by guaranteeing them fully legitimate citizenship. This jealously guarded right was the proper code for the interpretation of the auspices, and was kept from the plebs by the fathers (NS 598). The properness of the fathers' interpretation was guaranteed by an unbroken line that connected them to heaven. If the plebs were to become full citizens, then they needed to have access to the auspices, which meant having the right to interpret them. The demand of the plebs can therefore be understood in terms of a plea for generalized interpretation (of the auspices). This plebian demand had two effects. First, it had the effect of showing the interpretation of the fathers was, after all, just a form of human interpretation; it broke the ancient line that connected the fathers to the gods in heaven, and that guaranteed the paternal interpretation of the auspices:

> The ancient Romans must also have had such a Solon [According to Vico, poetic character representing the plebs] among them. For the plebeians in their heroic struggles with the nobles, ... kept saying that the fathers of whom Romulus composed the senate (and from whom these patricians were descended) *non esse caelo demissos*, 'had not come down from heaven'; that is, Jove was equal [just] to all. This is the civil history of the expression *Iupiter omnibus sequus*, into which the learned later read the tenet that all minds are equal and that the differences they take on arise from differences in the organizations of their bodies and in their civil education. By this reflection the Roman plebeians began to achieve equality with the patricians in civil liberty, until they entirely changed the Roman commonwealth from an aristocratic to a popular form. (NS 415)

Thus it was that interpreting a *text* – a text written by the behaviour of birds – became the first site of class unrest. In breaking the fathers' link to heaven, the plebs unleash the radical and revolutionary power of interpretation. The power of interpretation lies in displacing the originality, legitimacy, and primacy of the fathers' correct and proper interpretation and reinscribing it within a more general economy of interpretation. Insurrectionary interpretation reaches past the originality of (one) interpretation. Not only that, but generalized interpretation serves to confirm the auspices as text, since it displaces the filiation of the fathers and gods to the extent that it goes beyond the interpretive will of the fathers who were the gods' putative heirs.

The textual scene of Vico's revolutionary generalization of interpretation can be understood to inform the interpretive strategies used to read the hen's letter in *Finnegans Wake*. Here, the text disrupts the filiation of paternal interpretation and regenders it by inscribing the reader in the position of a young girl:

> Gee up, girly! The quad gos-
> pellers may own the targum but any of the Zingari shoolerim
> may pick a peck of kindlings yet from the sack of auld hensyne.
> (112.6–8)

In wresting the interpretation of the letter from the quadgospellers who 'own' the targum (the authorized translation and interpretation of sacred text), the 'Zingari shoolerim' (Italian, *zingari*, gypsies; shoolerim: shoolers, vagrants, but also German, *Schülerin*, schoolgirls) may also compete for something from the mother-hen's sack. Further, if the 'owners' of the targum correspond to the fathers and their interpretation of the auspices that guaranteed them power, then the 'Zingari shoolerim' correspond to the *famuli* who desire to read it. These were seen as the 'second comers' to society and were regarded by the fathers as no better than vagrants, since they lacked a proper home or property entitlement. From a Vichian perspective, the desire of the 'Zingari shoolerim' corresponds to the plebeian demand for *connubium* – the ability to marry, which could only be celebrated before the auspices.

The breach in the filiation of fatherly interpretation and will comes about through the structure of the sensory and imaginative constitution of the topic itself. In other words, the plebs could disrupt the structure of the animating or divine will that guaranteed the fathers' interpretation only because 'a wholly corporeal imagination' makes possible something like the proper interpretation of the topic in the first place (NS 376, 180). The divine animating will comes *after* the corporeal imagination, which amounts to saying that the corporeal is interpretive, and that the topic only 'exists' at all because it is the (non)product of the corporeal imagination. The corporeal imagination writes the topic *as* (an) interpretation, which is in turn taken to be the will of the divinity. As such, the topic cannot be said to exist in a pristine hermeneutic space that interpretation would then discover because the hermenuetic drive to discover the animating will or intention of the divinity can only be an after-effect of the (written) text. The imagined topic is structurally organized so as to allow other interpretations to supplement those of the fathers. Interpretation of the topic without animating intention is already other than itself as *re*interpretation.

The question now arises: if it is possible to displace the intention and will as the products of an animating consciousness in Vico's corporeal interpretation, is it possible to go even further? After all, we have already seen in previous chapters that, as far as the *Wake* and *Glas* are concerned, the senses always seem to be either impaired or indistinct. In order to confront what may be at issue in these imperfect senses, I propose extending the analysis of the sensory topics in terms of what Nietzsche refers to as 'perceptions in general' (*The Will to Power* 505).[15] For Nietzsche, 'perception,' or what we grasp as the 'sum of all those perceptions the becoming-conscious of which was useful and essential to us and the entire organic process,' does not exhaust 'perceptions in general (e.g., not the electric); this means: we have senses for only a selection of perceptions – those with which we have to concern ourselves in order to preserve ourselves. Consciousness is present only to the extent that consciousness is useful. It cannot be doubted that all sense perceptions are permeated with value judgements (useful and harmful – consequently, pleasant or unpleasant)' (ibid.). When viewed through the Nietzschean lens, general perception opens up a 'beyond' of the senses concerned with self-preservation and consciousness. This beyond would no longer simply be concerned with the life of the organism beyond the narrow confines of consciousness: it would also concern itself with death and 'unconsciousness.' It is on the basis of this Nietzschean 'beyond' of 'perception in general' that I wish return to the *amore* of the plebs' demand beyond a simple desire for self-preservation and its various modifications (cf. NS 341). This extension will perhaps go part of the way towards understanding the Vichian corporeal imagination as it is reworked by the texts of both *Finnegans Wake* and *Glas*, where, as I have already suggested, this lack of concern for self-preservation inscribes and marks the reader of both texts with the mark of a dead Christ. Further, insofar as the desire for self-preservation is displaced in this process, the sensory topics bound to *amore* must themselves be displaced by a 'topics' (if there can still be topics that are no longer simply sensory) that is grounded in 'perception in general.'

The 'gl' of *Glas* – which is composed of the rhythm of the flowing 'l' that tries to protect the organism against the 'skzz' of the strangulating 'g' by doubling to issue a 'gl [to] protect against the schiz that gl produces' (237b), cannot be confined to the sort of conscious or sensory preservation Nietzsche outlines above, precisely because as 'gl' tries to preserve itself, it also repeats the strangulation that puts it into danger to begin with. 'gl' can only try protecting itself from the *différantial* split by doubling itself. In doubling itself in order to protect itself, it also kills itself: the rhythm of constriction and flow tries to bandage the cut of 'skzz,' which it can only bandage as it cuts. The play of 'gl' therefore already exceeds the structure of sensory topic through which an organism shows *amore* for its welfare through a series of value judgments controlled by consciousness. Thus, the rhythm of imaginary discharge and release may be read as a dislocation of the value of consciousness insofar as it is not saturated by self-preservation. Rhythm would therefore correspond to Nietzsche's broader interpretation of life beyond consciousness as the will to power:

> Physiologists should think again before postulating the drive to self-preservation as the cardinal drive in an organic being A living thing desires above all to *vent* its strength – life as such is will to power –: self-preservation is only one of the indirect and most frequent *consequences* of it. – In short, here as everywhere, beware of *superfluous* teleological principles! – such as is the drive to self-preservation (we owe it to Spinoza's inconsistency). For this is a requirement of method, which has essentially to be economy of principles. (*Beyond Good and Evil* 13)[16]

In other words, for Nietzsche, the will to power is not just concerned with the simple 'life' of self-preservation: as such, the will to power dislocates teleology. In displacing teleology, the will to power exceeds the 'conceptual tenor' of the dialectical model of meaning that seeks to reduce text through the saturation of meaning (D 20). Insofar as it is concerned with power, it will forfeit life to gain it:

> The will to power *interprets* (– it is a question of interpretation when an organ is constructed): it defines limits, determines degrees, variations of power. Mere variations in power could not feel themselves as such: there must be present something that wants to grow and interprets the value of whatever else wants to grow. Equal *in that* – In fact, interpretation is itself a means of becoming master of something. (The organic process constantly presupposes interpretations.) (WP 643)

Interpretation, as the will to power, precedes even the sense organs. Without its a-teleology, there could be no sense organs. Interpretation, as Nietzsche formulates it here with reference to the will to power, shapes the organism's very organs, thereby permitting a look beyond what he calls here the 'organic process.' In groping past the organic process the will-to-power – which is also a will to interpretation – radicalizes Vichian interpretation beyond the Vichian interpretation of *amore* and the sensory topics.

As I have already indicated, in *Finnegans Wake*, the dislocation of the value of (self-present) consciousness is to be found inscribed in the textual body. In II.3, the *Wake* associates writing with a certain 'ownconsciousness.' A good example of this 'ownconscious writing' is found in II.2, where Shem writes yet another version of the letter (300.9–301.1). As he writes, his cufflinks are 'ownconsciously grafficking' 'sinister cyclopes after trigamies and spirals' wobbles pursuiting their roving-hamilton selves and godolphing in fairlove' (300.25–8) behind his back. At the same time, the text reveals that Shem's scene of 'ownconscious' writing is simultaneously his brother's scene of writing by inscribing their interactive writing in terms of the 'Same' (Shem) and 'Other' (Shaun) from Plato's *Timaeus* (36b–d).

The scene of writing in this passage is further complicated by a nod to Yeats's *A Vision*, which attempts to separate the mind, the mask, and the body. Here the brothers – Same and Other – try to separate themselves. The 'Other's' (Shaun's) 'creactive mind' (Creative Mind) (300.12–13) tries to 'deleberate' the 'mass' (Mask) from the 'booty of fight' (Body of Fate) (300.14), while the 'Same' (Shem), with the help of the 'bounty of food,' seeks to 'delubberate' his 'corructive mund' of the 'mess' (300.14–16) by 'ownconsciously grafficking' out at least two letters. The inability to separate the mask from the body exerts a pressure on the writer that causes his 'juggaleer's veins (quench his quill!) in his napier scrag' to stand 'out bursthright tamquam taughtropes' (300.34–1.1). As he strains himself further, the 'feacemaker' (301.4) finally squeezes out enough to leave the residue of a text on some toilet paper:

> Dear and he went on to scripple
> gentlemine born, milady bread, he would pen
> for her, he would pine for her, how he would
> patpun fun for all with his frolicky frowner
> so and his glumsome grinner otherso. And how
> are you, waggy? My animal his sorrafool!
> And trieste, ah trieste ate I my liver! *Se non é*
> *vero son trovatore.* O jerry! He was soso, harriot
> all! He was sadfellow, steifel! He was mister-
> mysterion. Like a purate out of pensionee with
> a gouvernament job. All moanday, tearsday,
> wailsday, thumpsday, frightday, shatterday till
> the fear of the Law. Look at this twitches!
> He was quisquis, floored on his plankraft of

shittim wood. Look at him! Sink deep or
touch not the Cartesian spring! Want more
ashes, griper? How diesmal he was lying low
on his rawside laying siege to goblin castle.
And, bezouts that, how hyenesmeal he was
laying him long on his laughside lying sack
to croakpartridge. (Be thou wars Rolaf's intes-
tions, quoths the Bhagavat biskop Leech) Ann
opes tipoo soon ear! If you could me lendtill
my pascol's kondyl, sahib, and the price of a
plate of poultice. Punked. With best apolojigs
and merrymoney thanks to self for all the
clerricals and again begs guerdon for bistris-
pissing on your bunificence. Well wiggy-
wiggywagtail, and how are you,yaggy? With
a capital Tea for Thirst. From here Buvard to
dear Picuchet. Blott. (301.10–2.10)

The process of letter-writing is outlined here in detail. The letter
becomes a piece of faeces ('feace') and of 'shittim wood.' This kind of
writing causes the writer a week-long series of moans, tears, wails,
thumps, frights that leaves the shitter shattered and twitching on
the floor. When the letter finally appears, it only seems to produce a
'Punkt' (German, spot or dot), which the writer 'blotts' the paper with
in an act that simultaneously signs the letter with a brown (tea) stain.[17]

As Shem struggles with constipation, book IV of the *Wake* evokes the
scene of writing as a scene of rhythmic evacuation. Letter-writing, this
time, however, binds the Vichian theme of the wisdom of birds, the
body, and the notion of the remainder as textual excrement in some
eggs:

Our wholemole millwheeling vicociclometer, a tetradoma-
tional gazebocroticon (the 'Mamma Lujah' known to every
schoolboy scandaller, be he Matty, Marky, Lukey or John-a-
Donk), autokinatonetically preprovided with a clappercoupling
smeltingworks exprogressive process, (for the farmer, his son and
their homely codes, known as eggburst, eggblend, eggburial and
hatch-as-hatch can) receives through a portal vein the dialytically
separated elements of precedent decomposition for the verypetpurpose of subsequent recombination so that the heroticisms,

catastrophes and eccentricities transmitted by the ancient legacy
of the past, type by tope, letter from litter, word at ward, with
sendence of sundance, since the days of Plooney and Colum-
cellas when Giacinta, Pervenche and Margaret swayed over the
all-too-ghoulish and illyrical and innumantic in our mutter nation,
all, anastomosically assimilated and preteridentified paraidioti-
cally, in fact, the sameold gamebold adomic structure of our
Finnius the old One, as highly charged with electrons as hophaz-
ards can effective it, may be there for you, Cockalooralooraloo-
menos, when cup, platter and pot come piping hot, as sure as
herself pits hen to paper and there's scribings scrawled on eggs.
Of cause, so! And in effect, as? (614.27–15.11)

This complex passage is of interest here primarily because it identifies
letter-writing with the actions of the body's entrails; this association of
the letter with excretion begins with the characterization of the letter
as 'scribings scrawled on eggs' (615.10). Not only does the egg-letter
recall the auspicial directives of I.5, it also fuses the life-cycle of man –
'the farmer, his son and their homely codes' (614.31–2), who are patterned after the life-cycle of their chickens – 'eggburst, eggblend, eggburial and hatch-as-hatch can' (614.32–3). The *Wake*an 'life' is
patterned on an egg – an *hommelet* – which is indissociable from its
destruction – burst, blent, buried, and hatched – is *mortal*. Insofar as it
is mortal, it recalls what Derrida calls both the trace, the 'mortal germ'
(WD 230), and the disseminative χ, which corresponds to the textuality of 'the preface, as *semen*,' which 'is just as likely to be left out, to
well up and get lost as seminal *différance*, as it is to be reappropriated
into the sublimity of the [dialectical] father' (D 44, translation slightly
modified). In other words, the egg is *différantial* lifedeath; as such it is
neither simply semen nor pure loss since it can give rise to both. Further, 'Finnius the old One' (615.7), insofar as he is the ever-receding
Finnegan, cannot be a dialectical father: the text makes clear that
despite his great age, he is preceded by, prefaced by *textual* mechanisms – both mechanical and bodily – that generate *both* the entire text
of *Finnegans Wake* (the 'smeltingworks exprogressive process,' which
of course recalls Joyce's name for the *Wake* while writing it, the '*Work
in Progress*') and the hen's letter, both of which are here identified with
(her) eggs or her zig-zag Xs. Here, digestion acts upon the more
ancient eggs/Xs to create the 'separated elements of precedent decomposition for the verypetpurpose of subsequent recombination' that

makes his 'sameold gamebold adomic structure' possible: the hen, her eggs/Xs, bodily mechanisms, writing, and so on, are that which the same old atomic structure of the receding father must take for granted. The text once more invokes the textual body, allowing the letter-egg to be simultaneously subjected to both writing and the digestive process. Because the letter-egg is eaten, it is no longer simply worked over by the mind; in being digested, the body's excretory system takes over: blood vessels that are connected to each other by cross-branches in anastomosis feed the larger hepatic portal vein, which 'takes [the] products of digestion from [the] gut to [the] liver' (*Annotations* 614). Other processes of excretion like that of 'dialysis,' hidden in the 'dialytics' of 614.33, then kick in. Dialysis, according to McHugh's *Annotations*, refers not only to the 'separation of colloids and crystalloids,' but also to the process whereby the impurities are filtered from the bloodstream. In the human body, this excretory function is performed by the kidneys.

All of this might be taken to suggest that it is perhaps the egg/X, since eggs/Xs are edible, that precedes digestion. The problem with such an interpretation is that the relationship between the eggs/Xs and digestion is caught in the cycle of a repetition that destroys the possibility on settling on either the body or the egg/X as that which 'comes first': there is only egg-letters and digestion – the textual body, whose excretory process allows the text to both shift and exploit the writing of the Vichian topic, or 'tope' (615.1), converting it into written 'type.' As the text guides the reader from 'tope' to 'type,' the reader discovers the 'letter' in 'litter' (615.1). And yet, there is one more turn to these eggs/Xs. They also give the egg-shells upon which the scribings are scrawled: the eggs/Xs are also indigestible. In being indigestible, they foreground their status as the Christic/excremental remains discussed above and chapters 2 and 3: the remains that remain inassimilable to speculative dialectics. As will become clear momentarily, the eggs/Xs are linked with at least two sets of remains: the shitty ink excreted and the inedible remainder that the shitty-ink writes upon. In the interval of the remains of the egg/Xs the *Wake* writes/is written.

To the extent that letter-writing is thus once again fused with the processes of bodily discharge, its shitty writing can no longer be comprehended by the conscious will, purpose, or intention of a writer-reader. Thus, these processes of discharge do not only overwhelm the values of consciousness and intention; they exceed the opposition of both conscious/unconscious, intentional/unintentional. As such, their 'causality' – 'Of cause, so! And in effect, as?' (615.11) – can be usefully compared to Nietzsche's analysis of what the relation of conscious causal intention to the 'deed' takes for granted. Nietzsche views causal intention, purpose, or motive as but a small part of an action. This results in a doubled structure of action wherein our '"knowledge" and our "deed"' lie 'coldly apart, as if in two different domains' (WP 665). The smallness of purpose or intention in relation to the deed allows it to be grasped as a series of 'interpretations whereby certain points in an event are emphasised and selected at the expense of other points, which, indeed, form the majority' (666). In the chain of an action these 'other points,' which constitute the deed, are of the body and they remain simultaneously parallel but 'coldly apart' from, and incomprehensible to, the realm of conscious intentional reflection. It is these 'other points' that adhere to the Vichian analysis of the imagination of giants in their auto-affective relations with their bodies: 'The [early] human mind is naturally inclined by the senses to see itself externally in the body, and only with great difficulty does it come to understand itself by means of reflection' (NS 236). Reflection ignores the traces of these myriad other points, which nevertheless remain legible. Nietzsche's analysis goes beyond Vico to the extent that he is no longer simply concerned with the senses, but with 'perception in general.'

If one now folds Vico's understanding of God's creation – the physical world of nature – back into the Nietzschean analysis of the will to power that man's organism uses to actually shape the constitution of that organism through the process of interpretation (WP 643), then it becomes possible to say that interpretation as interpretation *makes* the natural body. And, since man's body is a part of the natural world, interpretation makes him even more God-like insofar as he makes something natural through interpretation beyond the senses and self-preservation. Man's organism reinscribes God's creation that was without discharge within the (non)productive praxis of residual discharge. Nietzsche's ruminations on corporeal perception radicalize the possibilities of Vico's art of the topics beyond certain limits imposed by Vico on his own text.

To the extent that it may be reread in a manner that is no longer concerned with simple self-preservation, the *Wake*an art of the topics is no longer either simply Vichian or even concerned with 'topics.' The *Wake*an 'topics' form an art of the topics on the other scene of conscious intention, imposing on the reader a reconsideration of the 'obedient and trained tools' – the organism, the body, and its energies – that conscious intention and interpretation must presuppose (WP 666). These tools are also the 'subordinates' that correspond to 'the enormously greater part' of the energy that the sun 'squanders' (665, 666). These points/tools that do not make a profit are structurally identical to the prefatory text that dialectical philosophy must presuppose. The act of rereading the text of these 'obedient and trained tools' constituted by these myriad 'other points' gropes towards the knowledge of organic nature, a gesture that would appear to fall outside of the (non)productive theatre of the Vichian *verum-factum* principle ('the made is the true'). Physical nature is, as I suggested above, from man's productive point of view, discharged and knowable only to God because it was him, and him only, who made it. Since man did not make nature, Vichian man cannot know it. At this juncture, then, the text of *Finnegans Wake* must be read as radicalizing the Vichian art of the topics in a direction that is no longer simply sensory even as it tries to try to read the organs made by nature through its obsessive preoccupation with the functions and discharge of these natural organs as they constitute the writing practices in the text:

> *Primum opifex, altus prosator, ad terram viviparam et cuncti-*
> *potentem sine ullo pudore nec venia, suscepto pluviali atque discinctis*
> *perizomatis, natibus nudis uti nati fuissent, sese adpropinquans,*
> *flens et gemens, in manum suam evacuavit* (highly prosy, crap in his
> hand, sorry!), *postea, animale nigro exoneratus, classicum pulsans,*
> *stercus proprium, quod appellavit deiectiones suas, in vas olim*
> *honorabile tristitiae posuit, eodem sub invocatione fratrorum gemino-*
> *rum Medardi et Godardi laete ac melliflue minxit,psalmum qui*
> *incipit: Lingua mea calamus scribae velociter scribentis: magna voce*
> *cantitans* (did a piss, says he was dejected, asks to be exonerated),
> *demum ex stercore turpi cum divi Orionis iucunditate mixto, cocto,*
> *frigorique exposito, encaustum sibi fecit indelibile* (faked O'Ryan's,
> the indelible ink). (185.14–26)[18]

The organic discharge here provides the ink, and the body the paper, that Shem the author-forger writes with in so plain a manner. These discharges are perhaps best understood as the gifts of the non-conscious work performed by what are termed organs: discharge comes unwilled, and unbidden, without asking for thanks, through the rhythmic opening of a sphincter; it does not try to fulfil anything like an intention, even if its (non)product begs interpretation.

This understanding of the *Wake*an scene of writing makes it impossible to say that the text constructs the body as an unconscious hanger-on to the business of a more or less fully conscious speaking and writing. The non-conscious body, written and read after Nietzsche and Vico, is inscribed in the *Wake* as text:

> But vicereversing thereout from those palms of perfection to
> anger arbour, treerack monatan, scroucely out of scout of ocean,
> virid with woad, what tornaments of complementary rages rocked
> the divlun from his punchpoll to his tummy's shentre as he dis-
> plaid all the oathword science of his visible disgrace. He was
> feeling so funny and floored for the cue, all over which girls as
> he don't know whose hue. (227.19–25)

Here, the textual body becomes the allegorical site that reworks the Catholic notion of a 'sacrament': an 'outward and visible sign' pointing to 'an inward and spiritual grace' (*A Catechism of Catholic Doctrine* 77).[19] Here, the sacrament is reinscribed in the belly and bodily processes, as the 'oathword science of his visible disgrace,' problematizing the sacrament's calm and assured distinction between an inside/outside, sign/spirit, and visible/invisible in its concern for the 'outward' and 'visible.'

In offering the 'science' of the legible actions of the entrails to be read in this manner, *Finnegans Wake* also recalls the interpretative activities of Vico's Gauls and Druids: 'Caesar reports that the Gauls also offered sacrifices of human victims, and Tacitus in the *Annals* relates of the Britons that the divine science of the Druids (who, according to the conceit of the scholars, were rich in esoteric wisdom) divined the future from the entrails of human victims' (NS 517). In I.7 Shaun, in the guise of a butcher, displays a similar talent for reading the organs and entrails of his brother, Shem the penman:

> [Johns is a different butcher's. Next place you are up town pay
> him a visit. Or better still, come tobuy. You will enjoy cattlemen's
> spring meat. Johns is now quite divorced from baking. Fattens,
> kills, flays, hangs, draws, quarters and pieces. Feel his lambs! Ex!
> Feel how sheap! Exex! His liver too is great value, a spatiality!
> Exexex! COMMUNICATED.] (172.5–10)

Here, Shaun the butcher recalls the eminent spatialist of I.6.11 to the extent that he represents himself as 'spatializing' in his brother's liver. Death is never far away with these twins: Shaun 'kills, flays, draws, quarters and pieces' the meat he sells. He quarters his carcasses in his shop by making X-shaped cuts in their flesh. These cuts, due to their shape, recall the 'pierced butnot punctured' (124.1) carcass of the (split) reader, which exhibits the 'crosskiss' wounds inflicted by the professor's breakfast fork and hen's beak as she 'ygathers' the missing letter-phallus in I.5. In I.7, Shaun's butchery also recalls the figure of 'Pope Adrian' of I.6.11 insofar as his X-shaped cuts also serve to cut Shem off from the Church by 'ex'-communicating him. In the hands of this butcher, Shem becomes an 'abortion':

> [Jymes wishes to hear from wearers of abandoned female cos-
> tumes, gratefully received, wadmel jumper, rather full pair of
> culottes and onthergarmenteries, to start city life together. His
> jymes is out of job, would sit and write. He has lately commited
> one of the then commandments but she will now assist. Superior
> built, domestic, regular layer. Also got the boot. He appreciates
> it. Copies. ABORTISEMENT.] (181.27–33)

As such butchered abortion meat, Shem, at the hands of Shaun, becomes a remainder, a cast-off who suffers from the madness of a 'dislocated reason,' is without work, and is of no use to anybody. The messy residue of this auto-affective scene of fraternal butchery is remarked by one of the washerwomen in I.8, who, unable to get the gore stains out of Shaun's butcher's apron, hangs it in a tree, saying: 'And I'll tie my butcher's apron here. It's suety yet' (213.25).

Shem, Shaun goes on to say, suffers from a 'dislocated reason' (189.30). Shem's reason is dislocated due to compulsive meditation on his 'many scalds and burns and blisters, impetiginous sore and pustules,' which he interprets according to the model of taking the 'auspices of that raven cloud,' and 'by the auguries of rooks in parlament' (189.29–34). Shem's obsession with the auspices and augury then escalates into a desire to kill his 'pure' brother, Immaculatus (191.13), just so he can read his entrails:

> but him
> you laid low with one hand one fine May morning in the Meddle
> of your Might, your bosom foe, because he mussed your speller
> on you or because he cut a pretty figure in the focus of your

frontispecs (not one did you slay, no, but a continent!) to find
out how his innards worked ! (191.28–33)

As I argued above, the scene of legible innards has to do with a
bodily writing composed of a myriad other, non-conscious points that
come down to the actions of what Zarathustra calls the body's entrails:

> You [sentimental hypocrites] too love the earth and the earthly: I have
> seen through you; but there is shame in your love and bad conscience –
> you are like the moon. Your spirit has been persuaded to despise the
> earthly; but your entrails have not yet been persuaded, and they are what
> is strongest in you. And your spirit is ashamed at having given in to your
> entrails, and, to hide from its shame, your spirit sneaks on furtive lying
> paths. (*Thus Spoke Zarathustra*, part II, 'On Immaculate Perception')

The coils of the Zarathustran entrails are the 'feelful thinkamalinks'
(613.19) that precede, support, and carry consciousness, even as they
dislocate its value and processes, particularly the relation of cause and
effect (cf. 615.11). For Nietzsche, the blind prioritization of cause and
effect must be questioned on the grounds that its structure makes possible the fantasy of an animating will, which is given over to having
intentions and purposes. In other words, these hallmarks of consciousness are thought to cause actions:

> In this regard, 'purpose' requires a more vigorous critique: one must
> understand that an action is never caused by a purpose; that purpose and
> means are interpretations whereby certain points in an event are empha-
> sized and selected at the expense of other points, which, indeed, form the
> majority; that every single time something is done with a purpose in view,
> something fundamentally different and other occurs; that every purpo-
> sive action is like the supposed purposiveness of the heat the sun gives
> off: the enormously greater part is squandered. (WP 666)

The critique of an action caused by the effect of a will that looks to
other points and squandering is also a critique of an eidetic model of a
fully present causal intention.

Nietzsche finds a similarly disruptive structure for critiquing cause
and effect in dreams, wherein 'often a whole little novel in which the
dreamer turns up as protagonist' is 'slipped under a particular sensation (for example, one following a far-off cannon shot)':

The sensation endures meanwhile in a kind of resonance: it waits, as it were, until the causal instinct permits it to step into the foreground – now no longer as a chance occurrence, but as 'meaning.' The cannon shot appears in a *causal* mode, in an apparent reversal of time. What is really later, the motivation, is experienced first – and the shot *follows*. What has happened? The representations which were *produced* by a certain state have been misunderstood as its causes.

In fact we do the same thing when awake. Most of our general feelings – every kind of inhibition, pressure, tension, and explosion in the play and counterplay of our organs, and particularly the state of the *nervus sympathicus* – excite our causal instinct: we want to have a reason for feeling this way or that – for feeling bad or for feeling good. (*Twilight of the Idols*, 'The Four Great Errors' 4)[20]

When this sensation is grafted on to Vico's conception of the topics, it becomes possible to see that it is not so much the present experience of Jove's thunder that composes the first topic of poetic history. It is rather the non-present, or non-experiential enduring tremor of a sensation that is always already theorized and mediated as the 'inhibition, pressure, tension, and explosion in the play and counterplay of our organs' that constitutes the originary multiplicity of *topics* in a non-present that reaches beyond the split of consciousness/unconsciousness and culture/nature. This *différantial* play and counterplay of the organic process is, says Nietzsche, a threatening 'unknown.' Against this unknown, and in the interests of self-defence, the dreamer calls upon the balm of 'memory which swings into action in such cases' and 'brings up earlier states of the same kind, together with the causal interpretations associated with them' ('The Four Great Errors' 4). The cause and effect of this kind of memory is the desire for comfort, protection: 'To derive something unknown from something familiar relieves, comforts, and satisfies, besides giving a feeling of power. With the unknown, one is confronted with danger, discomfort, and care; the first instinct is to abolish these states' (ibid., 5). The play and counterplay of the organs is disconcerting and threatening to the organism.

However, this soothing scene of memory cannot be said to correspond to the irruption of shamrock-flowers examined in chapter 3 that come to dress the wounds of history. Like the 'gl' of *Glas*, the irruption of these plants can only ever re-cut the cuts they come to dress precisely because they are composed of the holey fetish writing that 'erects the hole.' The dressing can never be dissociated from the wound. Thus, in the postal imaginary, it is impossible for the reader-writer to separate out from the text an experience of pleasure or pain:

> The normal satisfaction of our drives, e.g., hunger, the sexual drive, the drive to motion, contains in it absolutely nothing depressing; it works rather as an agitation of the feeling of life, as every rhythm of small painful stimuli strengthens it ... This dissatisfaction, instead of making one disgusted with life, is the great stimulus to life.
>   (One could perhaps describe pleasure in general as a rhythm of little unpleasureable stimuli.) (WP 697)

Here Nietzsche names a sort of repression, which is, according to Derrida, an 'absurdity' that 'upsets the logic implicit in all philosophy: it makes it possible for a pleasure to be experienced – by the Ego – as unpleasure' (*The Post Card: From Socrates to Freud and Beyond* 288, 289). Repression can also be understood to structure the Vichian bond of marriage that precedes Hegel's dialectical reading of marriage. I will explore this relation in the next chapter. Here, the repression that bonds as the rhythmic alternation of pleasure and pain contracts itself into the rhythm of the 'continuous little jerks' of *Glas* and the rhythm of the postal imaginary in *Finnegans Wake*. In the *Wake* the letter is encountered by the reader as a 'social something' that 'bowls along bumpily, experiencing a jolting series of prearranged disappointments, down the long lane of (it's as semper as oxhousehumper!) generations, more generations and still more generations' (107.32–5). These 'jolting disappointments' are figured on the textual level as those little cuts made in the 'singleminded men's asylum' (124.7) by the hen's beak, the obeli (120.14), and 'bi tso f b rok en engl a ssan dspl itch ina' (124.7–8) that are 'cayenne-peppercast over the text, calling unnecessary attention to errors, omissions, repetitions and misalignments' (120.14–16).

But there is yet another *Wake*an reinscription of this '*rhythmic sequence of little unpleasureable stimuli*,' associated by Nietzsche with 'the sexual tickling in the act of coitus' (WP 699). It is found in the staccato rhythm of the Vichian stutter. The roll of thunder caused the first men, by way of protecting themselves, to 'subject themselves to a higher power which they imagined as Jove' (NS 1097). Such men were caught

> between the powerful restraints of frightful superstition and the goading stimuli of bestial lust (which must have been extremely violent in such men), as they felt the aspect of the heavens to be terrible to them and

hence to thwart their use of venery, they had to hold in conatus the impe-
tus of the bodily motions of lust [340, 504]. Thus they began to use human
liberty, which consists in holding in check the motions of concupiscence
and giving them another direction; for since this liberty does not come
from the body, whence comes concupiscence, it must come from the mind
and is therefore properly human. The new direction took the form of forc-
ibly seizing their women, who were naturally shy and unruly, dragging
them into their caves, and, in order to have intercourse with them, keeping them there as perpetual lifelong companions. Thus with the first
human, which is to say chaste and religious, couplings, they gave a beginning to matrimony. Thereby they became certain fathers of certain children by certain women. (1098)

The roll of thunder inscribes the first men as the site of conatus,
wherein they feel guilt and shame before the god. Since the first men
could only express their 'violent passions by shouting and grumbling'
(377), the roll of thunder seemed to them to be the expression of violent
passions by the sky, which they 'pictured to themselves as a great animated body' (377). The thunder causes them to feel ashamed of their
open promiscuity, and they try to make their sexual activity more
pleasing to the god by consecrating it in marriage. In other words, the
shock of thunder, the thundering voice of the god's disapproval, permits sexual pleasure to be experienced as something unpleasureable,
and as such it opens the detour of conatus.

   In the face of this feeling of shock, the first men begin to talk, imitating onomatopoeically what they heard in the sky (NS 447): 'Human
words were formed ... from interjections, which are sounds articulated
under the impulse of violent passions. In all languages these are monosyllables. Thus it is not beyond likelihood that, when wonder had been
awakened in men by the first thunderbolts, these interjections of Jove
should give birth to one produced by the human voice: *pa!*; and that
this should be doubled: *pape!*' (NS 448). Vico here imagines a wonderfully complex primal scene where the human response to the shock
created by a roll of thunder takes the form of 'processual mimesis'[21]
that allows itself to be read as a form of repetition compulsion. The
human voice repeats and reproduces the trauma of the thunderous in
the syllable '*pa!*' but as it does so, it doubles the traumatic sound as
'*pape!*' In this scene, it is as if the repetition calls for another repetition
that repeats the 'first.' In so doing, the first human voice tries to apotro-
paically protect itself against that shock. As Vico makes explicitly clear,

this form of protection is lodged in the repeated interjections reproduced by the voice, which can only double that which it hears and
reproduces in its reproduction, in a sort of verbal embroidery. This
doubling is also what permits the interpretation of the auspices by the
fathers to be disputed by the plebs in their demand for *connubium*. The
trauma of the thunder calls for *connubium* and speech. But because
speech and *connubium* repeat the trauma – the *pa!* of thunder becomes
the stuttered and repeated *pape!* of human speech – in trying to cope
with it, the trauma is never over with, and is constantly re-enacted as
such. This reiterative *connubium* is represented as such in setion III.4 of
the *Wake*, which tries seven times to paint a picture of $\triangle$ and Ш[22] in the
marriage bed (555.5–58.31), before finally arriving at a more stable
view in book IV, which still rumbles:

> Pharoah with fairy, two
> lie, let them! Yet they wend it back, qual his leif, himmertality,
> bullseaboob and rivishy divil, light in hand, helm on high, to
> peekaboo durk the thicket of slumbwhere, till their hour with
> their scene be struck for ever and the book of the dates he close,
> he clasp and she and she seegn her tour d'adieu, Pervinca calling,
> Soloscar hears. (O Sheem! O Shaam!), and gentle Isad Ysut gag,
> flispering in the nightleaves flattery, dinsiduously, to Finnegan,
> to sin again and to make grim grandma grunt and grin again
> while the first grey streaks steal silvering by for to mock their
> quarrels in dollymount tumbling. (580.12–22)

Such iterability opens speech and *connubium* to renegotiation and reinterpretation, shaping in its very form the guilty mute speech of the first
men: 'Mutes utter formless sounds by singing, and stammerers by
singing teach their tongues to pronounce' (NS 228). Such stammering
first speech finds its way into *Finnegans Wake* also as the result of 'the
root of some funner's stotter' (96.31).

Finnegans Wake brings the reiterative stuttering of the organism into
alignment with the scene of a recalled trauma in I.1, which, as I pointed
out in chapter 3, explores Mutt's stuttered attempt to recover from the
'hauhauhauhaudibble' peal of thunder (16.14–18). The 'horrible' thing
that Mutt 'remembers' causes him to 'trumple' anew with fear: 'Urp,
Boohooru! Booru Usurp! I trumple from rath in mine mines when I
rimimirim!' (16.26–28). In other words, Mutt both stutters and shudders at the image of this thunderer conjured by his 'mines I.' If one

takes Nietzsche's word that the *différantial* play and counterplay of the organic process is a threatening unknown, then the stutter – as the *Wake* (re)formulates it here – can itself be read as the *différantial* relation of the known to the unknown.

This *différantial* memory is therefore not the comforting sort of memory 'which swings into action in such cases' (Nietzsche, 'The Four Great Errors' 4). The comfort of memory tries, as I mentioned above, to bring up earlier states of the same kind, together with the causal interpretations associated with them, in an effort to relieve the discomfort of the *différantial* play in the organic process. It attempts to derive the unknown from the known. In the text of the *Wake*, this comforting memory is always already affected by the irruption of its disruptive and *différantial* other. Just like the irruption of the shamrock-flowers, this other makes itself felt in a scene of originary doubling that calls the 'original' trauma into question. The act of remembering the original shock only (re)produces it in the effort to abolish it. This (re)production itself calls for another (re)production in an attempt to derive comfort, and so on. In this way, the comforting memory of cause and effect fails. The failure of soothing memory is marked throughout the text by the obsessively recurrent textual motif in the *Wake* that denotes all those things that go 'doublin their mumper all the time' (3.21–2). 'Doublin' allows itself be read as a scene that vainly attempts to overcome the wounds of difference through a memory that can only ever dismember itself in the effort to re-member.

The *Wake* explicitly connects rhythmic 'stottering' to the operation of the imagination when it exhorts its reader to imagine the Museyroom episode's primal scene of the 'sinful' encounter between HCE, a 'stotterer,' and two women and three men in the Phoenix Park:

> Imagine twee cweamy wosen. Suppwose
> you get a beautiful thought and cull them sylvias sub silence.
> Then inmaggin a stotterer. Suppoutre him to been one bigger-
> master Omnibil. Then lustily (tutu the font and tritt on the boks-
> woods like gay feeters's dance) immengine up to three longly
> lurking lobstarts. (337.16–21)

This scene is the very one that causes the vicious cycle of rumour that the hen tries to quash by writing the letter. According to James Atherton, stuttering implies 'guilt' and a 'fall' from 'innocence' (*The Books at the* Wake 31). In this way the 'stotter' doubles for the originary 'totter' from the ladder that gets the whole book under way (3.15–24).

The stuttering of guilt, with its reiterative series of jolts, is formed by the brittleness of the imagination, which does not necessarily belong to the father:

> Sonly all in your imagination, dim. Poor little brittle magic
> nation, dim of mind! Shoe to me now, dear! Shoom of me! While
> elvery stream winds seling on for to keep this barrel of bounty
> rolling and the nightmail afarfrom morning nears. (565.29–32)

In keeping the non-present, reiterative, echoing roll of thunder rumbling, the imagination is brittle, shattered, and shattering, but it also pulls together in a 'togethergush,' so as to create the guiltily reiterated image of *connubium* that toys with the four Aristotelian causes (581.15–36). And it is this (s)tottering that is very much of the body:

> Well, even should not the framing up of such figments in the
> evidential order bring the true truth to light as fortuitously as
> a dim seer's setting of a starchart might (heaven helping it!) un-
> cover the nakedness of an unknown body in the fields of blue
> or as forehearingly as the sibspeeches of all mankind have foli-
> ated (earth seizing them!) from the root of some funner's stotter
> all the soundest sense to be found immense our special mentalists
> now holds (*securus iudicat orbis terrarum*) that by such playing
> possum our hagious curious encestor bestly saved his brush with
> his posterity, you, charming coparcenors, us, heirs of his tailsie.
> (96.26–35)

For the *Wake*, as for Vico, the 'sibspeeches' take root in the genus of 'some funner's stotter' that ironically and abysmally gives 'all the soundest sense to be found immense,' which is, in turn, attached by the text to the uncovered 'nakedness of an unknown body.' What is the reader to make of this unknown naked body? Can it be construed along the lines of a metaphoric home? Does it offer a genealogical checkpoint that would arrest for once and for all the play of the long implicit sentence of *différance* in some sort of bodily truth?

The body is neither a metaphoric home nor a genealogical checkpoint that would act as a guard rail to halt the play of *différance*. The scene as it occurs here corresponds to Vico's imaginary composition of the emergence of man's first speech. As such, it may also be taken as the very first scene of writing that composes the first men, first speech, the first sensory topic. But I have already indicated how the consciousness of the first sensory topic is purchased at the expense of the silence of a host of other bodily *topics*. In this way, the unknown naked body can only present itself as the *différantial* play of *topics*, which is to say, it cannot appear according to the modes of presence at all. It is written and cannot bring *différance* to a halt because it is composed by it. It is precisely this *différance* that permits the stutter to graft itself onto the series of little jerks of ejaculatory monosyllables made by Joyce's Vichian man, Tim Finnegan, who perpetually relives, without ever relieving, his traumatic fall into shame. But even this 'fall' remains suspended: man 'stotters' but does not fall. The rhythm of this scream may be usefully compared to what Nietzsche called above the repressive 'sexual tickling in the act of coitus' (WP 699).

Nietzsche's theoretical project of following 'every kind of inhibition, pressure, tension, and explosion in the play and counterplay of our organs' ('The Four Great Errors' 4) thus offers a tremendously useful way of expanding Vico's art of the topics beyond the *ama* of self-preservation in the sensory topics. This exploration and exploitation of the topics, as it turns out, is already mapped and developed as such by the text of *Finnegans Wake* in its reinscription of Vico's conception of conatus, auspicial sacrifice, the constipated mode of production, the process of education, and the rhythmic ejaculatory stuttering of mutes. These reinscriptions toy with the written body by opening up the interpretability or, better, legibility of its entrails and discharge. The rhythm of peristalsis and the sphincter constitute the last stop on the route of discharge. The sphincter is that constrictive holding in of the sphigma that must eventually yield because it cannot hold forever: its constrictive squeeze, even as it holds, is always moving in the direction of an expulsion, rather than an interiorization. But there is another aspect of rhythmic expulsion by the sphincter that has yet to be discussed. That scene is birth, where yet another sphigma passes. I will turn to this scene in the course of the final two chapters under the respective titles of 'Imagination, Representation, and Religion' and 'The Remains of Time.'

5 Imagination, Representation, and Religion

I Conatus ... Repression

In the previous chapter I argued that *Finnegans Wake* radicalizes Vico's conceptions of the art of the topics and the bodily imagination. Because the scene of writing and reading in the *Wake* takes into account the death and mutilation of the reader-writer, it became necessary to seek out a more radical art of the topics beyond the *amore* of simple self-preservation in Vico. Nietzsche's will to power provided the framework for that radical extension of Vico's topics. This extension of Vico via Nietzsche, however, should in no way be taken as a rejection of Vico's text or the art of the topics. To the extent that the topics are bound up with the imagination that shapes primary operation of the human mind (NS 496, 699) that auto-affectively sees itself externally in a body (236), Vico's analysis remains absolutely indispenable for this study. Increasingly, over the course of the remaining two chapters, both Vico's text and Joyce's use of it in *Finnegans Wake*, will assume something of the status of a 'commentary' on Hegel's speculative philosophy. And it is this status of commentrary that will bind *Glas* and the *Wake* together, permitting a much broader conception of their shared textuality.

In order to illustrate this broadened conception of the shared textuality of Joyce and Derrida, I want to turn my attention once again to where God and man meet in the bodily tension of the 'conatus points' (NS 340), where man writes himself. This process of bodily writing is, as I have been arguing, incommensurable with philosophical reflection in that its imaginary nature is the exercise of judgment without reflection (NS 184–8). In particular, I wish to consider what these conatus points share with the process that *Glas* calls 'repression.' 'Repression,' however, cannot simply be understood in the psychoanalytical sense of 'repression,' which would leave an unreconstructed opposition between consciousness and unconsciousness intact. Rather, 'repression' here is a type of 're-strict-ure' that 'remains a confused imagination' (191a). Since the text of *Glas* examines repression as a structure of 'confused imagination' as a remains that is incommesurable with Hegelian dialectic, connecting repression to Vico's conatus points will make it possible to expand further the non-dialecticizable imaginative writing of *Finnegans Wake*. To that end, the 're-strict-ure' of conatus and repression will be compared to the constrictive rhythm of the *Wake*an imaginary examined above. This comparison, I will argue, may be usefully organized around those responsible for writing the *Wake*'s letter – mother and son(s). Further, this comparison will also make it possible to explore how the writing of conatus-repression intervenes in the speculative dialectics of marriage, the family and religion through a *différantial* relation that imaginatively relates dialectical knowledge to the unknown (M 19). Finally, in concluding this chapter, I will argue that since conatus/repression precedes speculative dialectics, it weaves yet more of that textual or written remainder/excess that, even though dialectics tries to master it by saturating it with the teleology of meaning, cannot be appropriated by dialectical thought.

Commentary: Points ... Bands

To the extent that one continues to consider the art of the topics as an art of the middle term without comment or commentary, one perpetuates the Hegelian dialectic, because that dialectic is a powerful philosophy of the middle understood in terms of consciousness. This can be readily seen, for example, in those passages of *Glas* that consider the role the middle point plays in the formation of consciousness. Consciousness is primarily eidetic, since it is 'the Idea's or absolute beings's return to self' (108a). Consciousness is also 'spirit's return to itself,' and as such is also 'the simple and immediate contrary of itself': that is, it is both active and passive to the extent that consciousness is what it is conscious of, and therefore is its own 'proper opposite' (118a). Thus, 'as the two opposites *and* the movement of opposition, the differents and the difference, consciousness is *Mitte*, mediation, middle, medium' (ibid.). Like the *Aufhebung* (which means both 'negation' and 'lifting up'), consciousness 'idealizes nature in denying it, produces itself *through* what it denies (or relieves)' (ibid.).

For Hegel, the individual (man and animal) in nature, the 'singularity,' 'rejoins, repairs or reconciles itself with itself within the genus. The individual "continues itself," in another, feels and experiences itself in another,' which begins with 'need and "the feeling of this lack"' (110a). The genus is 'in the individual as a gap [*écart*], a tension (*Spannung*).' The process or operation that consists of 'filling in the gap, of uniting one to the other ... is *copulation*': 'the operation of the genus (*Gattung*), the generic and generative operation' (ibid., Derrida's italics). In the copulation of two individuals of the same species 'the nature of each goes throughout both,' and this effaces their sexes, making them bisexual (ibid.). 'Copulation relieves the difference. *Aufhebung* is very precisely the relation of copulation and the sexual difference' (111a). Consciousness and copulation come together in a topic: 'And in the 'mediation or middle term' of the syllogism is the gap [*écart*] (*Spannung*), the inadequation between the individual and the genus, the necessity for the singular to look for the 'self-feeling' in the other' (ibid.). In copulation, male and female are not 'opposed as two differents, two terms of the opposition, but as indifference and difference (opposition, division). The sexual difference is the difference between indifference and difference. But each time, in order to relieve itself, *difference* must be determined in/as *opposition*' (112a, Derrida's italics).

Given this, it can readily be seen that a concern for the 'middle,' the gap or tension, in itself, does not yet necessarily escape the clutches of the Hegelian dialectic, since that dialectic capitalizes on the middle term by determining its meaning as consciousness. For *Glas*, this is a problem that is analogous to the rhythm of the dialectic:

> This [dialectical] structure – discontinuous jump, breaking-in and allayed stay in a form open to its own proper negativity – has no outer limit. Thanks to its own inner limit, to this contraction, or this strangulation it gives *itself*, this structure avoids losing itself in abstract determination ...
>
> And this structure organizes in the same stroke the Hegelian text. All commentary is disqualified that, as commentary, would not follow its prescription or would hang about hesitating between explication and rupture, within all the oppositional couples generally maintaining the history of the historians of philosophy. No displacement is possible of this history without displacing ... what in the text called Hegelian imposes

this rule of reading, say a displacement that itself escapes the dialectic law and its strict rhythm ...

The event cannot be as noisy as a bomb, as garish as or blazing as some metal held in the fire. Even were it still an event, here it would be – strict-ure against strict-ure – inapparent and marginal. (107a)

What needs to be carried out, then, is a 'marginal' commentary. Such a commentary would no longer be governed by the prescription of the dialectic, the precipitation and saturating teleology of meaning. '[H]esitating between explication and rupture,' it works quietly in the margins of the dialectic, neither fully explicating Hegel's text, nor explosively rupturing it. It is a commentary that remains bound by the structure of 'strict-ure,' a commentary that remains marginal in order to avoid the 'proper' breaks in the Hegelian text that perpetuate its dialectical system. The commentary would dangle between explication and rupture – as remains – since they are not simply either outside or inside the Hegelian text. The place that begins this commentary would then be the shared notion of a 'point' where something is drawn into a relation with its other.

I want to proceed here by reading what Vico has to say on the conatus points and their relation to religion, marriage, and the family as a marginal commentary on Hegel's speculative dialectics. For Vico, religion, marriage, and the family form the first stages in the heroic education of early man. This education, is, as I argued above, purely imaginative and prior to philosophical reflection. What I want to explore here is the manner in which these stages in Vico's consideration of heroic education can be understood to resist the traditional philosophical readings of these institutions. To the extent that these sites of resistance may be read in the *Wake*, they may be understood to form a series of textual excesses that remain inassimilable to speculative dialectics.

As I argued above, conatus points are always points of restraint caused by the 'frightful thought of some divinity which imposed form and measure on the bestial passions of these lost men and thus transformed them into human passions. From this thought must have sprung the conatus proper to the human will, to hold in check the motions impressed on the mind by the body, so as either to quiet them altogether, as becomes the wise man, or at least to direct them to better use, as becomes the civil man. This control over the motion of their bodies is certainly an effect of human choice, and thus of free will ...

When informed by justice, the will is the fount of all that is just and of all the laws dictated by justice' (NS 340). Man, 'fallen into despair of all the succors of nature, desires something superior to save him' (NS 339). For men under the control of such beastly passions, the awesome sound of thunder that must signal the deity's displeasure gives rise to fear (NS 504). Through the 'bond' of conatus, form, measure, and control bind the body. Men, says Vico, even if they are always acting for private utility, end up, in the formation of institutions, observing their social nature. In so doing, they accomplish something other than what they intend (the pursuit of private utility), which (paradoxically) is also the accomplishment of what they intend (the pursuit of private utility). Thus, in consciously pursuing what is natural (private utility), man unconsciously pursues what is beyond the 'natural' (but which is, nevertheless, still within 'nature'). In other words, Vico's argumentation is not bound by the nature/culture dichotomy.

Nevertheless, an interpretive difficulty arises here that requires some attention. On the one hand, man tires of nature, and turns to divinity. On the other hand, nature is 'an abundance' (NS 1106), and, says Vico, 'law exists in nature' and man's nature is most properly expressed in 'being social' (NS 2). Thus, man becoming tired of nature, is wholly natural, which implies that nature can be understood to step outside itself 'naturally' through the intervention of 'human choice' or 'free will,' which builds first a family, then a city, then a nation-state (NS 2, 341). The logic of conatus would then exemplify what Derrida calls the 'logic of the supplement': on this reading conatus, like the supplement, 'adds itself without adding anything to fill an emptiness which, within fullness, begs to be replaced' (OG 292). However, just as the supplement of conatus can 'first' restrain man into acting socially, there would appear to be little that would stop it from *preventing* man from acting socially; indeed, this seems to be what brings about the catastrophe of the *ricorso* wherein men once again act like beasts in what Vico calls the 'barbarism of reflection':

> 1106 For such peoples, like so many beasts, have fallen into the custom of each man thinking only of his own private interests and have reached the extreme of delicacy, or better, of pride, in which like wild animals they bristle and lash out at the slightest displeasure. Thus no matter how great the throng and press of their bodies, they live like wild beasts in a deep solitude of spirit and will, scarcely any two being able to agree since each follows his own pleasure or caprice ... [T]hrough long centuries of barbar-

ism, rust will consume the misbegotten subtleties of malicious wits that have turned them into beasts made more inhuman by the barbarism of reflection than the first men had been by the barbarism of sense ... [T]he [beasts of the barbarism of reflection], with a base savagery, under soft words and embraces, plot against the life and fortune of friends and intimates. Hence peoples who have reached this point of premeditated malice, when they receive last remedy of providence and are thereby stunned and brutalized, are sensible no longer of comforts, delicacies, pleasures, and pomp, but only of the sheer necessitites of life.

It is possible to see the relaxation of conatus here if one rereads the *ricorso* in the light of what Vico elsewhere refers to as the bond of conatus in terms of a 'force' or 'power' by which 'bodies' 'approach their centers of gravity, as the ancient mechanics had it, or depart from their centers of motion as modern mechanics has it' (NS 340). This description gives the bond of conatus a certain elasticity or tension. Understood in this manner, the supplement of conatus can therefore be understood in terms of sphincteral contractions. Its odd structure makes it possible to say (somewhat paradoxically) that the relaxing of the bonds of conatus is, simultaneously, a restraining of itself. This elastic tension permits the barbarism of reflection to (re)emerge: man, the once social being, restricts his decisions to himself, and is no longer concerned with anything beyond his own self-interest, which, given the analyses in chapter 4, can no longer be understood in terms of simple self-preservation.[1] In what follows, I will first explore how Vichian marriage, religion, and the family is reinscribed in *Finnegans Wake*. I will then consider how this reinscription of Vico's text in the *Wake* relates to the non-dialectical structure that *Glas* calls repression.

In section III.3 of the *Wake*, the four old men finally make contact with the absent Ш in a *séance*, and the absent giant delivers his famous 'Amsatdam' address, which comes from beyond the grave through the medium of his son, Shaun the post. In this address Ш recounts the scene of his first arrival as a Danish invader at the future site of Dublin. He tells of how he tamed the site that would eventually become Dublin. The taming started as soon as he reached the Liffey's mouth: 'I did raft her flumingworthily and did leftlead her overland the pace, from lacksleap up to liffsloup' (547.15–16). Already erect ('But I was firm with her' [547.13]), Ш's arrival at △'s mouth is both sexual and repressive. He forcefully 'rafts' up the narrow opening of the river, binding her, his bride to be, between bridges and banks as she runs from the town of Leixlip on the edge of County Kildare, to the Loopline Bridge. The Loopline is the first bridge on the Liffey moving East to West inland, and carries the train track that rings and loops about Dublin. These rings recall the speculations about ⊔ and △'s marriage by the gossipy washerwomen of I.8:

> Who blocksmitt her saft anvil or yelled lep to her pail? Was her
> banns never loosened in Adam and Eve's or were him and her
> but captain spliced? For mine ether duck I thee drake. And by
> my wildgaze I thee gander. Flowey and Mount on the brink of
> time makes wishes and fears for a happy isthmass. She can show
> all her lines, with love, license to play. And if they don't remarry
> that hook and eye may ! O, passmore that and oxus another!
> (197.11–17)

The marriage as it is celebrated here is complex and threefold. The ceremony is performed over an anvil after the fashion of Gretna Green. △'s 'anvil' is covered in 'saft' (German, juice), just as it is 'blocked' by ⊔, who is now a blacksmith. This association of squeezing a woman with squeezing juice is found elsewhere in the text that links 'lebbensquatch' (270.L4–5) with 'woman squelch' (392.36) to recall Eve with her apple. The anvil then starts to become a ship when the couple are said to be 'spliced' by a captain, an event consistent with ⊔'s nautical wanderings. After this wedding at sea, the two then exchange vows and rings according to the rhythm of the Anglican marriage service, which recalls ⊔'s Protestant ancestry, but the words are substituted with the language of ducks and geese.

However, it is constriction that interests me here. It is first suggested by ⊔'s 'blocking' △'s anvil, and can just as easily be seen to attach to the text's 'happy isthmass.' An isthmus names either a neck of land, or narrow passage, and on looking closer, it can be seen that it is ⊔ who is constricted by Flowey, or △, in the guise of water. The constriction of ⊔ by △ then forms the ring of the wedding banns-bands that squeezes the Isthmus of Sutton, itself doubling for the buried ⊔'s neck. This constriction recalls the scene of the heliotrope outlined above in that Flowey's constriction gives rise to the erection of ⊔'s 'mount,' or Howth Head. This tightening then spreads to affect the 'marriage lines' (which also denote the marriage certificate [*Annotations* 196]) at 196.16. These 'lines' pass through the constriction of a 'hole' in a 'hook's eye.'

Now this hole recalls the nearby constricting hole of the 'O' (196.1) through which this entire watery chapter flows. The restriction gives rise to both an erection – the built city – and the outpouring through the river's mouth bounded by piers and breakwaters, according to the rhythm of the stricturing wedding banns/bands. These rings call forth, according to the postal structure of the heliotrope and *bander* examined above, yet more erections that, in their turn, call for even more rings:

> I upreized my magicianer's puntpole, the tridont
> sired a tritan stock, farruler, and I bade those polyfizzyboisterous
> seas to retire with hemselves from os (rookwards, thou seasea
> stamoror!) and I abridged with domfine norsemanship till I had
> done abate her maidan race, my baresark bride, and knew her
> fleshly when with all my bawdy did I her whorship. (547.22–7)

Here, ⨆ subjects himself to the whore-river-woman in 'whorship' as he 'abates' and 'abridges' her in the form of the Annunciation of the Angel of the Lord gushing forth to tell of his glory:

> I did reform and restore for my smuggy
> piggiesknees, my sweet coolocked, my auburn coyquailing one,
> her paddypalace on the crossknoll with massgo bell, sixton
> clashcloshant, duominous and muezzatinties to commind the fit-
> ful: doom adimdim adoom adimadim: and the oragel of the lauds
> to tellforth's glory: and added thereunto a shallow laver to slub
> out her hellfire and posied windows for her oriel house: gospelly
> pewmillieu, christous pewmillieu: zackbutts babazounded, ollguns
> tararulled: and she sass her nach, chillybombom and forty bon-
> nets, upon the altarstane. May all have mossyhonours! (552.21–30)

Here, HCE sees himself as the coming of the 'oragel of the lauds' (angel and German *Orgel* organ). As such he must again pass through ALP's 'ringasend,'

> the widest circulation round the whole universe. Echolo choree
> choroh choree chorico! How me O my youhou my I youtou to
> I O? Thanks furthermore to modest Miss Glimglow and neat
> Master Mettresson who so kindly profiteered their serwishes as
> demysell of honour and, well, as strainbearer respectively.
> And a cordiallest brief nod of chinchin dankyshin to,well,patient

> ringasend as prevenient (by your leave), to all such occasions,
> detachably replaceable (thanks too! twos intact!). As well as
> his auricular of Malthus, the promethean paratonnerwetter which
> first (Pray go! pray go!) taught love's lightning the way (pity
> shown) to,well,conduct itself (mercy, good shot! only please
> don't mention it!). (585.3–14)

Once again, the constricting mechanics of the ring or band is of both genders. As ш binds and restricts △, he erects the city, but as he does so, he forms the bands (which, as I showed above, are *of* the mother) that erect *her* as *his* 'holey' erection. The building of the city here re-inscribes the scene of the erection of the fetish.

These rings that build cities allude to the site of the first circular sacrificial altars (*arae*, which gives rise to *arable* land [NS 775]) and cities, which were, according to Vico, cleared by the ringed board of the first ploughs:

> For even the philologists say the walls were traced by the founders
> of the cities with the plough, the moldboard of which, by the origins of
> language above discovered [428ff.], must have been first called *urbs*,
> whence the ancient *urbum*, curved. Perhaps *orbis* is from the same ori-
> gin, so that at first *orbis terrae* must have meant any fence made in this
> way, so low that Remus jumped over it to be killed by Romulus and
> thus, as Latin historians narrate, to consecrate with his blood the first
> walls of Rome. (NS 550)

Intruders found on these circular asylum-fields were, like Remus's twin, Romulus, sacrificed and consumed by fire (NS 776). This is the scene of the 'city in the country,' or '*Urbs in Rure*' (551.23), cleared by ш and criss-crossed by his 'terminals four,' the four great railways of Ireland, the 'Geenar, the Greasouwea, the Debwickweck, the Mifgreawis' (552.1–3). These criss-crossed fields 'sept up' his 'twinminsters,' who oppose each other as

>   the pro and the con, my
> stavekirks wove so norcely of peeled wands and attachatouchy
> floodmud, now all loosebrick and stonefest, freely masoned
> arked for covennanters and shinners' rifuge: descent from above
> on us, Hagiasofia of Astralia, our orisons thy nave and absedes,
> our aeone tone aeones thy studvaast vault; Hams, circuitise!

Shemites, retrace!: horns, hush! no barkeys! hereround is't
holied! (553.3–10)

In this way, Ⅲ himself recognizes and declares the sacredness and
emptiness of these traced rings – 'hereround is't holied' – which are
born of the fires set by Hercules to clear the primeval forests and reveal
the clouds to the eyes of those who would take the first auspices (NS
391, 539ff.).[2] But what is clear here is that these fiery rings crop up on
both sides of the opposition (pro and con), and actually clear the way
for opposition.

City building takes place as the scene of squeezes and the contractions that also constitute the banns or bonds of marriage. These
'carnal bridal ring[s]' (U 17.1205–6) that erect the city also allude to the
Vichian bond of marriage, which binds man (in)to the social:

> 513 Juno is called *jugalis*, 'of the yoke,' with reference to the yoke of sol-
> emn matrimony, for which it was called *conjugium* and the married pair
> *conjuges*. She was also known as Lucina, who brings the offspring into the
> light; not natural light, for that is shared by the offspring of the slaves, but
> the civil light by reason of which the nobles are called illustrious. And she
> is jealous with a political jealousy, that from the Romans down to the
> 309th year of Rome excluded the plebs from *connubium*, or lawful mar-
> riage [110, 598].

This, the binding of *connubium*, gives *hereditas* or inheritance (NS 513)
and the article of Roman law that states, 'As the family father has dis-
posed concerning his property and the guardianship of his estate, so
shall it be binding [*legassit*].' 'The disposing was generally called *legare*,
which is a prerogative of sovereigns; thus the heir becomes a "legate"
[legatee] who in inheriting represents the defunct *paterfamilias*' (NS
513).[3] Thus does the binding-bond of Juno once again crop up on the
other side of the gender gap, with the *paterfamilias*.

But the binding bond of *connubium* also crops up on both sides of the
natural-social divide:

> [The] opinion that the sexual unions which certainly take place between
> free men and free women without solemn matrimony are free of natural
> wickedness [i.e., do not offend the law of nature], all the nations of the
> world have branded as false by the human customs with which they all
> religiously celebrate marriages, thereby determining that this sin is bes-

tial, though in venial degree. And for this reason: such parents, since they are held together by no necessary bond of law, will proceed to cast off their natural children. Since their parents may separate at any time, the children, abandoned by both, must lie exposed to be devoured by dogs. If humanity, public or private, does not bring them up, they will have to grow up with no one to teach them religion, language, or any other human custom. So that, as for them, they are bound to cause this world of nations, enriched and adorned by so many fine arts of humanity, to revert to the great ancient forest through which in their nefarious feral wander-ings once roamed the foul beasts of Orpheus, among whom bestial venery was practiced by sons with mothers and by fathers with daughters. This [incest] is the infamous *nefas* of the outlaw world, which Socrates ... tried to prove was forbidden by nature, whereas it is human nature that forbids it; for such relationships are abhorred naturally by all nations, nor were they ever practiced by any save in their last stage of corruptions as among the Persians. (NS 336)

Without the restrictive bond marriage places on nature – the prohibi-tion of incest – human society falls to pieces. Children are abandoned to be consumed by wild dogs. They wallow in their own filth, which re-fertilizes the great forest and (re)starts the cycle of forming giants. In other words, without marriage's tightened grip, there would be no society. The process of prohibition is natural, a natural extinguishing of the natural, which reaches into the socio-cultural: '[B]y His eternal counsel [God] has given us existence through nature, and through nature preserves it to us' (NS 2).

For Vico, matrimony is the first step taken by society to prohibit incest. In *Finnegans Wake* this prohibition appears in the attempt to cur-tail the interpretation of the letter's writing in so far as it which might deflect the crossing of nature/culture towards a certain 'passion':

> And, speaking anent Tiberias and other
> incestuish salacities among gerontophils, a word of warning
> about the tenderloined passion hinted at. Some softnosed per-
> user might mayhem take it up erogenously as the usual case of
> spoons, *prostituta in herba* plus dinky pinks deliberatively summer-
> saulting off her bisexycle, at the main entrance of curate's per-
> petual soutane suit with her one to see and awoh! who picks her
> up as gingerly as any balmbearer would to feel whereupon the
> virgin was most hurt and nicely asking: whyre have you been so

grace a mauling and where were you chaste me child? Be who,
farther potential? and so wider but we grisly old Sykos who have
done our unsmiling bit on 'alices, when they were yung and
easily freudened, in the penumbra of the procuring room and
what oracular comepression we have had apply to them! could
(did we care to sell our feebought silence *in camera*) tell our very
moistnostrilled one that *father* in such virgated contexts is not
always that undemonstrative relative (often held up to our con-
tumacy) who settles our hashbill for us and what an innocent all-
abroad's adverb such as Michaelly looks like can be suggestive
of under the pudendascope and, finally, what a neurasthene nympholept, endocrine-pineal typus, of inverted parentage with a
prepossessing drauma present in her past and a priapic urge for
congress with agnates before cognates fundamentally is feeling
for under her lubricitous meiosis when she refers with liking to
some feeler she fancie's face. And Mm. (115.11–35)

Here, the passion in question is related to the incest of a father with a
daughter. But this interpretation is deemed to be 'erogenous.'[4] On this
'incorrect' interpretation, the 'father' in the letter, a 'priest' named
'Father Michael,' becomes the object of his prostitute-daughter's affec-
tions. This interpretation of the passion in the letter, performed by
'grisly old Sykos who have done our unsmiling bit on 'alices, when
they were yung and easily freudened,' is psychoanalytic. In this reading, Father Michael is no longer simply a priest. Rather, he does (at
least) double duty as the father or 'undemonstrative relative' who settles our hashbill. The text then pokes fun at the incestuous insinuations
made by students of psychoanalysis by offering a diagnosis of the
daughter's sexual problems in psycho-babble, where she becomes a
'neurasthene nympholept, endocrine-pineal typus, of inverted parentage.' But as soon as this type of interpretation is advanced, it is
retracted: 'Yet what need to say? 'Tis as human a little story as paper
could well carry ... ' (115.35–6). Thus, the reader would be in error if
s/he were to read this scene as 'erogenous.' But what is happening
here? What exactly is the text shutting down when it declares a psychoanalytic reading that implies an incestuous relationship between
the father and the daughter to be wrong? Could it be trying to shut
down incest itself? If so, it is possible to say that this scene enacts, in a
powerful manner, the incest prohibition, just as Vico's text does. It is
therefore a scene of marriage transcoded.

But neither the repression nor its interpretation takes. They are subject to constant renegotiation, because they are seduced by the 'pineal' gland, a gland that when diseased leads to hypersexuality. In this hypersexuality the reader is exposed to a 'drauma' of hypersexual femininity that rewrites the female 'priapic urge' and the procreation it engenders as a slippery ('lubricitous') meiosis. If meiosis names the 'reduction division of [the] nuclei' in the sexual organs (*Annotations* 115), then the above scene relates the incest prohibition (Vichian marriage itself) to the disruption of both the nature/culture and male/female dichotomies. Because the disrupted dichotomy of male/female always seems to attach itself to the shifting power structures of either the heliotrope or marriage, it should not surprise the reader that the prohibition, as soon as it is uttered, and insofar as it is related to marriage, simultaneously and rhythmically opens itself to the process of its renegotiation. This renegotiation is called for by the plebeian renegotiation of the fathers' contract with heaven in marriage that recalls the traumatic experience lying at the heart of the origin of Vichian marriage and speech: the thundering anger of the god. However, as I argued in chapter 4, the prohibition called for by marriage cannot simply be set once and for all because marriage (re)enacts the trauma over again, which in turn calls for another attempt to soothe the trauma. The contraction of (re)striction is on both sides of the issue.

Shem, in the games chapter, sets about tearing this bond apart when he realizes that he is unable to guess the colour of the Maggies' knickers. His frustrations turn to thoughts of revenge against his parents. To that end, he would

> Go in for scribenery with the satiety of arthurs in S.P.Q.R.ish
> and inform to the old sniggering publicking press and its nation
> of sheepcopers about the whole plighty troth between them, ma-
> lady of milady made melodi of malodi, she, the lalage of lyon-
> esses, and him, her knave arrant. (229.7–11)

The key to dissolving the bond, he reasons, is to start a series of public rumours about the disunity of his parents:

> Maleesh! He would bare to untired world of Leimunconon-
> nulstria (and what a strip poker globbtrottel they pairs would
> looks!) how wholefallows, his guffer, the sabbatarian (might

faction split his beard!), he too had a great big oh in the
megafundum of his tomashunders and how her Lettyshape, his
gummer, that congealed sponsar, she had never cessed at waking
malters among the jemassons since the duft that meataxe delt
her made her microchasm as gap as down low. (229.17–24)

This schismatic writing also splits Shem, the author, in exile. But the
same X that splits the exiled author leaves but a temporary wound.
Shem may 'split' (228.5),

But, by Jove Chronides, Seed of Summ, after at he had bate
his breastplates for, forforget, forforgetting his birdsplace, it was
soon that, that he, that he rehad himself. By a prayer? No, that
comes later. By contrite attrition? Nay, that we passed. Mid
esercizism? So is richt.
And it was so. And Malthos Moramor resumed his soul. With:
Go Ferchios off to Allad out of this! An oldsteinsong. He threwed
his fit up to his aers, rolled his poligone eyes, snivelled from his
snose and blew the guff out of his hornypipe. The hopjoimt jerk
of a ladle broom jig that he learned in locofoco when a redhot
turnspite he. (231.23–33)

Shem 'rehas' his split parts through a strange exercise/exorcism that
throws him into a fit where his feet come up to his ears or arse ('aers'),
and causes him to roll his eyes and spin as if he were on a spit.
In other words, by contracting himself into a ring, Shem starts to
overcome his being split by the exile he imposed upon himself when
he fails to guess the colour of the girls' knickers. His circuit, however, is
only completed when he receives a message calling him out of exile, a
message of love calling him back home:

When (pip!) a message
interfering intermitting interskips from them (pet!) on herzian
waves, (call her venicey names! call her a stell!) a butterfly from
her zipclasped handbag, a wounded dove astarted from, escaping
out her forecotes. Isle wail for yews, O doherlynt! The poetesser.
And around its scorched cap she has twilled a twine of flame to
let the laitiest know she's marrid. And pim it goes backballed. Tot
burns it so leste. A claribel cumbeck to errind. Hers before his
even, posted ere penned. (232.9–17)

The circular message is a letter from the Maggies, who have contracted themselves into Issy. Issy's letter is circular, and bound shut by a band of flame. This band is also a wedding ring that lets Shem know 'she's marrid.' It is only when Shem is called out of exile, called back home, through the circuit of the letter/marriage band or ring that he finds the 'treatment' (232.7–8) that finally cures his split. Thus, exile remains, ultimately, a stage on the return home, facilitated by the circuit of the letter, mirrored here in the wedding band. Exile was a homecoming before it was exile. The wedding band guarantees the return home, the healing of the split. The band is thus found on both sides of the split. As such it must be older than the split, making possible both the split itself and its re-joining.

This band-bond recalls the familiar scene in Vico of the plebeian renegotiation of their bond with their owner-fathers. In order to escape from living in constant fear of dismemberment, the plebeian *famuli* disputed the fathers' natural right to be the sole interpreters of the auspices (NS 598). The disputes were thus an argument for being placed on equal footing as citizens, and, because of this, quickly came to be centred on their being denied '*connubium,* or the right to contract solemn nuptials, whose chief solemnity was the auspices of Jove.' It was *connubium* that 'was the prerogative of the heroes' and guaranteed full legitimacy and citizenship (NS 414, 508). In seeking the right to interpret the auspices and celebrate *connubium*, the plebs sought to have sacrifice sacrifice itself in marriage, for in marriage, as enjoyed by full citizens, the plebs were safe from sacrifice.

But the battleground for interpretation and connubium in Joyce and Derrida can be understood to be bound by the structure of bonds: that is to say, there is always more than one singular bond. The plebs' insistence on their rights meant that the exclusive bond that the fathers enjoyed with heaven had to be broken. As I argued in chapter 4, breaking this exclusive bond found voice in the formula '*non esse caelo demissos,* had not come down from heaven' (NS 415), which meant that the natural interpretation of the auspices was just another, different interpretation, and therefore already open to negotiation. But it also meant that the bond of the fathers with heaven was only capable of being broken on the basis of another contracted bond or band: marriage. It is clear from this that in this dispute, the contraction of the band is found on both sides of the war of interpretation. As such, it must be older than the dispute itself, making both sides possible as positions for the disputants. It is with these doubled scenes of restrictive banding and binding in mind that I now wish to graft onto what the text of *Glas* calls 'repression.' Because *Glas*'s left-hand column (a) deals in great detail with Hegel's dialectic reading of marriage and the family, this graft makes it possible to see how the Vichian and *Wake*an matrimonial conatus provides a non-dialecticizable marginal commentary on the Hegelian dialectic and its relation to marriage.

According to the text of *Glas*, the Hegelian analysis of marriage builds on the analysis of labour with the tool (123a). Labour with the tool gives the structure of 'desire.' Desire is that which 'holds in check the destruction of what it desires.' In other words, it is dialectical and economical in that it wishes to make a profit, wants to 'wants to keep what it wants to lose' (120a); thus, it cannot be the simple annihilation of an object. That is why desire – as desire – can 'never [be] satisfied, and [therein] lies its "practical" structure':

> 'Desire does not come to its satisfaction in its operation of annihilation.' Its object stays, not because it escapes annihilation, ... but because it stays *in* its annihilation. *Desire remains inasmuch as it does not remain.* Operation of *mourning*: idealizing consum(mat)ing. This relation is called labor. Practical consciousness *elaborates* in the place where it annihilates and holds together the two opposites of the contradiction. In this sense labor is the middle (*Mitte*) of the opposition intrinsic to desire. (122a, Derrida's italics)

The practical place of labour, making, production is the 'middle' of desire. In keeping with the powerful metaphorics of production identified in previous chapters, Hegelian marriage interiorizes ('consum[at]es') the 'exteriority' of the tool/implement (123a), and is therefore the 'labor of desire without an instrument.' For Hegel, both marriage and love are indistinguishable from the operation of the *Aufhebung*, since all of them 'relieve' the two sexes by permitting them to 'pass into each other,' which 'constitutes the ideal, the ideality of the ideal' (123a–4a). In the love of marriage, 'desire frees itself from its relationship with enjoyment' and this 'relief' is the '"repression" of the natural pressure' (124a).

It is in this matrimonial context that *Glas* asks, 'How does monogamy intervene in the system opposing ... the masculine and the feminine?' Monogamy interferes as repression, but also as *Aufhebung*:

> Does the heterogeneity of all the restrictions, of all the counterforces of constriction (*Hemmung, Unterdrückung, Zwingen, Bezwingung, zurückdrän-*

gen, Zurücksetzung) always define the species of general negativity, forms of *Aufhebung*, conditions of relief? ... Can repression be thought according to the dialectic? The response is necessarily affirmative ... If one asks: '*what is* repression?' '*what is* the re-strict-ure of repression?' in other words, 'how is that re-strict-ure *to be thought*?' the response is The Dialectic.

But to say that re-strict-ure – under its name repression – today remains a confused imagination, that is perhaps only to designate, in regard to philosophy, what does not let itself be *thought* or even arraigned [*arraisonner*] by a question. The question is already strict-uring, is already girded being. (191a)

What this passage recalls here is the 'strict-ure' of the marginal commentary that marks the formal structure of the Hegel column of *Glas* noted above (107a). It goes on to connect this strict-ure with a doubled form of 'repression' that is at once 'inside' and 'outside' the dialectic. That is, the confused imagination of 'repression' is not thought (*itself*), and it is not thought within the dialectic; not only that, but imaginative repression as re-strict-ure precedes and constitutes the force that the philosophical question *par excellence* – 'what is ... ?'[5] – needs in order to form the strict-ure of a question. The 'confused imagination' of repression or re-strict-ure is, gives (dialectical) thought while remaining outside it. Derrida notes this doubling:

Hegel also condemns 'repression': in the name of freedom of spiritual consciousness, and so on. But – for the same reason – he prescribes the 'repression' of animal pressures, which makes possible spiritual liberation, and so on. One repression for another, one restriction for an erection, one compresses on the one side so that it (*ça*) rises on the other. Repression – here the relief – is not on one side or the other, on the left or the right: it 'is' that relationship between two accounts, the two registers, the two ledgers, the two operations of this economy. (197a)

As such a doubled moment in *Glas*, 'repression' or 're-strict-ure' recalls what I have suggested in the previous chapter about the text, remains, and the signature. Here, repression/re-strict-ure, joins with them to form a growing chain of that which 'must be assigned two locations and two sorts of scope,' since each 'belongs to both the inside and outside of the concept' (D 11). As that which is both inside and outside, these 'doubles' always run the risk of being reappropriated by the negativity of dialectics as *'its own* outside'; but they are also that which belongs to the outside of philosophy in the 'critical gap between the logical or scientific development of philosophy and its empirical or formalist lag' (ibid.).

The empirico-formalist lag of 'repression' is also here explicitly referred to as 'a confused imagination' that cannot be *thought* within the dialectic. It is its status as empirico-formalist that I now wish to consider. 'Empirico-formality' also names the mere formality of a marriage contract in which something is signed, slipping outside of the dialectics of marriage, which is, for Hegel, 'the free inclination of both sexes' (124a). Furthermore, 'marriage excludes any contract. Such an abstract juridical bond could in effect bind persons only to (dead) things, could not by right commit two living freedoms. In marriage there can be no empiric determinations, 'pathological' inclinations, but that is inessential' (124a). The two living freedoms do not need this dead and deadening bond, the 'empiric limitations of freedom' (ibid.). This is why Hegel's philosophy does not need to 'state anything at all about the sex difference between the spouses. Nothing more logical: everything must happen as if the spouses were the same sex, were both bisexual or asexual. The *Aufhebung* has worked' (124–5a).

Derrida suggests that one who comments on sexual difference in marriage remains, like Kant, 'outside' the dialectical interpretation of marriage, 'which has no possible housing in the Hegelian philosophy of spirit' (131a). To the extent that the *Wake* sketches the antagonistic marriage of both HCE and ALP in terms of the constrictive rhythm of the *bander* discussed above, its protagonists could no longer be regarded as '*true* spouses, as the essence of marriage is not accomplished' (ibid., Derrida's italics). The *Wake*an take on marriage, like Kant's, 'would remain no further along than this nondialectical conjunction of an empiricism and a formalism,' stuck at the level of description without understanding essence. It piles trait upon trait in its description, since it does proceed 'from the essential unity of marriage,' all it can do is accumulate and isolate 'without order the descriptive traits' (131a). One would also remain confined to the empirico-formalist wilderness of the signature and the signed contract: 'To confine oneself to the signature's formality is to believe that marriage (or divorce) depends on that formality, is to deny the ethics of love and return to animal sexuality ... To rivet oneself to the contractual formality of the signifier is then to be held back by instinct or to let nature – without restriction – take its course: the complicity of formal-

ism and of empiricism is confirmed once again' (196a). The formality
of the signature retards marriage because it lacks the inner feeling that
makes the bond both spiritual and sincere.[6] However, on closer inspection, it would appear that Hegel's idea of repression in the context of
marriage is no longer simply that of simply repressing the animal:

> When it 'goes out of its naturalness,' monogamous conjugal conscious-
> ness escapes immodesty; which could let it be thought that immodesty is
> natural and that going out of nature suffices for recovering it. And yet
> immodesty supposes the understanding, the formal relation with the con-
> cept and the law. Immodesty is not only sensible, natural, inferior, an
> object more base than another; its baseness is the object of an interdict, of
> a repression whose counterforce (of law) does not have the form of dis-
> tancing from nature, of a simple raising above animality, in the ontologi-
> cal hierarchy, of a negativity. But nothing is ever homogeneous in the
> different ruptures, stances, or saltations of speculative dialectics. Is this
> heterogeneity of the interdict heterogeneous to the *general* (thus homoge-
> neous) heterogeneity of the whole set of the ontological system? Can one
> ever speak of a *general heterogeneity*? Does the interdictory repression only
> introduce a flection of heterogeneity in addition (a reflection of the alter-
> ity)? Or else a heterogeneity that no longer lets itself be interned in a
> reflection?
>
> Since the concept of general heterogeneity is as *impossible* as its con-
> trary, such a question cannot *pose itself*. The question's posit(ion)ing is the
> question's annulment.
>
> ('Hegel''s) *text* is offered (up), open to two responses, to two interpreta-
> tions. It is text, textualizes itself rather, in as much as it lays itself open to
> the grip and weight of two readings, that is to say, lets itself be struck with
> indetermination by the impossible concept, divides itself in two. (198–9a)

Dialectical repression here attempts to repress 'immodesty' that both
treads and fractures the desire to draw a simple line between nature
and culture. The repression of 'immodesty' is therefore neither purely
natural animal sexuality nor simply cultural, since it 'supposes understanding, the formal relation with the concept of the law' – 'contractual
formality.' In aiming to repress 'contractual formality,' Hegel, says
Derrida, does something different to the usual attempts to repress
animality and create a distance from nature. This 'innovation' would
therefore no longer have 'the form ... of a negativity homogeneous to
all the other forms of [dialectical] negativity.' 'Repression' here would

be different from the other forms of Hegelian repression. But this causes a difficulty: does the 'innovation' constitute a just add another bend in speculative reflection or is it inassimilable to that reflection? Derrida suggests that an answer to this question is undecidable, since it is impossible to formulate a 'concept of a *general* (thus homogeneous) heterogeity' to even ask this question. Here, the repression of the empirico-formal-animalistic contractual bond makes clear that 'speculative dialectics always has the form of a general critique of the contract, or at least of the contractual formality, of the *contract* in the *strict* sense' (195a, my emphasis). One can already glimpse, therefore, the non-dialectical strict-ure in the contract, a binding relation with the law that is not filled with spiritual content.

If the contractual bond cannot therefore be dialectically repressed as the product of the animal or the natural, then it reaches towards 'the incest prohibition [which] is at once the example and the pivot [*charnière*]' (199a). This doubleness marks the 'pivot of a system that is contradictory within itself – with a contradiction of which one cannot say whether it operates *in* or *against*. The "opposition" plays two times and with it, each conceptual determination.' In other words, the incest prohibition marks the space of marginal commentary, the space between the two readings of Hegel's text. The incest prohibition 'breaks with nature, and *that is why* it conforms to nature. What appears as formal incoherence ... critically denounces at the same time, but without its knowing, the absence of a concept of nature, or reason, or of freedom, and posits, but without its knowing, the necessity of accounting for [the] "dark feelings" [of incest]' (199a).[7] If the Vichian attempt to break with nature is understood in this way, then the texts of *Finnegans Wake*, *Glas*, and *The New Science* all construct the same site, that of the 'confused imagination,' a site that is 'supplemental':

The supplement adds itself, it is a surplus, a plenitude enriching another plenitude, the *fullest measure of presence* ...

But the supplement supplements. It adds only to replace. It intervenes or insinuates itself *in-the-place-of*; if it fills, it is as one fills a void. If it represents or makes an image, it is by the anterior default of a presence. Compensatory [*suppléant*] and vicarious, the supplement is an adjunct, a subaltern instance which *takes-(the)-place* [*tient-lieu*]. As substitute, it is not simply added to the positivity of a presence, it produces no relief, its place is assigned in the structure by a mark of emptiness. Somewhere, something can be filled up *of itself*, can accomplish itself, only by allowing itself to be filled through sign and proxy. The sign is always the supplement of the thing itself.

This second signification of supplement cannot be separated from the first ... But their common function is shown in this: whether it adds or substitutes itself, the supplement is exterior, outside of the positivity to which it is super-added, alien to that which, in order to be replaced by it, must be other than it. (OG 145)

This play of the supplement is explictly associated by Derrida with the 'catastrophe' of Vico's *ricorsi*, which is incompatible with the dialectical progress of history: 'This play of the supplement, the always open possibility of a catastrophic regression and the annulment of progress, recalls not only Vico's *ricorsi*. Conjugated with what we have called geometric regression, it makes history escape an infinite teleology of the Hegelian type' (OG 298). Understood thus, tension, conatus, supplement, ricorsi, the incest prohibition, and so on, would constitute something of a supplemental and textual chain in the margins of Hegel's dialectic.

The case of the supplemental *ricorsi* is not much different from the crossed 'X' of the letter's writing in *Finnegans Wake*: 'Such crossing is antechristian of course, but the use of the homeborn shillelagh as an aid to calligraphy shows a distinct advance from savagery to barbarism' (114.11–13). The X of the letter's writing alludes to the Vichian 'advance,' which is no 'advance' at all since it devolves into an even more inhuman 'barbarism of reflection' (NS 1106). This serves to explicitly ally the text of the 'oldworld epistola of their weatherings and their marryings and their buryings and their natural selections' (117.27–8) with Vico's imaginative and non-philosophical formulations of the heroic institutions. But the epistola, on 'closer inspection' (107.23–4) also bears the traces of 'some prevision of virtual crime or crimes' (107.25–6). This 'crime' that automatically seems to erase itself as a crime (107.26–8), 'marks' the point where one might see 'a multiplicity of persons' or individuals, which then, 'under the closed eyes of the inspectors,' immediately seem to 'coalesce' into a 'stable somebody' or 'social something.' The slipperiness of this crime that is not a crime, or this multiplicity that is not a multiplicity, seems to mark the shift from individual savagery to society. If, in the Vichian schema, the point where the savage raw nature of the promiscuous giants succumbs to the first conative stirrings of men in society marked by religion (NS 177), and the 'crime or crimes' that the letter refers to also occur at the point where many act as one, then the letter inscribes a simultaneous innocence and guilt at the origin of the social. This point corresponds once more to what Vico considers as the prohibition that inaugurates marriage and the family: that is, the 'natural' (in)junction of the natural in its putative opposite, the socio-cultural (which nevertheless remains 'natural'): '[The] opinion that the sexual unions which certainly take place between free men and free women without solemn matrimony are free of natural wickedness [i.e., do not offend the law of nature], all the nations of the world have branded as false by the human customs with which they all religiously celebrate marriages, thereby determining that this sin is bestial, though in venial degree' (NS 336). The guilt and innocence of sexual union are yoked by conatus in the institution of matrimony.

And yet – and not surprisingly – even this supplemental, confused imagination is always, according to the text of *Glas*, in danger of being dominated once more by the *Aufhebung* in a 'dialectics of nature' (200a). This sentence inscribes the text of *Glas* in the space of analyses of the play of the supplement in Rousseau carried out in *Of Grammatology*.[8] In dealing with the Hegelian text, which continues to 'pick itself up' and continue, even when a 'deconstructed moment' has 'happened,' the supplement remains marginal. As marginal, it is therefore doubled and pivotal in that it occupies two different 'places' simultaneously: the inside and the outside of Hegelian dialectics. In offering commentaries that must remain marginal, and in continuing to explicate the Hegelian text, the text of *Glas* slowly builds a chain of true remains: remains that do not simply fall, but which are 'passed over' or left behind by the Hegelian dialectic. And it is on this cusp, hanging between 'explication and rupture' (107a), that the text of *Glas* dangles yet another thread of the fraying fabric of the dialectic in front of its reader, enticing him/her to pull on it when it asks 'what if the *Aufhebung* were a Christian mother?' (201a). The reinscription of the *Aufhebung* in/as a Christian mother will begin to preoccupy this analysis, since she permits the text of *Glas* to once more inscribe itself in the *Wake* (and vice versa).

II The Holy Family of Text

A blind person can deal with the frame, the canvas, the varnish of a picture; can know the story of painters, the fate of a picture, its price, into what hands it has fallen, and can see nothing of the picture itself.

What obstructs religion in our epoch is that science has not been recon-
ciled with it. Between the two is found a barrier [*cloison*]. (*Glas* 218a)

Before I come to the Christian mother herself, it is perhaps useful to
linger over some of the other explorations of female figures in the text
of *Glas* that are, quite often, associated with irony and laughter. As
such, the female figure's laughter may be understood to recall the
laughter of both the Bataillean sovereign and that which Derrida hears
in the *Wake*. The woman's laughter takes place in the context of the
Hegelian analysis of the dialectical opposition of the natural, divine,
nocturnal, and feminine law of singularity and the social, human, diur-
nal, and masculine law of universality, which is also an opposition of
the sexes (142a, 169–70a). This dialectic is framed by the dramatic conflict between Antigone and Creon in Sophocles' *Antigone*. Antigone,
the embodiment of the feminine law of the woman, is allied to both the
unconscious and 'the night of the subterranean world.' Antigone's law
is opposed to the 'masculine, conscious law' of civil bourgeois society,
embodied by Creon. The space in which this battle takes place is the
family, which acts as a sort of a *charnière* that prevents the family from
being completely relieved without remains. The difficulties for the dialectic start when the 'copulation of these two "opposite movements"
appeases nothing. There's no reconciliation.' In the space of this unresolved opposition, 'tragedy begins' because one acts ('operation is
action' [171a]) under the jurisdiction of two laws in such a way as to
'produce' both consciousness and unconsciousness. If the 'ethical life'
(*Sittlichkeit*) is supposed to unite the 'two laws,' nevertheless 'the operation always comes down to a singular individual. So the operation
always recreates the split, the opposition of the divine and the human,
of the woman and the man. Each on his or her side, Antigone and
Creon hear or read only one law; they lack and betray the other' (ibid.).
This split is 'why the unconscious does not let itself be reduced.' The
'unconscious constitutes itself, in the order of *Sittlichkeit*, from this
double articulation of the law: one can never know what the other does
on the two sides at once, on the side of human law and on the side of
divine law, that is, on the side of man and on the side of woman. The
other counts' (ibid.). In acting, then, both the conscious and the unconscious are generated: there are always two texts, one supplementing
the other, and it is in acting that one applies pressure, strict-ure: 'No
operation can actualize itself in the (day)light of consciousness without
having structurally to restrain (shall we say repress, gird, suppress,

push back into darkness, un-think, un-know) the other law' (ibid.). The structure of the law is thus indissociable from the motif of strict-ure discussed in the previous section.

The structure of the law – 'no law without double law, without opposition' – simultaneously gives rise to both crime and guilt because, even if one is obeying the law, one is always already acting against (the 'other') law (172a). This gives rise to the by now familiar structure of the unconscious 'delay' of spatio-temporality: 'An *after-effect* [*un effet d'*après] offers endless resistance there':

> The crime has taken place, the culpability remains. Even if the agent [here, the example is Oedipus] did not know what he killed, whom he killed. More than elsewhere, the unconscious here seems unamenable to simple nonconsciousness. Perhaps one could use this as the authority for removing from the *Aufhebung* the identifying marks of the meaning-(to say) [that is, from the teleology of meaning as *eidos*, of consciousness] of Hegel. (ibid.)

Antigone, however, goes a little further here than her father: no longer simply bound by unconsciousness, she (even though she remains *unconscious* law) *consciously* disobeys the other law: she reads both tables of law: '*sur ses deux tableaux*' (173a). Antigone, who sides with her brother Polynices against his brother Eteocles's, is 'also Eteocles enemy brother' (175a). 'Two brothers' – and this comes as absolutely no surprise to a reader of *Finnegans Wake* – 'going head to head, can only kill themselves' (176a). They fight to the death, since they are both identical and universal, because complete, male individualities. Government, which, says Hegel, 'does not tolerate the duality of individuality,' must now step in in the form of the other brother, Eteocles, who fights for the city, since 'there cannot be two – two foundations, two discourses, two *logoi*, two accounts, two reasons, two heads – they are both wrong ... They must each fall (on the other)' (ibid.).

But it does not stop there: the government punishes the other brother by 'depriving him of a burial (place), in abandoning his corpse to the "dogs" and the "birds"' (176–86a). However,

> [t]he universal [i.e., government], by doing this, only 'grazes lightly' the 'pure tip of its pyramid' the moment it carries off its victory over the rebel principle of singularity and over divine [that is, feminine] law. That is because the continuous struggle of the 'conscious spirit' with the 'uncon-

scious spirit' has not come to an end. The unconscious has not been destroyed, only 'wounded,' injured, offended ... So the deceased continues to act; the *deceased is wounded*, returns to the charge from the mute and unconscious substance in which one wanted to repulse, reduce, curb, restrain him. The return of the dead, the vengeance of the suppressed comes to its prominence in wild nature: the birds and the dogs eat the morsels of the corpse abandoned without burial, left to the earth's surface, and then are going to 'defile' with these the altars of other communities. The morseled corpse dribbles, bleeds [*saigne*], and spits on the cultic places ... What the community has killed, in order to maintain itself, they are, under the name brothers, still women – family representatives. Human law, the law of the rational community that institutes itself against the private law of the family, always supresses femininity, stands up against it, girds, squeezes, curbs, compresses it. (186–7a)

This image recalls the *Wake*an association of squeezing a woman with squeezing juice that links 'lebben-squatch' (270.L4–5) with 'woman squelch' (392.36). Here, as with the *Wake*, the masculine power has a limit, a hole. The weapons of the community are unable to combat the dead brother-sister-woman's weapon, '*irony*.' The brother-sister-woman's irony lies in the fact that government can only preserve itself by trying to absorb 'the singularization into independent families presided over by womankind, femininity.' However, since the feminine family is also 'the universal acting ground of the singular consciousness,' the community as 'universal self-consciousness' can only produce itself 'in what it suppresses,' 'femininity in general, its eternal enemy' (187a). This is also how the womb-tomb discussed below operates in the *Wake*: the masculine restriction of the river-y, flowing femininity of ALP by HCE is only ever played out against that which was waiting for him and into which he flows as already dead. In other words, the *Wake*, just like *Glas*, understands 'suppression' in a specific manner: 'So supression produces just what – the singularity of the unconscious, the irony of femininity – it suppresses as it own 'essential moment.' It traps itself, and glues, limes itself in its own essence. Whence the eternal burst [*éclat*] of laughter of the unconscious – or of the woman, the exclamation that indefinitely harrasses, questions, mocks the essence, the truth (of man)' (188a). However, this does not mean that one should see in this femininity 'precipitantly, the end of phallocentrism, of idealism, of metaphysics.' This is not only because femininity forms the internal limit or closure (in the Derridean sense) of all of these '-isms,' but also because this space is still that of a 'ruse of reason or the woman's eternal irony, each able to take itself for the other and *to play the other*. If God is (probably) a man in speculative dialectics, the godness of God – the irony that divides him and makes him come off his hinges – the infinite disquiet of his essence is (if possible) woman(ly)' (ibid.). This reinscribes the dialectic within both Kant's take on the domestic war of man and woman,[9] and, once again, the double science of textuality.

Woman, the *différantial* 'godness of God,' that which has the power both to make and harass him as God, the unconscious feminine law of the family, is also the law of the non-dialecticizable hinge that unhinges God and plays with/in sexual opposition in the family. That is her irony:

> The 'eternal irony' of the woman will never let itself be reached behind the absolute entrenchment of this already [what Derrida has just called the 'absolute already nonwritten laws ... engraved in the heart from always, their orginating event cannot be determined'], which is further back than the origin, older than birth, and attends death.
>
>   As irony, the woman is at once a *moment to be passed* and the very form of *Sa* [*Savoir Absolut*, Absolute Knowledge, the self conscious return of knowledge to itself in the Hegelian concept]. Double mark and double place. (190ai)

Ironic woman, obsessed with death, the heart, and engraving, is the absymal double. As double, she is also catachrestic: that is to say, she is the abyss, both figure and ground, the destruction of both figurative and philosophical language.[10] She marks the double point that is both a 'stop' along the way in the system and the entire system itself, a 'place' that also permits her to function as the quasi-empirico-formal mime of Hegelian speculative dialectics: 'Absolute woman, absolute irony, absolute evil lightly graze and mime *Sa*' (ibid.). The extent of her irony stretches across the entire system of Hegel's dialectics to the extent that she is both part and whole. This also means, however, that she cannot be 'surpassed' by the progression of speculative dialectics towards *Savoir Absolut*. Thus, even though she is 'natural,' she is also a manifestation of the law and therefore culture. The woman, therefore, grafts herself onto the incest prohibition through her very undecidability, which prevents her from ever settling down as either natural or cultural.

Given that the woman is the form of the Hegelian *Savoir Absolut*, it is perhaps only when Derrida asks, 'And what if the *Aufhebung* were a Christian mother?' (201a) that it becomes possible to understand that the Christian mother is also the ironic reinscription of the form of Hegelian dialectics: the *Aufhebung*. The Christian mother is the hymen of *Dissemination* insofar as she binds together the desire of/for maternity *and* of/for virginity, where the 'one – the veil of virginity, where nothing has yet taken place – remains in the other – consummation, release, and penetration of the *antre* [French, cave, recalling of course the cave in which Antigone is encrypted at the end of Sophocles' play]' (D 215). As both part and (w)hole of the woman, that which is neither inside nor ouside the woman (D 213), she is also 'productive imagination':[11]

> The Hegelian dialectic, mother of the criticism, is first of all, like every mother, a daughter: of Christianity, in any case Christian theology. She returns ceaselessly to it, as if to its *lap*. *Aufhebung* is a Christian daughter-mother. Or else: the daughter mother, the Christian holy mother is named *Aufhebung* ... [Feuerbach's] *The Essence of Christianity* establishes an equivalence between the categories of miracle, imagination, and relief. The transformation of the water into wine, of wine into blood, transubstantiation, resurrection above all are *Aufhebung* operations: what is destroyed preserves itself, what dies can be reborn. Wonderful and miraculous, *Aufhebung* is the productive imagination. Likewise, the dogma of the Virgin Mary sees its contradiction lifted, cancelled [*lever*], or cleaned up, cleared [*laver*], by an *Aufhebung* that suspends what it keeps, what it guards, or reg(u)ards what it lifts, what it cancels. 'Here we have the key to the contradiction in Catholicism, that at the same time marriage is holy and celibacy is holy. This simply realises, as a *practical contradiction*, the *dogmatic contradiction* of the *virgin Mother* or the mother Virgin.' (203–5a; citing Feuerbach, *The Essence of Christianity*, 138)[12]

At first glance, *Glas*'s reading of Feuerbach's text pursues the operation of the imagination back to its Eucharistic roots. However, these Eucharistic roots – insofar as they are textual – are subject to the citational or 'simple play of quotation marks' that exceeds the difference between 'prescription and description' (198a). This play – which can always affect text – creates the 'predicaments in which citationality, quotation marks, and signature place the theory of the performative' (198a). Here, the imagination is no longer simply allied to the performative aspect of the Eucharist in the sense of the word given to it by Speech Act theory, where form is act.[13] It/she is written, textual, struck with indeterminacy. In the insert that covers 203–5ai, the 'wondrous unity' of 'virginity and maternity' 'contradict[s] Nature and reason, but in the highest degree accordant with the feelings and imagination' (204ai). She comes between nature and all its philosophical others – culture, reason, techne, etc. – as she reinscribes the textuality of the incest prohibition in the *Aufhebung*. She is therefore the pure *différance* through which 'the very project of philosophy, under the privileged heading of Hegelianism, is displaced and reinscribed. The *Aufhebung* – *la relève* – is constrained into writing itself otherwise. Or perhaps simply into writing itself. Or, better, into taking account of its consumption of writing' (M 19). Imagination may therefore be said to be the same for *Glas* as it is for Vico: a writing that comes before philosphical reflection.

All of this brings the undecidability of the image into line with the writing in the letter of *Finnegans Wake*. As I pointed out above, Vico's conception of marriage as a restrained 'break' with nature that ultimately remains somewhat 'natural' also takes the form of the incest prohibition. The prohibition, the nub of marriage's restraint, puts it within the familiar orbit of the Vichian conatus points. The false exit from nature is also to be found nestled in the letter of *Finnegans Wake*, where it projects the origins of heroic education and its relation to the prohibition of incest onto religion. This projection is traced by the letter's 'antechristian calligraphy [which] shows a distinct advance from savagery to barbarism' (114.11–13). The interval that the letter's calligraphy opens lies *between* savagery and barbarism, between what Vico calls the '*barbarism* of sense,' which is also 'a generous *savagery*' (NS 1106, my emphasis). The advance marked in the letter is not really an advance because it merely traces the sameness 'of the law in nature' (NS 2). By grafting the letter's calligraphy onto Vico's nature, *Finnegans Wake* marks the matrimonial, dialectical, religious, cross-point of nature's false exit from itself as culture (117.27–30). The letter's scene of writing, as I argued in chapters 2 and 3, is one of (non)production without model – what I have been relating to 'building,' mimicry, etc. – in which the reader-writer writes only by following the mother-hen. Since the mother–son relation is inscribed by the text as one of 'Madonagh and Chiel' (490.6), and of the Vesica Piscis (293), its writing figures the image that constrains the Hegelian *Aufhebung* to write itself otherwise, in a non-dialectical manner. In this way the doubled writing of *Finnegans Wake* plays with the Christian mother in a manner that is both anti-Christian and ante-Christian.[14]

Over the remainder of this chapter, I want to examine the scene of writing that takes place between the mother and her son(s) as a site that grafts a bond with the contradictory and double-crossed imaginary site of the Christian as discussed in the previous section. I will argue that the scene of writing corresponds to the written image of the ironic *Aufhebung*. To read only the written image of the *Aufhebung* is, according to the text of *Glas*, to read as a Jew. Jews 'consider the family nomination of the relation of God to men or to Jesus as images (*Bilde*), in the most external sense, as ways of speaking or imagining. Thus do they disqualify what essential the advent of Christianity can include in the history of the spirit' (84a). In reading the family relation of Jesus as imagery, the Jew reads the 'imagination without truth' (85a). The 'Jew stands by this objectivism that, incapable of leaving the finite closure of the understanding or the imagination, also remains a subjectivism. Enclosed in this nondialectic one-sidedness, he has access neither to the divine nor to the spiritual sense of filiation. For the spirit has not yet spoken in him. He has not yet become an adult in himself. At bottom no matter how much the Jew strives to be [*a beau être*] a kind of executioner, he is also a child. And what characterizes childhood is that it cannot think childhood as such, filiation as such. As long as he is child, the son is blind to the father son relation ... The Jew is not filial (*kindlich*) because he is puerile (*kindisch*). Not at all childlike, but childish' (85a). By grafting the 'risk[y]' 'Jewish reading' (84a) of the image – that is, the empty form – of the *Aufhebung* onto the *Wake's* scene of letter-writing, it becomes possible to see the compositional processes of the *Wake* as a site of the *différantial* reinscription of the Hegelian *Aufhebung* that is, in many ways, remarkably similar to *Glas's* reinscription of the *Aufhebung*.

'not-yet': Anticipating 'Anticipation'

The 'not-yet' or 'anticipation' I am referring to here should not be confused with the sort of teleological anticipation of meaning that drives the Hegelian dialectic. On the contrary, this sort of 'anticipation' must be understood to play both within and without Hegelian dialectics in the same double manner that I have been considering for some time now. In order to come to grips with this reinscribed 'anticipation,' it is necessary to return to an analysis of the imagination. As I argued above in chapters 2 and 3, the imagination constitutes a profoundly problematic space wherein 'images' – in a sense that has yet to be fully explored – are incompatible with the anticipation of meaning. As such, they bear the taint of 'absolute death,' marking the point of no return, where the 'instance of an expenditure without reserve which no longer leaves us the resources with which to think of this expenditure as negativity' (WD 259). The imagination can, at the same time, be understood as a site where Hegel's 'debate with Kant resembles most an explication and least a break.'[15] This suggests that the site where intuition and conception 'meet' in the Kantian imagination acts as a palimpsest, a site of 'marginal commentary' on the Hegelian dialectics mentioned in *Glas* (107a). In this section, then, I will begin following the thread of the imagination as that which 'hesitat[es] between explication and rupture' in order to explore further how the imagination functions as the empirico-formal textual site wherein Hegelian dialectics take shape.

The text of *Glas* reports an imaginary speech given by Kant,[16] where he speaks of the conditions for the impossibility of Freud's attempt to link the 'negative conception' of the taboo (*Standard Edition* 13, xiv) to his 'positive conception' of the *Impératif Catégorique* (denoted in *Glas* by the siglum *IC*)[17] (215a):

[The *IC* could] never be a process of idealization and interiorization passing from the negative to the positive, from one object to the other, from the unconscious to the conscious, from constraint to autonomy, from the psychological to what is given as nonpsychological, nonphenomenal, never will such a process be able to give an account of the properly infinite leap that produces the object of pure morality. (216a)

However, a nearby textual judas intervenes in, and comments on, Kant's opinion of this impossibility:

unless, following a deconstructive displacement of all the oppositions on which the Kantian discourse bets, in order to make impossible in that discourse an analogical process (sensible/intelligible, phenomenal/noumenal, intuitus derivatus/intuitus originarius, and so on), psychoanalytic discourse determines – in Kantian logic – the sensible point: the point of sensibility where the two terms of the opposition touch and do without the [speculative] leap [*saut*]. For example, *respect* of the moral law belongs to neither the rational order of the law nor the order of psychological phenomena; the *interest* of reason and in general the whole schematism of transcendental imagination is still what, raising the opposition, *suspends the leap*. (216ai)

In other words, the text of *Glas* suggests that Kantian and Freudian discourses may be usefully combined in order to uncover what it refers to here as 'the sensible point,' which it goes on to associate with Kantian 'schematism of transcendental imagination.' This suggested combination comes five pages after a discussion of Freud's account of fetishism, which, as 206–17a makes clear, provides the basis for Hegel's criticism of the Kantian philosophy of religion and vice versa. The fetish is 'undecidable' and its 'power' lies in the fact that it constitutes an 'excess in relation to the opposition (true/nontrue, substitute/nonsubstitute, denial/affirmation, and so on)' (211ai). It is the site of a speculation that is 'not dialectical, but plays with the dialectical' (210ai). Thus, if the Kantian discourse of the imagination is bound to the Freudian account of the fetish, where both terms of an opposition touch in nondialectical undecidablility, what *Glas* here refers to as the 'the point of sensibility where the two terms of the opposition touch and do without the [speculative] leap [*saut*]' can once again be understood as the site of the fetishistic imagination discussed in chapter 3.[18]

Fetishism must therefore be understood to perform a crucial role in a text that is concerned with the role religion plays in/with the dialectic:

> To found *or* destroy religion (the family production) always comes down to wanting to reduce fetishism. Fetishism, to form against itself the unanimity of founders and destroyers, must indeed somewhere constitute the opposing unity: the unveiling of the column, the erection of the thing itself, the rejection [*rejet*] of the substitute. The same desire works (over) the Christian mother, her ancestry, and her descendants. As long as fetishism will be criticized – for or against religion, for or against the family – will the economy of metaphysics, the philosophy of religion, have been tampered with? (206–7a)

Here, fetishism, which is bound up with both the woman and the *Aufhebung*-Christian mother is seen as the force that constitutes the 'thing itself' – the very thing that is supposed to relieve the fetish. Fetishism remains irreducible precisely because it constitutes the thing itself. Further, since it is associated with the mother, it not surprising to see it allied by both Hegel and Kant with 'sensible representations' of those supposedly properly infinite objects – 'the law, God the father, and so on' – that are 'no longer (present), no longer appear' (216a). I want to consider here the issue of representation and religion, which is indissociable from Christianity.

The issue of religious representation is explicitly bound up with time: 'Religion is representative because it needs time' (220a). Religion is the last step in the Hegelian dialectic of *Savoir Absolut* (or 'absolute knowledge,' the completion of Hegel's philosophical system where everything is bound together, this is siglumed in *Glas* as '*Sa*': 'its' or its homophone *ça*, 'it,' itself the French word for the Freudian Id); and 'the identity of philosophy with religion finds its ultimate mediation in the philosophy of religion' (218a). In this 'last step' *Savoir Absolut* (*Sa*) is not identical with 'Absolute religion' or Christianity:

> Absolute religion is not yet what it is already: *Sa*. Absolute religion (the essence of Christianity, religion of essence) is already what it is not yet: the *Sa* that itself is already no more what it is yet, absolute religion.
>
> The already-there of the not-yet, the already-no-more of the yet cannot agree [*s'entendre*]. (218a)

This inability to hear or understand itself introduces a 'gap' in understanding. This gap is legible in a 'not-yet' that cannot be subsumed by the '*absolute* already-there of the not-yet or the *absolute* already-no-more of the yet,' which should 'describe an eternal or intemporal circle,' no longer belonging to time (ibid; Derrida's italics).

It is the '*absolute* already-there of the not-yet or the *absolute* the already-no-more of the yet' that *Glas* 'de-temporalizes' as '*not-there* [pas-là] (the being-there (*Da*) of the *not* [pas] that, being there, is not, *not there*)':

> If one hears Hegel, understands him, if one comprehends (from inside the picture) the sense of what his text means-(to say) [*entends*], one cannot reduce the *absolute* already-there of the not-yet or the *absolute* already-no-more of the yet to what one believes one knows familiarly of the family ... So the *not-there* cannot be reduced to the circle of a family about which what it is and means-(to say) would already be familiarly known. On the contrary, the absolute essence of the family can be reached only in thinking the absolute of the *not-there*. (219a)

Here, the family is between, double: it is 'between' because 'the absolute sense of the family's being-family hands itself over only (in) (to) the passage between absolute religion and *Sa'* (ibid.). It is 'double' because it is that which one believes one knows 'familiarly' – which is not to understand the family *absolutely* – and that which is yet to be fully understood: it is not yet there. This thinking of the family puts it 'inside and outside,' 'at the hinge [*charnière*] of the next-to-last [religion] and the last chapter [*Sa*]' (ibid.). The 'family between' is neither the absolute family nor what one believes one knows familiarly as family.

It is the doubleness of the family that leaves its marks on 'absolute religion' as unresolved or unreconciled opposition that is marked as 'anticipatory representation':

> In effect: in absolute religion, division in two (*Entzweiung*) is *not yet* absolutely overcome by reconciliation. An opposition (*Entgegensetzung*) stays, determines itself as an anticipatory representation (*Vorstellung*). The ultimate limit of the absolutely true, absolute, revealed religion: it remains no further than the *Vorstellung*. The essential predicate of this representation is the exteriority of what presents itself there ... The unity of the object and the subject does not yet accomplish itself presently, actually; the reconciliation between the subject and the object, the inside and the outside, is left waiting. It represents itself, but the represented reconciliation is not the actual reconciliation. There is nothing fortuitous to this representative exteriority being, at the same time, time. If in the absolute religion of the absolute family, there is an already of the not-yet or a not-yet of the already (of *Sa*), that is very simply, if this can be said, because there is – yet again – time. (219a–20a)

The relation of religion to *Sa* can, of course, be understood as imaginative to the extent that religion 'anticipates' philosophy in an image, a representation a *Vorstellung* (219a). In representation there is no present unity or reconciliation of subject/object or inside/outside. There is both time and the object that remains exterior to, alienated from, the subject.

If reconciliation can be said to have taken place at all in representation, then it has taken place only as a representation:

> The reconciliation has produced itself, and yet it has *not yet* taken place, is *not present*, only represented or present as remaining in front of, ahead of, to come, present as not-yet-there and not as presence of the present ... [O]ne has to say that in religion, in the absolute revelation, presence is

present as representation. Consciousness has the representation of this presence and of this reconciliation, but as it is only a representation of what is outside consciousness (in front of or behind it, here that comes to the same), this representation remains outside it. (220a)

To this extent, religious consciousness is Jewish in the sense discussed in chapter 3:

> The fact of the representation, the *Vor-stellen*, forms an opposite (*Gegan-satz*), an object, a desire, or a nostalgia, absolute religious consciousness remains in the opposition, the split. Reconciliation remains a beyond. The temporal motif (movement of transcendence), relation with a nonpresent future or a past, depresentation) is the truth of a metaphorically spatial motif (the 'distant,' the nonproximate, the nonproper). The family proper has not yet, in the absolute family, found its identity or proximity to itself ... This dehiscence of the family proper forms an ellipse that parts [*écarte*] the religious focus from the philosophical, Christianity from *Sa*. And if philosophy – *Sa* – was considered to be the myth of absolute reappropria-tion, of self-presence absolutely absolved and recentered, then the abso-lute of revealed religion would have a *critical* effect on *Sa*. It would be necessary to keep to the (opposite) bank, that of religion and the family, in order to resist the lure of *Sa*. (221a)

The absolute family is thus *différantial* spatio-temporality that does not return to itself: it is the 'family between' insofar as it is not simply familiar and not yet properly dialectical. It is also a site of dessemina-tion or dehiscence that spaces, distances, and tears the dialectic apart. The image is non-presently 'anticipatory,' or 'in advance' (KPM 64); it is also the non-present allegorical reinscription of the *Aufhebung* dis-cussed in chapters 2 and 3 above.[19] In this gap there emerges a 'not-yet' that continues to mark time by translating what is supposed to be intemporal 'into a temporal grammar, into the syntax of adverbs of time and negation' (218a). It is this 'not-yet' that Hegel tries to deter-mine as 'the fall [*chute*] of sense into the body, outside the circle imme-diately carried back into the circle' (219a). The undecidability of the 'not-yet' affects the family as yet another hinge, *charnière*, which recalls the other hinge, that of the pivot or *charnière* of the incest prohibition, and it is the *charnière* that is also given over to the citationality that rup-tures the performative (198a) of the speculative system: 'the pivot of the system that is contradictory in itself – with a contradiction of which one cannot say whether it operates *in* or *against*. The "opposition" plays two times and with it, each conceptual determination' (199a). To the extent that the absolute family is doubled and between, it makes legible a 'formal incoherence' that 'critically denounces' the absence of any speculative 'concept' of family.[20] It is, then, the absence of a specu- lative concept of the family that pushes it into the exteriority of a repre- sentative image formed in the imagination. If the image is understood in this manner, then the text of *Glas* explores the anticipatory image of absolute knowledge in terms of the representation of the family scene of absolute religion immediately prior to its becoming *Sa* as a fetish, which is, in its turn, indissociable from the question of time since 'there is no time but the family's': 'The opposition of the already, of the not- yet, of the already no more, everything that forms the time of not being present (*not-there*), everything that constitutes time as the *Dasein* of a concept that is not(-)there [(*n')est pas là*], the being-there of the not- there (one not more – not-not-there – or less), all that is a family scene' (221a). The woman who watches over the family and its laws also watches over this temporal syntax and grammar of non-presence. Just like its contact with the woman, the dialectic's contact with the abso- lute family '"grazes lightly" the "pure tip of its pyramid"' (186a). This graze is also a written mark (233a).

The absolute family scene is, of course, that of the Immaculate Con- ception, which *Glas* also siglums as *IC*. To the extent that the Immacu- late Conception is a family scene, it therefore is dominated by the woman and the syntax of her spatio-temporal grammar. This syntax, says Derrida, punctuates the German of Hegel's text: 'The *noch* and the *nur* that punctuate these statements (only this, yet that, remains this, remains that) mark well the limit – temporal and structural – that holds absolute religion back in the opposition and separates it absolutely from *Sa*: a barely visible limit, nevertheless, a next-to-nothing that parts the present from its representation and that does that in its [*sa*] very (re)presentation' (222a). This temporal grammar links up with the ticking of the empty German *noch nicht* (not-yet) (cf. 228a), which pre- vents the absolute family from ever being completely at one with itself, ellipses and prevents its circle from rejoining with itself. This ellipsis is found at a structural level in *Finnegans Wake* in the form of its famous last sentence, which is supposed to link up with the first. On closer reading, however, it becomes clear that the sentence, does not form a perfect circle, even though it could still be said that it evokes one: 'A way a lone a last a loved a long the ... riverrun, past Eve and Adam's, from swerve of shore to bend of bay, brings us by a commodius vicus of recirculation back to Howth Castle and Environs' (628.15–16 to 3.1–3). To read this sentence as a seamless circle is to read the *Wake* dialectically and to ignore both the reference to Vico and the work the text does in order to dislocate and reinscribe dialectical thinking by lodging fetishism within representation. This first/last 'sentence' never settles down into a stable piece of discourse or vehicle for proper meaning to the extent that it dislocates the grammatical subject of the sentence through the reiterated punctuation of ALP's 'a-a-a-a-a,' a repeated movement away from or towards (a shore), negation, pluralization, affixing, in which one can also hear an analogue of Molly's orgasmic 'Yeses' at the end of *Ulysses*. The 'subject' is 'a way a lone a last a loved along,' sent off, broken, separated, alienated, distanced, distributed, *différantial*, and subject to affect, the heart, in the form of love. The heart, which is associated throughout *Glas* with nature and the mother, like the father in the absolute family, does not exist: 'the heart, is truly not there' (220bi), is 'not an object for consciousness' (223a).

The ellipsis affects and punctuates the absolute family scene, and these effects are once more concentrated on/in the 'mortal seed,' the disseminative χ of the 'singular divine man – Christ – [who] has a father who is in (it)self, and with whom he has no actual relation. Only his relation with his mother is actual' (222a). Insofar as there is no reconciliation with the father-reason-concept, the family scene of Jesus-χ remains an image, a representation of the scene of the production of absolute knowledge, the reconciliation of 'the heart and reason' (223a). This happens because in the Immaculate Conception of the absolute family, Jesus has a relationship with his mother that here corresponds to the immediacy of intuition, the heart and natural immediacy (223a), but has no 'relationship' with his father, who 'remains beyond phenomenal actuality, invisible,' 'absent, transcendent, hidden, separated, severe, *not-there*' (222a). Jesus, who also marks the site of the reader of the *Wake*, is therefore not graspable as a site of dialectical reconciliation in *Glas*. Supplementing (in the Derridean sense) this dialectical reconciliation, however, is a natural, affectionate, and unconscious reconciliation with the mother in 'worldly immediacy' (223a). This familiar incompletion affects the 'reconciliation, in the son, of the father and the mother. Jesus also suffers from the divorce of his parents' (ibid.). Jesus remains a mortal seed to the extent that he does not come back to the father, which is also, says *Glas*, 'the problematic place of an Annunciation' (223a).

mutter: 'Annunciation'

It is easy enough to trace the structure of the Immaculate Conception in the text of *Finnegans Wake*. However, in order to do so, it is necessary to consider the various scenes of death, burial, rape, and *bander* in the text. As I pointed out in chapter 1, throughout book I of the text Finnegan can only ever appear in the text as the absent 'goodridhirring,' the antithesis of the 'Real Presence' of the Eucharist (7.12–18). Section I.2 nevertheless continues the search, and comes across the 'The Ballad of Persse O'Reilly' (44.23–47.34), which is of little help because it is merely the product of rumour drunkenly overheard at a racecourse (40.5–6). Next, I.3 interviews several witnesses, and the diversity of their impressions serves only to confuse the evidence even further. In I.4 the mode of investigaton becomes more formalized, and takes the form of a trial that tries to 'bring the true truth to light' (96.27). The first mention of Finnegan is at the end of I.1 as 'that samesake sibsubstitute of a hooky salmon, there's already a big rody ram lad at random on the premises' (28.35–6), 'Humme the Cheapner, Esc' (29.18–19), and 'he is ee and no counter he who will be ultimendly respunchable for the hubbub caused in Edenborough' (29.34–6). As this quote makes clear, Earwicker, an avatar of ⊔ who never exists outside rumour, is already a substitute for the (already) dead and dying *Finn* McCool/Tim Finnegan. Finnegan thus never actually presents himself, but is instead carried off in a long implicit *sentence* that functions, therefore acts, as an *image* in the sense that I have been pursuing all along: only because he is a general picture that overflows all particular incarnations/actual presentations can he constantly recede in the face of the Mamalujo's search for him.

The investigation seems to finally get a break when it comes across the only remaining historical document related to the whole affair, the hen's letter of I.5. The letter holds out the promise of new life, or 'refleshmeant' (82.10); as such it is also the enveloping mailbag womb of 'Mrs Hahn' (German, *Hahn*, rooster):

> Will it bright upon us,
> nightle, and we plunging to our plight? Well, it might now, mircle,
> so it light. Always and ever till Cox's wife, twice Mrs Hahn, pokes
> her beak into the matter with Owen K. after her, to see whawa
> smutter after, will this kiribis pouch filled with litterish frag-
> ments lurk dormant in the paunch of that halpbrother of a herm,
> a pillarbox? (66.21–7)

This 'womb,' however, is so contradictory and overdetermined as to be utterly illogical. First, it is a 'womb' that is also a 'polysexual' *Hahn*'s 'paunch' belonging to a 'herm.' This 'herm' is also a herm-aphroditic pillar/column that supports a bust. Thus does the 'refleshing womb-paunch' oscillate between the sexes. As it oscillates between the sexes, the post-bag also recalls one of the hen's sons, Shaun the Post. Nor is it only a postal bag: since it is also a 'kirbis pouch filled with litterish fragments,' it can become 'a pillarbox.' Through the mailbag, the hen's Isis-like agglutinative 'ygathering,' which picks up the fragmentary refuse of words and world after the holocaust, is reinscribed as postal. The rapidity and complexity of the changes of languages, sex, position, gender, occupation, kinship, and so on, that the text subjects this scene to are perhaps best understood in the terms of what Derrida, in the context of his study of Bataille, calls the 'destruction of discourse,' a wake:

> It multiplies words, precipitates them one against the other, engulfs them too, in an endless and baseless substitutuion, whose only rule is the sover-iegn affirmation of the play outside meaning. Not a reserve or a with-drawal, not the infinite murmur of a blank speech erasing the traces of classical discourse, but a kind of potlatch of signs that burns, consumes and wastes words in the gay affirmation of death: a sacrifice and a chal-lenge. (WD 274)

However, a thread may still be picked up here: once again, it is the auspices. If the reader-writer (once again) follows Mrs Hahn's lead, as she pokes her beak into the mailbag, s/he will be able to 'see whawa smutter' (66.24–5). What matters, in other words, is seeing the 'mother' (German, *mutter*) in/as her mailbag. Thus, if the reader once more fol-lows the text according to the textual structure of taking the auspices, s/he may learn more about the 'refleshing paunch' of the mother-son-hen-rooster by observing what s/he does with it. The *Wake* presents the work of the mother-hen as it falls to △ in terms of agglutinatively 'ygathering' rubbish and putting it into her mailbag-pouch. This bag, which also houses and agglutinatively 'refleshes' the 'litterish frag-ments' of Osiris that 'lurk dormant' (66.25–6), expands rapidly to become the whole woman-hen who mothers Ш:

> she ... shuttered him after
> his fall and waked him widowt sparing and gave him keen and

made him able and held adazillahs to each arche of his noes, she
who will not rast her from her running to seek him till, with the
help of the okeamic, some such time that she shall have been after
hiding the crumbends of his enormousness in the areyou looking-
for Pearlfar sea. (102.1–7)

In (s)mothering the letter-man, the bag-woman envelops him as/in 'a
protem grave in Moyelta' (76.21). This nurturing makes it clear that the
tomb-coffin that shelters ⊔ after his fall is also a motherly enveloping
womb, just like the womb-tomb Stephen Dedalus rolls around his
mouth in *Ulysses* 3:

> Mouth to her kiss. No. Must be two of em. Glue em well. Mouth to her
> mouth's kiss.
>   His lips lipped and mouthed fleshless lips of air: mouth to her moomb.
> Oomb, allwombing tomb. His mouth moulded issuing breath, un-
> speeched: ooeeehah: roar of cataractic planets, globed, blazing, roaring
> wayawayawayawayaway. Paper. The banknotes, blast them. Old Deasy's
> letter. Here. Thanking you for the hospitality tear the blank end off.
> (3.399–405)

This odd womb-mouth that is only ever doubled – and which is composed of the simultaneity of life and death – provides the opportunity
for writing, just as the coffin that promises the 'refleshmeant' of the
corpse attaches to a fetishistic hen-mother. However, because she enve-
lopes, the mother who encloses the lost man-child within her darkened
womb-tomb, is felt in the heart of the child: 'My heart, my mother! My
heart, my coming forth of darkness!' (493.34–5). This feeling of heart-
felt immediacy offered by the womb is, insofar as it is simultaneously
life and death, *différantial* (M 19).

This scene of burial and birth is at once very close to and very far
from the text of Hegel as it is presented in *Glas*. The mother in *Glas* also
has a relation of 'immediacy' to the child insofar as she too is 'felt' in
the 'heart' by the child (223a). 'Feeling' has to do with relationships
that are at once 'natural, sensible, worldly immediacy' (164a, 223a),
and as such is always tending towards disseminative loss of 'natural
desire' that 'loses itself, does not come back as spirit.' Throughout *Glas*,
the 'natural' is that which, time and again, always seems to be 'destined to lose itself, to be incapable of reflecting itself in its naturalness.
If natural desire were to do so, it would no longer be what it reflects –

natural' (148a). As such loss, it attaches to the relation between parents and children, which retains 'a certain natural contingency [that] does not let itself be reduced' because it is 'still affected by the remains of a nonreturn.' The 'seed' of the child 'does not go back to the source, it no longer circulates' (ibid.). The natural desire/child would, on this reading, be analogous to the death from which the dialectic cannot make a profit. The life of the natural relationships and desire are always tainted by death. The womb always brings with it burial in the tomb: 'In herself: under the earth, but the night of the subterranean world is the woman, Hegel specifies. Freud will also have shown the reverse side of this desire: the fear of being engulfed in the maternal womb is represented in the agony of bring buried alive' (143a). The mother's womb in *Glas* is also that which, as engulfing, envelops the dead (erection) wrapped in bands: 'Entrusting with death, the guarding of a marrowless body, on the condition that the woman erect his burial place after shrouding the rigid corpse (unction, bandages, etc.), maintaining it thus in a living, monumental, interminable surrection' (143a). This is why the 'erection of the burial place would be the feminine work' (144a). The dialectic of the dead one must here pass through the woman who, working the corpse into an erection, lets the dead man live on (cheat death) in his name by suppressing the 'unconscious desires' that would otherwise be destoyed by these desires (144a). Her labour writes – engraves – his name 'on the stele or slab' (ibid.).[21]

The complexity of the 'name' that the hen inscribes on the tomb of the dead/missing one once again plays in the margins of the Hegelian dialectic, opening it up, extending it beyond the play of its proper outside. This play can be seen in the hen's writing of her letter, which, insofar as it fails to exonerate her absent husband by 'crush[ing] the slander's head' (102.17), does not save his (proper) name. The same writing comes to en-grave the coffin that merges with her mailbag-womb:

The coffin, a triumph of the illusionist's art, at first blench
naturally taken for a handharp (it is handwarp to tristinguish
jubabe from jabule or either from tubote when all three have just
been invened) had been removed from the hardware premises of
Oetzmann and Nephew, a noted house of the gonemost west,
which in the natural course of all things continues to supply
funeral requisites of every needed description. Why needed,
though? Indeed needed (wouldn't you feel like rattanfowl if you

hadn't the oscar!) because the flash brides or bride in their lily
boleros one games with at the Nivynubies' finery ball and your
upright grooms that always come right up with you (and by jingo
when they do!) what else in this mortal world, now ours, when
meet there night, mid their nackt, me there naket, made their
nought the hour strikes, would bring them rightcame back in the
flesh, thumbs down, to their orses and their hashes. (66.28–67.6)

Here, the scene is once again that of the postal imagination: the coffin
appears in the narrative as part of the on-going attempt to find clues as
to the whereabouts of the resolutely non-present Finnegan/Earwicker.
Since the coffin seems to offer a clue in the investigation in his whereabouts, it would appear to hold out the promise to bring Finnegan 'back
in the flesh.' However, on 'closer inspection' (107.23–4), the promise of
the coffin turns out to be insincere, a con. And not just because Finnegan
will never – can never – return, because he was never 'present' to begin
with. The coffin's promise is insincere because it invites many anonymous others of both genders to come dance on his grave. The hen writes
'Finnegan's' name in such a manner as to lose it in a flurry of others: the
funeral rites become a wedding party ball where anonymous and
'upright grooms' 'game' with an indeterminate number of women in
the guise of 'flash brides or bride.' The bride/s, not unlike the Maggies
later in the text, ring to form a naked 'nought' at midnight, which, encircling the grooms, 'who always come right up with you,' makes them
erect and brings them 'back in the flesh.' The 'nought' of this dance-
coffin that is not a sarcophagus prevents the eating of the flesh. It is a
bander in that the pressure it applies re-erects the penis-corpses that
come to the wedding-funeral. Its bands are not unlike the tabernacle.
The promise of the coffin, once again, warps the performative/Eucha-
ristic structure of the promise to the extent that it remains insincere. Further, seeing that HCE is never-present, he can only inhabit the inside of
the tabernacle-coffin without ever touching it because he is constantly
receding and withdrawing his presence: he is, like the father analysed in
Glas, *pas-là*. What the hen writes on the tomb is therefore not in any simple sense what might be understood as a name: rather, it is a death that
cannot be reappropriated by the dialectic.[22]

As I suggested above, *Finnegans Wake* inscribes the feeling of/for the
mother in the non-conscious processes of heart and the womb. The
womb and the vagina are consistently yoked together by the text as
the site of HCE's 'first' penetrating landing at Dublin Bay:

> Well, ptellomey soon and curb your escumo.
> When they saw him shoot swift up her sheba sheath, like any
> gay lord salomon, her bulls they were ruhring, surfed with
> spree. Boyarka buah! Boyana bueh! He erned his lille Bunbath
> hard, our staly bred, the trader. He did. Look at here. In this wet
> of his prow. Don't you know he was kaldt a bairn of the brine,
> Wasserbourne the waterbaby? Havemmarea, so he was! H.C.E.
> has a codfisck ee. Shyr she's nearly as badher as him herself.
> Who? Anna Livia? Ay, Anna Livia. (198.2–10)

Here, the gush that shoots forth from HCE's prow is caught by △'s vagina (Latin, sheath). However, his arrival is reinscribed by the text in sexual indeterminacy and in terms of a virgin-birth to △, suggested in the passage by the prayer to the Blessed Virgin, the 'Havemmarea' ('Ave Maria'). In other words, HCE's arrival as father-son takes the form of a fusion of the Immaculate Conception and the Annunciation, where Mary receives God's oral message-seed via her ear and into her motherly 'refleshing paunch.' It is appropriate, then, that Mary-Anna as Virgin-wife-mother should give birth to a fishlike water-baby-husband with a 'codfisck ee': this fish's eye recalls α (alpha), another symbol of χ (Christ).

The reinscription of HCE's arrival and founding of the city of Dublin also reappears in the passage cited above where he outlines his general policy of reforms:

> I did reform and restore for my smuggy
> piggiesknees, my sweet coolocked, my auburn coyquailing one,
> her paddypalace on the crossknoll with massgo bell, sixton
> clashcloshant, duominous and muezzatinties to commind the fit-
> ful: doom adimdim adoom adimadim: and the oragel of the lauds
> to tellforth's glory: and added thereunto a shallow laver to slub
> out her hellfire and posied windows for her oriel house: gospelly
> pewmillieu, christous pewmillieu: zackbutts babazounded, ollguns
> tararulled: and she sass her nach, chillybombom and forty bon-
> nets, upon the altarstane. May all have mossyhonours! (552.21–30)

What I am interested in here is the way in which HCE brings about his reforms: he binds the river to give rise to the city. His 'coming' is signalled as the rumbling of the 'sixton clashcloshant,' the six-o'clock tolling of the Angelus. In elaborating the city of Dublin 'from next to nothing' (5.1), Ш appears in the guise of the six o'clock 'oragel [angel, but also German, *Orgel*, organ] of the lauds [Lord]' unto Mary to 'tell-forth's glory,' of 'christous,' who will wash (*laver*) away the sins ('hell-fire') of △'s world. And because this parodic 'Annunciation' is also, as I discussed above, yet another reinscription of the heliotropic *bander* that sheathes the river in order to erect the city, it is also a reinscription of the *charnière* of conatus-repression. The woman who deals in/with death is, according to *Glas*, always allied to 'the night of the subterranean world' in the *Aufhebung* that desires the dissolution of the family into its essence – civil bourgeois society. On the way to society, the woman represents the natural 'feminine, unconscious law,' or law of the family, which is opposed to the 'masculine, conscious law' of the community. Within the *Aufhebung* of the family into the civil bourgeois society, the family, as I mentioned above, acts as a sort of a *charnière* that prevents it from being relieved without remains. To the extent that the feminine represents the unconscious law of the family, it also represents the law of the non-dialecticizable hinge that plays with sexual opposition in the family and prevents it from being relieved into civil bourgeois society.

The Frustrations of Joseph: Virgin-Text

If the scene of Annunciation in the *Wake* reinscribes the imaginary rhythm of *bander* and conatus, then the constriction of the virginal womb-tomb-bag, the O-△ of 196.1–6, must pass around an χ, the site of the reader-Christ discussed in chapter 2. As such, its constriction of the χ also makes it the site for inscription in the text. The text allegorizes this scene of writing in III.3 during Shaun's questioning by the Mamalujo. Shaun's answers (re)cast the relationship between the author-forger son and the mother in terms of the 'Tiberiast duplex' of Madonna and Child:

> – Madonagh and Chiel, idealist leading a double life! But who,
> for the brilliance of brothers, is the Nolan as appearant nominally?
> – Mr Nolan is pronuminally Mr Gottgab.
> – I get it. By hearing his thing about a person one begins to
> place him for a certain in true. You reeker, he stands pat for
> you before a direct object in the feminine. I see. By maiden
> sname. (490.6–12)

The maternal bond here marks Shem as a fetish in that 'he' becomes the mother's 'direct object in the feminine,' recognizable by his 'maiden sname.' But this reinscription of the scene of the 'Havemmarea' of the writer's generation also suggests that the writer-child is 'formed' as 'the direct object of the feminine' only. The writer has no patronym, only a 'maiden sname.' This scene of writing takes place after the father-figure is 'Gee. Gone' from the letter-writing process:

> Letter, carried of Shaun, son of Hek, written of Shem, brother
> of Shaun, uttered for Alp, mother of Shem, for Hek, father of
> Shaun. Initialled. Gee. Gone. (420.17–19)

The relation that exists between the writer and the mother is all that remains. It is one of 'dictation' and 'writing' in the absence of the father, HCE, or 'Hek,' who, I have argued, nowhere presents himself in the text. This scene of writing also allegorizes the situation of the one reading the text of *Finnegans Wake*. In the absence of the father-figure of James Joyce, who is dead and gone, the reader writes both the text and him- or herself by following the textual traces left behind by a mother-hen. This would imply that the reader-writer of the *Wake* is gestated in an 'Immaculate Conception.'

This space is also the site of the imagination formed by the imagery that is in advance of the (present) thing. It is also formed by the fact that the Immaculate Conceptions are never the same twice. This means that each shows itself, according to a by now familiar mode, in exactly such a way as to be an *image* of the Immaculate Conception, rather than the actual Immaculate Conception itself. There is no present Immaculate Conception. It will be remembered that in an image, 'something' 'must not necessarily appear as it does.' Rather, an image 'shows us "only" the "as ..." in terms of which' an Immaculate Conception, in order to be an Immaculate Conception, 'can appear' – in a non-present fashion – as one. Thus, what is perceived 'is the range of possible appearing as such, or, more precisely, ... that which cultivates this range, that which regulates and marks out how something in general must appear in order to be able,' as an Immaculate Conception, 'to offer [a] look' (KPM 67).

If one of the essential components in the Immaculate Conception of the reader-writer is an alienation or separation from the father, then there must also be a lack of clear knowledge on the part of the mother regarding the absented father. In other words, the non-present father does not furnish any present knowledge. That △ suffers from a certain 'nonconsciousness' regarding the father is ironically underlined in I.8, where the two washerwomen gossip about the fact that △ herself cannot recall the identity of the man with whom she lost her virginity:

> Waiwhou was the first thur-
> ever burst? Someone he was, whuebra they were, in a tactic attack
> or in single combat. Tinker, tilar, souldrer, salor, Pieman Peace
> or Polistaman. That's the thing I'm elwys on edge to esk. Push
> up and push vardar and come to uphill headquarters! Was it
> waterlows year, after Grattan or Flood, or when maids were in
> Arc or when three stood hosting? Fidaris will find where the
> Doubt arises like Nieman from Nirgends found the Nihil. Worry
> you sighin foh, Albern, O Anser? Untie the gemman's fistiknots,
> Qvic and Nuancee! She can't put her hand on him for the mo-
> ment. Tez thelon langlo, walking weary! Such a loon waybash-
> wards to row! She sid herself she hardly knows whuon the annals
> her graveller was, a dynast of Leinster, a wolf of the sea, or what
> he did or how blyth she played or how, when, why, where and
> who offon he jumpnad her and how it was gave her away.
> (202.12–26)

The inability to recall the circumstances of the loss of virginity as well as the name of the father reinscribes the scene of the Annunciation as a scene of what might be called 'virginal enantiosis.'[23] If one cannot remember when one lost such a thing, did one lose it? What (exactly) is lost after all? Mary-Anna had a child, and some non-present one was the father. But who? These questions are perhaps the frustrations of Joseph, but they only serve to bolster Mary's 'immaculacy' all the more.

If the child who follows the mother is also without a father, unable to presently know him, the s/he is a childish child, in the position of what the text of *Glas* calls a 'Jew' (85a). Reading in this blind manner, the child-reader-writer follows the text according to 'the logic of obsequence' (255a), a logic in which the textual matrix (mother-text) is followed by a reader-writer who is also troped throughout *Glas* as the '*je suis*,' or Jesus without the I/eye:

The Torah wears a robe and a crown. Its two rollers are then parted [*écartés*] like two legs; the Torah is lifted to arm's length and the rabbi's scepter approximately following the upright text. The bands in which it had been wrapped had been previously undone and entrusted, generally, to a child. The child, comprehending nothing about all these signs full of sense, was to climb up into a gallery where the women, and old women especially, were and then to pass them the ragged bands. The old women rolled them up like crape bands for infants, and then the child brought them back to the Torah. (241–2bi).

In following the folds between the legs of the feminine text without comprehending the sense of signs, the child writes without present knowledge. S/he does not properly know his/her father. The text of *Glas* explores this Christ child (χ – the disseminative mortal germ) in the context of speculative reconciliation that would seek to complete the speculative family by fusing the father and the mother, 'the heart and reason,' the 'for-(it)self and the in (it)self' (222a). Christ, like the reader-writer of the *Wake*, 'has a father who is in (it)self, and with whom he has no actual relation. Only his relation with his mother is actual' (222a). Jesus, on the one hand, has a relationship with his mother, who 'makes the child without knowledge' of the father (223a). On the other, he does not yet have a 'relationship' with the father, who, as concept/knowledge is not-there, 'does not present himself' (223a). The family scene of absolute religion 'does not yet accomplish itself,' precisely because the father is not-there. This 'incompletion then affects the reconciliation, in the son, of the father and the mother.' Jesus remains child-like and 'suffers from the divorce of his parents,' where 'the father (knowledge) is cut off [*coupé*] from actuality' and 'the mother (affect) is too natural and deprived of [*sevrée de*] knowledge' (222a).

The lack of knowledge regarding the father is associated by the text of the *Wake* with promiscuity, even as it maintains a certain virginal 'immaculacy.' In fusing promiscuity and virginity, the text of the *Wake* may be understood as grafting the entire scene of the IC onto the *khora* in Plato's *Timaeus*.[24] In the *Wake* this *khora* is where the twins, in the guise of the demiurgic interaction of the 'Same' and the 'Other,' come together in an auto-affective way and cannot be separated from each other (300.9–1.1, citing *Timaeus* 36 b–d). This *khora*, according to Derrida's *Dissemination*, is 'a matrix, womb, or receptacle that is never and nowhere offered up in the form of presence, or in the presence of form, since both of these already presuppose an inscription within the mother' (D 160). In the text of *Glas*, this receptacle is also the clapper of the bell where the *seing* of the 'mother' and the 'nurse' is doubly struck, which makes it no longer possible to tell their signatures or breasts apart (71b):

> [This nurse] must always be called the same, for, inasmuch as she receives all things, she never departs from her own nature and never, in any way or at any time, assumes a form like that of any of the things that enter into her; she is the natural recipient of all impressions (*ekmageion*), and is stirred and informed by them, and appears different from time to time by reason of them. But the forms which enter her are the likenesses of eternal realities (*ton onton aei mimemata*) modeled within her after their patterns (*tupothenta*) in a wonderful and mysterious manner ... And we may liken the receiving principle to a mother, and the source to a father, and the immediate nature to a child, and may remark further that if the model is to take a variety of form, the matter in which the model is fashioned will not be duly prepared unless it is formless and free from the impress of any of these shapes which it is hereafter to receive from without ... (*Timaeus* 48e–51b, cited in D 160–1)

The promiscuous but virginal *khora* is not, therefore, an authentic mother precisely because her promiscuity means that she can always be confused with a nurse in the tolling of a bell. This bell-ringing can be understood to correspond to what *Glas* calls 'the place of Gabriel, the problematic place of an Annunciation' (223a). In this problematic place, which is also the place of the Christ child or χ in the text(s), the reconciliation of the father and mother does not take place. They are still held in opposition to each other:

> The opposition of father and mother is equivalent to all the other opposi- tions of the series. Equivalent, then, to *opposition itself* as it constitutes the structure of representation. What holds back this side of *Sa* while arriving there already, the null and infinite difference would therefore be sexual difference *as opposition*: what *Sa* will have relieved, to which up to there *Sa* is answerable [*relève d'*].
>
>   And if the sexual difference as opposition relieves difference, the oppo- sition, conceptuality itself, is homosexual. It begins to become such when the sexual differences efface themselves and determine themselves as *the* difference. (223a)

In other words, to the extent that the mother and father – as intuition and conception – remain opposed, they cannot be relieved without remains. The traces of their opposition are still legible and they once again underline the way in which the family acts as a *charnière* that plays 'two times' with 'opposition' (199a). Here, the familial *charnière* is 'homosexual,' and it plays with the structure of the Immaculate Conception, exploiting its non-dialecticizable remains:

> [The Immaculate Conception is] a phantasm of [the] infinite mastery of the two sides of the oppositional relation. The virgin-mother does without the actual father, both in order to come and to conceive. The father in (it)self, the real author, the subject of the conception ... does without the woman, without that in which he passes without touching. All the oppositions that link themselves around the difference as opposition (active/ passive, reason/heart, beyond/here-below, and so on) have as cause and effect the immaculate maintenance of each of the terms, their independence, and consequently their absolute mastery. (223a)

This 'phantasm of infinite mastery of the two sides of the oppositional relation' 'makes the moment of absolute religion [the Immaculate Conception] appear as simple representation (*Vorstellen*)' (223–4a). This *Vorstellen* remains (paradoxically, unorthodoxically, badly) 'Jewish' insofar as it remains blind to the structure of filiation that exists in 'the father/son relation' (85a). The Jew, who sees only images, or idols (84a), does not yet grasp the life of filiation because he is caught between the 'double nondialectic onesidedness' of 'objectivity' and 'subjectivity' (85a). An 'opposition' 'stays' in the *Vorstellen* and 'determines [itself] as an anticipatory representation (*Vorstellung*)' (219a). The Immaculate Conception is the 'anticipatory representation,' that is to say, image in the sense that I have defined it in chapters 2 and 3, of *Sa* (218a):

> The ultimate limit of the absolutely true, absolute, revealed religion remains no further than the *Vorstellung*. The essential predicate of this representation is the exteriority of what presents itself or announces itself there. It poses in front of it(self), has a relation with an object that is present, that arrives before only inasmuch as the object remains outside. The unity of the object and the subject does not yet accomplish itself presently, actually; the reconciliation between the subject and the object, the inside and the outside, is left waiting. (219a–20a)

If there is not yet a reconciliation between 'being and the selfsame, between the being itself of being and the being-same of being,' at the most there is a

reconciliation [that] puts itself forward there as an object for consciousness that *has* this representation, that has this representation *in front of* it.
The reconciliation has produced itself, and yet it has *not yet* taken place, is
not present, only represented or present as remaining in front of, ahead of,
to come, present as not-yet-there and not as presence of the present. But
as this reconciliation of being and the selfsame (reconciliation itself) is
absolute presence, absolute parousia, one has to say that in religion, in the
absolute revelation, presence is present as representation. Consciousness
has the representation of this presence and of this reconciliation, but as it
is only a representation of what is outside consciousness (in front of or
behind it, here that comes to the same), this representation remains outside it. Consciousness represents to itself the unity, but it is not there. In
this does it have, it must be added, the structure of a consciousness, and
the phenomenology of spirit, the science of the experience of consciousness, finds its necessary limit in this representation. (220a)

Not only does this non-present 'anticipatory representation' invoke the
above analyses of the imagination, it also puts this imagination into
contact with the *différantial* futural memory of allegory. Further, it dislocates once again the structure of the performative by preoccupying
its space with the to-come, the non-present future, giving it the structure of an (allegorical) promise.

Religion and representation here come together as split, which
recalls the split that was earlier located in the split figure of Christ
(92a): 'So absolute religion guards yet some negativity and remains in
conflict, the split, the disquiet. The critique of antecedent religions or
philosophies of religion receives some disqualification from this: they
were always reproached with not going beyond division, with not
attaining reconciliation' (221a). Religion is always divided by a 'not-
yet,' and this is what allies it to 'anticipatory representation' (219a). But
this anticipation is not teleological because its 'product' nowhere presents itself (220a): it is no longer a 'product' at all. Since there is no
present *eidos* in this understanding of religion, it quickly becomes
allied with mere imagination,[25] the realm of the Jew, who can never get
past the cut or split that forever marks his consciousness. However,
because the non-present 'not-yet' mimics the ideal and fully present
teleology of *Sa*, the fully present 'not-yet' where everything that is not-
yet *Sa* will be (eventually), anticipatory representation becomes a very
powerful structure, one within which *Sa* takes place without (presently) taking place. This has the effect of reinscribing the Hegelian text

within non-present anticipation, and opens it up as a vast array of non-present imagery. As such, *Glas* asks, what could possibly 'limit' the phantasm?

> In front of what would the phantasm of the *IC* [Immaculate Conception] have failed? In front of 'reality'? But measured by the power of the greater logic that thinks the truth of the *IC*, this notion of 'reality' also remains very confusedly empiric. Who would dare say that the phantasm of the *IC* has not succeeded? Two thousand years, at least, of Europe, from Christ to *Sa*, without speaking of retroactive effects, of representations, of edging and de-bordering effects [*effets de bordure et de débordement*], of all that could be called the imperialism or the colonialisms and neocolonialisms of the *IC*. Will it be said, to determine the *IC* as phantasm, that the *IC* is not *true*, that that (*ça*) does not happen like that (*comme ça*), that this is only a myth? That would indeed be silly, and the silliness would again claim 'sexual experience' as its authority ... [The *IC* as phantasm] gives the measure of truth itself, the revelation of truth, the truth of truth. Truth is the phantasm itself. The *IC*, sexual difference as opposition (thesis against thesis), the absolute family circle would be the general equivalence of truth and phantasm. Homosexual enantiosis.
>
> This difference determined as contradiction or opposition, isn't it justly the religion (the representation) resolved in *Sa*? Does *Sa* not permit, precisely, thinking the limit of this limit, of making this limit appear as such, of *seeing* the phantasm in, as its truth [*en sa vérité*]? *Sa*, resolution of the absolute opposition, reconciliation of the in-(it)self and the for-(it)self, of the father and the mother, isn't the very *Sa* of the phantasm, is it? (224–5a)

The non-presence of the phantasm affects/is affected by the (failed) reconciliation of father and mother in absolute religion, the last stop of speculative philosophy before *Sa*. As *Glas* points out, it is very difficult to limit or 'check' the IC, the scene of the fetish-*cum*-Christian mother (cf. 206a). To the extent that the fetish/IC is infinite, it is coextensive with, but other than, *Sa*: 'No longer can it be said that the infinite phantasm is *nothing but*. *Sa*'s discourse disqualifies the *nothing-but*' (225a). Like the woman, the IC, the space of the Christian mother, is the ironic double: 'As irony, the woman is at once a *moment to be passed* and the very form of *Sa*' (190ai). As both part and whole, that which parts the series of woman/Christian mother/IC as phantasm, representation, image, from the system of *Sa*, is figured as a veil: 'Such would be the bar (opposition and rudder) of the religion/philosophy. Between them,

IC's *voiles*, its veils, its sails, virginity's or truth's, for the spirit to spirit (away) to inspire [*souffle*] there' (225a). These *voiles* recall the hymen ('a closeness and a veil') that runs between Plato and Mallarmé in *Dissemination* (D 208).

According to the text of the *Wake*, the problematic place of the allegorical-futural *Annunciation* (223a), which is also the problematic space of representation without presence, is marked by a specific time – six-o'clock in the evening. In the *Wake*, just as it was in *Glas*, this time is also marked by the tolling of a bell:

> Fieluhr? Filou! What age is at?
> It saon is late. 'Tis endless now senne eye or erewone last saw
> Waterhouse's clogh. They took it asunder, I hurd thum sigh.
> When will they reassemble it? O, my back, my back, my bach!
> I'd want to go to Aches-les-Pains. Pingpong! There's the Belle
> for Sexaloitez! And Concepta de Send-us-pray! Pang! Wring out
> the clothes! Wring in the dew! Godavari, vert the showers! And
> grant thaya grace! Aman. (213.14–21)

The reader is alerted to the text's concern for establishing the time. But the time that is established is not, strictly speaking, conventional time. Conventional time is in the process of being dismantled. Its textual figure, the 'clogh' has been taken 'asunder.' Rather, the time that the bell tolls is the 'Sexaloitez,' or the six-o'clock Angelus, itself the moment of the Annunciation, of virginal conception, of conception without (the) knowledge of the father. But this 'Annunciation' speaks double in two different languages: it hears the German 'Fieluhr?' or '*Vie viel Uhr?*' ('What is the time?'), in French as '*Filou!*' or 'Scoundrel!' Embedded in this passage is the commemoration of the Immaculate Conception itself, as it is spoken in saying the 'Angelus' – 'And Concepta de Send-us-pray!' (Latin *et concepit de Spiritu Sancto*: 'And she conceived of the Holy Ghost'). But, as it does so, it brings with it the chiming contractions and back pains of labour, which, according to Catholic tradition, Mary never experienced. The concern for time here empties the scene of the Immaculate Conception of present content: time attaches itself to six o'clock, the conventional time of the Annunciation, which commemorates in a prayer when Gabriel spoke to Mary. Thus, it is the non-present memory of the time of the Immaculate Conception, rather than the actual hour or, for that matter, the precise tenet of Catholic dogma regarding the virgin birth, that the text marks. It is the promise-structure of the Immaculate Conception that is temporal, and the emphasis on the Angelus displaces the actual moment of Christ's arrival in his mother. This promise is also that held out by the text regarding the reappearance of the lost giant, Finnegan, who never presents himself. And, as I argued in chapter 1, Finnegan, as the paradigm for (non)appearance in the *Wake*, affects the structure of time in the opening pages of the *Wake* with the 'not-yet' of non-presence.

This returns us to the text of *Glas*, which is also concerned with the problematic of time in the context of the Hegelian dialectic that was touched upon briefly above: 'There is nothing fortuitous to this representative exteriority being, at the same time, time. If in the absolute religion of the absolute family [in the Immaculate Conception], there is an already of the not-yet or a not-yet of the already (of *Sa*), that is very simply, if this can be said, because there is – yet again – time. Religion is representative because it needs time' (220a). Here time is the condition for the representative nature of religion and the family. In other words, it is the time of the *charnière* (incest prohibition, imagination, Jewish, homosexual, etc.) *and* the family insofar as it does without filiation:

Family time: there is no time but the family's. Time only happens in the family, as family. The opposition of the already, of the not-yet, of the already no more, everything that forms the time of not being present (*not there*), everything that constitutes time as the *Dasein* of a concept that is not(-)there [(*n')est pas la*], the being-there of the not-there (one not more – not-not-there – or less), all that is a family scene. (221a)

The non-presence of the not-there and the not-yet affects the family, inscribing it. But the futural nature of this 'Annunciative' not-yet plays (allegorically) with the χ, emptying it of any presence, of any teleological anticipation of eidetic content or meaning:

The condition on which the future remains to come is not only that it not be known, but that it not be *knowable as such*. Its determination should no longer come under the order of knowledge or of a horizon of preknowledge but rather as a coming or an event which one *allows* or *incites* to come (without *seeing* anything come) in an experience which is heterogeneous to all taking note, as to any horizon of waiting as such: that is to say, to all stabilizable theorems as such. It is a question of this performative to come whose archive no longer has any relation to the record of what is, to

the record of the presence of what is or will have been *actually* present. I
call this the *messianic*, and I distinguish it radically from all messianism.
(Derrida, *Archive Fever: A Freudian Impression* 72)

The not-there/not-yet is similar to the 'general economy' discussed in
chapter 1 insofar as it has to do with dislocating 'meaning, or the relation oriented from the unknown to the known or knowable, to the
always already known or to anticipated knowledge' (WD 270–1).[26] The
messianic 'to come' doubles for the Hegelian teleological 'messianism'
of meaning: it is the 'empty form' of the *Aufhebung* that rings at the end
of that essay on Bataille. What is announced in this peculiar Annunciation can no longer be understood as the teleology of meaning. Like the
text of Bataille, the Annunciation, as I read it here,

> can only utilize the *empty* form of the *Aufhebung* in an analogical fashion,
> in order to designate, *as was never done before*, the transgressive relation-
> ship which links the world of meaning to the world of nonmeaning. This
> displacement is paradigmatic: within a form of writing, an intraphilo-
> sophical concept, the speculative concept par excellence, is forced to
> designate a movement which properly constitutes the excess of every
> possible philosopheme. (WD 275, Derrida's italics)

The messianic *Aufhebung* is precisely *différantial* to the extent that it
exceeds all eidetic schema, and its event never comes to pass (as
present): it is always (playing at) coming, and cannot be grasped by
any form of present knowledge. In fact, the messianic may be understood as that which precisely exceeds Hegelianism by doubling for its
teleological messianism.

On the reading being developed here, then, the messianic is made to
link up with the peculiar form of *différantial* temporalization – spatio-
temporality, time's not-yet (*nicht noch*)/not-there (*pas là*) – which
religion nevertheless needs. At the same time, however, the outline
of something 'beyond' the Immaculate Conception, the 'absolute
phantasm,' may be glimpsed:

> What can there be outside an absolute phantasm? What can one yet add
> to it? Why and how does one desire to get out of it?
>
> It is necessary to give oneself time. Time's remain(s).
>
> Time's remain(s) – for the seminar(y) of *Sa* – that is nothing. (225–6a)

If anything lies 'outside' the IC, the text implies, it has to do with 'time's remains.' But what remains of time? Such temporal remains, if they are to remain non-dialectical, must have to do with the analysis of the imagination carried out above. As such, they must also have to do with the general economy, *différance* and the messianic. It is with all of this in view that this study now turns to 'time's remain(s)' for its final chapter.

6 'What is the ti..?': The Remains of Time

I

The all-riddle of it? That that is allruddy with us, ahead of schedule, which already is plan accomplished from and syne. (274.2–5)

'time jings pleas'

In this final chapter I want to compare the vicissitudes of time in both *Finnegans Wake* and *Glas* in order to consider how 'time' or, more precisely, 'temporalizing' may be thought about in conjunction with the rhythm discussed in chapters 3 and 4. 'Temporalization,' as was argued in chapter 2, is that aspect of the imagination that corresponds to auto-affection as it is reworked by Derrida's analyses of Husserl in *Speech and Phenomena*, while rhythm in *Finnegans Wake*, as was argued in chapters 3 and 4, exploits both squeezing and the sphincter, drawing the reader into a scene of writing conceived as an emptying and evacuation of the body. This scene of writing that gives rise to *Finnegans Wake* is, as I argued in chapter 4, a reinscription of the Vichian art of the topics and the faculty of the imagination that has 'its roots in the body' (NS 819). However, in bringing the imagination and rhythm together in this way, I want to suggest that *Finnegans Wake* makes recourse to a certain conception of 'temporality' – the quotation marks serving as a warning – that is indispensable for coming to grips with its scene of writing. The *Wake*an conception of imaginative temporality may be usefully compared to a reading of the treatment of time – or, more accurately, 'time's remains' (226a) – in Derrida's *Glas*. As I argued in the previous chapter, a certain temporality, insofar as it may be read in the text of *Glas* as attaching to the imaginary structure of the messianic – that is, a non-teleological anticipatory representation that exceeds presence – offers the reader a temporal framework for reading *Glas* that, to the extent that it both exceeds and empties itself of the animating presence of the *eidos* or *logos* of meaning, remains incommensurable with Hegel's project of appropriative philosophy. By considering both *Finnegans Wake* and *Glas* together on the basis of temporality, I hope to show how 'time's remains' may be said to provide something of a privileged context for understanding the imaginative framework that makes possible this study's broadened understanding of the intertextual 'laughter' that *Glas* and *Finnegans Wake* share in the face of an anticipatory and appropriative desire for meaning.[1]

The concern with temporality may be understood to offer itself as the *Wake*an analogue of the eidetic excess and emptiness of *Glas* discussed in the previous chapter. This emptiness is first glimpsed at what Clive Hart calls the 'naturalistic level' of the text, which is preoccupied by a temporality that seems to give a 'detailed account of a single day's activities' (S&M 70). The temporality of the naturalistic level of the text is emptied of its significance as a result of its being overlaid with other 'time-schemes,' which compete with each other and render each other defunct. In its simplest form, this competition causes the day time-schema to 'grind' against the schema of both 'a typical week of human existence' and that of a 'full liturgical year' (S&M 70). These competing time-schemas converge, according to Hart, to form the 'Eternal Now' in Saint Kevin's repose at Glendalough:

> The timeless nature of Book IV is perhaps most clearly expressed in the St. Kevin episode. At Glendalough Kevin retires:

> 'centripetally ... midway across the lake surface to its supreem epicentric lake Ysle, whereof its lake is the ventrifugal principality. (605.15)

> St. Kevin's hermitage, as described by Joyce in these pages, is a very effective symbol of renunciation and spiritual stillness. At the mid-point of the universe – the 'no placelike no timelike absolent' (609.02) – Kevin, at one with Brahman, gives himself over to memoryless meditation: 'memory *extempore*' (606.08) – *ex tempore* since no memory can exist in an Eternal Now. (S&M 76–7)

The 'Eternal Now,' where all 'events which seem to be "spaced" in a temporal succession are present simultaneously – or, rather, out of time altogether,' is also the absence of time: time is 'resolved' and 'all the complex time-schemes of *Finnegans Wake*' exist in a space without memory (S&M 75). It is an absolute standpoint that disregards the ordinary experience of time (ibid.). Hart's conception of the 'Eternal Now' is particularly interesting here because it is rooted firmly in the problematic of time discussed at length in chapter 2. In many ways, Hart's conception of the 'absence' of time corresponds to the traditional philosophical conception of the non-Being of time, where Being is understood only in terms of the presentness of the 'now' (M 50–3). At the same time, however, Hart's formulation of the *absence* of time in terms of *space* opens it up to the problematic of doubling and 'the movement of temporalization' as 'spacing' (M 55; SP 86). It is this detour through *différance*, spacing, doubling, the imagination, the messianic, laughter, and so on, that prevents any simple consideration of 'time itself' outside of the problematic of 'space.' As I argued in chapter 2, this 'spaced-time' appears again and again in *Finnegans Wake* as the conflict between Shem and Shaun. It provokes Shaun's attack on Shem at I.6.11, and causes him to accuse '[de]graded intellecktuals' such as Shem of 'falsely' believing 'dime *is* cash and the cash system.' This scandal

> means that I cannot now have or nothave a piece of
> cheeps in your pocket at the same time and with the same man-
> ners as you can now nothalf or half the cheek apiece I've in mind
> unless Burrus and Caseous have not or not have seemaultaneous-
> ly sysentangled themselves, selldear to soldthere, once in the
> dairy days of buy and buy. (161.6–14)

The problem with the time thinkers, says Shaun, is that they think time is space. This causes them to think in terms of 'spaced-time,' and this 'spaced-time' is experienced as something of a scandal for space. Time and space, say the time thinkers, are like two brothers, Burrus and Caseous, who are also doubles in that they are indistinguishable from one another because they were 'seemaultaneously sysentangled themselves, selldear to soldthere, once in the dairy days of buy and buy.' Only this originary temporalizing doubling can explain how one object can occupy – here, a piece of 'cheeps' – can 'hide' in two different spaces (*cache*: cash) at once: the reader's pocket and Shaun's mind. It is this *différantial* understanding of 'spaced-time' therefore, that guides the reading of 'time' in both *Finnegans Wake* and *Glas* throughout this final chapter. Thus, instead of focusing on the philosophical under-standing of the problem of time, this chapter opts to read the traces of 'time's remains' (225–6a) – or as the *Wake* designates them on at least one occasion, 'ti..?' (501.5) – as they are generated/spaced in the *dif-férantial* processes of the imagination.[2] These processes, as I have been arguing, are an impure originary contamination of 'space-time.' They 'space' 'time' by extending it and writing it beyond the boundaries of the 'now,' presence and present-ness. What I am suggesting here is that the 'not-yet' of *Glas* may be read as the doubled remains of the purely temporal 'not-yet' of Hegelian semiology as it is analysed in '*Ousia* and *Grammé*' (M 52). On this reading, the 'not-yet' in *Glas* shares an affinity with what I referred to in the previous chapter as the *différantial* 'messi-anic promise' of *Archive Fever* (72), inasmuch as it can be understood to mimic and double for the 'messianism' of both the Hegelian and Pla-tonic anticipated return to/of meaning.

However, time also has another peculiar property, and this is bound up with what might be termed the ruined metaphorics of ordinary time. A brief consideration of Derrida's analysis of Husserl's under-standing of time as a primordial self-engendering impression is 'primal creation' suffices to make this clear. However, since primal cre-ation is a creation that creates no-thing, in that the new 'now' is not an empirically 'produced' 'object,' 'every language fails to describe this pure movement other than by metaphor[;] that is, by borrowing its concepts from the order of the objects of possible experience, an order this temporalization makes possible' (SP 84). In other words, even if it were 'pure' (which is impossible), the primordial emptiness of time can only ever be designated by the space of ruined metaphors according to the structure of what 'The White Mythology' calls 'catach-resis.'[3] What this amounts to is a situation where a pure primordial time is rendered impossible through an originary contamination of space; at the same time, however, this pure/ly impossible time – its no-thingness – is only expressible in the form of a metaphorics. In the next sections of this chapter, I want to explore not only how spaced-time functions as an index of the *Wake*'s semantic void, but also how this void is legible in the traces of the ruined metaphors of ordinary time in the text. This means that the text of the *Wake* uses 'degraded' metaphors of time to express an impossibly pure time that it simulta-neously crosses out through the mechanism of 'temporalization.' I will focus on two such metaphors of ordinary time – the heliotrope and clock-time. These incarnations of 'time,' I will argue, are systematically voided by the text of both the *Wake* and *Glas* in order to affect the scene of the Annunciation with the sort of 'temporalization' that marks it as a peculiarly empty 'space' in the text.

'Heliotropic Time'

Spaced-time in *Finnegans Wake*, insofar as it is 'ordinary' time, can be measured in any way that a day or night can.[4] The measurement of ordinary time makes use of days, hours, seconds, etc., in a sliding scale of periodizations, and there is ample textual evidence that shows *Finnegans Wake* taking place over a day. That day appears to be a Friday: 'Then we'll know if the feast is a flyday' (5.24); 'his soufflosion of oogs with somekat on toyast à la Mère Puard, his Poggadovies alla Fenella, his Frideggs à la Tricarême' (184.32); *'It was of a wet good Friday too she was ironing and, as I'm given now to understand, she was always mad gone on me'* (399.21); and 'Never hate mere pork which is bad for your knife of a good Friday' (433.12) (Cf. S&M 70). Over the course of the book's 'day' the reader is posted regular time checks: for example, the reader is told in ALP's letter of book IV that book I begins at 11.32: 'Femelles will be preadaminant as from twentyeight to twelve' (617.23). This may be read as a reference to the opening sentence of the book, where Eve comes before Adam: 'riverrun, past Eve and Adam's, from swerve of shore to bend of bay' (3.1). Book I ends with the six o'clock Angelus ringing (213.18–16.6), and book II begins at about 8.30 p.m., or 'lighting up o'clock sharp' (219.1). The children's pantomime lasts about an hour: they pray for 'sleep in hour's time' (259.4), and so on.

But spaced-time is also marked by the heliotrope of II.1 as the heliotropic maggies turn towards Shaun-Mick the sun-god in 'heliolatry.' In awaiting the Annunciative word from Shaun, the sun-worshipping maggies heliotropically mark the ordinary time of (a) day as they track the course of the sun across the sky. But because the course of the sun marks a day, the other things in the text that wait for the morning sun can be understood to take the form of the heliotrope. Heliotrope always seeks the sun, and a good example of this reinscribed heliotrope may be found in the 'trancedone boyscript' of the letter in II.3. This 'boyscript,' perhaps younger than a 'manuscript,' will accuse, pass judgment on, and eventually sentence HCE in much the same way that 'The Ballad of Persse O'Reilly' did in I.2. The card-like letter statement, which is 'obviously inspiterebbed by a sibspecious connex-ion,' threatens to arrive 'tomorrow, marn, when the curds on the table':

> A trancedone boy-
> script with tittivits by. Ahem. You'll read it tomorrow, marn,
> when the curds on the table. A nigg for a nogg and a thrate for
> a throte. The auditor learns. Still pumping on Torkenwhite Rad-
> lumps, Lencs. In preplays to Anonymay's left hinted palinode
> obviously inspiterebbed by a sibspecious connexion. Note the
> notes of admiration! See the signs of suspicion! Count the hemi-
> semidemicolons! Screamer caps and invented gommas, quotes
> puntlost, forced to farce! The pipette will say anything at all for
> a change. And you know what aglove means in the Murdrus due-
> luct! Fewer to feud and rompant culotticism, a fugle for the glee-
> men and save, sit and sew. And a pants outsizinned on the
> Doughertys' duckboard pointing to peace at home. In some,
> lawanorder on lovinardor. Wait till we hear the Boy of Biskop
> reeling around your postoral lector! Epistlemadethemology for
> deep dorfy doubtlings. As we'll lay till break of day in the bunk of
> basky, O! (374.1–19)

The letter arrives like a newspaper that relates the news from around the globe with the sun and the milk in the morning.

If turning towards the sun constitutes the criterion for heliotropism, then the heliotropic 'epistlemadethemology' of the letter can be gener-alized to include the entire nighttime itself. If night is given over to sleep, it always turns the sleeper's face towards waking and the rising of the sun. One sleeps in order to wake again, rested and refreshed. However, once generalized in this manner, the heliotrope becomes inflected in an odd way. In the *Wake*an nighttime, heliotropism takes place 'under the closed eyes of the inspectors' (107.28–9). It therefore follows a sun that is obviously out of sensory range. That which brings with it a loss of clear and certain knowledge returns the text to the scene of sensation in Aristotle's *Topics* V, 3, 131b20–30, which Derrida analyses:

> Every object of sensation, when it passes outside the range of sensation,
> becomes obscure; for it is not clear whether it still exists, because it is com-
> prehended only by sensation. This will be true of such attributes as do not
> necessarily and always attend upon the subject. For example, he who has

stated that it is a property of the sun to be 'the brightest star that moves above the earth' has employed in the property of something of a kind which is comprehensible only by sensation, namely 'moving above the earth'; and so the property of the sun would not have been correctly assigned, for it will not be manifest, when the sun sets, whether it is still moving above the earth, because sensation then fails us. (M 250)

Similarly, metaphor, defined by Aristotle as 'giving the thing a name that belongs to something else' (M 231),

> risks disrupting the semantic plenitude to which it should belong. Marking the moment of the turn or of the detour [*du tour ou du détour*] during which meaning might seem to venture forth alone, unloosed from the very thing it aims at however, from the truth which attunes it to its referent, metaphor also opens the wandering of the semantic. The sense of a noun, instead of designating the thing which the noun habitually must designate, carries itself elsewhere. (M 241)

The 'wandering of the semantic' opened by metaphor turns the sun into a star. If one turns towards the sun at night, it 'begins no longer to function as a sun, but as a star, the punctual source of truth or properness remaining invisible or nocturnal' (M 244). The proper sun is lost, and the heliotrope is sent wandering in the long implicit sentence that is composed of a system of catachreses, relays, and legates. In other words, the punctual source of solar truth is replaced – in much the same manner as the topics chapter 4 – by an ever-expanding series of constellations.

Thus it is with the *Wake*. The maggies look to Mick-Shaun the sun-god and try to catch 'in their calyzettes' 'those parryshoots from his muscalone pistil,' 'while, dewyfully as dimb dumbelles, all alisten to his elixir' (237.2–9). In other words, the fertilizing Annunciative word delivered by the son-sun-god is heard by turning towards the sun. Because this scene takes place at night, the nocturnal sun-god cannot be grasped as the real sun. Shaun's imposture is made clear during his evidence to the Mamalujo in III.3. Shaun tries to pass himself off as the writer of the letter, but he is not believed by the Mamalujo, who twice associate him with the false Esau, Jacob: 'The gist is the gist of Shaum but the hand is the hand of Sameas. Shan – Shim – Schung. There is a strong suspicion on counterfeit Kevin and we all remember ye in childhood's reverye' (483.3–6); and 'Hood maketh not frere. The voice is the voice of jokeup, I fear. Are you imitation Roma now or Amor now' (487.21–3). The heliotropism of the maggies therefore does not always follow the real sun, and in not doing so, heliotropism begins to lose its sense. But what value has the heliotrope if it cannot follow the true sun, but rather a nocturnal fake? It starts to function as an empty mode of temporal marking.

Clock Time, Échec, and χ

The heliotropic sun-letter's sentence is 'to be carried out tomorrow-morn by Nolans Volans at six o'clock shark' (558.17–18), the purported time of the sun's arrival. In other words, the time of the sentence's passing is the same as that of the letter's arrival at six a.m. And as the reader of *Finnegans Wake* is soon made aware through the rhythm of the 'Hail Mary,' six a.m. is yet another time for the tolling of the Angelus:

> It is
> not even yet the engine of the load with haled murries full of
> crates, you mattinmummur, for dombell dumbs? Sure 'tis
> not then. (603.9–11)

Thus, the text and the dreamer await the arrival of the morning, the letter, and the Annunciation. The association of the letter's arrival with the Annunciation might imply that the delivery of the son-seed-letter is somehow guaranteed by the rising sun. But, as I have already noted, the heliotropic structure that traces the structure of delivery also works to waylay or defer delivery. In turning towards an absent sun, the 'epistlemadethemology' of the *Wake*'s heliotropism inscribes the sun as a star. As such, it ceases to function as the proper sun. If the sun is no longer a sun, then the temporal mode of the heliotrope voids itself in no longer having the sun as its point of reference. In a similar manner it can be shown that the hour of the Annunciation (and resurrection), six o'clock, never arrives.

The fact that six o'clock never arrives is underscored by the 'not-yet' in the text of the *Wake*. This 'not-yet,' which functions as both the spaced-time discussed in chapter 2 and the temporalized opening of the book (3.4–14) discussed in chapter 1,[5] is also legible as 'time's remains' in *Glas* (226a). This time is also essentially empty, without a fully present meaning: 'The question of time is indecipherable in the chapter of *Sa*: there it is at once annulled and relieved' (227a). To seek a 'way out' of *Sa* is impossible 'if one fills with thought the words of the phenomenology of spirit and of the logic ... [T]here is no means of getting out of the absolute circle.' 'If one believes or means (*meint*) to get out of it, that is pure verbalism: one cannot think what one says; one cannot conceive the signification of words that then remain void, empty' (227a). To read thus is to read Hegel badly, to remain 'immobilized in representation, in empty signification' (227a).

It is time, the 'not-yet' of time, that fulfils the role of 'pure verbalism,' and therefore offers the 'way out' of the phantasm of *Sa*, the Immaculate Conception:

> The *Da* of the concept (time) marks, at last with the stroke of time [*du coup*], its incompleteness, its inner default, the semantic void that holds it in motion. Time is always of this vacancy with which *Sa* affects itself. Because it affects itself with this, *Sa* empties itself with a view to determining itself, *it gives itself time*. It imposes on itself a gap [*écart*] in signing itself. The *Da* of *Sa* is nothing other than the movement of signification. (229a)

Annulled time is empty signification, but it is also of representation, of the image. The image is deemed to be incomplete and lacking full meaning. It can be said that *Glas*'s reading of Hegel is one that is primarily interested in imagery. *Glas* makes use of the temporality of the image's status as 'not-yet,' as the anticipation in which the next stage in Hegel's dialectic is represented. It cultivates these anticipatory images in order to give itself a repository, or battery, of images with which to read the figurative points in the Hegelian project that are forever destined to have incomplete meaning. For this reason, the image of *Sa* itself, the incomplete representation of Absolute Knowledge, full meaning, is to be found in the step before *Sa*, in religious iconography where the empty self-affection of time fuses the power of representation and religion: 'Religion is representative because it needs time' (220a). In particular, it is 'the moment of absolute religion [that] appear[s] as [the] simple representation (*Vorstellen*)' of *Sa* (224a). The moment of Absolute Religion is, as I argued in chapter 5, that of the Holy Family, the Immaculate Conception. And, once the Holy Family is on the scene, the question of reading χ is unavoidable: 'How – for example – is one to read the Lord's anointed in the text, at the threshold of *Sa*, at the end of the next-to-last chapter of the phenomenology of spirit?' (228a). χ can be read as corresponding to Hegel's 'abstract void': 'Absolute essence that is not grasped as spirit is merely the abstract void, just as spirit that is not grasped as this movement is only an empty word' (230a). This is the position of religion, which 'brings into the realm of pure consciousness the natural relationship of the Father and the Son' (231a). In other words, this religion returns us to the voided scene of the Immaculate Conception and χ:

> Previously, already as regards the 'actual mother' and the father 'being in (it)self,' these relations were represented as 'drawn from natural genera- tion.' Religion, as religion, never absolutely gets beyond representation or nature. It is necessary to relieve, in(to) the concept, both the figure of nat- ural representation (for example, that of the fall, of the son, and so on) and the arithmetic formality (for example, the number of moments). Christ's death marks at once the destruction of his natural being and the end of the abstraction of divine essence. God himself is dead, but the knowledge of his death produces this 'spiritualization' by which the 'substance has become subject' the moment the abstraction and the cadaveric frigidity (*Leblosigkeit*) raise themselves to the hot and glorious light of life. The triumphal moment of mourning.
>
> At the angle of the phenomenology of spirit and *Sa* (of the greater logic), at the hinge [*charnière*], the tomb of the Son. (231a)

Insofar as the empty tomb of χ is another hinge in the Holy Family, it forms the 'not-yet' of *Sa*. χ remains an incomplete representation of *Sa*. And because χ is an empty, abstracted image of *Sa*, it corresponds to time. Empty time affects *Sa*, and emptying it of its semantic plenitude affects it as text: 'It remains that, in this play, the signifying significa- tion gap [*écart*] always permits a text to work empty, to no effect. The concept can always not come back to itself in a text. The triangle or the circle can remain open when *Sa* arrives at the text. The text then will be what *Sa* cannot always give itself, what happens [*arrive*] to *Sa*, rather than *Sa* arriving there itself' (229a).

The paradoxical nature of this textual time-schema *plays with* Hegel- ian time, the future anterior or the future perfect progressive tense, which describes a future, ongoing action that will already have occurred before some specified future time.[6] In *Finnegans Wake*, the Hegelian/speculative form of time is displaced by that which is, first and foremost, *written* – the hen's letter. The *Wake*'s written artefact dis- places Hegelian temporality and inscribes it as/in *writing*. In other

words, even though we read the hen's letter at 615.12–19.19, its writing
is such that it remains possible to say that it has *not yet* arrived:

> Rased on traumscrapt from Maston, Boss. After rounding his
> world of ancient days. Carried in a caddy or screwed and corked.
> On his mugisstosst surface. With a bob, bob, bottledby. Blob.
> When the waves give up yours the soil may for me. Sometime
> then, somewhere there, I wrote me hopes and buried the page
> when I heard Thy voice, ruddery dunner, so loud that none but,
> and left it to lie till a kissmiss coming. (623.36–24.6)

In its play of its writing, the 'not yet' announced in the buried letter is,
like a child's Christmas, always coming. Further, in playing at coming,
the letter exceeds Hegelian and speculative time by holding itself in
the realm of a promise, one that may never be fulfilled. It is only
through being written in the manner that it is that the letter, due to
arrive at six o'clock in book IV, can be *read* even though it does not
actually arrive.

A similar paradox occurs with the textual 'clock' in the final chapter,
which never quite gets around to actually striking six:

> Tim!
> To them in Ysat Loka. Hearing. The urb it orbs. Then's now
> with now's then in tense continuant. Heard. Who having has
> he shall have had. Hear! Upon the thuds trokes truck, chim,
> it will be exactlyso fewer hours by so many minutes of the
> ope of the diurn of the sennight of the maaned of the yere of
> the age of the madamanvantora of Grossguy and Littleylady,
> our hugibus hugibum and our weewee mother, actaman house-
> truewith, and their childer and their napirs and their napirs'
> childers napirs and their chattels and their servance and their
> cognance and their ilks and their orts and their everythings that
> is be will was theirs.
> Much obliged. Time-o'-Thay! But wherth, O clerk?
> Whithr a clonk? Vartman! (598.27–99.4)

Thus, even though the text repeatedly asks about the time, and the
whereabouts of Tim Finnegan – 'Tim!' – it can be said that no definite
answer is forthcoming: thus six a.m. is inscribed in the schema of the
'not-yet' just as the letter was. This is made even clearer by the text

when the time is further obscured by the sound of the 28 rainbow-girls as they toll in the form of church bells:

> S. Wilhelmina's, S. Gardenia's, S. Phibia's, S. Veslandrua's,
> S. Clarinda's, S. Immecula's, S. Dolores Delphin's, S. Perlan-
> throa's, S. Errands Gay's, S. Eddaminiva's, S. Rhodamena's, S.
> Ruadagara's, S. Drimicumtra's, S. Una Vestity's, S. Mintargisia's,
> S. Misha-La-Valse's, S. Churstry's, S. Clouonaskieym's, S. Bella-
> vistura's, S. Santamonta's, S. Ringsingsund's, S. Heddadin
> Drade's, S. Glacianivia's, S. Waidafrira's, S. Thomassabbess's
> and (trema! unloud!! pepet!!!) S. Loellisotoelles!
>   Prayfulness! Prayfulness!
>   Euh! Thaet is seu whaet shaell one naeme it!
>   The meidinogues have tingued togethering. Ascend out of
> your bed, cavern of a trunk, and shrine! (601.21–32)

It is impossible to discern the hour in the middle of this 28 bell(e) racket. These bells call in vain for HCE to awaken: 'Ascend out of your bed, cavern of a trunk, and shrine!' Because he does not arise (yet), and six is the hour of his expected resurrection, it cannot yet be six o'clock. In other words, the bell(e)s toll, but six does not arrive. It is therefore caught in the time of its tolling, a tolling that paradoxically, does not tell the time in any real sense. This peculiar mode of time is, according to Clive Hart, due to the fact that book IV

> begins and ends at 6 a.m. It is a timeless moment which yet contains all
> the seeds of the book. In the yearly frame of reference *Finnegans Wake*
> begins and ends at the vernal equinox, so that in Book IV the sun rises at 6
> a.m. exactly. The sun is in fact rising as Book IV opens (593–4) and is still
> rising as it ends. All the substance of the chapter is in a state of momen-
> tary change-over from one cycle to the next and is here 'frozen' in the act.
> Book IV is indeed the most important of a number of 'stills' in 'this
> allnights newseryreel' (489.35). (S&M 73)

This 'frozen time' also explains how, some eighteen pages later in the text, △ is still trying to coax her 'man of the hooths' to 'Rise up' (619.25). Rising time – six o'clock – is thus always, like a child's Christmas, com-ing, and the text haemorrhages time insofar as the allotted time does not arrive. 'Time' is no longer itself. Once again, the text reinscribes 'time' as 'non-time,' space. And because the paradigm of spaced-time is the not-yet, this sort of 'time' affects the scene of the Annunciation or Immaculate Conception, as one of a (non)Annunciation. In other words, the 'time' of the Annunciation makes it a (non)Annunciation of the child, a situation that provokes the legal controversy surrounding the legitimacy of the child in the family firm in III.4.

This scene of legal wrangling has here to do with someone's having passed a bad cheque. Two individuals, D'Oyly Owens and F.X. Coppinger, bring a suit against HCE and ALP (who here become the 'firm' of 'Brerfuchs [Fox] and Warren [Rabbit]') over their liability for a certain 'joint deposit' (574.3). The 'foreign firm' that they form is said to be 'disseized' because it has not paid its legitimate debts:

> D'Oyly Owens
> holds (though Finn Magnusson of himself holds also) that so
> long as there is a joint deposit account in the two names a
> mutual obligation is posited. Owens cites Brerfuchs and Warren,
> a foreign firm, since disseized, registered as Tangos, Limited,
> for the sale of certain proprietary articles. The action which was
> at the instance of the trustee of the heathen church emergency
> fund, suing by its trustee, a resigned civil servant, for the pay-
> ment of tithes due was heard by Judge Doyle and also by a com-
> mon jury. No question arose as to the debt for which vouchers
> spoke volumes. The defence alleged that payment had been made
> effective. The fund trustee, one Jucundus Fecundus Xero Pecun-
> dus Coppercheap, counterclaimed that payment was invalid
> having been tendered to creditor under cover of a crossed cheque,
> signed in the ordinary course, in the name of Wieldhelm, Hurls
> Cross, voucher copy provided, and drawn by the senior partner
> only by whom the lodgment of the species had been effected but
> in their joint names. (574.1–18)

The duplicitous pair – whose 'firm' is now called 'Tangos,' Latin for 'I touch, I cheat' – has tried to pay its debts using a 'crossed cheque.' In trying to pay off their debts with counterfeit money, the pair, allege their creditors, shirk their fiscal responsibilities: simply to offer, but not to pay, is insufficient to acquit the debt. In case the reader might suspect that a crossed cheque from a firm of touchers and cheaters is crossed merely to prevent its being cashed by just about anyone (such crossing would be useless in the face of a forger), the text makes clear that the 'crossed cheque' is null and void, a 'D you D,' a dud:

> Since then the cheque, a good washable pink, em-
> bossed D you D No 11 hundred and thirty 2, good for the figure
> and face, had been circulating in the country for over thirtynine
> years among holders of Pango stock, a rival concern, though not
> one demonetised farthing had ever spun or fluctuated across the
> counter in the semblance of hard coin or liquid cash.
> (574.25–30)

The joint-deposit cheque is therefore a dud that never comes to presence as either 'hard coin' or 'liquid cash' that might pay off a debt. The
dud cheque, which has been circulating for thirty-nine years without
being cashed, is what causes an action to be brought against the firm's
partners by their creditors. However,

> only the junior partner Barren could be found, who entered an
> appearance and turned up, upon a notice of motion and after service
> of the motion by interlocutory injunction, among the male jurors
> to be an absolete turfwoman, originally from the proletarian class,
> with still a good title to her sexname of Ann Doyle. (575.2–6)

Here, the null and void 'D you D' cheque affects the name of one of the
partners in the firm: Warren becomes Barren. Barren is in turn revealed
to be 'Ann,' the mother-hen-writer of the letter in I.5. Ann-Barren-
Warren takes the stand in the suit brought against her firm in order to
defend her absent senior partner, Brerfawkes. If the mother is a 'junior
partner,' then the 'firm' in question can be read in terms of a family,
which reinscribes the 'Holy Family' in which HCE plays the absent
father, who no longer has any physical contact with what the text calls
the 'matter of tact' – the tactility of the 'actual' mother (576.1–2). In this
'Holy Family,' the crossed cheque is the joint deposit of the father and
mother: a Christ-child. However, because this cheque is a dud, it is also
crossed (out). This cross simultaneously crosses out, or cancels, the
cheque, and marks it with a 'χ.' Here, the cross cancels Christ as a dud
even as it marks him as Christ: it strikes through, or voids, the cheque-
child, reinscribing it as a scene of (non)Annunciation, where a dud
cheque, which cannot be said to arrive, remains without value in that it
cannot pay for what it was written for.

Thus does this reinscription of the scene of the (non)Annunciation
hinge here on the nature of the debt incurred by the Holy Family that
issues cheques it cannot guarantee. Ann tries to account for her inabil-

ity to pay her firm's debts by stating that she was paid with many 'blank assignations' by other 'payers-drawers,' which she also issued to her creditors:[7]

> Doyle (Ann), add woman in,
> having regretfully left the juryboxers, protested cheerfully on the
> stand in a long jurymiad *in re* corset checks, delivered in doy-
> lish, that she had often, in supply to brusk demands rising almost
> to bollion point, discounted Mr Brakeforth's first of all in ex-
> change at nine months from date without issue and, to be strictly
> literal, unbottled in corrubberation a current account of how
> she had been made at sight for services rendered the payee-
> drawee of unwashable blank assignations, sometimes pinkwilliams
> (laughter) but more often of the *crème-de-citron, vair émail paon-
> coque* or marshmallow series, which she, as bearer, used to en-
> dorse, adhesively, to her various payers-drawers who in most cases
> were identified by the timber papers as wellknown tetigists of the
> city and suburban. (575.7–20)

Aside from what the Holy Family may actually be owed by its debtors, the debt incurred by the Holy Family has, therefore, everything to do with the absent husband's 'lack of issue' after 'nine months.' In other words, the child-cheque is a dud that cannot be honoured by the absent father, who may or may not be impotent. The mother, Ann, in an effort to defend her husband against these allegations of impotency, tells the court that in the father's absence many lodgments in and withdrawals from the firm were made by other toucher-cheaters over the years, implying that all the other lodgments also failed to produce the magical bond of filiation. However, her evidence has a two-fold effect: first, it reinscribes her virginity as that of the promiscuous nurse-mother of the *Timaeus*; second, it means that neither parent is capable of guaranteeing the child's value. The debt is incurred by arrival of a dud-cheque-bastard-child who, simultaneously, does not arrive in order to pay off a debt. The non-arrival or (non)Annunciation of the child inscribes it once again as being 'Jewish' insofar as it is made by the mother in the absence of the father, and without knowledge (of him).[8]

Perhaps aware that her evidence cannot help her husband's case, Ann tries a different approach. She offers her services to Coppinger, who has now been transformed into 'Monsignore Pepigi' and who has

taken an interest in her. When she consents to enter into a new 'par-
donership' with him, Ann hopes he will 'pardon' her family of its
problematic debt. Thus, she offers

> to reamalgamate herself,
> tomorrow perforce, in pardonership with the permanent suing fond
> trustee, Monsignore Pepigi, under the new style of Will Break-
> fast and Sparrem, as, when all his cognisances had been estreated,
> he seemed to proffer the steadiest interest towards her ... (575.26–31)

Just as Ann is about to offer herself as payment for the non-arrival of
her child, the dud-cheque, the court intervenes and her

> prepoposal was ruled out on appeal by Judge Jeremy Doyler, who,
> reserving judgment in a matter of courts and reversing the find-
> ings of the lower correctional, found, beyond doubt of treuson,
> fending the dissassents of the pickpackpanel, twelve as upright
> judaces as ever let down their thoms, and, occupante extremum
> scabie handed down to the jury of the Liffey that, as a matter of
> tact, the woman they gave as free was born into contractual in-
> capacity (the Calif of Man *v* the Eaudelusk Company) when, how
> and where mamy's mancipium act did not apply and therefore held
> supremely that, as no property in law can exist in a corpse,
> (Hal Kilbride *v* Una Bellina) Pepigi's pact was pure piffle (loud
> laughter) and Wharrem would whistle for the rhino. (575.31–76.7)

It would seem that in the eyes of the court, Ann's offering her services
to Pepigi is drawn from an insufficient fund for acquitting the debt
incurred by the Holy Family for its dud cheque. However, this solution
is not sufficient for Judge Doyler and his 'judaces,' who throw out
D'Oyly Owens-Coppinger-Pepigi's suit. The judge rules that 'no property in law can exist in a corpse.' The attempt to pay off the debt is
unsatisfactory to the court because it cannot break the contract of marriage to the non-present father. His non-presence cannot simply be 'fastened or promised' by 'Pepigi' (Latin *pepigi*, I have fastened, promised,
driven in), who would simply fill the void.

The judge's ruling regarding the lack of property due a corpse also
recalls the structure of Jewish law discussed in chapter 2. For Derrida,
Jewish law is governed by non-presence because at its heart one looks
in vain for a centre 'under a sensible cover [*enveloppe*] – the tent of the

tabernacle, the stone of the temple, the robe that clothes the text of the covenant' (50a). This is because there is nothing to be discovered beneath the shroud: it is 'an empty room, [which] is not uncovered, never ends being uncovered, as it has nothing to show' (50a). Because it is void of all proper content and sense, its 'vacant center ... signif[ies] that the Jewish essence is totally alienated. Its ownness, its property would be infinitely foreign to itself' (50a). In other words, the Jew is always already dead insofar as his relation to the law remains external, written without the life of spirit because the 'Jewish tongue [*langue*] speaks without yet knowing how to speak, without being able to develop fully the sperm of the [Christian] *logos*. It is the childhood of the tongue' (73a). Under this ruling of Jewish law, the new family – that of 'Wharrem' and 'Pepigi' that seeks the acquittal without remainder of debt incurred by non-presence – can 'whistle for the rhino [money]' because the wife-partner was born into 'contractual incapacity' in being already bound to an (older) contract with the non-presence and lack of knowledge regarding the father. Thus, it is due to the non-presence of the Holy Family-firm's senior partner, and the mother's lack of knowledge regarding him, that the (law)suit falls. In its turn, this non-presence and unknowable and broken (af)filiation fuels the rumours and questions about the filiation of the crossed dud-child-cheque. This dud cheque is a dud because it does not even arrive. And even if it did arrive (which is impossible), there are insufficient funds for it to be cashed. In other words, it cannot be guaranteed by either parent, and can only take place in the text according to the a/temporal structure of a (non)Annunciation.

II Reading-Writing: 'Contractations' and Morsels

Emptying: From Topic to Type

In this section, I will argue that the emptiness of 'time' or, better, spaced-time explored in the previous section affects all the other forms of emptiness in these texts with a generalized (non)Annunciated fetishism that overflows the image of the Immaculate Conception. As I argued above, the Immaculate Conception is already to an extent overflowed by the way in which it grafts itself onto the mother-nurse of the *Timaeus*. However, I want to open this emptiness up even further by indicating some of the ways in which the emptiness of time-space sketches reading-writing in these texts. This emptiness, I will argue, calls for a reconstruction of reading with respect to some of the essential textual operations in both *Finnegans Wake* and *Glas*. Next, I will explore the ways in which these operations can be traced in both texts by considering the games each text plays with squares and the contraction of rings, and how the interaction of both line and curve may be explored through the ancient art of manuscript illumination. I will conclude by considering this analysis's major preoccupations with non-eidetic writing, the spaced-time of *différance*, the series of X's of letter writing, manuscript illumination, and so on, all converging in the 'X' of the Book of Kells's *Tunc* page. This X-point, I will argue, forges a written relation to an unknown beyond philosophy, in a sort of unceasing temporal algebra that is no longer grasped in terms of 'meaning' understood in either the Hegelian or Platonic sense.

Thinking about spaced-time, or rather its 'remains,' offers a way out of the image of the Immaculate Conception. This happens, as I mentioned in the previous section, through the so-called temporal 'not-yet' of both the *Wake* and *Glas* that grafts the non-dialectical remainder in all its non-present forms. In other words, because it is non-dialectical, time can be understood as being essentially empty, without meaning for the project of speculative philosophy: 'The question of time is indecipherable in the chapter of *Sa*: there it is at once annulled and relieved' (227a). Read in this way, the text of *Finnegans Wake* becomes the site of a temporal writing devoid of sense that seeks a way out of the speculative project of *Sa*. Escape from *Sa*, however, is impossible 'if one fills with thought the words of the phenomenology of spirit and of the logic ... [T]here is no means of getting out of the absolute circle.' Instead of this attempt to think itself out of the nets cast by *Sa*, both the *Wake* and *Glas* turn to the interplay of 'belief' and 'pure verbalism': 'If one believes or means (*meint*) to get out of it, that is pure verbalism: one cannot think what one says; one cannot conceive the signification of words that then remain void, empty' (227a). To read thus is to read (Hegel) badly, since reading in this manner remains 'immobilized in representation, in empty signification' (227a). Further, to read thus is to be preoccupied with the letter of the law rather than its life-force or spirit. In short, by reading thus the reader writes.[9]

This is due to the difficulty involved in 'thinking' the remain(s) of time, especially when these remains form a mode of time 'that would not come under [*relèverait d'*] a present, under a mode of being or presence, and that would not fall from it as *its* negative' (226a). Time's remain(s) are not 'permanent, substantial, subsistent,' nor are they 'the residue' or 'scrap that falls' from speculative dialectics: 'The remain(s), here, rather, would provoke the action' (226a). In provoking the dialectical action of *Sa*, the remain(s) would no longer come under its power because the dialectic would be after the fact of the remain(s). As such, the remain(s) is/are 'suspended' between permanence, substance, subsistence, and the impermanence of a scrap that falls from the dialectic. This suspension tears the remains into two 'senses,' into 'morsels': 'Let us give ourselves the time of this suspense. For the moment time will be nothing but the suspense between the regularity and the irregularity of the morsels of what remains' (226a). So, according to this structure, time, in its suspended form, has something to do with the 'morsel,' or play of morsels. In *Finnegans Wake* suspended time attaches to the (non)Annunciation of both the Angelus and heliotropism. But what has this suspended time to do with the operation of cutting into morsels? And what have squares to do with reading?

In order to offer an answer to these questions, I want to return to the scene of the letter's composition in order to reconsider its *envelope*:

> Has any fellow, of
> the dime a dozen type, it might with some profit some dull even-
> ing quietly be hinted – has any usual sort of ornery josser, flat-
> chested fortyish, faintly flatulent and given to ratiocination by
> syncopation in the elucidation of complications,of his greatest
> Fung Yang dynasdescendanced,only another the son of, in fact,
> ever looked sufficiently longly at a quite everydaylooking stamped
> addressed envelope? Admittedly it is an outer husk: its face, in
> all its featureful perfection of imperfection, is its fortune: ... (109.1–9)

The envelope is the disseminative empty 'husk,' or 'space' into which a letter is placed, and as such it corresponds to the play-space of the turning-toward discussed in relation to Heidegger's analysis of the imagination in Kant, which composes the schema-image.

> Admittedly it is an outer husk: its face, in
> all its featureful perfection of imperfection, is its fortune: it ex-
> hibits only the civil or military clothing of whatever passion-
> pallid nudity or plaguepurple nakedness may happen to tuck it-
> self under its flap. Yet to concentrate solely on the literal sense or
> even the psychological content of any document to the sore

neglect of the enveloping facts themselves circumstantiating it is
just as hurtful to sound sense (and let it be added to the truest
taste) as were some fellow in the act of perhaps getting an intro
from another fellow turning out to be a friend in need of his, say,
to a lady of the latter's acquaintance, engaged in performing the
elaborative antecistral ceremony of upstheres, straightaway to run
off and vision her plump and plain in her natural altogether, pre-
ferring to close his blinkhard's eyes to the ethiquethical fact that
she was, after all, wearing for the space of the time being some
definite articles of evolutionary clothing, inharmonious creations,
a captious critic might describe them as, or not strictly necessary
or a trifle irritating here and there, but for all that suddenly full
of local colour and personal perfume and suggestive, too, of so
very much more and capable of being stretched, filled out, if need
or wish were, of having their surprisingly like coincidental parts
separated don't they now, for better survey by the deft hand of
an expert, don't you know? Who in his heart doubts either that
the facts of feminine clothiering are there all the time or that the
feminine fiction, stranger than the facts, is there also at the same
time, only a little to the rere? Or that one may be separated from
the other? Or that both may then be contemplated simultaneously?
Or that each may be taken up and considered in turn apart from
the other? (109.13–36)

The envelope-knickers, which are empty, are to be 'stretched, filled
out.' It/they is/are that which 'clothe(s)' (*band*) the (wo)man wearing
them, preventing the viewer from envisioning him/her too quickly in
'her plump and plain in her natural altogether.'

The colour of these garments provides a way for coming to grips
with these knickers within the framework of a non-Hegelian reading
of the *Wake*. The empty knickers, the reader is told, are 'full of local
colour and personal perfume' (109.25–6). In combining both colour
and scent, the knickers recall the both the heliotrope (the smell of its
flower), as well as the heliotropically hued knickers of II.1 that draw
forth the other's '(s)prich.' Not only that, but the non-present emptiness of the knickers allows them to reinscribe the postal space discussed in chapter 3 wherein non-present *Wake*an objects come to stand
without presence. Thus do the knickers function as a schema-image, an
anticipatory representation without presence. As such, they are nothing: they enact the turning-toward that lets-stand-against, the 'premo-

nition' that 'cannot be a [present] being,' which if it is not a being, is 'just a nothing [*ein Nichts*]. Only if the letting-stand-against of ... is a holding oneself in the nothing can the representing allow a not-nothing [*ein nich-Nichts*], i.e., something like a being if such a thing shows itself empirically, to be encountered instead of and within the nothing' (KPM 51). Thus, the play-space of the envelope-knickers is also the space where something comes to stand, and be what it is. In this sense the envelope captures precisely the structure of the postal imaginary: that which comes to stand in it is eminently postable.

Taken in this fashion, the envelope-knickers explicitly draw(s) together postal space – insofar as it/they is/are an envelope – with the non-present mechanics of the heliotropic 'rossy banders' (250.3) to the extent that they can be 'stretched, filled out.' These articles of feminine underwear exert an equal and opposite tension that binds, holds in, and constricts 'accourdant to the coursets of things feminite' (236.26–37.1). In the 'corsetry' of their *bander* the knickers also bind and constrict in order to give rise to both the erection and gush of (s)prich which is, as I have been arguing, both male and female, sheathing the fetish of the author-forger, bandaging him/her erect. They therefore (re)enact the constrictive arrest followed by the emptying flow of an image that constitutes the rhythm of the Joycean postal imaginary.

This gushing outpouring recalls what Heidegger calls the 'gift of the outpouring as libation': 'The consecrated libation is what our word for a strong outpouring flow, "gush," really designates: gift and sacrifice. "Gush," Middle English *guschen*, *gosshen* – cf. German *Guss*, *geissen* – is the Greek *cheein*, the Indoeuropean *ghu*. It means to offer in sacrifice' (*Poetry Language Thought*, 172). But the outpouring does not only return the text to a concern with the sacrifice of chapters 2 and 4. This gushed outpouring also attaches to the text of the *Wake*, which is made up of the familiar textual rhythms that constitute the 'next to nothing' of the words of others.[10] These words are emptied of their present sense and become unreadable to the extent that reading remains an activity whereby one refills words with pre-existent sense.[11] Voided of the Hegelian 'messianism' of sense, they become what the *Wake* calls 'typtopies':

> A bone, a pebble, a ramskin; chip them,
> chap them, cut them up allways; leave them to terracook in the
> muttheringpot: and Gutenmorg with his cromagnom charter,
> tintingfast and great primer must once for omniboss step rub-

rickredd out of the wordpress else is there no virtue more in al-
cohoran. For that (the rapt one warns) is what papyr is meed
of, made of, hides and hints and misses in prints. Till ye finally
(though not yet endlike) meet with the acquaintance of Mister
Typus, Mistress Tope and all the little typtopies. Fillstup. So you
need hardly spell me how every word will be bound over to carry
three score and ten toptypsical readings throughout the book of
Doublends Jined (may his forehead be darkened with mud who
would sunder!) till Daleth, mahomahouma, who oped it closeth
thereof the. Dor. (20 5–18)

The reader confronts a non-present text of 'typtopies,' a combination of
type and topics, emptied of its present sense. In other words, the
reader is a reader-writer who proceeds to 'bind' (20.14) in a hen-like
fashion 'all the little typtopies' together in order to generate multiple
'toptypsical readings' of the 'book of Doublends Jined.' In 'jining' or
'binding' the parental 'typus-topes' together, the reader-writer-child
fabricates or forges the text. In order to be able to do so at all, the
reader-writer must be able to see and hear those textual topics on
the basis of a non-present prior readerly-writerly familiarity with the
words of others embedded in the type of the text.

The text offers a neat synopsis of what actually happens to the meaning of the original phrases once they are encrypted in typographical
topics:

> To tell how your mead of, mard, is made of. All old
> Dadgerson's dodges one conning one's copying and that's what
> wonderland's wanderlad'll flaunt to the fair. A trancedone boy-
> script with tittivits by. Ahem. You'll read it tomorrow, marn,
> when the curds on the table. A nigg for a nogg and a thrate for
> a throte. The auditor learns. Still pumping on Torkenwhite Rad-
> lumps, Lencs. In preplays to Anonymay's left hinted palinode
> obviously inspiterebbed by a sibspecious connexion. Note the
> notes of admiration! See the signs of suspicion! Count the hemi-
> semidemicolons! Screamer caps and invented gommas, quoites
> puntlost, forced to farce! The pipette will say anything at all for
> a change. And you know what aglove means in the Murdrus due-
> luct! Fewer to feud and rompant culotticism, a fugle for the glee-
> men and save, sit and sew. And a pants outsizinned on the
> Doughertys' duckboard pointing to peace at home. In some,

lawanorder on lovinardor. Wait till we hear the Boy of Biskop
reeling around your postoral lector! Epistlemadethemology for
deep dorfy doubtlings. As we'll lay till break of day in the bunk of
basky, O! (374.1–19)

In reading the letter's 'trancedone boyscript' (or 'automatic writing'),
'the auditor learns' the letter's textual process of 'epistlemadethemology.' This epistlemadethemology is a duplicitous and doubled writing
that is written by an anonymous left hand that both accuses 'the auditor' and retracts in the form of the palinode. If its writing both admires
and casts suspicion (at the same time) on 'the auditor,' then the typographic *topics* are 'obviously inspiterebbed by a sibspecious connexion'
to the words of others. These words are subjected to a writing in which
the 'quoites [are] puntlost, forced to farce.' In other words, in this
epistlemadethemology, quotes are punished until the point is lost, and
farce becomes over-stuffed, the farce of farce, which supplements the
Hegelian conception of meaning.

But how is the Hegelian conception of meaning supplemented?
Meaning is supplemented through an excess, or over-stuffing of meaning. The text trades on the reader-writer's prior familiarity with the
words or phrases of others, reinscribing the readerly-writerly relation
to the phrase in terms of the anticipatory nature of the image. By anticipating the phrase-images, the reader-writer is also heliotropically
drawn through the text, turning to the next occurrence of the phrase-
image. There can only be a next occurrence of the phrase-image if there
is a certain excess already in the phrase-image. Thus, the reader-writer
is drawn through the text by the anticipated excess of the phrase-
image. Further, the excess of the rhythmic phrase-image causes it to
show itself as 'other than what it is.' This structure will be recognized
as that of the generalized image discussed in chapters 2 and 3.

If the excessive rhythmic image is to be understood in this way, then
it must also be grasped as emptying itself of any pre-existing present
semantic content. This emptying, which recalls the functioning of Earwicker's paradigmatic and Dionysian ear (70.36), occurs on the basis of
the image that exceeds the particular occurrence: the image 'shows us
"only" the "as ..." in terms of which [something] can appear' (KPM 67).
The general (non-present) rhythmic image is then inherently empty,
open, and representational without presence.[11] The general nature of
the rhythmic image overflows any prior semantic content that could be
construed as original. This scene of overflowing rhythmic imagery that

empties itself is associated in the *Wake* with the structure of the 'amplified' echo (533.33) as well as that of the tabernacle:

> Armigerend everfasting horde. Rico! So the bill to the bowe.
> As the belle to the beau. We herewith pleased returned auditors'
> thanks for those and their favours since safely enjoined. Coco-
> ree! Tellaman tillamie. Tubbernacul in tipherairy, sons, travel-
> lers in company and their carriageable tochters, tanks tight anne
> thynne for her contractations tugowards his personeel. Echo,
> chorec chorecho! O I you O you me! (584.28–34)

Here Issy's echoing heliotropic-tabernacle is composed of 'contractations.' These rhythmic 'contractations' of the scene of *bander* are composed of the Latin for handling stolen goods, *contractatio*. The stolen
bands of the *Wake*an tabernacle graft themselves onto the text of *Glas*,
where the tabernacle is also a site emptied of ontological and eidetic
meaning (49a). The 'contractated' rhythm of the text cannot house the
semantics of presence, and its voided rhythm operates according to a
logic that is incommensurable with the 'messianism' of meaning.

'Reading': Squares

Agglutination, as I argued above, is concerned with a reduction of any
present model of sense. A splendid example of agglutination is found
in *Glas*'s playful consideration of the words of (an)other, Jean Genet's
phrase *'le voile du palais.'* In the text of Genet (and therefore *Glas*), the
'glosses' of the phrase *'le voile du palais'*

> resound in every sense and direction under the vaults of a *palais* [palace,
> palate]. The glue of chance [*aléa*] makes sense. All the ca(u)ses deploy
> their discourses, their effects, their substance there in *voiles* of every kind
> or gender [with a masculine article, veils; a feminine one, sails], in cob-
> webs or trousers. (140b)

This *palais* recalls Issy's mouth at 249.5, which also resounds with the
echo of her word:

> There lies her word, you
> reder! The height herup exalts it and the lowness her down aba-
> seth it. It vibroverberates upon the tegmen and prosplodes from

pomoeria. A window, a hedge, a prong, a hand, an eye, a sign, a
head and keep your other augur on her paypaypay. (249.13–17)

Thus, in both *Glas* and *Finnegans Wake*, non-present echoes (i.e., recurrent amplified sounds that void present sense) 'glom' together to make
up the 'signifying paste' that 'also sticks to the sense' (147–9b). In other
words, the voided 'ringing' of the text also affects sense with its ringing (*Glas*, 149b–60b). In this way, the text becomes (re)motivated. But 'a
determination, hence a motivation, hence a univocal semantics are
impossible ... "[because] there is no simple and exclusive correspondence between a drive and a given sound." The drive that seeks to
motivate always finds something with which to be nourished and frustrated at once. Its result necessarily contradicts the drive because the
drive itself, by itself, diverges [*s'écarte*] into two columns' (159bi). The
frustration of the drive for univocality is itself due in part to the
(re)motivating drive that splits itself in two. This split results in the loss
of meaning insofar as there is 'no simple and exclusive correspondence
between a drive and a given sound' (159bi).

The loss of a present referent in *Glas* is perhaps most readily grasped
as a theft: the theft [*vol*; but also flight] attaches to an old woman
[*vielle*], an 'old thief' [*vielle voleuse*], who robs the semantics of presence
of its referent:

[A]s always semantic necessity, giving rise to a hermeneutics, a semiotics,
verily a psychoanalysis, remains undecidably suspended from the chance
of an agglutination called formal or signifying. The flight, the theft [*vol*] of
this suspense, and its necessity, derails semanticism as well as formalism.
Voleuse takes up *veilleuse* [night light] in mid-flight [*au vol*] and fixes it a
little farther on in *vielle voleuse*. Marvellous [*merveilleuse*] writing. Incredibly precious. (147bi)

Theft, or the 'contractations' (584.33) of Issy's 'Tubbernacul' (584.31)
make off with non-present sounds of a phrase, setting its present
semantic content on a long implicit sentence (M 257). The empty
phrase is then refilled with other words. When the reader sets about
(re)filling the phrases, s/he is precisely, according to *Glas*, reading:
'because *reading* has been defined simultaneously as semantic (ful)fill-
ing and as remain(s) of semantic void' (228a). In other words, as the
reader fills the rhythmic void, s/he reads the text. In this way,
the rhythmically voided semantic content is paradoxically 'read on the

condition of not being read' (228a), because the present meaning of the phrase is lost. And it is here that the square intervenes in reading as 'representation' and 'empty signification':

> What happens if one is immobilized in representation, in empty significa-tion? Or if one deviates [s'écart] from the three, the deviation, the écart, as its name indicates [écart: gap, quarter (of a shield), é-cart, etc.], cutting the text up and out into squares [en carrés] or squaring it, dividing it into quarters more or less regular, exalting it (on the contrary or thereby even) or revering the charter in it, unless the deviation deals the text out like playing cards. What about the text as remain(s) – ensemble of morsels that no longer proceed from the whole and that will never form altogether one? That is no longer a question. (227a)

According to the text of *Glas*, in tearing the text into squares the reader reads, becoming embroiled in a game of cards that does without present meaning. The text of book III section 4 plays this game as it offers the reader four tableaux, each of which projects the spectacle of the parents, △ and Ш, during sex from the point of view of each of the four evangelists, Matthew, Mark, Luke, and John. Matthew is the first to present his tableau to the reader:

> A time.
> Act: dumbshow.
> Closeup. Leads.
> Man with nightcap, in bed, fore. Woman, with curlpins, hind.
> Discovered. Side point of view. First position of harmony. Say!
> Eh? Ha! Check action. Matt. Male partly masking female. Man
> looking round, beastly expression, fishy eyes, paralleliped
> homoplatts, ghazometron pondus, exhibits rage. Business. Ruddy
> blond, Armenian bole, black patch, beer wig, gross build,
> episcopalian, any age. Woman, sitting, looks at ceiling, haggish
> expression, peaky nose, trekant mouth, fithery wight, exhibits
> fear. Welshrabbit teint, Nubian shine, nasal fossette, turfy tuft,
> undersized, free kirk, no age. Closeup. Play! (559.17–29)

It will be noticed that Matthew's tableau freezes the couple in what seems to be a sexual act, and forms something of an obscene *ekphrasis*. But this *ekphrasis* – perhaps paradoxically – also contains the stage direction 'Play!', which can be understood to open the frozen tableau onto other more game-like tableaux.

The tableau opens onto a table, 'a flat board, a plank, a board to play on, a writing tablet, a written tablet, a writing, a list, an account, a painted tablet, a painting, a votive tablet, a flat piece of ground' (OED). In this textual instance, however, the table in question is composed of the squares of what the text calls a 'Tabler' (559.30), a Joycean coinage that seems to derive from *tablier*, the French word for chessboard:

> By the sinewy forequarters of the mare Pocahontas and by the white shoulders of Finnuala you should have seen how that smart sallowlass just hopped a nanny's gambit out of bunk like old mother Mesopotomac and in eight and eight sixtyfour she was off, door, knightlamp with her, billy's largelimbs prodgering after to queen's lead. Promiscuous Omebound to Fiammelle la Diva. Huff! His move. Blackout.
>
> Circus. Corridor.
>
> Shifting scene. Wall flats: sink and fly. Spotlight working wall cloths. Spill playing rake and bridges. Room to sink: stairs to sink behind room. Two pieces. Haying after queue. Replay.
>
> The old humburgh looks a thing incomplete so. It is so. On its dead. But it will pawn up a fine head of porter when it is finished. In the quicktime. The castle arkwright put in a chequered staircase certainly. It has only one square step, to be steady,yet notwith-stumbling are they stalemating backgammoner supstairs by skips and trestles tiltop double corner. Whist while and game.
> (559.32–60.12)

Here, in this sexual scene, the strategy of chess is related to the manipulation of stage scenery and props. These props are presented by the passage in terms of the manipulation of the pieces of the strategic games of chess, draughts, and cards. The passage is also shot through with the vocabulary of these games. For instance, a 'gambit' (559.34) is the opening move in a game of chess. 'Huffing' (560.2) captures an opponent's pieces (560.5) in both draughts or checkers, and the 'rake and bridges,' or rook and bishop, are 'Two pieces' used in chess. A pawn (560.8) is an oft-sacrificed chess piece. 'Stalemate' (560.11) and 'Check' (hidden in the word 'chequered' [560.9]) name certain chess moves. 'Chequered' itself recalls the look of the 8 × 8 = 64 ('eight and eight sixtyfour' [559.35]) squares of the chess/draughtboard, and on any given chess/draughtboard, the 'top double corner' square is, obviously, the cornermost one. 'Backgammon' (560.11) is a strategic game of chance 'played on a board consisting of two tables (usually united by a hinge), with draughtsmen whose moves are determined by throws of the dice' (OED).

But the tableau is not exhausted by playing on all these tables. It also names 'the arrangement formed by the cards laid out on the table in the game of patience' (OED). Patience, or solitaire, is a game of cards that requires both strategy and patience. And it is patience that the letter chapter of I.5 counsels the reader in:

> Now, patience; and remember patience is the great thing, and above all things else we must avoid anything like being or becoming out of patience. A good plan used by worried business folk who may not have had many momentums to master Kung's doctrine of the meang or the propriety codestruces of Carprimustimus is just to think of all the sinking fund of patience possessed in their conjoint names by both brothers Bruce with whom are incorporated their Scotch spider and Elberfeld's Calculating Horses. (108.8–16)

If the strategic manipulation of cards in the solitary game of patience is borne in mind, it then becomes possible to see the text as something dependent on the woman-hen and 'Her Move[s]' (559.30) within a generalized field of strategic squares. In other words, the squares or leaves of text can be played like a game of patience. Indeed, the game of patience with chopped squares of text is one played by Joyce and his son: 'The piece for the Criterion [I.5, the "hen" chapter] nearly drove me crazy. It came back from the typist (to whom I was too blind to explain the labyrinth) in a dreadful muddle. Yesterday with three magnifying glasses and the help of my son we chopped it up and today Mr. Morel will come and sew it up again on his sewing machine.'[13] Thus, chopping up and sewing back together text is a game played with the text of the hen. Chopping and joining together again may also be grafted onto *Glas*'s textual operation of 'strewking': 'To incorporate all sexes at once ... assumes cutting [*coupure*] and the supplement within the double band. But as soon as there are two bands, by reason of supplementary strewking, *coupture*, (grafted flower), a double, undecidable sex activates itself sheathing father and mother all at once' (247–8b). 'Strewking' is *Glas*'s word for the simultaneous cutting and sewing of the 'morsels' or remains of text, an operation it performs with Genet's text: 'The morsels, which I cut [*coupe*] and sew [*couds*] in the text designated by the one named Genet, must neither destroy its form or quash it (prompting) breath ... nor recompose or recapture [*reassaisir*] its integrity in one of those nets – formal or semantic: [but] only in order to show how or rather to draw beyond any manifestation that the net operates only insofar as it is beholden to a remain(s)' (169b). However, according to *Glas*, 'strewking' is not merely the citation of another's text (here, Genet's): it is also the originary citation that stitches the semantic and formal nets, making them possible. But, as can be readily seen, originary citation, or strewking, fuses citation with the undecidable sex hidden in the fetish (247–8b). Sexual undecidability in the fetish is not formed by weaving the 'fleece of hair [*la toison*]' (210ai), because such weaving concerns itself with the '"disavowal" that protects the child against the threat of castration' and allows him/her to believe in 'the substitute (*Ersatz*) for the woman's (the mother's) phallus' (210ai). Derrida implies here that the threat of castration is, to a degree, controlled, resolved in this weaving, where it could act as a 'sign of triumph' over castration (210ai). In contradistinction to the triumphant operation of weaving, *Glas* offers instead Freud's other, 'purely speculative,' remarks on the fetishist's 'oscillation' between 'the denial and the affirmation (*Behauptung*), the assertion or the assumption of castration. This at-once, the in-the-same-stroke, the *du-même-coup* of the two contraries, of the two opposite operations, prohibits cutting through to a decision within the undecidable' (210ai). The undecidability of the cut is strengthened by the action of sewing, which rejoins the cut, and makes *Glas* mistrust 'the textile metaphor. This is because it still keeps – on the side of the fleece, for example – a kind of virtue of naturality, primordiality, cleanliness [*propreté*]. At least the textile metaphor is still more natural, primordial, proper than the metaphor of sewing, of the seam [*couture*]. The sewing metaphor still supervenes on an artifact' (208b), a text.

The 'digamma,' the original sixth letter of the Greek alphabet that looks like an 'F,' but has the sound value of 'W,' can be said to continue the work of the 'strewking.' Insofar as it is allied to one of the agglutinative zigzag hen-letters, W and X, it too can be understood as plotting the hen's trajectory across the surface of the midden heap. Digamma

stalks all over the
page, broods Ⅎ sensationseeking an idea, amid the verbiage,
gaunt, stands dejectedly in the diapered window margin, with
its basque of bayleaves all aflutter about its forksfrogs, paces

with a frown, jerking to and fro, flinging phrases here, there, or
returns inhibited, with some half-halted suggestion, Ŀ, dragging
its shoestring; (121.2–8)

Those 'Fs' name the 'fret pattern' of Sullivan's introduction to the Book
of Kells:

> [The] fret pattern, which is employed in a considerable number of forms
> as a filling for panels in both borders and initials. The peculiarity of the
> Celtic fret, which is strongly distinguished from the square type so usual
> in Greek art, lies in the bending of links, at a certain point, at angles of 45°
> instead of 90°. The whole assumes in this way a peculiar Chinese charac-
> ter.
>
> Diaper work is occasionally used to brighten small spaces lying
> between the larger designs of more extended elaboration. (39)

This fretwork leads to the word 'fretty,' a term derived from heraldry,[14]
which has to do with the letter's 'diapered window margin.' Diaper
work is a form of decoration of heraldic origin that recalls the squares
of text insofar as it makes use 'of squares or lozenges.'[15] The *Wake* thus
invites the reader to think about the marks of the notches of the fret-
work left in the text by 'that fretful fidget eff' (120.33) as it 'stalks all
over the page' (121.2–3). As it moves, its rhythmic 'effing' is traced out
in an ungrammatical sentence in the text as the 'jerking to and fro
flinging phrases here, there, or returns inhibited, with some half-halted
suggestion' (121.6–7). This rhythmic 'effing' conforms to the processual
'jerking' of the bodily sphincter that opens and closes the imagistic
flow so disruptive of the present sense of words in the text. In disrupting the smooth operation of present sense, the 'fretful' F's cut into and
scar the surface of the text. In a similar fashion, these 'frets' also 'tattoo'
the typographic columns in *Glas* with the seeds of their betrayal: judas-
holes and religious imagery:

> At the beginning, then, the phallic columns of India, enormous forma-
> tions, pillars, towers, larger at the base than at the top. Now at the out-
> set – but as a setting out that already departed from itself – these
> columns were intact, unbreached [*inentamées*], smooth. And only later
> (*erst später*) are notches, excavations, openings ... made in the columns, in
> the flank, if such can be said. These hollowings, holes, these lateral
> marks in depth would be like accidents coming over the phallic col-

umns at first unperforated or apparently unperforatable. Images of gods (*Götterbilder*) were set, niched, inserted, embedded, driven in, tattooed on the columns. (2–3a)

Fretting thus both cuts and plays with images, and playing with images remains caught at the level of the image and religion, the imagination. Imaginative cutting illuminates the phallic column of *Glas* as it does the illuminated text of the *Wake*, the new Book of Kells.

'Cherchons la flamme!' (64.28)

Fretting cuts into the smooth flanks of *Glas*'s phallic columns, decorating them with flowers and jewels in a reinscription of the scene of 'antherection' (129–30b). *Finnegans Wake* offers, as I suggested above, a similar scene in terms of the Quinet sentence, where flowers come to dress and decorate the cuts, scars, and wounds of war left on the cities of men, their cut-down erections:

> *Aujourd'hui comme aux temps de Pline et de*
> *Columelle la jacinthe se plaît dans les Gaules,*
> *la pervenche en Illyrie, la marguerite sur les*
> *ruines de Numance et pendant qu'autour d'elles*
> *les villes ont changé de maîtres et de noms, que*
> *plusieurs sont entrées dans le néant, que les*
> *civilisations se sont choquées et brisées, leurs*
> *paisibles générations ont traversé les âges et sont*
> *arrivées jusqu'à nous, fraîches et riantes comme*
> *aux jours des batailles.*
>   Margaritomancy! Hyacinthinous pervinci-
> veness! Flowers. A cloud. (281.4–15)

The city has been razed by the wars of men, leaving nothing but a shattered, smoking ruin after being (literally) cut off by a terrible battle. All that remains are the flowers that continue to laugh and smile even as they did on the days of battles.

But how does this cutting and dressing get started? In order to answer this question, I will turn again to the scene of excrement in *Finnegans Wake* in which Issy, the daughter of HCE, offers her comments on Quinet's sentence:

Translout that gaswind into turfish, Teague, that's a good bog and you, Thady, poliss it off, there's nateswipe, on to your blottom pulper. (281.F2)

Issy counsels translating the 'gaswind' of the sentence into 'turfish.' This translation, as I argued above, recalls the insult made by either a foreign intruder or usurping rival who wipes his backside after defecating with a sod of turf representing one's territory. This gesture ignites a war of erections, ejaculations, and shit, all of which is fuelled by the explosive 'gaswind' of the Quinet sentence. This scene is also heliotropic to the extent that one crection-ejaculation calls for another. On the battlefield, for example, the general's defecation provokes Buckley's shit/shot/ejaculation.

In the face of this mess, Issy calls for something that will 'poliss it off, there's nateswipe, on to your blottom pulper.' The turf is also a sheet of blotting paper, and this paper is connected to that of the letter through the *Wake*'s use of Sheridan Le Fanu's *The House by the Churchyard*. In Le Fanu's book, a sod of turf, 'so much as a good sized sheet of letterpaper might cover,' was 'trod and broken' by an intruder. Turf, green turf, is also Ireland, 'the oul' sod,' which is always that which is ruined by an intruder, just as it was when the Russian general 'blotted' his backside with it. The national sod of turf, thus connected by Le Fanu's text to a letter, becomes the *Wake*'s 'goodish-sized sheet of letterpaper originating by transhipt from Boston (Mass.)' (111.8–10), a 'nationalistic letter.'[16]

Book IV expands upon the nationalistic theme of the oul' sod-letter as it further inflects the Quinet sentence in its reinscription of the scene of antherection discussed above. During the battle between St Patrick and the 'Archdruid Berkeley,'[17] the Archdruid expounds on the

> all too many much illusiones
> through photoprismic velamina of hueful panepiphanal world
> spectacurum of Lord Joss, the of which zoantholitic furniture,
> from mineral through vegetal to animal, not appear to full up to-
> gether fallen man than under but one photoreflection of the
> several iridals gradationes of solar light, that one which that part
> of it (furnit of heupanepi world) had shown itself (part of fur of
> huepanwor) unable to absorbere, whereas for numpa one pura-
> duxed seer in seventh degree of wisdom of Entis-Onton he savvy
> inside true inwardness of reality, the Ding hvad in idself id est,

all objects (of panepiwor) allside showed themselves in trues
coloribus resplendent with sextuple gloria of light actually retained, untisintus, inside them (obs of epiwo). (611.12–24)

The illusory world and all the 'zoantholitic furniture' in it only shows
itself to man under one of the 'seven iridals gradationes of solar light,'
the one it is 'unable to absorbere.' In contradistinction to such ordinary men, the Archdruid proposes the existence of a 'numpa one
puraduxed seer in seventh degree of wisdom' who knows the 'inside
true inwardness of reality,' the 'thing-in-itself,' the Kantian *noumenon*.
This 'thing-in-itself,' the very opposite of the fetish, is the fabulous
beast of the metaphysics of presence to which Berkeley himself never
subscribed, holding rather that *esse est percipi*, and that nothing lies
outside the senses. The Archdruid is perhaps more Newton than
Berkeley.

Either way, the seven colours of the true inwardness of reality show
themselves to the seer in an odd way because six of the colours, the
very rays of the 'sextuple gloria of light,' are 'actually retained inside,'
held inside the presence of those things-in-themselves. The result is a
world that presents itself only in shades of green – saffron takes on the
same hue as 'boiled spinasses' – and is to be ruled over by the overtly
phallic Highking Leary, a large, jewel encrusted 'Big Cockwocky,' who
lights a green fire while wrapped in swathes of green cloth fashioned
from various leaves:

High Thats Hight Uberking Leary his fiery grassbelong-
head all show colour of sorrelwood herbgreen, again, nigger-
blonker, of the his essixcoloured holmgrewnworsteds costume
the his fellow saffron pettikilt look same hue of boiled spinasses,
other thing, voluntary mutismuser, he not compyhandy the his
golden twobreasttorc look justsamelike curlicabbis, moreafter, to
pace negativisticists, verdant readyrainroof belongahim Exuber
High Ober King Leary very dead, what he wish to say, spit of
superexuberabundancy plenty laurel leaves, after that com-
mander bulopent eyes of Most Highest Ardreetsar King same
thing like thyme choppy upon parsley, alongsidethat, if please-
sir, nos displace tauttung, sowlofabishospastored, enamel Indian
gem in maledictive fingerfondler of High High Siresultan Em-
peror all same like one fellow olive lentil, onthelongsidethat, by
undesendas, kirikirikiring, violaceous warwon contusiones of

facebuts of Highup Big Cockywocky Sublissimime Autocrat, for
that with pure hueglut intensely saturated one, tinged uniformly,
allaroundside upinandoutdown, very like you seecut chowchow
of plentymuch sennacassia Hump cumps Ebblybally! Sukkot?
(611.33–12.15)

Patrick, who initially drank up the Archdruid's words (611.11), now
'no catch all that preachybook' (611.25). The green fires of nationalism
are lost on him, and he thus sets about starting another fire, a counter-
fire, one of his own:

Punc. Bigseer, refrects the petty padre, whackling it out, a
tumble to take, tripeness to call thing and to call if say is good
while, you pore shiroskuro blackinwhitepaddynger, by thiswis
aposterioprismically apatstrophied and paralogically periparo-
lysed, celestial from principalest of Iro's Irismans ruinboon pot
before, (for beingtime monkblinkers timeblinged completamen-
tarily murkblankered in their neutrolysis between the possible
viriditude of the sager and the probable eruberuption of the
saint), as My tappropinquish to Me wipenmeselps gnosegates a
handćaughtscheaf of synthetic shammyrag to hims hers, seeming-
such four three two agreement cause heart to be might, saving to
Balenoarch (he kneeleths), to Great Balenoarch (he kneeleths
down) to Greatest Great Balenoarch (he kneeleths down quite-
somely), the sound sense sympol in a weedwayedwold of the
firethere the sun in his halo cast. Onmen. (612.16–30)

But Paddy ('blackinwhitepaddynger') has already appeared on the
other side of the divide, in the colourblind 'Bigseer' Archdruid, who
'refrects the padre.' The scene of this 'Irismans ruinboon' of nationalism and its fetishistic worship of snakes are perhaps not so easy to
erase. The rainbow-fire conjured by Patrick tries to show the Archdruid and his followers the mystery of Father, Son, and Holy Ghost. In
order to do so, he makes the sign of the cross, and summons three rainbows, or 'Balenoarchs.' The bright colours of these rainbows are not
the conflagration itself, but rather the 'sound sense sympol' of that
conflagration that is such a potent burning that it sacrifices the sacrifice
of Christ on the cross. The conflagration is that of the figure-less fire of
the Trinity, 'the firethere the sun in his halo cast.' There, the 'Son in his
holocaust' is consumed by blinding burning of all that still echoes

nationalism in its 'Good safe Firelamp! hailed the heliots' (613.1), an echo of the words of an Irish rebel song, '"God Save Ireland," Say the Heroes.'

In this green (in Irish, *glas*) and turfish place is to be found the 'gaswind' Issy speaks of. But what is Issy pointing to in the translation of the gaswind of the Quinet sentence into a sod of turf-letter with which to wipe one's arse? Fire. The sod of turf-letter is itself a fuel that keeps burning after it has been itself ignited by the explosive fuel of the 'gaswind.' This is the scene of the war for turf. Thus, in this green place there is a circle of fire: the gaswind ignites by provoking the shots that call for each other. After they are fired, the turf-letter continues to burn, and results in a conflagration that ends up burning even the sun/son.

But where there is sun, there is also the structure of the heliotrope, and here, in this burning, the heliotrope is that of the after-effect, the delay of the conflagration, the rainbow. As I have been arguing, the structure of the heliotrope is always that of *bander* in which the linked chain of heliotropic flower-girls tightens in a ring around the other, squeezing it in order to 'make hims prich' (249.34). This squeezing that erects recalls 'local colour' (109.26) that shades the items of 'feminine clothiering' (109.31), the 'coursets' and the knickers of the maggies. Their constrictions are thus not surprisingly figured in

> Catchmire stockings, libertyed garters, shoddyshoes, quicked
> out with selver. Pennyfair caps on pinnyfore frocks and a ring on
> her fomefing finger. And they leap so looply, looply, as they link
> to light. And they look so loovely, loovelit, noosed in a nuptious
> night. Withasly glints in. Andecoy glants out. They ramp it a
> little, a lessle, a lissle. Then rompride round in rout.
>   Say them all but tell them apart, cadenzando coloratura! R is
> Rubretta and A is Arancia, Y is for Yilla and N for greeneriN. B
> is Boyblue with odalisque O while W waters the fleurettes of no-
> vembrance. Though they're all but merely a schoolgirl yet these
> way went they. I' th' view o' th'avignue dancing goes entrancing
> roundly. Miss Oodles of Anems before the Luvium doeslike. So.
> And then again doeslike. So. And miss Endles of Eons efter Dies
> of Eirae doeslike. So. And then again doeslike. So. The many
> wiles of Winsure. (226.24–27.2)

But this 'RAYNBOW' that constricts, bandages, and binds in stockings, garters, loops, and nooses also corresponds to the squeezing ring of the

sphincter in the enigma of excretion. The emptying of the text's meaning through a rhythmed squeezing draws attention to the letter's
empty envelope. If the scene of war and its aftermath is one of ejaculation and evacuation, then there must, according to Issy, be a wiping up
after the carnage, and it is the letter that appears in Issy's formulation
as toilet paper. This means that the letter is both that which, as turf,
provokes the war and sets the fires of nationalism going even as it
wipes up after it. As such, the letter-turf of the Quinet sentence seems
to come both before and after the war: the letter is thus also a ring that
envelops the war by passing on both sides, and hence around it.

The relationship between Ireland as site of burning, the burning letter, and the bandaging rainbow is neatly captured where the text
stages Shem's circuit of exile and return. The bandaging power of this
constrictive 'noose' of the RAYNBOW is also one that splits Shem
(228.5) and sends him into voluntary exile because he cannot guess the
colour of the rainbow-girls' knickers during the game of II.1. Because
of this splitting that is prompted by the knickers, Shem can only
'rehave' (231.25) himself through a strange exercise/exorcism that
throws him into a fit where his feet come up to his ears or arse ('aers')
and causes him to roll his eyes and spin as if he were roasting over a
fire on a spit. In other words, Shem can only overcome his being split
by contracting himself into a sort of ring.

But the promise of the completion of the circle of exile and return is
only held out by Shem's receipt of a message from the rainbow-girl-
maggies, who have themselves contracted into Issy:

> Cokerycokes, it's his spurt of coal. And may his tarpitch dilute
> not give him chromitis! For the mauwe that blinks you blank is
> mostly Carbo. Where the inflammabilis might pursuive his com-
> burenda with a pure flame and a true flame and a flame all too-
> gasser, soot. The worst is over. Wait! And the dubuny Mag may
> gang to preesses. With Dinny Finneen, me canty, ho! In the lost
> of the gleamens. Sousymoust. For he would himself deal a treat-
> ment as might be trusted in anticipation of his inculmination unto
> fructification for the major operation. When (pip!) a message
> interfering intermitting interskips from them (pet!) on herzian
> waves, (call her venicey names! call her a stell!) a butterfly from
> her zipclasped handbag, a wounded dove astarted from, escaping
> out her forecotes. Isle wail for yews, O doherlynt! The poetesser.
> And around its scorched cap she has twilled a twine of flame to

let the laitiest know she's marrid. And pim it goes backballed. Tot
burns it so leste. A claribel cumbeck to errind. Hers before his
even, posted ere penned. (232.1–17)

The message that comes to call him out of exile is complicated and
bound by a series of other interlaced bands. The message is itself bound
by a twine, a band of fire that quickly becomes a wedding band to let
everyone know 'she's married.' It is this interplay of bands that makes it
possible to speak about Shem's exile's 'cumbeck to errind,' insofar as it
anticipates, or promises, the (metaphorical, dialectical) circuit of exile's
return: 'Hers before his even, posted ere penned' (232.16–17). Read in
this way, the promise of the double band that does not deliver marks the
very first appearance of the band in the *Wake*, the circular Vichian contracting band of history, which first erects Finnegan's erection/tower
even as it truncates it, causing him to fall from presence, home.[18] These
bands that call home are the promise of a return to propriety and presence, which they cannot fulfil because they are that which cuts off
presence and propriety, losing it in the carnival of rings and bands.

This fiery band – which anticipates return home in all the senses discussed in chapter 1 – recalls the bands of halo-rainbows, which are figured in the gauze-like veil of clouds (281.15) that dress the burning
fires of book IV. However, in anticipating as well as bandaging the
flames, the rainbow-band, like the letter, also envelops those flames. It
is thus the constricing/contracting band itself (contract of marriage,
conatus, repression, corsets, stockings, rings, restriction, knickers,
sphincters, etc.) that is found on both sides of the fire. As such it must
be more or less than the fire itself, making possible both the fire and its
bandaging. The 'sound sense sympol[s]' that band-age the fire perform
the same role as the *flowers* in the Quinet sentence. Indeed, when these
'selfreizing flower[s],' which spontaneously irrupt after the phoenix
who sits on his pyre 'flaming away in true prattight spirit' is consumed
(265.6–8), are grafted onto Vico's rings of history, they become the
flowers of imaginative humanity that spring up just after the 'folgor of
frightfools' (613.28). After this frightful Italian lightning of Vico's
march of civilizations, there emerge both 'Monogynes' (613.35) and
'Dianders' (613.36), which, according to the Linnaean classification of
plants, denote flowering plants that have either one pistil (*Monogynia*)
or two stamens (*Diandria*).

These 'flower-people' are subject to an affective sway of time that
does not admit of human being:

Forbeer, forbear! For nought that is has bane
bane. In mournenslaund. Themes have thimes and habit reburns.
To flame in you. Ardor vigor forders order. Since ancient was
our living in possible to be. Delivered as. Caffirs and culls and
onceagain overalls, the fittest surviva lives that blued, iorn and
storridge can make them. Whichus all claims. (614.7–12)

There is no being ('bane') as a present, past, or future. The memory-
anticipation of the frightful thunder is kept burning in the breasts of
the flower-people who emerge after the conflagration. The fire burns in
accordance with the Vichian structure analysed in chapter 4, whereby
the first men try to protect themselves from trauma by repeating it, and
once again, this imaginary fire quickly becomes 'nationalistic':

Fennsense, finnsonse, aworn! Tuck upp those wide shorts.
The pink of the busket for sheer give. Peeps. Stand up to hard
ware and step into style. If you soil may, puett, guett me prives.
For newmanmaun set a marge to the merge of unnotions. Inni-
tion wons agame.
What has gone? How it ends?
Begin to forget it. It will remember itself from every sides, with
all gestures, in each our word. Today's truth, tomorrow's trend.
Forget, remember!
Have we cherished expectations? Are we for liberty of peru-
siveness? Whyafter what forewhere? A plainplanned liffeyism
assemblements Eblania's conglomerate horde. By dim delty Deva.
Forget! (614.14–26)

Here the *Sinn Féin* slogan, '*Sinn Féin, Sinn Féin Amháin*' (Ourselves,
ourselves alone), merges with Parnell's 1885 Cork speech when he said
that 'No man has a right to fix the boundary of the march of a nation'
(*Annotations*). Finally, the call is for Ireland to become, as the nationalistic song has it, 'A Nation Once Again.' This process is not one of a conscious remembering or forgetting: this fire of nationalism remembers
itself from all sides in our every gesture and word. It simply returns.

However, as the flame 'reburns' within the breasts of the flower-
people, they 'play a game' with this nationalistic fire. The ring of fire
initiates ('Innition wons agame') the flower-people into a recon-figura-
tive game of nationalism that recasts the 'marge' of the 'nation' as the
site of 'e-merge-nce,' a field of 'un-notions' where the rainbow of

colours or laughing flowers come to play. They come to play by *band-aging* and dressing the wounds and scars left by the conflagration, and by figuring, refracting, and cooling the white-hot light of the sun/son into the (at least) seven colours of light. As they do so, the uniformly green leaves of nationalism sprout flowers. And it is the play of these *Wake*an fires and rainbows of nationalism that make it possible to reinscribe the scene of *Glas*'s imaginary of religion prior to the Immaculate Conception in *Finnegans Wake*.

Glas casts flowers as the images or symbols used in the rituals of the pre-Christian 'religion of flowers,' the religion, according to Hegel, that follows the first moment of natural religion, the 'religion of the sun.' This religion is

> [p]ure and figureless, this light burns all. It burns itself in the all-burning [*le brûle-tout*] it is, leaves, of itself or anything, no trace, no mark, no sign of passage. Pure consuming destruction, pure effusion of light without shadow, noon without contrary, without resistance, without obstacle ... A pure essenceless by-play, a play that plays limitlessly, even though it is already destined to work in the service of essence and sense ... Play and pure difference, those are the secret of an imperceptible all-burning, the torrent of fire that sets itself ablaze. Letting itself get carried away, pure difference is different from itself, therefore indifferent ... Now here the sun does not set – or else it sets immediately ... This difference without subject, this play without labor, this example without essence, devoid of self (*Selbst*), is also a sort of signifier without a signified, ... a One at once infinitely multiple and absolutely different, different from self, a One without self, the other without self that means (to say) nothing, whose language is absolutely empty, void, like an event that never comes about itself. (238–9a)

Such a conflagration is then related to 'the gift: the sacrifice, the putting in play or to fire of all.' Even though it may appear that the gift [*don*] and its 'figures' are 'under the power of [*en puissance d'*] ontology,' '[w]ithout the holocaust the dialectical movement and the history of Being could not open themselves ... Before, if one could here count with time, before everything, before every determinable being [*étant*], there is, there was, there will have been the irruptive event of the gift [*don*]' (242a). Thus, the gift's irruptive event – rather than the gift of the thing (itself) – is what interests *Glas* here.

Such a 'giving' of the 'gift,' therefore, cannot be giving in the ordinary sense of the word, where someone gives something to somebody else (242a, 243a). Rather, because this gift is before the 'for-(it)self' (243a) (the Hegelian figure for self-consciousness [25–6a, 109a]), 'the gift, the giving of the gift, the pure *cadeau*, does not let itself be thought by the dialectics to which it, however, gives rise. The giving of the gift understands itself here before the for-(it)self, before all subjectivity and all objectivity. But when *someone* gives *something* to *someone*, one is already within calculating dialectics and speculative idealization' (243a). Because speculative dialectics can only 'think of the gift as a sacrifice' (243a), it becomes clear that sacrifice itself must be sacrificed, if the path and destiny of speculative philosophy is to be deviated (from). This happens with the chain:

> *Cadeau* means *chain*. The word designates, according to Littré, the 'Pen strokes [*Traits*] with which the masters of writing embellished their examples,' or also, 'Large letters placed at the head of acts or chapters in cursively written manuscripts.' Or too, 'Formerly, feast that one principally gave to women, a pleasure party.' The etymology, still according to Littré, would refer to '*Catellus*, small chain, from *catena*, chain ... because of the chained form of the pen strokes. Household management teaches us that making *cadeaux* is said for making things that appear attractive but are useless, metaphorically compared to those strokes of the hand of the writing masters. From there one passes without trouble to *cadeau* in the sense of diversion, feast, and finally, present.' (243–4a)

This gift or chain of presents, which clearly figures *différance*, or the concatenation of time and space, is taken up in the 'annulus, the ring or collar or necklace' (243a). Hence, 'to give means-(to say) to give an annulus' (244a). Rethinking the annular gift 'before the constitution of the *Selbst*,' or the self-consciousness of the self/subject, requires seeing how the 'annular movement re-stricts the general economy' of the Hegelian dialectic, giving it its circular shape, wherein the spirit unceasingly returns to itself:

> The contraction, the economic restriction forms the annulus of the self-same, of the self-return, of reappropriation. The economy restricts itself; the sacrifice sacrifices itself. The (con)striction no longer lets itself be circumscribed [*cerner*] as an ontological category, even were it a trans-category, a transcendental. The (con)striction – what is useful for thinking the ontology or the transcendental – is then [*donc*] *also* in the position of

transcendental trans-category, the transcendental transcendental. All the more because the (con)striction cannot not produce the 'philosophical' effect it produces. There is no choosing here: each time a discourse *contra* the transcendental is held, a matrix – the (con)striction itself – constrains the discourse to place the nontranscendental, the outside of the transcendental field, the excluded, in the structuring position. The matrix in question constitutes the excluded as the transcendental of the transcendental, as imitation transcendental, transcendental contraband [*contre-bande*]. The contra-band is *not yet* dialectical contradiction. To be sure, the contra-band necessarily becomes that, but its not-yet is not-yet the teleological anticipation, which results in it never becoming dialectical contradiction. The contra-band *remains* something other than what, necessarily, it is to become.

Such would be the (nondialectical) law of the (dialectical) stricture, of the bond, of the ligature, of the garrote, of the *desmos* in general when it comes to clench tightly [*serrer*] in order to make be. Lock [*Serrure*] of the dialectical. (244a)

Since the gift of (con)striction (and hence the re-striction discussed in chapter 5 in relation to the city and marriage) is both inside and outside of, and gives (rise to), the dialectical circular return of the same, it would seem possible to say that just as its priorness structures the Hegelian dialectic, so its priorness would figure, according to a by now familiar structure, the image of the dialectic. But the burning remains figureless insofar as it must return, in a circular trajectory, to the third moment of natural religion – that of the artisan, because (con)striction 'cannot not produce the "philosophical" effect it produces' (244a). If the reader wishes to trace the figure or image in this dialectic of pre-Christian religion, s/he must move beyond the annulus while following its tracks. These tracks lead directly to the second moment of the dialectic of natural religion, which follows the conflagration: 'Then in the place of burning all, one begins to love flowers. The religion of flowers follows the religion of the sun' (240a). In a strikingly similar gesture to *Finnegans Wake*, the text of *Glas* offers a bouquet and places its flowers at the site of the burning-all, at the site of the wound or scar its burning leaves behind. This scene is antherection. These flowers, which bandage or soothe the all-burning, also mark, as I have already mentioned, the 'mediation between the first and the second moment of natural religion, between the religion of the pure luminous essence and that of the plant or animal. This is also the passage to the for-(it)self'

(245a). But the for-(it)self of the flower merely anticipates the for-(it)self of the animal, which is given over to the war of species (109a) because 'the plant, as such, lives in peace: substance to be sure, and there was not yet any substantiality in the light, but peaceful substance, without this inner war that characterizes animality. Already life and self, but not yet the war of desire. Life without desire – the plant is a sort of sister' (245a).[19] But the plant is not yet the flower: it is 'uprooted from itself, toward the outside, by the light.' In other words, the plant will never become anything like a for-(itself). That is the job of the

> flower [that] sets free an advance in the movement of reappropriation and subjectivization. A moment of relief: the light no longer comes to provoke or uproot from the outside; on the contrary, the light engenders itself spontaneously from inside the plant. This passage is analogous to the one that relieves the outer resonance of noise (in)to the voice. Instance of *Klang*. The *color* of the flower manifests this phenomenal auto-determination of the plant. 'Consequently, the plant now engenders (*gebiert*) light from itself, as *its own* self. It does this in the *flower*, in which the neutral colour, green, is from the outset determined as a specific color.' (246a)

The process of the spontaneous emission of colour from green – the emergence of the flower from the plant – can also be seen as the one that generates St Patrick's flowering rainbow from the uniform of Berkeleyan green. And it is these coloured flowers that project the very image of the self without authentic self. However, they do not only represent the subject or self without presence; they also represent representability, representation itself:

> Flower religion is innocent insofar as the war internal to animality is not yet unchained in it. The relation to self does not yet trigger the war because it does nothing but *represent itself* in the flower. Flower religion (like the flower, as the flower) mimes and anticipates the true self, contains itself in this 'self-less representation of the self (*selbstlose Vorstellung des Selbsts*).' ... But as the flower has already begun to subjectivize the luminous essence and the plant, it no longer simply falls (entombed) into dissociative exteriority. The flower is neither an object nor a subject, neither a not-I nor an I, neither pure alterity without relation to self nor a '*Selbst*.' Innocent to be sure, therefore not culpable, not guilty, but its innocence is declared (what could not be done of the sun or the plant) only

insofar as the flower is capable of culpability, culpable [*coupable*] of being
able to become culpable, cuttable [*coupable*]. Among all these opposites,
the essence of the flower appears in its disappearance, vacillates like all
the representative mediations, but also excludes itself from the oppositional structure. The flower gives the example of every possible representation, but the circular system of the between-representation permits
making the flower the trope of every representative middle or saying that
every representation is anthomorphous. (246a)

Understood in this way, the game of colours played by the twins and
the ring of Maggies in II.1 can be seen to take part in an imaginary
game that religiously plays at becoming subjective. Such playful, imaginary, pre-Christian flowers go beyond the absolute phantasm of the
Holy Family because they occupy the anteriority within the religious
image with respect to the absolute phantasm. As such, the scene of
antherection – or that of the Quinet sentence – is doubly imaginary, an
anterior image of an image. This structure of the image of an image can
never point the way back to reality: it has the structure of the enigma
(M 243). Such imaginary flowers are also heliotropic in that they follow
the sun. But once again, their heliotropism is not simple: it remains
within the voided time of heliotropism in that it is a nocturnal heliotropism that emerges after the 'sun goes down' because burning all
'must also consume the blaze,' even the sun itself (241a). In the place of
this scar, the flowers gush forth, erupting in a flow that dresses the
wound, just like the *Wake*'s Maggies who play at sunset and rhythmically encircle the other in order to 'make hims prich.'

Insofar as they are specifically pre-Christian images, the ornamental
flowers and columns that fret both the *Wake* and *Glas* are also represented by the *Wake*'s 'Ophidian' reptiles, whose knots and curves make
up the 'strange exotic serpentine, since so properly banished from our
scripture' (121.20–1). St Patrick, according to the legend, cleared the
way for Christianity in Ireland by driving all the snakes, which were
worshipped by the pre-Christian inhabitants, out of the country. Yet
here they are once again offering themselves to be read in the letter. All
of this suggests that the traces of pre-Christian serpentinism cannot
simply be erased, and Patrick's attempts to 'purify' Ireland of both
snakes and nationalism are doomed to failure. It is perhaps the use to
which the *Wake* puts the celebrated *Tunc* page of the Book of Kells[20]
that most economically draws together and succinctly illustrates the
complexity of the reasons for, and what is at stake in, Patrick's failed

attempt to restore purity to Ireland. In many ways, the *Wake*'s framing of the *Tunc* page may also be read as a sort of allegorical image for what is at stake in Joyce-Derrida intertextuality when these texts are brought into sustained contact with each other.

Tunc

The celebrated *Tunc* page recalls text from Matthew 27:38: '*Tunc cruci-fixerant XPI cum eo duos latrones*' ('Then were there two thieves cruci-fied with him'). According to Atherton, the '"tenebrous *Tunc* page" [122.22–3] has a serpentine capital T in the top half, followed by a line of capitals reading *UNCCR*, and then a smaller capital u. The deco-rated capital T Joyce calls "Big Whiggler" (284.25) following this by "NCR"' (*The Books at the* Wake, 65). Understood in this fashion, the Book of Kells' writing traces both the pre-Christian fetish worship of snakes mentioned above, which it uses to illuminate and intertwine the Celto-Christian 'word.' It is therefore a site of contamination, where its loops, sweeps, and coils, 'as pipless as threadworms,' point to an improperly repressed Ophidian 'unconscious':

> strange exotic serpen-
> tine, since so properly banished from our scripture, about as freak-
> wing a wetterhand now as to see a rightheaded ladywhite don a
> corkhorse, which, in its invincible insolence ever longer more and
> of more morosity, seems to uncoil spirally and swell lacertinelazily
> before our eyes under pressure of the writer's hand: (121.20–5)

These coiled, serpentine designs 'swell,' in yet another scene of antherection, under the pressure exerted by the writer's hand to per-vert the Christian text and cast doubt on the pure origin and pious communication of the authentic Christian message:

> The prouts who will invent a writing there ultimately is the
> poeta, still more learned, who discovered the raiding there origin-
> ally. That's the point of eschatology our book of kills reaches
> for now in soandso many counterpoint words. (482.31–4)

In this way, the Celto-Christian word of the letter-Book of Kells is always already the site of an original but fatal betrayal. The Celto-Christian 'word' is betrayed by its inability to be a true origin, because it is already only a 'raiding' of another text that it tries to hide by an unsuccessful attempt at appropriating and 'killing' the coils and spirals of the exotic serpents that it parasites. Unable to overcome the tendrils of the 'strange exotic serpentine' that it needs to survive, the authentic *verbum* of Celto-Christianity is fatally compromised by any attempt to isolate a 'pure' Christian message in the text.[21]

'Raiding' marks the impossibility of ever arriving at a text's pure message, and this is why it can always betray the pious intentions of its writer, who, just like the infant Dolph discussed in chapter 2, can only ever be a figure who 'misappropriates' the words of other:

> To conclude purely negatively from the
> positive absence of political odia and monetary requests that its
> page cannot ever have been a penproduct of a man or woman of
> that period or those parts is only one more unlookedfor conclu-
> sion leaped at, being tantamount to inferring from the nonpre-
> sence of inverted commas (sometimes called quotation marks)
> on any page that its author was always constitutionally incapable
> of misappropriating the spoken words of others. (108.29–36)

The verbal thievery that literally makes up the letter is confirmed by Shaun as he gives evidence to the four old men (×) in III.1:

> Every dimmed letter in it is a copy and not a few of the
> silbils and wholly words I can show you in my Kingdom of
> Heaven. The lowquacity of him! With his threestar monothong!
> Thaw! The last word in stolentelling! And what's more right-
> down lowbrown schisthematic robblemint! Yes. (424.32–6)

If the writer is only ever a 'raider' s/he can only ever aspire to be a word thief. Authorial originality is lost in that the author is not the originator of his or her words, which are only ever stolen from another, whose traces poke through the writer's stolen word in the manner emblematized by the ophidian fetishism of the *Tunc* page of the Book of Kells. Joyce, therefore, and in keeping with Sullivan's thesis on the secrets of the Book of Kells, gives 'stolentelling' the value of fetishism: the presence of a word is no longer the guarantee of anyone's pure intentions or pristine originality. Every word acts as a sort of fig leaf, or better, a bunch of 'clee' (*clef*, key, but also German *Klee*, clover; 478.21) that dangles between one's legs, simultaneously hiding and showing what the writer-raider lacks: phallic authority.[22] *Glas* also considers the fetish as allied to the imagination (208ai), and associates it with what was discussed above in terms of 'the argument of the *girdle*, the *sheath* [gaine]' where sexual difference is no longer decidable (210ai–11ai):[23] in other words, a 'concept' of the fetish makes it impossible to say whether or not something is present or absent, aligning it with the *différance* that is troped elsewhere in the text as the 'the flight, the theft [*vol*]' of the 'agglutination' that 'derails semanticism' (147bi).

The *Wake*an scene of fetishistic 'stolentelling' that destroys the traditional oppositions of true/false, owned/stolen, and so on, and dislocates the eidetic model where a text's meaning would be guaranteed through an author's animating intention or will finds its place in a long tradition of texts. As has already been argued, its structure is sketched by Vico, who situates the operation of such a will within the *milieu* of the 'corporeal imagination' (NS 376), and Nietzsche, who critiques one of consciousness's favourite conceptions of itself as an animating will or intention that causes an action ('The Four Great Errors' 4–5). For Nietzsche, the will's assumption that it is the cause of an action through intention rests on the purely logical category of cause and effect. However, the intentionality of the will is but a tiny part of the story of an action or gesture, which nevertheless tries to erase the role played by the serpentine coils of the entrails (WP 666). It is these precisely Nietzschean entrails that *Finnegans Wake* considers in book IV as they unhook the cause-effect relations of conscious intention.[24] The *Wake*an and Nietzschean entrails of excretion do not just recall the Quinet sentence analysed above; they reinscribe their writing as an unconscious process of spontaneous motion ('autokinatonetically' [614.30]) of excretion fused with the Vichian cycles. And, as was discussed in chapter 4, through this process the reader moves from 'tope' to 'type,' and generates, in exactly the same manner as the hen on her midden-heap, the 'letter from litter.' Letter-writing is thus once again fused with the processes of bodily discharge in a fetishized writing that is no longer manipulated by the conscious will, purpose, or intention of a reader-writer. Insofar as these phenomena remain, they are moments of the more primordial forces of a more primordial '(non)production' that does not give, in any simple sense, a usable 'product.'

When writing becomes such a messy business, a certain amount of 'blottom pulper' is needed to 'poliss it off' (281.F2). Ever since *Ulysses*, this 'blotting paper' is composed of the words of another:

Quietly he read, restraining himself, the first column and, yielding but resisting, began the second. Midway, his last resistance yielding, he allowed his bowels to ease themselves quietly as he read, reading still patiently that slight constipation of yesterday quite gone. Hope it's not too big bring on piles again. No, just right. So. Ah! Costive. One tabloid of cascara sagrada. Life might be so. It did not move or touch him but it was something quick and neat. Print anything now. Silly season. He read on, seated calm above his own rising smell. Neat certainly. *Matcham often thinks of the masterstroke by which he won the laughing witch who now.* Begins and ends morally. *Hand in hand.* Smart. He glanced back through what he had read and, while feeling his water flow quietly, he envied kindly Mr Beaufoy who had written it and received payment of three pounds, thirteen and six ... He tore away half the prize story sharply and wiped himself with it. Then he girded up his trousers, braced and buttoned himself. He pulled back the jerky shaky door of the jakes and came forth from the gloom into the air. (U.4.507–40)

Thus, the rhythm of raiding and the rhythm of evacuation (which doubles here with the rhythm of the 'jerky shaky' jakes door) come together in this *Ulysse*an scene. Here, the sphigma passes through Bloom like the Holy Spirit through Mary, without 'touch[ing] him.' Bloom then tears a diapered sheet from what he rhythmically reads to wipe away the remains of the excrement that adheres to his backside. *Glas* also understands this function of the work when it asks (after Genet) '*what remained of a Rembrandt torn into small, very regular squares and rammed down the shithole*' (1b, 214b). In the text of the *Wake*, the raider-writer tears 'all the French leaves unveilable out of Calomnequiller's Pravities' (50.9).[25] These loose leaves later become the 'goodish-sized sheet of letterpaper' (111.8–9) that wipes the backside of both the Russian general on the battlefield (353.16) and Roderick O'Connor, who has been 'idylly turmbing over the loose looves leaflefts jaggled casuallty on the lamatory' (357.21–2).

This scene of excretion is also a scene of writing where the reader-writer writes him- or herself 'from scratch' (336.15–18), without the benefit of an eidetic model, on the paper in the form of 'a stinksome inkenstink, quite puzzonal to the wrottel. Smatterafact, Angles aftanon browsing there thought not Edam reeked more rare' (183.6–8). Both Shem and Bloom calmly meet the personal stink of their 'own rising smell' in a reinscription of the Vichian scene of composition 'from next to nothing' (4.36–5.1). This voided gas, according to *Glas*, is what does not becomes the fire of spirit, or *Savoir Absolut*: it merely gathers above the body of Christ as it begins to rot on the cross: 'Everything happens around a sepulcher. No doubt the memory of the rotting body was the first effaced in the institution of the glory, but it has returned, was insistent, to the very extent the split continued its work. The dead body resting there in the interminable decomposition of relics, the spirit never raises itself high enough, it is retained as a kind of effluvium, of gas fermenting above the corpse' (91a). But this gas, like Shem's and Bloom's stink, scratches out a scene of writing that remains ungraspable by any ontology of presence: 'How could ontology lay hold of a fart?' (58bi).[26]

The sheets of text that wipe and are smeared with the excretions of the entrails become the by now familiar site where the time of the history that the *Wake* is composed of hardens:

> Then, pious Eneas, conformant to the fulminant firman which
> enjoins on the tremylose terrian that, when the call comes, he
> shall produce nichthemerically from his unheavenly body a no
> uncertain quantity of obscene matter not protected by copriright
> in the United Stars of Ourania or bedeed and bedood and bedang
> and bedung to him, with this double dye, brought to blood heat,
> gallic acid on iron ore, through the bowels of his misery, flashly,
> faithly, nastily, appropriately, this Esuan Menschavik and the first
> till last alshemist wrote over every square inch of the only fools-
> cap available, his own body, till by its corrosive sublimation one
> continuous present tense integument slowly unfolded all marry-
> voising moodmoulded cyclewheeling history. (185.27–86.2)

A 'Then' watches over this whole scene of cubist historiography, where the body evacuates itself as the time of history that empties itself into the hollowed-out time of a 'continuous present tense integument.' The integument of the present is no longer a kernel, but a hollowed-out shell of a present thoroughly (de)composed of (by) caked-on shit where Shem's joyfulscatological song resounds and echoes without presence (185.14–26).[27]

This shell, as I have just suggested, is marked by a punctual 'Then,' a *'Tunc'* in Latin. 'Then' punctures the text in the same way as the break-fast fork or hen's beak inflict a sense of time on the hen's letter (124.8–28). In book IV this punctual *Tunc* (612.16) repeatedly tolls the expected hour of (re)awakening, 6 a.m. (611.4, 612.16, 612.36). The time of this reawakening, which brings together both hollowed-out forms of time in the text – the clock-time of the Angelus and the heliotropic turn towards the sun – also remains hollow because it can never become a present. Its coming remains, therefore, non-Annunciative. As such, its '*Tunc*' marks both the death of χ as well as his non-arrival, marking the text with the structure of what Derrida has elsewhere called a *différantial* 'messianic promise' (*Archive Fever* 72). And since χ has never arrived, his expected resurrection is also hollowed.

Conclusion: 'When ex what is ungiven.'

Finnegans Wake is a text that disrupts and dismantles the imitative eidetic schema that is central to the Western philosophical tradition. In its place, it proposes the problematic of an imagination that tries to picture the ever-receding figure of Finnegan, who is lost in a past that has never been present or a future that never arrives.[28] To the extent that Finnegan never presents himself, the imagination in *Finnegans Wake* imitates 'nothing.' The workings of this non-imitative or, better, non-eidetic imagination are elaborated upon in the famous letter-writing scene of book I, section 5, where the reader is counselled to follow the hen's lead as she composes a letter about her husband that promises to tell the 'cock's trootabout him' (113.12). Even though the hen's letter fails to deliver this truth, by orchestrating this scene in this way the *Wake* fuses the operation of the non-eidetic imagination with what Vico in *The New Science* considers to be one of the seminal activities that permitted the emergence of human institutions: taking auguries and observing the auspices (NS 9–10). The scene of writing that emerges from book I, section 5 therefore is one where the non-eidetic imagination disrupts the philosophical conception of the *eidos* insofar as it imagines without being constrained by a prior present model, whether that model is understood as an idea, thing-in-itself, meaning, animating will, or intention. From a theoretical standpoint, the operation of the non-eidetic imagination in book I of the *Wake* can be clarified in terms of *différance*, catachresis, mimicry, and doubleness, which in turn suggests that the *Wake* and certain texts of Derrida's share a common genealogy that is in part traceable to the role that Vico accords the reader in making *The New Science* (NS 349). Insofar as this making corresponds to the manner in which the hen composes the letter, it may be read as another scene of non-eidetic immarginative writing. This scene of non-eidetic imaginary writing can be analysed and given theoretical rigour by using Heidegger's analysis of the imagination in *Kant and the Problem of Metaphysics*.[29] Heidegger's text also makes it possible to understand the imaginative and temporal indebtedness of certain key Derridean strategies – *différance*, catachresis, and mimicry, for example – to temporalizing auto-affection.[30] In combining Vico and Heidegger it becomes possible to clarify and theorize both the theoretical framework of the non-eidetic imagination as well as the reader's role in it as a site of 'mimicry' and 'deconstructive performance.'

Since the operation of the non-eidetic imagination shares a structural affinity with certain key textual strategies found in Derrida's writing that are, to a certain degree, 'outside' what is taken to be the 'usual' terrain of Joyce-Derrida intertextuality – that is to say, 'outside' of the texts where Derrida either explicitly writes on Joyce or mentions him by name – this suggests an expanded zone of Joycean-Derridean intertextuality that stands in need of further exploration. Since Hegel is for Derrida the privileged heading under which 'the very project of philosophy' is 'displaced and reinscribed' (M19), his texts take on an important role for a reader of Joyce and Derrida because they provide a context for understanding the Hegelian underpinnings of Derrida's direct engagements with Joyce's texts in both 'Two Words for Joyce'[31] and 'Ulysses Gramophone: Hear say yes in Joyce.'[32] The appropriative 'hypermnesia' that Derrida reads in Joyce is a variation of the manner in which Hegel's philosophical system tries to 'include within itself and anticipate all the figures of its beyond, all the forms and resources of its exterior' (WD 252). Similarly, the 'laughter' that Derrida analyses in Joyce is a variation of the sovereign laughter that Derrida reads in Bataille's critical engagement with the Hegelian philosophical system (WD 256). What Hegel makes clear to a reader of Joyce and Derrida is that the disruption of Joycean hypermnesia is, first and foremost, a disruption of Hegelian philosophy.

The extensive applicability of Derridean strategies outside of the usual terrain of Joyce-Derrida intertextuality as well as the central role accorded to both Hegelian thought and the disruptive effects of laughter constitute the expanded conception of Joyce-Derrida intertextuality that this study sketches throughout. Chapters 2 to 6 have sought to test the general applicability and flexibility of the non-eidetic imaginative framework outlined in chapters 1 and 2 for reading this expanded understanding of the Joyce-Derrida intertext by using it to shape and guide a sustained comparative analysis of *Finnegans Wake* and *Glas*. *Glas* was chosen to test the imaginative framework not only because it is Derrida's most sustained analysis of the Hegelian philosophical system, but also because, as I have been arguing, it can be read as Derrida's most sustained meditation on the imagination. This comparative examination tried to show how the imaginative framework developed by this text could be used to account for the remarkable similarity of key traits and textual strategies employed in both *Finnegans Wake* and *Glas*. Both texts privilege a kind of writing that is inextricably linked to the site or space of the non-eidetic imagination, that is to say, a writing of laughter, non-presence, scatological bodily rhythms, fetishism, theft, religion, and time. The writing of *Glas* and *Finnegans Wake* may therefore be said to forge a long and perhaps somewhat odd chain of imaginary remainders that makes all forms of eidetic appropriation – hypermnesias included – im/possible, that nevertheless remains, according to *Glas*, 'immobilized in representation, in empty signification' without presence (227a).

It is in view of the imaginative site of immobilized representation and empty signification that I would like to close this study with the consideration of a scene of an algebraic writing offered by the *Wake*. On the one hand, this scene of algebraic writing functions as an emblematic device that draws together a number of the key motifs – temporalization, rhythm, the X, emptiness, non-presence, fetishism – as reversing the movement of eidetic philosophy from the unknown to the known. On the other hand, it is possible to read this algebra as an emblem of how the broadened conception of Joyce-Derrida intertextuality opens the way for a changed understanding of the *différantial* relation of the known (the *eidos*) to the unknown (M 19) with which this study began.[33]

The scene of algebraic writing I am referring to here is to be found in the italicized 'stage directions' of a television program featuring the warring twins – this time re-named as Butt and Taff. These directions set the scene for the moment in the program when the twins fuse together to shoot the Russian general, an avatar of Finnegan/HCE.[34] The text problematizes their union by troping it as a moment of 'presence' that is at the same time indistinguishable from the familiar mechanism of auto-affection:

> [*The pump and pipe pingers are ideally reconstituted. The putther and bowls are peterpacked up. All the presents are determining as regards for the future the howabouts of their past absences which they might see on at hearing could they once smell*

of tastes from touch. To ought find a values for. The must over-
listingness. When ex what is ungiven. As ad where. Stillhead.
Blunk.] (355.1–7)

Here, the stage directions lay bare the mechanism of the temporality of an ideally reconstituted homophonic presents/presence, and subject them/it to spatial and logical contortions that empty/empties them/it of meaning, reducing it to rhythmic blank 'Blunk.' 'Presents' is therefore problematized in these stage directions, not only by its designation as a 'blank,' a 'nothing,' but also by the manner in which 'presents' is tied to the 'howabouts of their past absences,' that is, to a past that is no longer 'there,' and withheld in a future that is always looked to, but which, as I have been suggesting throughout this chapter, never 'arrives' as such. Understood thus, 'presents' in the *Wake* is the 'Blunk' space 'between' two non-presences that also marks the divisions that space 'presence' into a multiplicity of 'presents.' 'Presents' is therefore always the time of the double: more than one and other than itself.[35]

However, this does not mean that 'presence' is simply an originary state that is somehow 'disrupted' by 'Blunks' that would come, 'after the fact,' to destroy its perfection. On the contrary, here 'presence' is reinscribed by the text as 'presents' that can only ever be 'ideally reconstituted' in a sort of retroactive fiction that cannot avoid both doubling and spacing. As I read it here, the text sets the reader the task of finding the value for this 'must,' an 'ought' ([n]ought). This task, even though the text prescribes it, is nevertheless also a sort of trick, an *'over-listingness'* (German *uberlisten*: to dupe), that the reader should be wary of. This is because the task of ideally reconstituting the value of the 'Blunk' of 'presents' resembles 'presence' so closely that it runs the risk of being turned into simple presence once more. Thus, in order to avoid being 'duped' into once more finding presence in its double, the reader must practise the imaginary algebra of 'Blunk' 'presents,' where presence gives way to the auto-affective, or *différantial*, spacing of time. In other words, the reader's task is to be aware of the effects of 'presents' that the imaginary algebra of the *Wake* produces as it voids – literally crosses out – presence with an 'ex': it is pure (non)production.[36]

Read in this way, this algebraic 'ex' on the one hand captures precisely the non-eidetic textual relations that have been discussed throughout this study. Algebraically speaking, the 'ex' recalls the 'eggs is to whey as whay is to zeed' (167.7–8), which in turn recalls the hen's digestible eggs on which the 'scribings' of the letter are 'scrawled'

(615.10). In this unheard-of 'eggy' algebra of '(n)oughts' and 'exes,' eggs are affected by the 'ex' of non-presence. As a result, they are no longer simply 'eggs,' and since they are non-present, they may also be understood to withhold themselves in the same manner as the non-dialectical gift discussed above.[37] On this reading, these 'ex-eggs' slide outside of the mode of 'Real Presence' in precisely the same manner that Finnegan withdraws from the text of the *Wake*.[38] The 'ex' of 'presents' also conforms to the strategy of doubling or simulation, where the double 'is separated from what it simulates only by a barely perceptible veil, about which one can just as well say that it already runs – unnoticed – between Platonism and itself, between Hegelianism and itself' (D 207). As such, the 'ex' would also follow the traces of *différance*, where the known is related to the unknown (M 19).

On the other hand, there is another fold in this algebra that, not content with crossing out presence in the 'presents' of auto-affection, strives to re-double the crossing out already discussed. This is because the 'ex' that crosses out presence as the 'Blunk' 'presents' in the *Wake* is *already* doubled. The 'ex,' insofar as it is an 'ex,' is haunted by its 'former' 'self' – an unknown 'x.' This 'ex' is extremely difficult to grasp not only because it is an ex 'x,' as it were, estranged from 'itself,' but also because it is already doubly erased, doubly unknown in that it is both an 'ex' and an 'x.' On top of all this, the 'ex' 'x' remains, as the text puts it, 'ungiven' (355.6): it is fundamentally incapable of becoming (a) present, but it is nevertheless still 'legible,' even if it is only in the traces of its not appearing as an unknown.

The criss-crossings of this 'ungiven' doubly 'unknowable' 'ex' that 'crosses' 'itself' 'out' – the quotation marks are necessary here to mark the imaginative distortions of language in this peculiar temporal algebra – are also an erasable trace, 'a seed ... a mortal germ' (WD 230). It is possible to read in the contours of this trace the broadened reconceptualization of the intertextual relations of Joyce and Derrida that arise from a sustained reading of Joyce alongside Derrida, and particularly a sustained comparison of *Finnegans Wake* and *Glas*. However, it may also be possible to say that this 'unknowable ex' begins to recast, at least in part, one of the key motifs of the Derridean project: *différance*. Such 'recasting' would suggest that *Glas* does not *simply* double (for) the *Wake* in the same manner as, say, Bataille's sovereignty doubles for Hegel's lordship, relating the 'known ... to the unknown, meaning to nonmeaning' (WD 271). By letting Derrida's *Glas* emerge as the *Wake*'s non-simple double, this study offers a glimpse beyond that which relates the 'known to the unknown.' In other words, this study sketches a textual relation of non-simple doubling wherein the text of *Glas* relates to those aspects of *Wake*an writing that *already* relate the 'known' to the 'unknown' and slip outside the Platonist order of appearance: thus, this textual relation is that which pertains between two unknowns. And it is perhaps this double relationship that is no longer expressible in terms of the singular unknown of *difference*: there is a *doubling* of unknowns insofar as both texts would be related on the basis of strategies that serve to disrupt the 'known.' The unknown 'x' of *différance* would in this strange relation perhaps be better written as the doubly erased 'ex' that offers the reader, instead of 'one' unknown, a relation between (at least) two. It is this 'ex,' I would like to suggest, that this study's framework of a broadened conception of Joyce-Derrida intertextuality brings into view. But this is not to say that the relation of two relations to the unknown would be legible without first passing through the texts of both *Finnegans Wake* and *Glas*. It is this passage that makes the 'ex' legible.

It is perhaps in the context of this 'passage' that the 'ex' suggests itself as the most fitting emblem with which to draw to a close this study's attempts to read *Glas* alongside *Finnegans Wake*, since it recalls the discussion in chapters 2 and 3 that compares the criss-cross motifs that characterize both the hen's style of writing and the situation of the reader in *Finnegans Wake* to what *Glas* calls the 'X, an almost perfect chiasm(us), more than perfect, of two texts, each one set facing [*en regard*] the other: a gallery and a graphy that guard one another and disappear from view' (43–4b). The difference this time, however, lies in bringing the 'ex' into contact with the chiasmatic X that puts texts into a relation with each other and allows the reinscription of the language of intertextual relations in the metaphorical language of broken romantic relationships. Reading the relationships that obtain between the writing of texts that (have a) regard (for) each other demands a reader who is '*bigle*,' or 'cross-eyed' (113bi), since, perhaps, it is only by having 'double vision' that the reader can have access to the space of the *regard*[39] that *Finnegans Wake* and *Glas* have for each other. In this regard, the X is doubled since both *Finnegans Wake* and *Glas* act as two fond but estranged 'Xs [that] must ... take account of one another, [and] reflect, record and inscribe themselves equally in one another' (59a). It is also in this regard that the cross-eyed reader reads both Joyce writing Derrida and Derrida writing Joyce, in a writing that is forever 'self-penned to one's other,' 'neverperfect everplanned' (489.33–4). This writing is 'neverperfect' despite being 'everplanned' because the regard each 'eX' has for the other must pass through a 'judas' (113bi) – which, as I have argued in chapters 2 and 3, doubles for the reader – through whom the 'eXs' fondly betray, and are fondly betrayed by, one another. And it is perhaps only after the careful reconsideration of the 'psycho/dynamics' of the regard, love, betrayal, and jealousy that the next chapter in Joyce-Derrida intertextual relations can be written.

Notes

Introduction

1 Page and line numbers are cited in the text: e.g., 3.15 is page 3, line 15.

2 Jacques Derrida, *Dissemination*, 194. Hereafter cited in the text as D.

3 *Finnegans Wake*, Book I, sections 1–4, passim.

4 *The Margins of Philosophy*; hereafter cited parenthetically in the text as M. Speech *and Phenomena, and Other Essays on Husserl's Theory of Signs*; hereafter cited in the text as SP. *Writing and Difference*; hereafter cited parenthetically in the text as WD. Of course, arbitrarily carving up Derrida's work into 'earlier,' 'more serious' texts and 'later,' 'playful' ones, is to be found as an operative division in Christopher Norris's *Derrida*. This division has been problematized by a number of later writers on Derrida. See, for example, Geoffrey Bennington and Jacques Derrida, *Jacques Derrida*, 41–2.

5 Derrida has also explored both the *Wake* and *Giacomo Joyce* in a more playful, fragmented fashion in the context of his ever-deferred exploration of the 'envois' in *The Post-Card: From Socrates to Freud and Beyond*. I hope to return to these texts in a future study on love in Joyce.

6 *Post-structuralist Joyce: Essays from the French*, ed. Derek Attridge, 145–60. Hereafter cited in the text as PSJ.

7 *Acts of Literature*, ed. Derek Attridge, 256–309. Hereafter cited in the text as AL.

8 Sam Slote, 'No Symbols Where None Intended: Derrida's War at *Finnegans Wake*' in Laurent Milesi, ed., *James Joyce and the Difference of Language*; Claudette Sartiliot, *Citation and Modernity: Derrida, Joyce, and Brecht*; and Susan Shaw Sailer, *On the Void of To Be: Incoherence and Trope in* Finnegans Wake; although not strictly speaking a 'Joycean,' special mention must be made of Geoffrey Hartman's *Saving the Text: Literature, Derrida, Philosophy,* esp. 33–

66. Christine van Boheemen-Saaf's *Joyce, Derrida, Lacan, and the Trauma of History: Reading, Narrative and Postcolonialism* is less sympathetic to Derrida's project and attempts to reclaim a post-colonial Joyce from Derrida's reading.

9 Notable in this vein are Shari Benstock's 'The Letter of the Law: *La carte postale* in *Finnegans Wake*' and Alan Roughley's *Reading Derrida Reading Joyce*.

10 Reed-Way Dasenbrock, 'Philosophy after Joyce: Derrida and Davidson'; Herman Rapaport, *Derrida and Heidegger*, 221–34. Christopher Norris, *Derrida*; Jacques Derrida and Geoffrey Bennington, *Jacques Derrida*; and Geoffrey Bennington, *Legislations, the Politics of Deconstruction*.

11 The reference is to Geert Lernout's *The French Joyce*.

12 What I am referring to here as the Platonic *eidos* is also commonly rendered as 'form' in English translations of Plato.

13 Derrida observes that within this metaphysics of presence 'there is no possible objection concerning this privilege to the present-now; it defines the very element of philosophical thought, it is evidence itself, conscious thought itself, it governs every possible concept of truth and sense.' *Speech and Phenomena*, 62.

14 Here, the word '*pré-séance*' ('precedence') is also a pun on the word 'presence.'

15 Derrida remarks this himself in the essay 'Violence and Metaphysics,' WD 79–153, where he cites 17.2098–9, 'Jewgreek is greekjew,' and refers to Joyce as 'perhaps the most Hegelian of modern novelists' (153). The *eidos* is that which is already known, and to which philosophy seeks to return. Derrida, in 'From Restricted to General Economy: A Hegelianism without Reserve' (WD 251–77), analyses the Hegelian project in terms of the relation of the 'unknown to the known' (271).

16 This association can, of course, be traced as far back in Derrida's work as 1969 and *Dissemination*'s thorough-going discussion of the relations of the Platonic *eidos* and memory. See particularly D 95–117. *The Post-card* also tropes the Platonic/Socratic debt in a similar way as a stamp that 'is simultaneously immense, imposes and is imposed everywhere' (101): 'Whatever I say, whatever I do, I must paste on myself a stamp with the effigy of this diabolical couple, these unforgettable comperes, these two patient impostors' (100). See also pp. 18–19.

17 Among many possible examples, see, *Of Grammatology*, 10–18.

18 The extent to which gramophoned memory caught in the 'ambiguity of written and oral marks' (AL 282) actively disrupts Platonic anamnesis can be clarified by considering it in conjunction with what Derrida, in his discussion of Plato's *Lesser Hippias* (368a–d) and the *Greater Hippias* (285c–e),

calls 'hypomnesis' (D 106–7). Hyponmnesis is not (Platonic) memory itself, but rather its supplement: 'monuments (*hypomnēmata*), inventories, archives, citations, copies, accounts, tales, lists, notes, duplicates, chronicles, genealogies, references' (D 107). It is the sophistical mechanical memory that Plato indicts because it substitutes mnemonic devices for 'living memory,' and contaminates the Platonic dream of a living 'memory with no sign' with the signs and marks of death (D 109, 111). The gramophoned *yes* – 'the space of writing, space *as* writing' (D 109, Derrida's emphasis) – disrupts the closed circuit of eidetic meaning precisely because it 'describes nothing, states nothing, even if it is a sort of performative implied in all statements' (AL 297). In other words, the *yes* is the writing 'prior' to the non-written *eidos* (AL 296). It is the very parodic double that 'sets in motion the anamnesic machine' and 'its hypermnesic overacceleration.' The gramophoned repetition of the *yes, yes* is not yet the hypermnesic machine of Joyce studies, but that which sets it in motion – that which it needs to get going. As such, both *yes*es cannot be simply separated from each other: they double (for) each other, 'call for and imply each other irresistibly' (AL 307). And yet, the hypomnesic *yes* is also that which ruins all reappropriative hypermnesia by opening its circuit to dialogical repetition, even as it risks being mistaken for it.

19 This writing is, of course, the one explored by Derrida in *Of Grammatology* (hereafter OG). See especially 6–93.

20 This study does not intend to suggest that Derrida's output 'stops' with *Glas*, but is rather intended to read these two texts alongside each other in a sustained manner for the first time.

21 Throughout this text I will cite material from columns (a) and (b) of *Glas* in parentheses. Thus, (99a) means page 99, column (a). When there is an insert into either column (a) or (b), the format will be as follows: (99bi) means the insert in column (b) on page 99. Even though it may be tempting to regard the columns of *Glas* as being inspired by the columns of book II section 2 of the *Wake*, it should be pointed out that Derrida's texts have long played with doubled or non-linear textual configurations. One obvious example is 'Tympan,' the introductory essay in M that has a marginal strip of text running alongside the main text. However, 'Tympan' is by no means unique in its utilization of non-linear text. For example, double columns are also found at the start of 'The Double Science' in D and in the alternating pages of French and English text in *Spurs*. In texts like *The Truth in Painting* and *The Post-Card*, doubled text takes the form of competing, multiple voices in the 'main body' of the text. In both WD and OG Derrida plays with the notion of the footnote as a sort of 'margin' that disrupts the linear flow of the main text. This textual form is given extended treatment by Derrida in

both his essay 'Living On: Border Lines' (*Deconstruction and Criticism*, 75–176) and *Jacques Derrida* (with Geoffrey Bennington).

22 Martin Heidegger, *Kant and the Problem of Metaphysics*. See especially 134–6. I will return to this in chapters 2 to 6 below.

1. 'Immargination'

1 What I am referring to here as the Platonic *eidos* is also commonly rendered as 'Form' in English translations of Plato. See, for example, the 'Theory of Forms' in F.M. Cornford's translation of *The Republic*, book 10.

2 Although Derrida is discussing Aristotle in *Margins*, it is the *eidos* that permits Derrida to suggest that the order of appearance remains unbroken throughout the history of Western philosophy, whether the *eidos* is taken to be 'a figure of the thing itself, as in Plato, a subjective representation, as in Descartes, or both, as in Hegel' (D 194).

3 As when, for example, Oscar Wilde argued that life imitates art in 'The Decay of Lying,' in *The Complete Works*, 982.

4 OG 11, citing Aristotle's *De interpretatione* 1, 16a.

5 When read in this manner, the act of creation or production can be understood to constitute what Derrida in his essay 'White Mythology' calls a metaphor of metaphor (M 207–1). This issue is an important one for understanding Derrida's relation to Heidegger's analyses in 'The Origin of the Work of Art,' where the philosophical notion of a 'thing' is shown to be philosophically rooted in the process of making/production. This issue lies beyond the scope of the present argument, which seeks to examine what *Finnegans Wake* shares with Derrida's problematization of the Platonic order of appearance. I intend to explore elsewhere what bearing this matter will have on the reading of Joyce and Derrida proposed here.

6 Derrida's analysis is of course close to and critical of Heidegger's well-known analysis of *logos* as speaking. See, for example, *Being and Time*, trans. John Macquarrie and Edward Robinson (Oxford: Basil Blackwell, 1962), 55–63.

7 Unfortunately, the hen's famous letter (93.24–7) also fails to clear anything up.

8 For a list of some of Finnegan's names and attributes, see 71.10–72.16 and 126.10–139.13.

9 See, for example, 108.8–112.8.

10 John Bishop, *Joyce's Book of the Dark*, 27.

11 See Derrida, *Positions*, 20 (hereafter cited in the text as P) and OG 20.

12 See also Bishop's fascinating discussion in *Joyce's Book of the Dark*, 28, 142, and Roland McHugh, *The Sigla of* Finnegans Wake, 103.

13 This of course has the same form of Derrida's analysis of the bobbin in 'To Speculate: On Freud' in *The Post-Card: From Socrates to Freud and Beyond*, 257–411.

14 Borrowing from Levinas, Derrida says the exact same thing twice on this page of *Margins of Philosophy*. He also repeats himself in *Memoires for Paul de Man*, 58. Hereafter cited in the text as Mem.

15 I will return to the complicated issue of time and temporalization in detail in chapters 2, 3, and 6.

16 The Wakean 'immargination' can also be understood as being concerned with a non-present space-time that even precedes the concept of 'property,' to the extent that a 'messuage' is also a dwelling house along with its adjacent lands and holdings.

17 See, for example, Derrida's discussion of *The Garden of Epicurus* by Anatole France, M 210–19.

18 I will return to this blindness and deafness below in the context of the body in both *Glas* and *Finnegans Wake*.

19 The term *usure* is certainly useful here, but with the reservations that Derrida notes in the first section of 'White Mythology,' M 215–19, regarding its position in the 'continuist presupposition' that sees metaphor as a gradual loss of meaning, rather than in terms of displacement, rupture, and reinscription.

20 Adaline Glasheen, *A Third Census of Finnegans Wake*, 94. It is also worth noting here, as Glasheen does, that Joyce did not make a distinction between the 'indications' and 'names' of persons in the text (See also *Letters of James Joyce*, vol. I, ed. Stuart Gilbert, 247–8). It is therefore clear that the loss of the 'proper' and its partial echo cannot be contained by any conception of 'personhood.'

21 See particularly, '*Différance*,' M 19.

22 D 222, footnote 36.

23 For an extended discussion of the rhetorical trope of catachresis in a semiotic and catechistic context, see Lorraine Weir, *Writing Joyce: A Semiotics of the Joyce System*, 29–53. Hereafter cited as WJ.

24 See also M 229: 'To permit oneself to overlook this *vigil* of philosophy, one would have to posit that the sense aimed at through these figures is an essence rigorously independent of that which transports it, which is an already philosophical *thesis*, one might even say philosophy's *unique thesis*, the thesis which constitutes the concept of metaphor, the oppostion of the proper and the nonproper, of essence and accident, of intuition and discourse, of thought and language, of the sensible and the intelligible.'

25 Joyce filters this creation through Yeats's use of the *Timaeus* in *A Vision*. See McHugh, *Sigla*, 72–3.

26 Clive Hart also documents Joyce's use of the scene of demiurgic creation from the *Timaeus*: 'The central passage of II.2 – where the marginal notes are allowed to dissolve into the main body of the text before their reappearance with exchange of tone – corresponds to the central point of contact on the sphere of development ... That in disposing his materials in this way Joyce had the *Timaeus* in mind is made clear by a whole shower of allusions to it' (*Structure and Motif in* Finnegans Wake, 132). Hereafter cited as S&M. Hart also notes that the use of the *Timaeus* interacts with the *Wake*an theme of the 'double-cross' (133f.).

27 And yet, at the heart of this scene of the carefree dance of affirmative openness there is the other 'yes-laughter' Derrida has identified in 'Ulysses Gramophone.' This 'yes-laughter' 'takes joy in hypermnesic mastery' that functions as an 'alpha and omegaprogramophone' wherein 'all the histories, stories, discourses, knowledges' would be prescribed in advance (AL 292). In this scene, both the absence of eidetic meaning and the chance similarities of words find themselves 'on the agenda' of the hypermnesic Joyce machine, the 'machine of filiation – legitimate or illegitimate – functions well and is ready for anything, ready to domesticate, circumcise, circumvent everything; it lends itself to the encyclopedic reappropriation of absolute knowledge' (AL 294). This 'yes-laughter of encircling reappropriation' (ibid.) can be heard as Dolph's finger-writing gives way to his recounting of the story of the 'the whole damning letter' (288.12–13), recalling the stages of Finnegan's/Here Comes Everybody (HCE)'s progress, before finally succumbing to the weight of memory and duty, and retelling (once again) the story of how HCE came to be in Ireland 'for the twicedhecame time' (288.14).

However, in staging the scene of Dolph's catachrestic gestural writing in this manner, the *Wake* performs a scene of writing that also stages the contamination of the two yes-laughters: 'The two yes-laughters of differing quality call the one to the other, call for and imply each other irresistibly; consequently they risk, as much as they request, the signed pledge. One doubles the other, not as a countable presence, but as a ghost. The yes of memory, with its recapitulating control and reactive repetition, immediately doubles the light, dancing yes of affirmation, the open affirmation of the gift' (AL 307–8). In Dolph's scene of writing, the 'manipulatory operation of hypermnesic reappropriation' (AL 304) that serves to recount (once again) the trajectory of the letter and to repeat the story of Finnegan occurs alongside the words of others gleefully 'chanched' by Dolph to say something other than what was meant by their speaker/author. But in staging both these possibilities at once in the scene of Dolph's catachrestic writing, *Finnegans Wake* also invites the reader to hear the other yes, the light, dancing yes that affirms the other, prior to Dolph's retracing of the hypermnesic circuit of both the letter and Finnegan's return.

28 On the conjunction between intention and the realm of the ideas in Artaud, see Derrida's *Writing and Difference*, 232–50. For a similar discussion in the context of Husserl, see SP, 18–19.

29 The textual body, however, is not simply 'anybody.' Catachresis can be understood to open the space of a sort of 'textual body' that is caught in language but not reducible to etymology because of the secondary origin of catachresis. I will return to this in chapter 2 below.

30 'Tinkling' of course reintroduces at this point yet another famous motif of urination in the *Wake*. See for example the scene in the Phoenix Park at 8.32.

31 See particularly the long footnote at D 181–2.

32 I will return to this scene of rhyme in detail in chapter 3 below.

33 See also M 225.

34 I will return to this issue in the final section of this chapter.

35 Hereafter cited as U. All quotations follow the Gabler format of chapter number and line number. E.g., 1.160 is chapter 1, line 160.

36 D 191. Once again, what I am referring to here as the Platonic *eidos* is also commonly rendered as 'Form' in English translations of Plato.

37 M 257. Although Derrida is discussing Aristotle in *Margins*, it is the *eidos* that permits Derrida to suggest that the order of appearance remains unbroken throughout the history of Western philosophy, whether the *eidos* is taken to be 'a figure of the thing itself, as in Plato, a subjective representation, as in Descartes, or both, as in Hegel' (D 194).

38 This is the 'little booklet' that Derrida refers to numerous times in this section of the 'The Double Session.' It was written by Paul Margueritte, and published, according to D 196, by 'Calmann-Lévy, new edition, 1886.'

39 See previous note.

40 See also OG 10–26.

41 Once again, for the reasons outlined above in relation to Finnegan's buildung, the status of what the Mime 'produces' is to be treated very carefully.

42 It should be noted here that the 'nothing' in Heidegger means Being, as it does in 'What Is Metaphysics?' As is clear from the context here, the 'nothing,' as Derrida is using it here cannot simply mean the concealed nothing of Being. It rather means the *différantial* 'nothing' of the text, which is not punctually 'present.' Margot Norris tackles the relationship between Joyce and Heidegger in her *The Decentered Universe of* Finnegans Wake, 73–97.

43 Hereafter cited as NS. All references to this edition will follow Vico's paragraph numbering. *The New Science* is a standard point of departure for reading the *Wake*. For a detailed discussion of Vico and Joyce see Bishop, *Joyce's Book of the Dark*, 174–215, and WJ, 54–81. *Vico and Joyce* also provides an

indispensable overview of Vico's importance for Joyce. For a more introductory approach to Vico and Joyce see James S. Atherton, *The Books at the
Wake*, 28–43, and S&M 49–52, 57–62.

44 The strategy that I am outlining here would also form the basis for a thorough-going analysis of the Plato-Socrates couple of *The Post-card* and
Joyce's work. Derrida's 'Two Words for Joyce' of course heavily hints in this
direction.

45 The other Hegelian 'laughter' will have to do with a loss that cannot be
capitalized upon: 'Contrary to the metaphysical, dialectical, "Hegelian"
interpretation of the economic movement of *différance*, we must conceive of
a play in which whoever loses wins, and in which one loses and wins on
every turn' (M 20). I will return to this below.

46 See Jacques Derrida, 'Before the Law,' in AL 183–220.

47 Cf. '*Différance*,' passim, M 3–27.

48 Hereafter cited as KPM.

49 I will explore this in more detail in chapter 2, below.

50 See OG 24.

51 See particularly OG 10–15.

52 As I noted in the introduction, Derrida himself underlines this in the essay
'Violence and Metaphysics' (WD 153), where he cites 17.2098–9 and refers
to Joyce as 'perhaps the most Hegelian of modern novelists.'

53 Among many possible examples, see OG 10–18.

54 See pages 7–8 above.

55 *Aufhebung* is Hegel's term for the simultaneous negation and conservation
of terms in the dialectical progression towards Absolute Knowledge (WD
255). *La relève* is Derrida's translation of *Aufhebung*.

56 History and meaning are inextricably bound together in Hegel insofar as
the history of the world is also the history of the emergence of truth and
meaning. This culminates in the emergence of the Spirit or Absolute
Knowledge, to which I will return in chapters 5 and 6, below.

57 G.W.F. Hegel, *The Phenomenology of Mind*, 234. Cited in WD 255.

58 Georges Bataille, *Hegel, la mort et le sacrifice*, 38. Cited in WD 258.

59 This writing is, of course, the one explored by Derrida in *Of Grammatology*.
See especially 6–93.

2. Following the Hen

1 Martin Heidegger, *Kant and the Problem of Metaphysics*.

2 This undecidability is accentuated later in I.2 when Finnegan (as HCE)
meets 'a cad with a pipe' in the Phoenix Park (35.11), who asks him for the

time. HCE's responds that the time is 'twelve of em sidereal and tankard time' (35.33–4). The exchange is gay slang for assent in an anonymous sexual encounter that implies erection. Indeed, HCE faces the cad 'standing full erect' (36.15).

3 Babel is, of course, the Old Testament story of the tower built by the Shem, the tribe of descendents from Noah's son Shem. This tower was intended to rival the beauty and complexity of Yahweh's creation. Yahweh, when he realized what was happening, decided to thwart the Shem's efforts by introducing foreign languages among the work crews. Presumably, with a confused language, communication would have broken down, construction would have stopped, and the tower would have remained a sort of truncated stump.

4 Among these thunder-words are the Japanese *kaminari*; Hindustani *karak*; Greek *brontao* (I thunder); French *tonnerre*; Irish *tórnach*; Portugese *trovao*; and Danish *tordenen*.

5 These giants and their shit are contrasted by Vico with the Hebrews, an originary distinction that splits the entire human race 'into two species: the one of giants, the other men of normal stature; the former gentile, the latter Hebrews' (NS 172). The Hebrews were smaller from the beginning 'on account of their cleanly upbringing and their fear of God and of their fathers.' Because of this they 'continued to be of the proper stature in which God had created Adam and Noah and his three sons; it was perhaps in abomination of giantism that the Hebrews had so many ceremonial rites pertaining to bodily cleanliness' (NS 371).

6 Hereafter, KPM and BP respectively. I will have occasion to return to the analyses in these texts in the present chapter and chapter 3.

7 For that reason, all of Heidegger's remarks must be treated carefully. This need for caution is especially necessary for a study such as this which seeks to compare *Finnegans Wake* to the work of Derrida, which has been extremely clear on the point of the problematic relation of Heidegger's work on Being to the trace (see, for example, OG 18–26 and M 63–7: these are but two of many other instances). The point here will be to take what is of use for the present study from Heidegger's texts. Far from being disrespectful, I see this gesture as being akin to Derrida's at M 62, where it is a matter of reading 'within the opening of the Heideggerian breakthrough, which is the only thought excess of metaphysics as such ... occasionally, and faithfully, beyond certain propositions within which the Heideggerian breakthrough has had to constrain itself.' I will try to make clear in the following discussion exactly where such a reading that goes 'beyond' the Heideggerian opening is necessary.

8 This catachrestic look is supplemented by another catachresis: the 'look' is also the *genos* (Greek, family, stock, generation) of the thing. Here, Heidegger's reinterpretation conjures all sorts of other questions. For example, how else does a 'look' become the *genos* of the object? Further, how else could nature's emergence from itself name the actualization of the thing produced? This would call for an entire rereading of the Heideggerian project from the point of view of catachresis. The point here, however, is *not* to pursue the Heideggerian project of the question of the meaning of Being: rather it is to appreciate how far Heidegger's destruction of the order of perception goes in the direction of the imagination and production. For example, it can easily be seen in the above excerpt that the values of nature and imitation still guide the interpretation Heidegger proposes: the 'actual thing arises out of phusis, the nature of the thing.' That is, the 'nature' of the thing emerges in imitation of the way in which nature (*phusis*) (naturally) emerges (*phuein*) from itself. I have already noted some of the issues with these concepts in chapter 1, but there is still a need to explore how reinterpreting the operation of nature and imitation as catachreses would affect what Heidegger undertakes in *The Basic Concepts of Phenomenology.* Unfortunately, this is not the place for such an undertaking.

9 Heidegger, it will be recalled from the long citation from BP, expressly says that the 'anticipated look, the proto-typical image, shows the thing as what it was before the production and how it is supposed to look as a product. The anticipated look has not yet been externalized as something formed, actual, but is the image of the imag-ination, of fantasy, phantasia.'

10 Here would be a interesting place to begin rereading all that Heidegger in *Being and Time* (hereafter cited as BT) has to say about the 'worldhood of the world' and the role that 'reference' plays in it (sections 15–18), in conjunction with both the analysis of the imagination I am sketching here and *différance*. Unfortunately, such a reading is beyond the scope of the present study.

11 Immanuel Kant, *Critique of Pure Reason.* Hereafter cited as CPR in the text.

12 For a full discussion of this, see BT, sections 15–18.

13 This paragraph also acts as a window that opens *Being and Time* onto the text of *Finnegans Wake.* While the interaction of these two texts would not add anything further here regarding Heidegger's discussion of time in KPM, the notion of 'Being-in' as it is analysed in *Being and Time* raises some interesting questions regarding the relationships between language in Heidegger's 'Origin of the Work of Art' the structure of language in both Derrida's *Speech and Phenomena* and *Of Grammatology,* and their relations to language in *Finnegans Wake.* These questions, however, are far beyond the scope of this analysis, and must be pursued elsewhere.

14 See, once again, BT, sections 15–18.

15 This text is also, of course, influenced by Bergson's *Time and Will*.

16 I will discuss this in greater detail in chapters 3 to 6 below.

17 The 'flow' of time is also associated with Bergson's conception of time in *Time and Will*. Bergson is disparagingly referred to by Shaun (echoing the words of Wyndham Lewis's *Time and Western Man*) at 149.20.

18 See also Roland McHugh's discussion of time in *The Sigla of* Finnegans Wake, 31–6.

19 Once again, Finnegan's 'absence' is not to be understood as a negative or real absence: his 'absence' functions in such a way that he is lost for/as presence. Nothing in the text guarantees that he will be found again in full *propria persona*. He can only ever come and go in/as a series of avatars that are borne on the series of lapping-flowing waves of time figured as a river.

20 This 'sensory' kernel is also explored by Derrida as a form of spacing in the context of Hegel's semiology and his analysis of Chinese writing and grammar in the essay 'The Pit and the Pyramid: Introduction to Hegel's Semiology' (M 71–108). See esp. 102–8.

21 This forms the structure of Derrida's reading of Nietzsche in *Spurs*. The 'spurs' in question motivate.

22 Joyce himself made several uses of the verb 'to come' in this sense. In *Ulysses*, Molly, she of the Latin blood, says, 'I never came properly till I was what 22 or so' (18.1050–1).

23 Another explanantion of how time can become money lies in Vico's *The New Science*. It was during the Vichian 'age of the heroes' that money was first invented (NS 342ff.). These hero-warriors were very war-like, but their speech was mute. In order to get around this muteness, the heroes communicated with each other through what Vico calls the 'mute speech' of heraldry and hoisted battle standards. Money derives from this culture of war and symbols. In bringing time and money together, the Questions and Answers chapter changes the Vichian battle standards into the 'intuitive symbols' of space and time. Finally, the references to money and war serve to alert the reader familiar with Vico that there is a battle brewing between space and time in I.6.

24 See, once again, McHugh's discussion of time in *The Sigla of* Finnegans Wake, 31–6. Both of us are endebted to Glasheen's 'Rough Notes on Joyce and Wyndham Lewis.'

25 See, for example, 104.22, 113.19, 158.1, 230.13, 279.F1, 389.24, 394.24, and 424.28.

26 See, for example, 292.11. The 'hatboxes' here also recall '□,' Joyce's symbol for the *Wake* itself in his composition notebooks. See McHugh, *Sigla*.

27 This is Roland McHugh's translation in his *Annotations to Finnegans Wake*, 168. Hereafter cited as *Annotations*.

28 See Derrida's *Geschlecht II*, 183.

29 For the full text of this poem see Richard Ellmann, *James Joyce*, 335–77.

30 This method is clearly seen in the various plates in David Hayman's *A First Draft Version of* Finnegans Wake. See particularly plates IV–VII. The 'X' also evokes Joyce's symbol in his composition notebooks for the Four Old Men, the 'Mamalujo.'

31 See also 18.33–4 of the *Wake*.

32 These considerations here would open up onto Derrida's consideration of non-linear writing in *Of Grammatology*. See, in particular, the discussion on 289.

33 OG 289.

34 In Vico, the first altars (*arae*), the fields of grain, were also the 'asylums' (NS 777) where the intruders, or *hostiae*, were either sacrificed, cut up, or subjugated as slaves by the *paterfamilias* (NS 776ff.).

35 Edward Sullivan, *The Book of Kells*, 24. See also McHugh, *Annotations to Finnegans Wake*, 120.

36 I have included the famous '*Tunc*' page of *The Book of Kells* manuscript (124 recto) as a plate (see p. x) to this study.

37 Once again, I refer the reader to the plate on p. x.

38 Michael J. O'Shea, *James Joyce and Heraldry*, 126. Hereafter cited in the text as JJH.

39 See M 262–3.

40 See Wendy Steiner, *The Colors of Rhetoric*, 191. For a consideration of Augustine and Cubism in this context, see WJ 30–33.

41 I will return to the question of the 'family' and the text in chapter 5 below.

42 Cf. *Glas* 93, column (a). Unless otherwise stated, all references to *Glas* will be given parenthetically in the text by page and column, e.g., 93a, 95b. References to a particular insert will also include the letter 'i,' e.g., 93ai, 95bi.

43 WD 196–231.

44 The translation used in Derrida's discussion in *Dissemination* is A.V. Miller's (New York: Oxford University Press, 1977).

45 D 4: Derrida is 'compelled' to 'apply the name "matter" to that which lies outside all classical oppositions and which, ... should no longer be able to assume any reassuring form.'

46 Insofar as the productive scene of contraband has to do with the rival-mother, it can also be related to the *Wake*an scene of letter-writing. I will explore this contraband and its tabernacle in relation to the letter's envelope-writing in more detail in chapter 6.

47 Jacques Derrida, *The Truth in Painting*. Hereafter, TP.

3. *To Hen*

1 Hereafter cited as Mem.
2 The first part of this paragraph is an attempt to reconstruct Hegel's complex conception of reflection in a limited space. For Hegel's full consideration, see the *Science of Logic*, book II, 'The Doctrine of Essence.'
3 Hegel uses a German pun, *Schein*, which means simultaneously both 'shine,' 'glow,' and 'semblance,' 'appearance' to convey this process. See also Hegel, *Hegel's Logic*, section 112A.
4 This can be clarified by pursuing the metaphorics of reflected light: when light strikes an object, it is no longer immediate, but reflected. Similarly, when the subject reflects on the object, the act of reflection produces a 'reflection' of the object's essence.
5 See also Hegel, *Philosophy of Nature*, sections 275A and 431ff. in particular.
6 This does not mean that the Hegelian *eidos* escapes the previously outlined schema of imitation, since the Hegelian project seeks to express and illustrate its pre-existent presence of its meaning or truth. See OG 10–24, and the discussion in chapter 1 above. The position of the Hegelian *eidos* here as that which bridges 'mental existence' and 'reality' is in many ways identical to the position of the sign and the imagination in Hegel, which lies between the interior and exterior and in may ways marks 'dialecticity itself' (M 77). I will return to the question of Derrida's uses of the imagination in Hegel in chapter 5 below.
7 'The Solar Anus,' in *Visions of Excess: Selected Writings, 1927–1939*, 5–9. Bataille's 'solar anus' parodies the role the intelligible sun plays in philosophical reflection from Plato to Hegel. See particularly M 253–4, 271.
8 See, for example, 14.24, 91.8, 294.1, 300.12, 310.9, 320.26, 351.23, 444.15, 490.20, 609.3, and 623.17.
9 I am endebted here to John Bishop's detailed and sensitive examination of the eye and the ear and their many permutations in his *Joyce's Book of the Dark*, 216–304. See particularly 296–9.
10 *A Third Census* of Finnegan's Wake, 'Earwicker' entry.
11 *Eternal Geomater: The Sexual Universe of* Finnegans Wake. Hereafter cited as EG.
12 See EG 64. △ is Joyce's shorthand in his composition notebooks for all the avatars of the mother in the text. For an extensive discussion of these symbols, see McHugh's *Sigla*.
13 For more on this, see EG, chapter 2. Solomon's analysis, to which I am endebted here, develops the coincidence of the two in a different manner.
14 Solomon also notes the metonymic relation between the body and the

phallus of HCE as they hang on the cross: 'The central majesty, the father-phallus, becomes a sugardaddy promising a Nobel prize to the two sons (thieves) hanging on each side: 'Heavysciusgardaddy, parent who offers sweetmeats, will gift uns his Noblett's surprize. With this laudable purpose in loud ability let us be singulfied. Betwixt me and thee hung cong' [306.6–7].' (EG 83).

15 For example, McHugh's *Sigla*, Hayman's *First Draft Version of* Finnegans Wake and The 'Wake' in Transit, and Solomon's *Eternal Geomater* all make this observation.

16 The major restatements of the letter crop up on pages 011, 111, 113, 116, 279.F1, 280, 301, 369–70, 413, 457, 615. There are far too many smaller restatements of the letter to list in this footnote. For a more complete list, see S&M 232–233.

17 This association is also well known. See for example S&M 204.

18 The reader will notice that Shaun's ejaculation scene is already a parody of the familiar father-mother-son conception scene of the Annunciation, where words are the fertile 'likequid glue' caught in the females' 'cups.' I will return to this 'Annunciation' below in chapters 5 and 6.

19 The ring-like 'contr-action' inflames the other, and as such forms the incandescent 'noose' of the 'RAYNBOW' (226.24–27.2). The rainbow, which is, as I will suggest in chapter 6, the after-effect of the holocaust (612.30), also becomes the flaming ring of the circular letter that calls forth Shem's 'spurt of coal' from his 'Old cocker' (232.27) as he 'comes back' to Ireland and himself (232.1–17).

20 Hebrew *letters* traditionally have the 'semantic' value of *things*. In the above list, the translated Hebrew word is followed by its equivalent letter. See McHugh, *Annotations* 249.

21 For a complex but fascinating discussion of the heliotrope in Joyce from 'The Dead' to the *Wake*, see Margot Norris, 'Joyce's Heliotrope,' in Beja, ed. *Coping with Joyce: Essays from the Copenhagen Symposium*, 3–24.

22 Re Heidegger, see KPM 35, noted above.

23 There are still some precautions to be taken here, however. The major difficulty for this reading of 'time' lies in the fact that the concept of time has been tied philosophically to particular teleo-spatial models such as the line in keeping with what Derrida calls the 'system of the founding oppositions of metaphysics' (M 61). To the extent that time is worked over by these oppositions, time can overcome this shuddering series of now-points that 'do not,' says Derrida, 'give time,' and which constantly threaten to arrest it. A clear example of this can be seen when Aristotle, who wants to get past the conception of the line or *gramme* 'as a series of points, as a composition

of parts each of which would be an arrested limit,' relies on the opposition of act/potential (59–60). In this gesture, the 'potential' *gramme* gives way to a teleology of the line that is in fact infinitely circular and therefore 'Hegelian' (60, 61):

> The point can cease to immobilize movement, can cease to be both beginning and end, only if the extremities touch, and only if the *finite* movement of the circle regenerates itself indefinitely, the end indefinitely reproducing itself in the beginning and the beginning in the end ... The *gramme* is *comprehended* by metaphysics between the point and the circle, between potentiality and the act (presence); ... *Time*, then, would be but the name of the limits within which the *gramme* is thus comprehended, and, along with the *gramme* the possibility of the trace in general. *Nothing* other *has ever been* thought by the name of *time*. Time is that which is thought on the basis of Being as presence, and if something – which bears a relation to time, but is not time – is to be thought beyond the determination of Being as presence, it cannot be a question of something that could still be called *time*. Force and potentiality, *dynamics*, have always been thought, in the name of time, as an incomplete *gramme* within which the horizon of an eschatology or a teleology that refers, according to the circle, to an archeology. (M 60)

Time, when it is tied to the teleology of the point-line-circle, cannot be thought outside the movement from potential to the presence of the act: the trace or *gramme* is already a *potential* circle – a point, a line. This presence dominates the *différance* of the trace that can only ever be a potential presence. The same problem also pertains to the embeddedness of certain terms that otherwise might be seen to hold out the possibility of displacing metaphysics – 'force,' 'potentiality,' 'dynamics,' and 'foreignness' (61) – in the 'founding oppositions of metaphysics.' When thought according to these founding oppositions, 'foreignness is thought as accident, virtuality, potentiality, incompletion of the circle, weak presence, etc.' (ibid.): all of these labels derive from the metaphysical opposition of essence/accident. Nevertheless, withdrawing these terms from the founding oppositions of metaphysics, even though it is difficult, would also appear to be a necessary manoeuvre. I say necessary because, despite all this, there remains a 'something – which bears a relation to time, but is not time' that makes itself felt through the complex and difficult problematic of time. This 'something – which bears a relation to time, but is not time' clears the way for a consideration of the now that cannot be contained by the opposition essence/accident since it is 'a constitutive part of time and an accidental part of time. It

can be considered *as such* or *as such'* (61). In other words, if one considers
the now as something that is related to time but is not time in the manner
that Derrida has, it becomes possible to see that the now has a problematic
relationship with the binary opposition that would seek to dominate it. If
one thinks of the now, or better, the shuddering 'coexisting-succession' of
now-points as 'that which bears a relation to time, but is not time,' it *exceeds*
the binary opposition that seeks to dominate it. It is thus no longer a case of
thinking the now as either potential or foreignness. And only by thinking of
the now-points in this way can they be thought in excess of 'everything that
the history of metaphysics has comprehended in the form of the Aristotelian *grammē*, in its point, in its line, in its circle, in its time, and in its space'
(67). In sum, the Aristotelian text has 'temporal' resources that cannot be
contained by its philosophy of time, which is dominated by the founding
oppositions of metaphysics.

If the philosophical concept of time is the 'name of the limits within
which the gramme is thus comprehended, and, along with the gramme the
possibility of the trace in general,' then the shuddering coexistence of now-
points that is related to time but is not time holds out the possibility of
understanding the gramme or trace in a way that no longer seeks to subor-
dinate them to their strict Aristotelian counterpart. This different understanding of the trace is also what make clear the links the now-points have
with the strategic but profound 'reversal' that Derrida sees as being necessary for displacing a reading of the gramme or trace that is dominated by
metaphysical opposition. In this reversal, presence is no longer treated as
'what the sign signifies' or 'what a trace refers to'; instead, presence
becomes 'the trace of the trace, the trace of the erasure of the trace' (66). In
other words, presence marks the erasure of the trace, the desire that seeks
to erase the trace, and 'on this condition can metaphysics and our language
signal in the direction of their own transgression' (ibid.). This is why, even
though the trace is 'erased,' it 'cannot be simply absent' since 'it would
give us nothing to think or it would still be a negative mode of presence.'
Its erasure is 'sheltered and visible in presence' and therefore remains
'absolutely excessive as concerns presence-absence' (65): that is, neither
present nor absent. Even so, 'all the determinations of such a trace' still
'belong as such to the text of metaphysics that shelters the trace and not
the trace itself' (66). In other words, the trace of the trace is only ever
named through the text of metaphysics, and this is what authorizes the
reading of time being proposed here: the now-points that are related to
time but do not give time are legible in the Aristotelian text. Thus, it is not
so much a question of 'wresting' the now-points, 'force,' 'potentiality,' or

'dynamics' from their domination by the founding oppositions of metaphysics, but rather one of rereading the metaphysical concept of time as
text.

24 It is this *'cum'* and the shuddering succession of now-points that are related
to both *différance* and time that will be of particular importance later in this
study's examination of 'agglutination' in *Glas* and the play of the band and
column in *Finnegans Wake*. This reading will also inform the reading of both
texts in the remaining chapters of this study.

25 I will return to the metaphors or, better, the catachreses of time under the
heading of what 'remains' of time – 'time's remains' (255–6a) – are legible in
Glas in chapters 5 and 6 below. The 'remains' of time is what is left once the
'now' has been set in the 'spacing' of the double.

26 This doubled relation is what Derrida has in mind when he notes that
'every text of metaphysics carries within itself, for example, *both* the so-
called "vulgar" concept of time *and* the resources that will be borrowed
from the system of metaphysics in order to criticize that concept ... It is on
the basis of this formal necessity that one must reflect upon the conditions
for a discourse exceeding metaphysics supposing that such a discourse is
possible, or that it announces itself in the filigree of some margin' (M 60–1).

27 It is also on the basis of this non-time that nonetheless bears a relation to
time that I wish to underline the necessity of rereading the role time plays
in Heidegger's reading of Kant. Time, as I have shown above, is of central
importance in Heidegger's consideration of the imagination in Kant. What
I am proposing here is the necessity of filtering Heidegger's reading of
Kant through what is related to time but is not time: the shuddering coexistence of now-points, the *cum*, the *hama*, *différance*. If this is not done, the
study risks comprehending the trace under the domination of metaphysics
and, as a result, would no longer be able to lay claim to its reading of Joyce
and Derrida.

There is one site in particular that suggests itself as a fitting one around
which I will organize this study's redeployment of Heidegger's work on
Kant: the relation between synthesis and the operation of the imagination.
For both Kant and Heidegger, '[s]ynthesis in general ... is the mere result of
imagination, a blind but indispensable function of the soul, without which
we should have no knowledge whatsoever but of which we are scarcely
ever conscious' (KPM 62–3, citing Kant, CPR A73/B105). What I am proposing here is a reinscription of the synthetic imagination – the power of
unconscious synthesis that precedes knowledge – in terms of the synthetic
spatio-temporal *cum* or *hama* discussed above. On this reading, the imagination becomes a synthesizing power that is inseperable from *différantial*

spatio-temporal *cum*. Once this reinscription of the imagination is under-
taken, it must then be understood to affect all other considerations of time
in Heidegger's reading of Kant. As mentioned in chapter 2, one of the most
important temporal sites in Heidegger's reading is the auto-affective 'inner
sense' of 'time': 'At the same time, however, we find givens of the 'inner
sense' which indicate no spatial shape and no spatial references. Instead,
they show themselves as a succession of states of our mind (representations, drives, moods). What we look at in advance in the experience of these
appearances, although unobjective and unthematic, is pure succession'
(34). Here the pure time of the 'inner sense' must be understood to undergo
a spatio-temporal, that is to say, a *différantial*, reinscription. Reread in terms
of *cum*, then, the sites of the imagination and temporal auto-affection are
reconfigured spatio-temporally with the *cum* of synthesis that can no longer
be conceived in terms of a pure, untroubled 'succession': 'succession' is displaced by the shuddering coexistence of now-points that mark the *force* of
the *gramme* beyond the teleo-geometry of the infinite circle.

28 For more on this in *Finnegans Wake*, see David Hayman, *The Wake in Transit*,
174–5.

29 The original sentence and translation read as follows: 'Aujourd'hui comme
aux temps de Pline et de Columelle la jacinthe se plaît dans les Gaules, la
pervenche en Illyrie, la marguerite sur les ruines de Numance; et pendant
qu'autour d'elles les villes ont changé de maîtres et de nom, que plusieurs
sont entrées dans le néant, que les civilisations se sont choquées et brisées,
leurs paisibles générations ont traversé les âges et sont arrivées jusqu'à
nous, fraîches et riantes comme aux jours des batailles. (Today, as in the
time of Pliny and Columella, the hyacinth disports in Wales, the periwinkle
in Illyria, the daisy on the ruins of Numantia; and while around them the
cities have changed masters and names, while some have ceased to exist,
while the civilizations have collided with one another and smashed, their
peaceful generations have passed through the ages and have come up to us,
fresh and laughing as on the days of battles)' (McHugh, *Annotations* 281).

30 S&M, especially 186–200.

4. 'Feelful thinkamalinks'

1 I am here using two translations of Vico's text. The first is that of *The New
Science* (3rd ed., 1744) by Thomas Godard Bergin and Max Harold Fisch,
which is the one I rely on throughout this study. The second is David
Marsh's 1999 translation, which I only make use of in the context of his rendering of 'imagination.' For Marsh, the 'imagination alters or recreates

things,' while ingenuity or invention merely put things in a suitable arrangement or context.' For Bergin and Fisch, the imagination more passively 'alters and imitates' things, whereas invention gives things a 'new turn *or* puts them into proper arrangement.' I have chosen to follow Marsh for his rendering of the imagination as the power to 'alter and recreate' things, and Bergin and Fisch for their rendering of invention as the power that gives things a 'new turn *or* puts them into proper arrangement.'

2 Donald Phillip Verene, *Vico's Science of Imagination*. Hereafter, VSI.
3 The 'sensibilities, feelings, metaphors and memories upon which human culture rests' (ibid., 40).
4 Obviously, there are a number of tensions that exert themselves between certain terms in Verene's vocabulary which this study has tried to put into question above – 'truth,' 'metaphor,' 'unity,' 'concept,' 'meaning,' etc. That being said, Verene's analysis shares a great deal with this study in that it sets out to explore in Vico an imagination that both knowledge and the concept must constantly presuppose. Thus, there is much in his analysis that remains of use for our reading of the remainder in Vico's imagination of creation. The point that I would like to focus on first is Verene's consideration of Vico's use of the 'topic' or 'middle term.'
5 See also WJ, chapter 5, especially the discussion of 'musica speculativa,' pages 85–91.
6 For reasons that will become clear momentarily, the topic is also the site where the Christian God of Providence blurs with the gods of the gentes.
7 See Bergin and Fisch, paragraph K5 of the introduction to the *New Science*.
8 This is, of course, Derrida's notion of 'supplementarity.' See OG 141–65.
9 This 'emptied scene' of ruined production recalls/anticipates the action of the sphincter, which is itself grasped by the 'folds' of the words *pro-duce* or *e-duce*. The 'pro-' part of 'produce' is derived from the Latin word meaning (1) 'for, in favour of,' and (2) 'for, in the place of, instead of' (*Oxford Dictionary of English Etymology*; hereinafter cited as ODEE). The 'e-' component of 'educe' derives from the Latin word *ex-*, shortened to *e-*, meaning 'out of' (ODEE). Both words derive from the Latin *ducere*, 'to lead.' *Ducere* is also related to the English word 'duct,' which can also mean 'course' or 'direction.' A 'duct' is both a 'stroke drawn' and 'a tube or canal in an animal or vegetable body' (ODEE), something that may be sealed off and opened by a sphincter.
10 See chapter 2 above, especially 124f.
11 'The Double Session' develops this doubled operational necessity of deconstruction: 'Operating necessarily from the inside, borrowing all the strategic and economic resources of subversion from the old structure, borrowing

them structurally, that is to say without being able to isolate their elements and atoms, the enterprise of deconstruction always in a way falls prey to its own work' (OG 24). This is also *'why a thought of the trace can no more break with a transcendental phenomenology than be reduced to it'* (OG 62, Derrida's italics).

12 See, for example, 39b.

13 See for example, 'The Origin of the Work of Art' in *Basic Writings*, ed. and trans. David Farrell Krell, 146, and 'The Thing' in *Poetry, Language, Thought*, trans. Albert Hofstadter, 167. The thingly character of the thing is, for Heidegger, bound up with the earth. One must be careful here not to equate earth with 'material,' but it would be at least theoretically possible to reconstruct this network of associations. Unfortunately, this is beyond the scope of the present argument.

14 This word also gives the name Sphinx, the mythological creature who poses riddles to Oedipus.

15 Hereafter, WP. All references to Nietzsche's texts utilize the aphorism/section number.

16 Hereafter, BGE. All references are to aphorism number.

17 Compare the stain that signs the letter at 114.29–15.6.

18 This passage translates as follows: 'First the artist, the eminent writer, without any shame or apology, pulled up his raincoat and undid his trousers and then he drew himself close to the life-giving and all-powerful earth, with his buttocks as bare as the day they were born. Weeping and groaning he relieved himself into his own hands. Then, unburdened of the black beast, and sounding a trumpet, he put his own dung which he called his "downcastings" into an urn once used as a honoured mark of mourning. With an invocation to the twin brethren Medard and Godard [the rain gods] he then passed water into it happily and mellifluously, while chanting in a loud voice the psalm which begins "My tongue is the pen of a scribe writing swiftly." Finally, from the foul dung, mixed, as I have said, with the "sweetness of Orion" and baked and then exposed to the cold, he made himself an indelible ink' (McHugh, *Annotations* 185).

19 See WJ, chapter 3 for a detailed discussion of the sacrament of the Eucharist.

20 All references are to aphorism number.

21 See also WJ, chapter 3.

22 ⊔ is the symbol Joyce uses in his composition notebooks to denote avatars of Finnegan, HCE, etc.

5. Imagination, Representation, and Religion

1 In other words, conatus, as I am rereading it here, must also be thought in

conjunction with the Nietzschean reinscription of the art of the topics in terms of the interpretative will to power.

2 I will return to these rings of fire in the context of 'the gift' in chapter 6.

3 The status of the legacy that binds opens the *Wake* onto Derrida's *The Post Card*, which explores the aporias of the debt Western thinking owes to Plato. Somewhat paradoxically, it is the language of contractual binding and the *khora* of the *Timaeus* 48e–51b that offer a chance to renegotiate this debt. I will pursue this opening elsewhere.

4 See also Bishop, *Joyce's Book of the Dark*, 393, and McHugh, *Sigla*, 30.

5 This is a familiar formula in Derrida's work. See, for instance, OG 18–19 among many possible examples.

6 See also *Glas* 47a.

7 It is also worth noting here that it is the incest prohibition that governs Hegel's analysis of the brother-sister bond (200a). I will consider this bond in some detail below.

8 See, especially, OG 298–9.

9 See 125–31a.

10 I refer the reader here to the discussion of catachresis in chapter 1.

11 Once again, it must be recalled that 'production' is here used catachrestically: there is no fully present 'product' 'produced' here. 'Imaginative production,' for all the reasons discuused thus far, would remain within the ambit of the '(non)productive' (D 296).

12 Trans. George Eliot (New York: Harper, 1957).

13 See WJ, chap. 3, esp. 34–6.

14 It will be recalled that in chapters 2 and 3 I argued that the X composes the writing of the hen's letter. In following the mother-hen's writing, the reader writes him/herself in the shape of the two warring sons who constantly cross each other in another X, which functions as the empty place in *Finnegans Wake* that the reader-writer occupies in order to set about making his/her way through the dense text. The reader-writer crosses him/herself and becomes a Christic figure who, like χ, is 'excruciated, in honour bound to the cross of your own cruelfiction!' (192.18–19). This cross, where reader and writer come together, composes the reader-writer as it plays – allegorically and catachrestically – with resurrection. 'Resurrection, which is always the formal element of "truth," a recurrent difference between a present and its presence, does not resuscitate a past which had been present; it engages the future' (Mem 59).

15 See 'The Pit and the Pyramid: Introduction to Hegel's Semiology' in M 71–108, 79.

16 The status of the fetish underscores the extraordinary imaginary dialogue that takes places between Hegel and Kant on 215–17a.

17 As Geoffrey Hartman notes on page 104 of *Saving the Text*, the treatment of
the 'IC' in the text of *Glas* is complex. Hartman's discussion makes for an
engaging early consideration of the IC. Although he notes that *Glas* abbre-
viates the Immaculate Conception as IC (see, for example, 223a), he does
not consider its relation to Kant's Categorical Imperative (in French,
L'Impératif Catégorique) (216a). Through the IC, both the Immaculate Conception and *L'Impératif Catégorique* playfully recall each other throughout
the text. Hartman's discussion also notes that in French, 'IC' is pronounced
the same as *ici* ('here'), and that it is found in conjunction with 'now' (*main-
tenant*) in the very first sentence fragment of *Glas* (1a). However, he does
not connect the 'here, now' of the IC/*ici* with the play of temporalization
discussed in detail in the previous chapters of this study. It is this spatio-
temporal ('here, now') play that sets the IC/*ici* ceaselessly wandering
because 'here' is always *différantially* split between a 'here,' a 'there,' a
'now,' and a 'then.' Read thus, the IC/*ici* marks the dislocation of (present)
meaning, opening it onto '*Il scie*' ('he saws'): IC/*ici* cuts/pierces the text,
invaginating it: 'I forced myself to say over and over, inwardly, with the
repetitiveness of a saw irritating the ear, He-re, He-re, He-re, He-re,
He-re … No drama could have taken the place in an area too narrow for
presence … They can trip him, can trip him, can trip him, cunt rip him, cunt
rip him … "Here cunt ripped him"' (258bi). Thus does the IC/*ici* pull on all
of the other markers of *différance* in the text that have already been discussed – judases, breaches, splits, Xs, inserts, knives, blades, cuts, fetishes,
and so on. To the extent that it recalls these *différants*, the IC opens onto the
difficult problem of the operation of the imagination in Hegelian dialectics.
I will return to this below.

18 It should also be remembered here that 'sensibility' is an overloaded word
in the context of the Kantian imagination: as should be clear from chapters
2 and 3, sensibility corresponds to the intuitive component of the imagination, which is, as Heidegger reminds us, 'original' in that it lets something
'spring forth' (KPM 99). Within the Kantian context, this originary springing forth is the intuition of time that has 'preeminence' because 'space gives
in advance merely the totality of those relations according to which what is
encountered in the external senses would be ordered' (34). However, 'time'
can no longer be considered as simply originary precisely for the reasons
that have been discussed throughout this study since chapter 2: Kantian
'time,' as I have been rereading it throughout this study, is reinscribed
within auto-affective spatio-temporality. Here, the text of *Glas* explicitly
names the operation of the Kantian imagination as that which suspends the
speculative leap, which also recalls Vico's conatus points, which also do
'without the speculative leap.' The imagination relates the finite to the infi-

nite non-speculatively in the operation of the imagination, which is no longer caught in the opposition of sensible/intelligible, phenomenal/noumenal, etc. The imagination displaces this opposition, connecting it in a non-speculative fashion in the 'point of sensibility.' Thus, when something, be it a geometric figure or a dog, is contemplated in this so-called 'inner sense,' it is always in conjunction with moods and drives. As I have already suggested, in the text of *Finnegans Wake* spatio-temporality is bound up with the mother.

But, on the surface of it, suggesting that spatio-temporality is allied to the mother might seem to contradict chapter 2's formulation where she was seen to correspond to conception, and her son to intuition. It should be remembered, however, that in the imagination, the auto-affective interaction of intuition and conception is more complex than simple opposition. The imagination is the non-simple productive site of both components in the image. As can be quickly seen at the level of the text, the mother (conception)-son (intuition) opposition is already compromised by the scene of letter-writing in which the author emerges as a 'Tiberiast duplex' (123.30–1). As the schema-image, the duplex is responsible for presenting (as a sensible, temporal image) the fused interrelation of the sensible (intuitive) and the intelligible (conceptual). Later in this chapter, I will consider the imaginary aspect of this scene, in order to inquire further into its spatio-temporality.

19 See also Mem 58–9.

20 Cf. 199a.

21 It is worth noting here that the woman at the tomb is not yet the Antigone of either Hegel or *Glas*. This is perhaps because the relation between the hen and Earwicker/Finnegan is not as 'desireless' as that of Antigone. I will, however, have occasion to return to Antigone and her sisters in the context of 'flowers' in chapter 6.

22 As such, the hen's writing recalls both Bataille's expenditure without reserve and death discussed in chapter 1 and the death that Derrida discusses on 139a.

23 This virginal bursting also recalls the discussion of Mary's aural conception in U.11.535–41.

24 In *Ulysses*, a similar graft is performed by Virag, Bloom's spectral grandfather:

VIRAG

(*A diabolic rictus of black luminosity contracting his visage, cranes his scraggy neck forward. He lifts a mooncalf nozzle and howls.*) Verfluchte Goim! He had a father, forty fathers. He never existed. Pig God! He had two left feet. He was Judas Iacchia, a Libyan eunuch, the pope's bastard. (*he leans out on tortured forepaws, elbows bent rigid, his eye ago-*

nising in his flat skullneck and yelps over the mute world) A son of a whore. Apocalypse (U.15.2570–76).

25 Compare 85–6a.
26 It is the *différantial* aspect of the 'not-yet' here that marks it as the double for the undeconstructed role of time and the 'not yet' that Derrida analyses in Hegel's philosophy in '*Ousia* and *Grammé*' (M 31–67) and, to a lesser extent, in 'The Pit and the Pyramid: Introduction to Hegel's Semiology' (M 71–108). See also my discussion of time in this context in chapter 2 above.

6. 'What is the ti..?'

1 The notion of 'time's remains' as I read it here would also open a reading of Derrida's *Given Time: I. Counterfeit Money* and *The Gift of Death*, both of which may be read as Derrida's rereading of the gift, excess, and time as they emerge in *Glas*. Such a reading would also have to include Derrida's comments on 'actuality' and 'events' in *Negotiations: Interventions and Interviews 1971–2001*. However, since my focus here is on both *Glas* and *Finnegans Wake*, such an analysis must remain beyond the scope of the present study. I hope to return to this elsewhere.
2 The 'ti..?' referred to here can also be read as a fragment of 'title' or 'tit.' As such, it fuses together issues relating to temporality, the relation to the breast, and the process of naming.
3 See chapter 1 above for an extended consideration of catachresis. I will return to this below.
4 For a more detailed précis of how the discussion of time relates to Joyce's ongoing argument with Wyndham Lewis, see George Otte, 'Time and Space (with the Emphasis on the Conjunction): Joyce's Response to Lewis.'
5 See pages 18–31 above.
6 See, for example, D 3–59.
7 Ann's name also recalls Christ as he appears in U.16.363 as 'Mr. Doyle': Doyle=oiled=anointed=Christ.
8 See my previous discussion of the Jewish figure in chapters 2 and 3 above.
9 This is similar to what Lorraine Weir calls the 'performance' of the Joyce text. For Weir, 'performance' is the keystone of the semiotics of the Joyce system. For a detailed discussion see WJ, pages 34–9, 41, and 49.
10 See *Finnegans Wake* 5.1 and compare 181.36–86.18 and 424.32–6.
11 Compare M 257.
12 See *Glas* 222a.
13 Letter to T.J. Brown, cited in Atherton, *The Books at the* Wake, 62.

14 The OED, citing Cussans, defines fretty as a surface '[C]overed with a number of narrow bars or sticks, usually eight, lying in the directions of the bend and bend-sinister, interlacing each other.'

15 '"*Diapre* or *Diapered*, in heraldry, a dividing of a field into planes, or compartments, in the manner of fret-work; and filling the same with variety of figures"' (OED). Diapering, which also decorates 'a flat surface, as a panel, wall, etc.' (OED), becomes even more complicated in 'fret-work': '**fret** fret, v.[2] Forms: Inf. 4–7 *frett(e*, (5 *freett*, 6 *freat*), 5– *fret*. Pa. t. 5 *fret*. Pa. pple. 4–7 *fret(t(e*, (5 *freit, freyt*), 4–5 *frettet, -it, -ut*, 4– *fretted*. Also pa. pple. 4 *ifreted*. [Perh. represents several distinct but cognate words. In part this word seems to be a OF. *freter* (used in pa. pple. *frete*, = Anglo-Lat. *frectatus, frictatus, frestatus*, in the sense 'ornamented with interlaced work, embroidered with gold, etc.', also Her. 'fretty'), f. *frete* ... In the architectural sense it agrees with *fretish* v.[2]; the two forms may be adoptions of the two stems of the OF. vb. **fraitir, fraitiss-*. There may also have been an independent English formation on *fret* sb.[1] The common view, that *fret* represents OE. *frætw(i)an*, to adorn, seems inadmissible phonologically; but it is possible that the OE. vb., though not recorded after the 12th c., may have survived in speech, and have been confused with the Romanic vb.] 1. a. trans. To adorn with interlaced work, esp. in gold or silver embroidery; in wider sense, to adorn richly with gold, silver, or jewels. Obs. ... b. transf. To variegate, chequer, form a pattern upon ... 2. Archit. To adorn (esp. a ceiling) with carved or embossed work in decorative patterns ... 3. Her. To interlace.'

16 For more on this see Atherton, *The Books at the* Wake, 110–13.

17 There is a strong case to be made that this scene presents neither Berkeley the philosopher nor his views on immaterialism. For more on this, see both Vitoux, 'Aristotle, Berkeley, and Newman in "Proteus" and *Finnegans Wake*' and Anghinetti, 'Berkeley's Influence on Joyce.'

18 See 3.1–24. As is well known in *Wake* scholarship, this whole scene takes place in the aptly named Phoenix Park in Dublin. This fiery park is the site where (truncated) erections pass through circular fire. The Wellington monument, a large obelisk ('the knock out in the park' [3.22]), doubles as the prostrate Finnegan's erection (*band*). Later, in I.1, the text draws attention to how 'the Willingdone git the band up,' his 'big Willingdone mormorial tallowscoop Wounderworker [which] obscides on the flanks of the jinnies' (8.34–5).

19 The reference here is to Hegel's analysis of Antigone's relationship to her brother, Polynices. The sister, or rather the *figure* of the sister, is without the desire that *is* the dialectic. Desire is the 'lack in self-feeling' (110a) that

prompts the one to go in search of, and incorporate, the other. Thus, the lack of desire is Hegel's '[f]ascination by a figure inadmissible in the system' (151a).

20 See p. x of the present text. See also the discussion in chapter 2 above.

21 This formulation is very similar to the thesis also formulated by Sir Edward Sullivan in his introduction to *The Book of Kells*: 'The frequently occurring presence of serpentine forms all through the decoration of the manuscript has given rise to the suggestion that these forms are in some way connected with the worship of Ophidian reptiles' (42, also cited in Atherton, *The Books at the* Wake, 65). If the 'word' of Christian revealed religion is embroiled in, and embroidered with, the decorative symbols of pagan ritual religion, then the Christian 'word' of the letter-book is itself 'derivative' and, to an extent, 'stolen' from the very moment of its first appearance.

22 See, particularly, chapter 3, above.

23 Ibid.

24 See above, chapter 4, section II.

25 The Book of Kells manuscript was also known as the Book of Columcille. See Atherton, *The Books at the* Wake, 63.

26 See also Derrida, *Of Spirit: Heidegger and the Question*, 99 and 136, and *Glas*, 8, 14, 15, 24, 59, 91, 235.

27 Compare Shem's shell to the 'cubehouse' of 5.14, his echoing 'haunted ink-bottle' 182.30–84.10, and Plato's pharmacy, D 169–71.

28 *Finnegans Wake*, book I, sections 1–4, passim.

29 See especially 134–6.

30 See Derrida SP, especially 60–9, and chapter 2 above.

31 PSJ 145–60.

32 AL 256–309.

33 This algebra would, of course, link up with the the disseminative (that is, non-Hegelian) reinscription of the 'lifeless numerical Unit' (D 21) in *Dissemination*.

34 See book II, section 3 of the *Wake*.

35 See, for example, SP 85 and M 21. See also the analysis of time and the double carried out in chapter 2 above.

36 This, of course, recalls Derrida's strategy of crossing out – placing *sous rature* – the verb 'to be' in *Of Grammatology.*

37 See *Glas* 242a.

38 See chapter 1.

39 Compare the 'regard' at 355.4 and 113bi.

Works Cited

Anghinetti, Paul. 'Berkeley's Influence on Joyce.' *James Joyce Quarterly* 19 (1982): 315–30.

Atherton, James S. *The Books at the* Wake. London: Faber and Faber, 1959.

– *Joyce Effects: On Language, Theory and History.* Cambridge: Cambridge UP, 2000.

Attridge, Derek, ed. *Post-structuralist Joyce: Essays from the French.* Cambridge: Cambridge UP, 1984.

Attridge, Derek. ed. *The Cambridge Companion to James Joyce.* Cambridge: Cambridge UP, 1990.

Bataille, Georges. *Hegel, la mort et le sacrifice. Deucalion* 5. Neuchatel, 1955.

– *Visions of Excess: Selected Writings, 1927–1939.* Trans. Allen Stoekl, Carl R. Lovitts, and Donald M. Leslie, Jr. Minneapolis: U of Minnesota P, 1985.

Beckett, Samuel, et al. *Our Exagmination Round his Factification for Incamination of Work in Progress, with letters of protest by G. V. L. Slingsby and Vladimir Dixon.* London: Faber and Faber Ltd, 1929.

Beja, Morris, ed. *James Joyce: The Centennial Symposium.* Urbana: U of Illinois P, 1986.

– *Coping with Joyce: Essays from the Copenhagen Symposium.* Columbus: Ohio State UP, 1989.

Bennington, Geoffrey. *Legislations: The Politics of Deconstruction.* London: Verso, 1994.

Benstock, Bernard, ed. *James Joyce: The Augmented Ninth, Proceedings of the Ninth International James Joyce Symposium, Frankfurt, 1984.* Syracuse: Syracuse UP, 1988.

Benstock, Bernard, ed. *The Seventh of Joyce.* Bloomington: Indiana UP, 1982.

Benstock, Shari. 'The Letter of the Law: *La carte postale* in *Finnegans Wake*.' *Philological Quarterly* 63 (1984): 163–85.

Bishop, John. *Joyce's Book of the Dark*. Madison: U of Wisconsin P, 1986.

Bloom, Harold, et al., eds. *Deconstruction and Criticism*. New York: Seabury, 1979.

Boheemen-Saaf, Christine van. *Joyce, Derrida, Lacan, and the Trauma of History: Reading, Narrative and Postcolonialism*. Cambridge: Cambridge UP, 1999.

Boheemen-Saaf, Christine van, ed. *Joyce, Modernity, and Its Mediation*. Amsterdam: Rodopi, 1989.

Brannigan, John, ed. *Re: Joyce: Text, Culture, Politics*. New York: Macmillan, 1998

Brown, Norman Oliver. *Closing Time*. New York: Random House, 1973.

Campbell, Joseph. *A Skeleton Key to* Finnegans Wake. New York: Harcourt, Brace and Co., 1944.

A Catechism of Catholic Doctrine. Dublin: M.H. Gill, 1951.

Cixous, Hélène. *The* Exiles *of James Joyce*. Trans. Sally A.J. Purcell. New York: D. Lewis, 1972.

Dalton, Jack P., ed. *Twelve and a Tilly: Essays on the Occasion of the 25th Anniversary of* Finnegans Wake. London: Faber, 1966.

Dasenbrock, Reed-Way. 'Philosophy after Joyce: Derrida and Davidson.' *Philosophy and Literature* 26(2) (2002): 334–45.

Derrida, Jacques. *Acts of Literature*. Ed. Derek Attridge. New York: Routledge, 1992.

– *The Archeology of the Frivolous: Reading Condillac*. Trans. John P. Leavey, Jr. Lincoln: U of Nebraska P, 1987.

– *Archive Fever: A Freudian Impression*. Trans. Eric Prenowitz. Chicago: U of Chicago P, 1996.

– *Dissemination*. Trans. Barbara Johnson. London: Athlone, 1981.

– *The Ear of the Other: Otobiography, Transference, Translation: Texts and Discussions with Jacques Derrida*. Ed. Christie V. McDonald. Trans. Peggy Kamuf. New York: Schocken Books, 1985.

– *The Gift of Death*. Trans. David Wills. Chicago: U of Chicago P, 1995.

– *Given Time: I. Counterfeit Money*. Trans. Peggy Kamuf. Chicago: U of Chicago P, 1992.

– *Glas*. Trans. John P. Leavey, Jr and Richard Rand. Lincoln: U of Nebraska P, 1986.

– *Margins of Philosophy*. Trans. Alan Bass. Chicago: U of Chicago P, 1982.

– *Mémoires: for Paul de Man*. Trans. Cecile Lindsay, Jonathan Culler, and Eduardo Cadava; translations ed. Avita Ronell and Eduardo Cadava. New York: Columbia UP, 1986.

– *Negotiations: Interventions and Interviews 1971–2001*. Ed., trans., with intro., Elizabeth Rottenberg. Stanford: Stanford UP, 2002.

– *Of Grammatology.* Trans. Gayatri Chakravorty Spivak. Corrected ed. Baltimore: Johns Hopkins UP, 1998.

– *Of Spirit: Heidegger and the Question.* Trans. Rachel Bowlby and Geoffrey Bennington. Chicago: U of Chicago P, 1989.

– *Positions.* Trans. Alan Bass. Chicago: U of Chicago P, 1981.

– *The Post Card: From Socrates to Freud and Beyond.* Trans., with notes and intro, Alan Bass. Chicago: U of Chicago P, 1987.

– *Resistances of Psychoanalysis.* Trans. Peggy Kamuf, Pascale-Anne Brault, and Michael Naas. Stanford: Stanford UP, 1998.

– *Speech and Phenomena, and Other Essays on Husserl's Theory of Signs.* Trans. with intro. David B. Allison. Preface by Newton Garver. Evanston: Northwestern UP, 1973.

– *Spurs: Nietzsche's Styles = Éperons: Les styles de Nietzsche.* Intro. Stefano Agosti; trans. Barbara Harlow; drawings by François Loubrieu. Chicago: U of Chicago P, 1979.

– *The Truth in Painting.* Trans. Geoff Bennington and Ian McLeod. Chicago: U of Chicago P, 1987.

– *Writing and Difference.* Trans., with intro. and additional notes, Alan Bass. Chicago: U of Chicago P, 1978.

– Ulysse *gramophone; Deux mots pour Joyce.* Paris: Galilée, 1987.

Derrida, Jacques, and Bennington, Geoffrey. *Jacques Derrida.* Trans. G. Bennington, Chicago: U of Chicago P, 1993.

Ellmann, Richard. *James Joyce.* Oxford: Oxford UP, 1982.

France, Anatole. *The Garden of Epicurus.* Trans. Alfred Allinson. New York: Dodd, Mead, 1923.

Gasché, Rodolphe. *The Tain of the Mirror: Derrida and the Philosophy of Reflection.* Cambridge: Harvard UP, 1986.

Genet, Jean. *Our Lady of the Flowers.* Paris: Morihien, 1949.

– *Miracle of the Rose.* New York: Grove P, 1966.

– *The Thief's Journal.* New York: Grove P, 1987.

Gifford, Don. Ulysses *Annotated: Notes for James Joyce's* Ulysses. Berkeley: U of California P, 1988.

Gilbert, Stuart, ed. *Letters of James Joyce.* Vol. 1. New York: Viking P, 1957.

Glasheen, Adaline. 'Rough Notes on Joyce and Wyndham Lewis.' *A Wake Newsletter* 8 (1969): 57–75.

– *A Third Census of* Finnegans Wake: *An Index of the Characters and Their Roles.* Berkeley: U of California P, 1977.

Groden, Michael, general ed. *The James Joyce Archive.* 60 vols. New York: Garland Publishing, 1977.

Hart, Clive. *A Concordance to* Finnegans Wake. Corrected ed. Mamaroneck:
Paul P. Appel, 1974.
– *Structure and Motif in* Finnegans Wake. London: Faber and Faber, 1962.
Hartman, Geoffrey. *Saving the Text: Literature/Derrida/Philosophy.* Baltimore:
Johns Hopkins UP, 1981.
Hayman, David. *A First-Draft Version of* Finnegans Wake. Austin: U of Texas P,
1963.
– 'The Joycean Inset.' *James Joyce Quarterly* 23 (1986): 137–55.
– 'Nodality and the Infra-Structure of *Finnegans Wake.'* *James Joyce Quarterly* 16
(1978): 135–49.
– *Re-Forming the Narrative: Toward a Mechanics of Modernist Fiction.* Urbana: U
of Illinois P, 1987.
– *The 'Wake' in Transit.* Ithaca: Cornell UP, 1990.
Hegel, G.W.F. *Hegel's Logic.* Trans. W. Wallace, intro. by J.N. Findlay. Oxford:
Clarendon, 1975.
– *The Phenomenology of Spirit.* Trans. A.V. Miller. Oxford: Oxford UP, 1977.
– *Philosophy of Nature.* Trans. A.V. Miller. Oxford: Clarendon, 1970.
Heidegger, Martin. *The Basic Problems of Phenomenology.* Trans., intro., and lexi-
con by Albert Hofstadter. Bloomington: Indiana UP, 1988.
– *Basic Writings: From* Being and Time *(1927) to* The Task of Thinking *(1964).*
Ed. with general intro. and intros. to each selection by David Farrell Krell.
San Francisco: HarperSanFrancisco, 1993.
– *Being and Time.* Trans. John Macquarrie and Edward Robinson. Oxford: Basil
Blackwell, 1962.
– *Early Greek Thinking.* Trans. David Farrell Krell and Frank A. Capuzzi. New
York: Harper & Row, 1975.
– *Kant and the Problem of Metaphysics.* Trans. Richard Taft. Bloomington: Indi-
ana UP, 1990.
– *Pathmarks.* Cambridge: Cambridge UP, 1998.
– *Poetry Language Thought.* Trans. Albert Hofstadter. New York: Harper & Row,
1971.
Joyce, James. *Finnegans Wake.* 3rd ed. London: Faber and Faber, 1964.
– *Giacomo Joyce.* London: Faber and Faber, 1983.
– *A Portrait of the Artist as a Young Man.* New York: Garland Publishing, 1993.
– *Ulysses. A Critical and Synoptic Edition Prepared by Hans Walter Gabler with Wolf-
hard Steppe and Claus Melchior.* 3 vols. New York: Garland Publishing, 1984.
Kant, Immanuel. *Critique of Pure Reason.* Trans. and ed. Paul Guyer and Allen
W. Wood. Cambridge, New York: Cambridge UP, 1998.
– *Foundation of the Metaphysics of Morals.* Trans. L.W. Beck. Indianapolis: Bobbs-
Merrill, 1959.
Leavey, John P. *Glassary.* Lincoln: U of Nebraska P, 1986.

Lernout, Geert. *The French Joyce*. Ann Arbor: U of Michigan P, 1990.

Lernout, Geert, ed. Finnegans Wake: *Fifty Years*. Amsterdam, Atlanta: Rodopi, 1990.

Loyola, Ignatius of. *The Spiritual Exercises of Saint Ignatius of Loyola*. Trans. W.H. Longridge. London: A.R. Mowbray, 1955.

MacCabe, Colin. *James Joyce and the Revolution of the Word*. London: MacMillan, 1978.

McArthur, Murray. 'The Example of Joyce: Derrida Reading Joyce.' *James Joyce Quarterly* 32 (1995): 227–41

McHugh, Roland. *Annotations to* Finnegans Wake. Baltimore: Johns Hopkins UP, 1980.

– *The* Finnegans Wake *Experience*. Dublin: Irish Academic P, 1981

– *The Sigla of* Finnegans Wake. Austin: U of Texas P, 1976.

Milesi, Laurent, ed. *James Joyce and the Difference of Language*. Cambridge: Cambridge UP 2003.

Nietzsche, Friedrich. *Beyond Good and Evil: Prelude to a Philosophy of the Future*. Trans. R.J Hollingdale. London: Penguin Books, 1990.

– *Thus Spoke Zarathustra*. Trans. Walter Kaufmann. Harmondsworth: Penguin, 1978.

– *Twilight of the Idols, or, How to Philosophize with a Hammer*. Trans. Duncan Large. Oxford, New York: Oxford UP, 1998.

– *Untimely Meditations*. Ed. Daniel Breazeale; trans. R.J. Hollingdale. Cambridge; New York: Cambridge UP, 1997.

– *The Will to Power*. Trans. Walter Kaufmann and R.J. Hollingdale. New York: Vintage, 1968.

Norris, Christopher. *Derrida*. London: Fontana, 1987.

Norris, Margot. *The Decentered Universe of* Finnegans Wake: *A Structuralist Analysis*. Baltimore: Johns Hopkins UP, 1976.

O'Shea, Michael J. *James Joyce and Heraldry*. Albany: State U of New York P, 1986.

Otte, George. 'Time and Space (with the Emphasis on the Conjunction): Joyce's Response to Lewis,' *James Joyce Quarterly* 22 (1985): 297–306.

Plato. *Timaeus*. Trans. Benjamin Jowett. Indianapolis: Bobbs-Merrill Educational Publishing, 1949.

– *The Republic*. Trans. F.M. Cornford. New York: Oxford UP, 1960.

Quinet, Edgar. *Oeuvres complètes de Edgar Quinet*. Paris: Pagnerre, 1857.

Rabaté, Jean-Michel. *James Joyce, Authorized Reader*. Baltimore: Johns Hopkins UP, 1991.

– *Joyce upon the Void: The Genesis of Doubt*. London: MacMillan, 1991.

Rapaport, Herman. *Heidegger and Derrida: Reflections on Time and Language*. Lincoln: U of Nebraska P, 1989.

Rose, Danis. *Chapters of Coming Forth by Day.* Colchester: A Wake Newslitter P, 1982.

– *The Textual Diaries of James Joyce.* Dublin: Lilliput P, 1995.

Rose, Denis, and John O'Hanlon. *Understanding* Finnegans Wake: *A Guide to the Narrative of James Joyce's Masterpiece.* New York: Garland, 1982.

Roughley, Alan. *Reading Derrida Reading Joyce.* Gainesville: UP of Florida, 1999.

Sailer, Susan Shaw. *On the Void of To Be: Incoherence and Trope in* Finnegans Wake. Ann Arbor: U of Michigan P, 1993.

Sartiliot, Claudette. *Citation and Modernity: Derrida, Joyce, and Brecht.* Norman: U of Oklahoma P, 1993.

Solomon, Margaret C. *Eternal Geomater: The Sexual Universe of* Finnegans Wake. Carbondale: Southern Illinois UP, 1969.

Steiner, Wendy. *The Colors of Rhetoric: Problems in the Relation between Modern Literature and Painting.* Chicago: U of Chicago P, 1982.

Sullivan, Sir Edward. *The Book of Kells described by Sir Edward Sullivan. With 24 colour reproductions from the original pages.* London, Paris, New York: The Studio, 1920.

Tagliacozzo, Giorgio, ed. *Giambattista Vico: An International Symposium.* Baltimore: Johns Hopkins UP, 1969.

– *Giambattista Vico's Science of Humanity.* Baltimore: Johns Hopkins UP, 1976.

Tindall, William York. *A Reader's Guide to* Finnegans Wake. New York: Farrar, Straus and Giroux, 1969.

Verene, Donald Phillip. *Vico's Science of Imagination.* Ithaca: Cornell UP, 1981.

Verene, Donald Phillip, ed. *Vico and Joyce.* Albany: State U of New York P, 1987.

Vico, Giambattista. *On the Most Ancient Wisdom of the Italians: Unearthed from the origins of the Latin language: Including the disputation with the Giornale de' letterati d'Italia.* Trans. L.M. Palmer. Ithaca: Cornell UP, 1988.

– *The New Science of Giambattista Vico.* Rev. trans. of 3rd ed. (1774) Thomas Goddard Bergin and Max Harold Fisch. Ithaca: Cornell UP, 1968.

– *The New Science of Giambattista Vico.* 3rd ed. (1774). Trans. David Marsh. Harmondsworth: Penguin, 1999.

Vitoux, Pierre. 'Aristotle, Berkeley, and Newman in "Proteus" and *Finnegans Wake,*' James Joyce Quarterly 19 (1981): 161–76.

Weir, Lorraine. *Writing Joyce: A Semiotics of the Joyce System.* Bloomington: Indiana UP, 1989.

Wilde, Oscar. *The Complete Works of Oscar Wilde.* London: Collins, 1966.

Yeats, W.B. *A Vision.* London: Macmillan, 1962.

Index